Wyatt Earp's
Cow-boy Campaign

Wyatt Earp's Cow-boy Campaign

The Bloody Restoration of Law and Order Along the Mexican Border, 1882

CHUCK HORNUNG

Epilogue by Jeffrey Wheat

McFarland & Company, Inc., Publishers

Jefferson, North Carolina

LIBRARY OF CONGRESS CATALOGUING-IN-PUBLICATION DATA

Names: Hornung, Chuck, 1943–
Title: Wyatt Earp's Cow-boy campaign : the bloody restoration of law and order along the Mexican border, 1882 / Chuck Hornung ; epilogue by Jeffrey Wheat.
Description: Jefferson, North Carolina : McFarland & Company, Inc., Publishers, 2016. | Includes bibliographical references and index.
Identifiers: LCCN 2016010009 | ISBN 9781476663449 (softcover : alkaline paper) ∞
Subjects: LCSH: Earp, Wyatt, 1848–1929. | Earp, Wyatt, 1848–1929—Family. | Peace officers—Southwest, New—Biography. | Frontier and pioneer life—Southwest, New. | Law enforcement—Southwest, New—History—19th century. | Cowboys—Southwest, New—History—19th century. | Outlaws—Southwest, New—History—19th century. | Southwest, New—History—19th century. | Cochise County (Ariz.)—History—19th century. | Southwest, New—Biography.
Classification: LCC F786.E18 H67 2016 | DDC 978/.02092—dc23
LC record available at http://lccn.loc.gov/2016010009

BRITISH LIBRARY CATALOGUING DATA ARE AVAILABLE

ISBN (print) 978-1-4766-6344-9
ISBN (ebook) 978-1-4766-2465-5

Front cover artwork by Bud Bradshaw, *Earp's Vendetta*, oil on board, 24" × 30", c. 1998 (courtesy of the artist, www.budbradshaw.com)

Printed in the United States of America

McFarland & Company, Inc., Publishers
Box 611, Jefferson, North Carolina 28640
www.mcfarlandpub.com

To my mother,
a woman who spoke with her life
as much as she did with words.

Table of Contents

Acknowledgments

Silent gratitude isn't much use to anyone.—Gladys Bertha Stern, novelist and critic

All Wyatt Earp–era fans owe thanks to trailblazer researchers like Stuart N. Lake, Walter Nobel Burns, and John Myers Myers. I was able to meet and correspond with Frank Waters, John D. Gilchriese, Ed Ellsworth Bartholomew, and Glenn G. Boyer. These men have passed beyond the veil but are not forgotten, as their research, opinions, and personal agendas still impact the field.

I have high regard for the groundbreaking research done by the late Al Turner, Bill Oster, Lee Silva, Mark Dworkin, and Roger Jay. Over the decades I have come to know and respect researchers Gary Roberts, Casey Tefertiller, Jeff Morey, Robert K. DeArment, Jeff Wheat, Jack Burrows, Paul Cool, Robert Palmquist, Woody Campbell, Peter Brand, Roger Peterson, Ben T. Traywick, Allen Barra, Roy B. Young, Scott Johnson, Tim Fattig, Steve Gatto, Gary McLelland, Paul Johnson, Bob Cash, David Johnson, John Bossenecker, Jim Peteresen, and Scott L. Nelson. I have benefited from the works of Lynn Bailey, Don Chaput, Ron Fischer, William B. Schillingberg, Gary Ledoux, Dave Cruickshanks, Nick Cataldo, Fred Holladay, and Neil Carmony.

Some excellent research and writing has been done by the ladies who have studied this era. The pioneers were Mrs. William Irvine, Vinnolia Earp Ackerman, Mabel Earp Cason, Susan McKey Thomas and Pat Jahns. Among today's leaders are Pam Potter, Sherry Monahan, Anne Collier, Rita Ackerman, Paula Mitchell Marks, S.J. "Cindy" Reidhead, Joyce Aros, Ann Kirschner, Sylvia Lynch, Emma Walling, and Karen Holliday Tanner.

A special thank you to the new group of western outlaw-lawmen history enthusiasts and researchers, because you continue to make the Earp era discussion so exciting. Keep moving the torch forward. Many of these individuals are members of the Wild West History Association.

My special appreciation goes to the late Mark Dworkin and his lovely Harriett. He read this volume in original draft form and freely offered his frank and insightful editorial advice to keep me honest and on track. Jeff Wheat and I have been friends for decades and have spent many hours discussing the Earp era and have shared copies of so much primary source material. He too read the early drafts, made many helpful editorial suggestions, and told me when I had gone down a rabbit hole.

Jeff Wheat and Gary Roberts were my traveling companions on our 1998 "voyage of discovery" into Wyatt Earp Country. We came from California, Georgia, and Texas to attend two western history association conferences. In the days between the meetings we visited with C. Lee Simmons at his Arizona home to see his Earp material; had our historic meeting with Glenn G. Boyer and his wife, Jane Candia Coleman, at their Cochise County ranch for lunch and a review of Glenn's original Earp-era documents and memorabilia collection; made the discovery of Frank Waters' original *Tombstone Travesty* manuscript at the University of New Mexico's Center for Southwest Research; conducted a private exploration of William A. Keleher's New Mexico History and Newspaper Collection in his Albuquerque home; and explored New Mexico sites related to Earp and Holliday adventures. Casey Tefertiller joined the fun in New Mexico. Thank you, my friends, for the fellowship and heated discussions. It was a great, once-in-a-lifetime 12 days and nights.

Gary, Jeff, and Casey were excited, as was I, a few years later with the discovery of the "Otero Letter." Gary gave the document the name it is now known by. These three men, along with Mark Dworkin, and others, helped to initiate the historical discussion and search for facts to prove or disprove the claims made in the Otero Letter. Thanks for handling this during my long recovery.

In New Mexico, I must acknowledge the late Katherine McMahan, Howard Bryan, and William A. Kelleher. These three individuals are greatly missed and fondly remembered for their gracious assistance in helping a young man develop his love for the history of this magnificent Land of Enchantment. Nancy Brown-Martinez, Christopher Geherin, Eileen Price and Jon Wheeler at the Center for Southwest Research and Special Collections at the University of New Mexico; Barbara Zamora, Bernalillo County Assessor's Office, Albuquerque; William B. Boehm, Rio Grande Historical Collections, New Mexico State University, Las Cruces; Judy Weinreb, Congregation Albert, Albuquerque; and Rachel Adler and Elena Perez-Lizano at the New Mexico State Records and Archives in Santa Fe were very helpful during my long years of research. Also helpful have been members of the Historical Society of New Mexico and the Wild West History Association.

A word of thanks to my friends Rabbi Hiam Richmond, Rabbi Sam Peek and Joe Good, excellent Torah teachers who helped me to understand the religious beliefs, customs, and traditions of the Jewish faith—orthodox, reformed and messianic. Their help takes center stage in the chapter dealing with Wyatt Earp, Josephine Marcus and religion. Over the decades, each of these men has helped to make my trips to the Holy Land both educational and spiritually meaningful.

Thank you to Bud Bradshaw who allowed his graphic *Earp's Vendetta* painting to be used on our cover, and Bob McCubbin for the use of his historic photo collection.

Ron Fuss, my brother-in-law, was with me when I bought the book that contained the Otero Letter and over the years he has encouraged me to document the truth or falsehoods behind the remarks contained in the letter. Thanks for the many gentle and not so gentle comments about finishing this book. Thanks to his wife, Pat, who has always welcomed me into her home.

Words are not powerful enough to thank my life-companion—*bashert* in Hebrew—for her support and for being my sounding board. Thanks for the many nights you let me stay up late and didn't complain; you were the spark that kept the flame alive. Sometimes you had no idea why I was excited about the new information I had found, but you listened even if you where half asleep.

A special thank you to my son Scott, who kicked me back into gear after a long health recovery that sidetracked me for a few years. God has blessed my family and I am thankful every day, so as my Lakota friends say, "*Wakan Tanka Kici Un*—May the Great Spirit Bless You."

Introduction

> Those who take no interest in the deeds of their ancestors are not likely to do anything worthy to be remembered by their descendents.—Walter M. Earp, *Past and Present of Jasper County (Iowa)*, 1912

My primary research and writing interest, for nearly a half century, has been the history of the New Mexico Mounted Police (rangers in the "Land of Enchantment"), so I never intended to write a book about Wyatt Earp, his brothers, or their central involvement in the Tombstone saga. That story has been told and mistold so many times since the early 1880s that the myths have taken on lives of their own. What could be learned from another retelling of that particular old chestnut? However, new revelations are constantly being discovered and thus strengthening the light cast upon what we look for: the truth. When the controversial "Otero Letter," containing revelations that alter traditional interpretations of the established outline of the saga, came into my life I was seeking information on my beloved New Mexico Mounted Police, not Wyatt Earp.

My friend Dr. Gary Roberts, a western history legend, and I first informed the Wild West history community about the Otero Letter in a coauthored article for *True West* magazine in 2001. This simple notification launched a debate on Tombstone history Web sites concerning this new information in relationship to the then-accepted version of the Earp–Cow-boys conflict. The validity of the letter was not a major issue, but it was discussed. The ramifications of the letter's contents became the focus of heated debate and launched new avenues of research to validate or debunk the letter's allegations. I was not an original bandwagon supporter of the letter and admit it took eight years before I presented my own paper on the Otero Letter at the history conference of the Historical Society of New Mexico in 2009. In the years since the Otero Letter was located, some researchers have quickly accepted the value of the letter's contents and, with noted caution, used its revelations in their scholarly works. I have now joined those ranks.

In this work I have combined the pro and con research done on the letter to reexamine Wyatt Earp's campaign to eradicate the Cow-boy confederation in Arizona and New Mexico territories in the early 1880s. The Earp–Cow-boy confrontation never was just a personal feud, as western fiction has promulgated for over a century and a quarter,

1

but was in fact a surgical seek-and-destroy mission, undertaken with the sanction of the Department of Justice's attorney general, the U.S. marshal and the governor of Arizona Territory. Simply stated, it was only after 18 months of inaction by corrupt county law enforcement officials and the 10-Percent Ring's expanded actions in league with the Cow-boys, the Cow-boy supporters' perjured court testimony, expanded livestock raids on both side of the international border, stagecoach holdups, and ambush murders that deputy U.S. marshal Wyatt Earp, acting upon direct orders, led a six-man federal strike force on a mission to restore law and order along the border with the Republic of Mexico.

Deputy U.S. marshal Wyatt Earp's lightning-strikes on Cow-boy hangouts lasted a month and destroyed the raiders' political and economic alliances. Acting upon the suggestion of federal district judge William Stilwell, Wyatt's warrants were served in lead. This sanguinary campaign ended the Cow-boys' feud with proper law and order authorities in southeastern Arizona Territory. The depth of Wyatt Earp's national political and financial support is a key element revealed in the Otero Letter and is mostly unexplored to date. If Wyatt Earp enjoyed some personal satisfaction from his determined effort then it was the icing on a successful mission.

This work is divided into three sections. The first part, "Frontier Paladins and Some Jokers," contains four chapters that establish the background of the major players prior to their converging on Tombstone, Arizona, in late 1879. Part two, "The Lion of Tombstone," contains chapters six and seven, which recap the Earp brothers' attempt to become Tombstone businessmen and their paths to law enforcement opposed to the Cow-boys; chapter eight, a monthly and daily account of the 18 months that led up to the final bloody field action, discussed in chapter nine with a day-by-day account of the March–April 1882 campaign; and chapter ten, a daily account of the Earp posse's journey from Arizona to New Mexico Territory.

The Otero Letter is discussed in detail in part three and comprises about half of the book. Chapter eleven is an overview of the war against the Cow-boys in New Mexico Territory. Chapter twelve deals with the provenance, authenticity and credibility of the Otero Letter. A concise history of Don Miguel Otero's family constitutes the chapter thirteen. Chapter fourteen is a detailed examination, pro and con, of each statement made in the Otero Letter, including the shotgun duel between Wyatt Earp and Cow-boy leader Curly Bill at Iron Springs and the reason behind the split in the friendship between Wyatt Earp and Doc Holliday that occurred during their April 1882 stay in Albuquerque. Chapters fifteen and sixteen discuss the arrangements for sanctuary for the Earp posse in Colorado and the struggle to stop Doc Holliday's extradition back to Arizona to face murder charges. Seventeen is a major chapter that discusses Wyatt Earp's covert Phase II action plan resulting in the death of Cow-boy leader Johnny Ringo. In chapter eighteen we investigate the social, cultural, and religious heritage surrounding the courtship and marriage of Wyatt Earp and Josephine Marcus. The final chapter, nineteen, contains my concluding observations.

The Commonwealth of Kentucky is my birthplace and I spent my youth there on a lovely family farm and an equally scenic New Mexico ranch. Unless I was seriously ill, I would always accompany Mom and my grandfather for the monthly shopping trip to Louisville. We always went to a certain large downtown department store where Mom would leave Pop, which is what I called my grandfather, and me on the book mezzanine to await her return. Over the years, sitting on the floor resting against a big overstuffed chair in the corner, with Pop taking a nap, I started and finished all eighteen of *The Lone Ranger* young adult novels and the one adult novel written by Fran Striker. This book series now has an honored place in my library.

After supper on Monday, Wednesday and Friday evenings the family gathered around the big Stromberg–Carlson standup radio in the living room as Dad adjusted the station selector knob to enjoy another adventure of the Masked Man and his faithful Indian friend, Tonto. (Fate has a twisted sense of humor. In later years, I had the honor to meet Mrs. Jeanne Cason Laing, who had an elderly Josephine Sarah Marcus Earp— Mrs. Wyatt Earp—living with her family when she was growing up in the 1930s; she told me Aunt Josie's favorite radio program was the award-winning *The Lone Ranger*.) In the early 1950s, television arrived in our rural part of the world and Thursday night saw the family also watching our heroes in action on the joint NBC/ABC television station broadcasting from Louisville. On Sunday we had the newspaper adventure comic strip to read. Hi-yo, Silver, away!

In the spring of 1955, I found another hero when I discovered Stuart N. Lake's biography of Wyatt Earp. The book's cover depicting the 1881 Tombstone streetfight, by Nick Eggenhofer, first caught my eye. Upon finishing the book, I made a close inspection of the dust jacket and noticed that the artist had not included Doc Holliday in the fight. I later discovered that Eggenhofer corrected the oversight for later editions when he did a slightly different second painting that included Doc Holliday. I did not know how to properly pronounce the hero's last name, but after I read the dust jacket introduction and the first few chapters, I wanted to own Lake's book. The problem was that I did not have the $3.50 book price, even if there was not any added sales tax in "those thrilling days of yesteryear."

I carefully replaced the Earp book when my mother came to get me. I told Mom I wanted to buy the book and hoped no one else bought it before I could earn the necessary money. In July, we made another trip to Louisville and this time I had $4.00 left from the money I had earned to go to Boy Scout camp and our church's summer youth camp. Good fortune shone upon me. No one had found the Earp book where I had placed it behind two other books. The saleslady finally located the listing in an old inventory log. She said that copy of *Wyatt Earp, Frontier Marshal* had been waiting for me to find it since the late 1930s, long before I was born during World War II.

In the fall of 1955, I finally discovered the proper way to say Wyatt's last name when I saw a promo for a new television western series. Our part of the commonwealth did not have a full-time ABC affiliate television station, so we couldn't view *The Life and Legend of Wyatt Earp* on its regular Tuesday night network broadcast time. Instead we viewed the program on a four-day delay on an NBC/ABC station following their Sunday evening local news.

In my youthful enthusiasm, I was so into the Wyatt Earp mystique that I kept notes on each TV show I was able to watch. Mom would sometimes finish the notes for me if I fell asleep before the show was over; we lived in the "stone age" before home recorders and I had school Monday morning. Yes, I knew the television series was more legend then fact. I had read the book, but the adventures of "Deacon Earp" were still moral-driven and exciting to watch. Even today the episodes have a nostalgic value to them and hearken back to a simpler era of innocence in our culture.

Until the Otero Letter found me I never intended to write a book concerning Wyatt Earp. More so, this volume is not intended to be a scholarly treatise on the man or his era, but an examination of the Otero Letter and the events it describes, so I have chosen not to burden this work with numerous endnotes. I have, however, included basic reference data in the text and placed source notations and author comments in a special section. This volume is suggestive rather then exhaustive. I hope others will use this work as a stepping-stone in an ongoing search for the truth surrounding the multilevel human drama set forth on these pages. The Nobel Prize winning physicist Albert Einstein is quoted as saying, "You never truly understand something until you can explain it to your grandmother." I wrote this examination of the Otero Letter with this concept in mind.

Frankly, this treatise is my interpretation of the facts discovered and how I understand them; it is not chimerical or a hagiography. I accept full responsibility for the judgments made in this examination of the facts. President Thomas Jefferson, in his second inaugural address, wrote that an "error of opinion may be tolerated where reason is left to combat it." Let the debate continue.

PART ONE

Frontier Paladins and Some Jokers

Shocking as it may seem to civilized souls, we had our code of honor on the frontier. When I speak of a fair fighter I mean a man who will not fight for what he knows to be a bad cause and who will not take his enemy at a disadvantage.—Wyatt Earp, *San Francisco Sunday Examiner*, 18 August 1896

1

Wyatt Earp: The Man, the Legend, the Myth

Early in his life Wyatt Earp seems to have adopted the words of Ralph Waldo Emerson as his credo: "Do not follow where the path may lead. Go instead where there is no path and leave a trail." His self-introduction was a simple, "I'm Wyatt Earp," and this style set the tone of the man himself. His parents christened this future daredevil frontier legend Wyatt Berry Stapp Earp following his birth in Monmouth, Illinois, on Sunday, March 19, 1848.

Today, many view Wyatt Earp as a tough peace officer and businessman who worked to bring law and order to the pioneer West. To others, he was a cold-blooded killer who hid behind his badge, a shady gambler, a saloonman, a pimp, a con artist, a petty thief, and a puffed-up blowhard. During different phases of his long life he may have been each of these individuals. One point is certain: he was not a typical frontiersman. He possessed a kaleidoscopic nature which allowed him to adapt, yet his core values rested upon a firm foundation of family and justice. Over a quarter of a century after his death, Wyatt Earp was still a memorable individual.

As a youthful reporter, renowned newspaper columnist and 1930s radio talk show host Adela Rodgers St. Johns interviewed Wyatt Earp in the late 1920s. She recalled the old lawman for an article published in the *Arizona Weekly* on May 22, 1960. She wrote, "He was straight as a pine tree, tall and magnificently built. I knew he was nearing 80, but in spite of his snow-white hair and moustache, he did not seem or look old. His greeting was warm and friendly, but I stood in awe. Somehow, like a mountain or desert, he reduced you to size."

Two decades after the Kansas cowtown era ended, Richard Cogdell, a clerk in the Smyth & Sons Store in the 1870s, recalled one of the men who had served on the Wichita police force during the rowdy trail driving years. The *Wichita Beacon* of December 4, 1896, printed Cogdell's memoirs: "He was a tall, slim man and as straight as an arrow. His complexion was fair, and he had blue eyes. He is a man who never smiled or laughed.

He was at the time the most fearless man I ever saw, and Satan and all his imps could not scare Wyatt Earp." Bat Masterson wrote in 1907, "Wyatt Earp is one of the few men I personally knew in the West in the early days, whom I regard as absolutely destitute of physical fear." Wyatt Earp's longtime friend John Clum, in an April 1929 article for the *Arizona Historical Review* honoring Wyatt's memory shortly after his death, recalled, "Wyatt's manner, though friendly, suggested a quiet reserve. His facial features were strong, positive and pleasing. His habitual expression was serious, with a gracious smile when the occasion warranted it—but his mirth was never boisterous."

John Ford, the legendary film director, claimed he knew Wyatt during his later years: "Men like Wyatt Earp had real nerve. They did not have to use their guns. They overpowered the opposition with their reputations and personalities. They faced them down." In a *True West* magazine interview for May–June 1959, Arthur M. King, Wyatt Earp's assistant, who worked with him on special law enforcement missions in the early 1900s in Southern California, remembered, "Earp was a very quiet fellow— a fine man, one of the coolest I've ever seen. He had a good sense of humor and didn't talk to[o] much. He was afraid of nothing. When he'd get angry the corner of his right eye would twitch just a little. His draw was only fairly fast, but his accuracy was uncanny."

Wyatt's oldest brother, his only half-brother, Newton Jasper Earp, was a partner with Wyatt in operating a family farm in Kansas. Newton was, like his famous younger brother, a Kansas peace officer. Wyatt cried at the news of his brother's death. Newton named one of his sons Wyatt and another Virgil. One of Wyatt Earp's Tombstone business partners named his son Wyatt. It is a high tribute for any man to have a child named in his honor.

Most western outlaw-lawmen history buffs know that Wyatt Earp first served as a peace officer in Lamar, Missouri. He was the township's constable from 1869 to 1871 and available records indicate that 21-year-old Wyatt Earp performed his duties with diligence; however, some writers have claimed that he was a thug with a badge and embezzled school tax funds.

Following the untimely death from typhus of his young wife and son while she was pregnant with the son, Wyatt Earp hunted buffalo, met the Masterson brothers, stole horses in Indian Territory, escaped jail in Arkansas, worked as a bouncer in an Illinois riverboat bordello, and learned the art of handling cards and gambling, using firearms, and the manly sport of frontier boxing. He also cultivated his lifelong love of fast horses and dog racing. Wyatt Earp developed into a physically fit young man who drank beer but not strong liquor, seldom used profane language, spoke as an educated individual, and became a voracious reader and fashionable dresser. Women of all ages enjoyed his company.

Wyatt S. Earp, "The Lion of Tombstone" (courtesy Robert G. McCubbin Collection).

Wyatt's second law enforcement job is the center of debate, as some western historians deny that he was involved in any way with the bold arrest of the renowned Texas gunman Ben Thompson at Ellsworth, Kansas, in August 1873. Earp detractors use this incident, as reported by Stuart Lake in his biography, to discredit Wyatt's entire law enforcement record. These debunkers claim that Earp had no part in the arrest and that his legend rests upon a foundation of sand. In his massive first book, *The Cowtown Years*, of his multivolume Earp biography, the late Lee A. Silva impressively analyzes all the known evidence concerning the "Ellsworth Incident" and offers readers strong evidence that Wyatt was in fact a central figure of the event.

Earp also has detractors concerning his job performance as an officer in Wichita, Kansas. In May 1874, he became a member of the cowtown's

James Cooksey Earp (courtesy Robert G. McCubbin Collection).

Virgil Walter Earp (courtesy Robert G. McCubbin Collection).

Morgan Seth Earp (courtesy Robert G. McCubbin Collection).

"private police force" and a year later the city council gave him an appointment as a deputy marshal or policeman. Wyatt proved to be an effective officer and eight years later Wichita "city dads" had glowing words concerning their former officer. They signed a testimonial stating, "Wyatt S. Earp was a good and efficient officer, and was well known for his honesty and integrity, that his character while here was of the best, and that no fault was ever found with him as an officer or as a man." Wyatt Earp's older brother James also recalled their days in Wichita: "In Wichita we [the Earp brothers] learned everything we needed to know about running a tough town."

There are folktales that the youthful deputy marshal Earp developed a sweet tooth and a lifelong love of ice cream while he lived in Wichita. There are stories of how he would stop in the ice cream parlor while on late afternoon patrol for a bowl of the vanilla-flavored icy confection; he always seemed to have some local kids as his guests. He did the same thing in Tombstone with his next door neighbor young Nona Neff and her friends.

Contained in Stuart Lake's research notes for his *Frontier Marshal* book is a comment that Wyatt Earp served as a member of a federal posse, led by a deputy U.S. marshal, that chased renegades in Indian Territory in 1875. An additional notation says Wyatt reportedly killed a man while riding in Indian Territory and might have also saved the life of a fellow posse member. Unfortunately, Lake did not elaborate on this adventure and, worse, he listed no source for the statements. The leader of the federal posse was most likely Mike Meagher, longtime peace officer in the Wichita area and a Wyatt Earp stalwart.

Wyatt Earp served three different terms as a marshal of Dodge City. His first time as a peace officer in the "Queen of the Kansas Cowtowns" was from May to early September 1876. That fall he and his younger brother Morgan left Dodge City and spent the next nine months gambling in Cheyenne, Wyoming, and cutting wood and prospecting in the Dakota Territory's gold fields. Through hard work, Wyatt and Morgan made a substantial profit selling firewood to the residents of Deadwood. Wyatt also served as a Wells Fargo shotgun messenger for bullion shipments sent from the mining camp, located in an outlaw-infested region, and all of his express guard consignments reached their destination.

Back in Dodge City in July 1877, Wyatt Earp was appointed assistant (chief deputy) city marshal and held that office until November, when he took a vacation from his Dodge City law enforcement duties to visit brother James in Fort Worth. During these months on the gambling circuit, Wyatt also worked as an undercover detective for the Atchison, Topeka and Santa Fe

Warren Baxter Earp (courtesy Robert G. McCubbin Collection).

Railroad and the Wells Fargo Express Company. It was during this Texas sojourn, while visiting at Fort Griffin, that Earp most likely first became acquainted with a Georgia-born dentist and gambler named John Henry Holliday. Earp knew Doc's gal-pal "Big Nose Kate" Elder from her time working as a prostitute in Wichita. (James Earp's wife operated a sporting house in Wichita.)

Wyatt was visiting James and gambling in the Cattle Exchange when one night he gave an unruly cowboy named Russell "a first class pounding" and was arrested for his trouble. The *Fort Worth Daily Democrat* of January 26, 1878, said that one of city marshal I.T. "Long-hair Jim" Courtright's policemen arrested Wyatt, who gave a bond to appear in court. Russell left town and the charges against Wyatt disappeared. While he was in Fort Worth, some writers claim that Earp sought employment as a Texas-based peace officer but to no avail.

During his extended stay in the legendary "Texas Cowtown" it is possible that Wyatt encountered Will McLaury—a local attorney and older brother to the men the Earps would kill in the 1881 Tombstone streetfight—who maintained a law office just a block away from the popular watering hole where James was the bartender. McLaury also served as an agent for some land speculators and Wyatt was still searching for a suitable ranch location. He failed to locate a ranch site, so he continued to gamble in "Cowtown" until spring, when he rejoined the Dodge City police force.[1]

The "Personal Mention" column of the *Wichita Eagle* for May 16, 1878, contained this item: "Wyatt Earp, well known in this city, and for a long time connected with our police force, received an offer of $200 per month to take the Marshalship of Dodge City which he went up to accept, with all its dangers and responsibilities last week." Wyatt was again serving as the chief deputy marshal, earning a $75 per month city salary, plus a two-dollar fee for each arrest made or complaint served. Local merchants may have augmented Wyatt's official city salary with some off-the-books supplemental funding, thus providing the $200 per month income and fees mentioned in the *Eagle*. The police court docket for Wyatt's last thirteen months on the Dodge City police force shows that he made thirty-five arrests and collected seventy dollars in arrest fees from the city court. In August of 1878, the *National Police Gazette* gave Wyatt Earp his first national recognition when it called him "a good fellow and brave officer."[2]

By the fall of 1879, assistant city marshal Earp held a well-deserved reputation as a strong-arm law enforcer, but not one as a man killer. He kept the peace in the Kansas cattle market towns by the psychology of the "unpressed trigger" and effectively used the skills he had learned as a boxer in railroad construction camps to enforce the law by a quick fist to the jaw or by "buffaloing" a suspect with a pistol to the head. These forceful tactics helped preserve the lives of the lawbreakers and of Earp and his fellow officers. More important, Dodge City fathers and local merchants (and if the truth be told, the cattle herders) liked Wyatt's arrest style, because a dead cowhand could not avail himself of their services. Police killings were bad for business.

In July 1910 Bat Masterson told a *Washington Post* reporter that during his Kansas Cowtown years Wyatt Earp had been a "terror in action, either with his fits or with his gun." Wyatt was proud of the fact that during his 27-month tenure on the Dodge City police force he was involved in only one incident that resulted in the death of a criminal suspect.

In the 1931 version of her memoirs, Kate Holliday claimed that during the months she and Doc were living in Dodge City she never saw or heard of Wyatt doing any noteworthy police work: "Most of the time Wyatt could be seen sitting at a table in a saloon playing cribbage with some rounder or a bartender. And some times taking a hand playing in a game of poker." Kate's remarks would imply that she did not read the local newspapers, socialize much in the Dodge City community, or was spinning a bitter personal revenge yarn.[3]

When Wyatt Earp lived in southeastern Missouri, he would often visit with his cousins who lived nearby. One of these young cousins was George Earp, later a lawman himself, who in old age recalled his visits with Wyatt: "My father was a farmer and I and my brothers grew up on a farm as typical 'hill-billy' boys of the Ozarks. There were many wild deer and turkey on the timbered portions of our farm and Wyatt often came to our farm to shoot deer and turkey." Wyatt had first learned the fine art of marksmanship on the plains of Iowa.

James Earp once recalled that his brother "was always dragging me out for target practice" while they lived in Wichita. He added, "I got enough target practice in the war [War Between the States]. So did the son-of-a-bitch that shot me." Adelia Earp Edwards remembered that her brothers Newton and Virgil were excellent marksmen due to their army training. They "would always win" shooting matches, she recalled. In a November 1880 match, held in Tombstone, Virgil finished fourth and won five dollars. Wyatt did not take part.[4]

On July 7, 1877, the *Dodge City Times* said, "It wasn't considered policy to draw a gun on Wyatt unless you got the drop and meant to burn power without any preliminary talk." Nineteen years later, the *San Francisco Call* of December 2, 1896, commented, "[I]t is not the safest thing in the world to impugn Earp's honesty when he has a 45-caliber Colt's revolver a foot long in his jeans...."

Stuart Lake wrote in his biography that while Wyatt was working in Dodge City he received a special edition Colt .45 pistol from New York State–born pulp magazine novelist Ned Buntline, a nom de plume for Edward Zane Carroll Judson. The pistol was unique because it contained a factory-installed, ten-inch-long barrel, which was two-and-a-half inches longer than the standard seven-and-a-half-inch barrel. Judson also provided a custom-made walnut rifle stock that could be attached to the pistol to help steady it for long-range shooting. This stock came with a buckskin carrying pouch that could be attached to the saddle. The name NED was engraved on the pistol's blackstrap and the weapon had an accompanying hand-tooled holster. The custom revolver was a gift-bribe meant to help recruit Wyatt and former buffalo hunters Charlie Bassett, Bill Tilghman, Neal Brown and Bat Masterson to join Buntline's Wild West stage show. All five men turned down the theatrical performance deal, but each kept his pistol. While the other four recipients found the barrel length cumbersome, Wyatt and his custom revolver became as one, and they became legendary. In her memoirs Josie Earp wrote about her husband's special pistol and said, "Wyatt loved this gift." Wyatt's sister Adelia claimed that Wyatt and Cody were friends, and Josie wrote of how Wyatt introduced her to Buffalo Bill when they attended his Wild West Show during their visit to the 1893 Chicago World's Fair.

Bat Masterson is quoted as saying Wyatt was a quality marksman with his long-barreled pistol and could hit a running coyote at 400 yards. In a 1955 letter to Robert Sisk, the producer of the Earp television series, Stuart Lake wrote about the Buntline Special, saying, "Wyatt told me once that he was not allowed to use it in the numerous target matches of his Kansas years."

Over the decades since Lake wrote his account of the "Buntline Special" numerous writers have tried to debunk the story. In the 1970s, western history collector John D. Gilchriese and gun historian William B. Shillingberg tried to convince the world an old model Smith & Wesson .44 pistol Gilchriese had acquired from John Flood, Wyatt's close friend, was the authentic "special gun" Wyatt Earp used. A prestigious national western history museum even bought the pistol for display. In the late 1990s, historians Jeff Morey and Lee Silva conducted a Herculean search to discover the truth about Wyatt Earp's special pistol. These two researchers published detailed accounts of their findings in popular gun magazines, western history journals, and in the first volume of Silva's multivolume Wyatt Earp biography. The factual information these two men discovered has rehabilitated the Buntline Special and the basic Stuart Lake narrative.[5]

> **Author's Perspective:** When all the current evidence is considered, I am left with one conclusion. I still believe that Wyatt Earp once owned and used a long-barreled Colt .45 pistol.

From 1877 to late 1879, James Earp worked as a bartender at the elegant Cattle Exchange Saloon on Houston and Second in Fort Worth. Pennsylvania-born Robert Jackways "Uncle Bob" Winders was the owner of the Cattle Exchange Saloon along with his son-in-law Origen Charles "Harelip Charlie" Smith. Winder and Smith would both play important roles alongside the Earp brothers during the Tombstone Cow-boy controversy. The *Fort Worth City Directory* noted that the James C. Earp family lived on the northwest corner of Ninth and Calhoun during their stay in north Texas.

Wyatt and James were always close as brothers and spent much of their adult life in close contact. "Jim Earp used to work in Jim Dagners' saloon [in Wichita] as a bar tender. Jim was not so tall as Wyatt, but he was a gentlemanly fellow like his brother," Kansas friend John Martin remembered in 1896. The Kentucky-born James Cooksey Earp, "Jimmy" to his friends and family, was the oldest of the children born to Nicholas Earp and his second wife, Virginia Ann Cooksey Earp. The Earp family Bible notes that James had been born on June 28, 1841, at Hartford, Kentucky. A contemporary account described James as "blond, blue eyes, light hair, about five feet six inches high, rather stout of build, has a heavy mustache."

Mrs. James C. Earp, commonly called Bessie, was notable in her prime as "a very beautiful brunette." James met the widow Nellie Bartlett Catchim on a visit to his grandparents in Illinois and married her on April 18, 1873, while also accepting her 10-year-old Harriet, called Hattie, and 12-year-old Frank as his own children. The couple had no children together.

By mid-year 1879 the financial crisis caused by the Panic of 1873 had turned a corner and the nation's economic system had rebounded enough to expand again. During the six-year economic downturn, 10,478 businesses, including large banking consortiums and brokerage houses, failed due to over-issuing paper money, inflated prices, and rampant speculation. Gold, silver, and other mineral and agricultural wealth of the southwest were in demand to fuel this new national growth and the Earp brothers wished to be part of the economic boom.

In late summer 1879, James and his family joined Wyatt at Dodge City to plan their trip to the railroad boom hub of New Town Las Vegas, New Mexico Territory. Later, they would continue on west to join Virgil and his wife in Arizona Territory for the family's chance to make their fortune in the new silver mining village named Tombstone.

Morgan joined his older brothers for the great adventure in late July 1880. Adelia Edwards recalled in her memoirs that at times her brother Morgan "had a terrible temper" but most of the time he was just a fun-loving young man. Allie Earp noted that her brother-in-law's "face wasn't lean like Jim and Wyatt's or heavy like Virgil's, but more sensitive. His thick straight hair never did stay combed and his mustache was always scraggly." Morgan's companion, the beautiful Louisa Houston, joined him in Tombstone six months after his arrival.

Warren, the youngest Earp brother, was unmarried. Unlike his blond-haired brothers, he was the only one in the family with dark hair. He arrived in Tombstone in early 1881.

2

John Henry Holliday, DDS

He was a dentist, but he preferred to be a gambler. He was a philosopher, but he preferred to be a wag. He was long, lean, and ash-blonde,
and the quickest man with a six-shooter I ever knew.—Wyatt Earp,
San Francisco Sunday Examiner, 2 August 1896

"While he never did anything to entitle him to a statue in the Hall of Fame, Doc
Holliday was nevertheless a most picturesque charter on the western border in those
days when the pistol instead of law courts determined issues," wrote W.B. "Bat" Masterson in the introduction to his reminiscences about the gambler-dentist in *Human
Life* magazine in May 1907. "Holliday had a mean disposition and an ungovernable temper, and under the influence of liquor was a most dangerous man. He was selfish and
had a perverse nature—traits not calculated to make a man popular in the early days
on the frontier."[1]

When Masterson knew Holliday, the young doctor "was slim of build and sallow
of complexion, standing about five feet ten inches, and weighting no more than 130
pounds. His eyes were a pale blue and his moustache was thin and of a sandy hue." The
bond between Bat Masterson and Doc Holliday was their mutual friendship with Wyatt
Earp. "While I assisted him (Holliday) substantially on several occasions it was not
because I liked him any too well, but on account of my friendship for Wyatt Earp, who
did."[2]

Even people who knew Holliday were confused about his birth state. In 1896, Wyatt
Earp is reported to have said that Doc "was a Virginian, but he preferred to be a frontiersman and a vagabond." The *Denver Republican*'s 1887 obituary for Holliday said that
Doc "had been well known to all the states and territories west of Kentucky, which was
his old home." The Henry B. Holliday family Bible shows that John Henry was in fact
a native of the State of Georgia, born on August 14, 1851, in Griffin, just south of Atlanta
in the state's original Henry County. The baby was baptized in the Presbyterian church
in March 1852.

Earp family researcher Woody Campbell has discovered that Daniel Earp and his
wife lived in Griffin, Georgia, about the time that John Henry Holliday was an infant
in that community. According to an advertisement in the *Griffin American News* of
September 1, 1855, Daniel Earp was "engaged in selling of slaves" and had hailed from

Anderson County, South Carolina. Daniel was a second cousin twice removed to the future lawman-gambler Wyatt Earp. It makes for interesting speculation as to whether Wyatt and Doc were ever aware of this location connection. When John was a young boy, the Holliday family settled in Valdosta, the county seat of Lowndes County, located in the Georgia coastal plain along the border with the Florida uplands.

The 1870 national census recorded John Henry Holliday as a "student." He would graduate from the Pennsylvania College of Dental Surgery, at Philadelphia, in March 1872 after writing a thesis entitled "Diseases of the Teeth."[3] Some researchers believe that young Holliday did some internship practice in St Louis, along with fellow dental school classmate Auguste Jameson Fuches, where he may have had his first encounter with a young Hungarian immigrate named Mary Katherine Haroney (aka Kate Fisher, Kate Elder or "Big Nose Kate"), who by the mid–1870s had joined Doc as his traveling companion and referred to herself as his wife. In fact, Kate would later claim that she married John in St Louis in 1870 while he was in dental school. At other times, she said they had wed in Georgia while on a visit to his family. To date, no public or private marriage record has been located in Georgia or Missouri.[4]

After Holliday graduated from dental school, he returned to Georgia and accepted a junior partnership with Arthur C. Ford and settled down to a budding practice in Atlanta. Sometime later, Holliday opened his own dental office in suburban Griffin. Doc and his uncle, Tom McKey, were involved in a shooting incident concerning some ex-slaves near McKey family-owned property on the Withlacoochee River in south Georgia. Whatever happened at the swimming hole, the young dentist suddenly developed a strong urgency to relocate.

Using family contacts and good references John was able to acquire a junior partnership with Dr. John A. Seegar, a former Georgian who had a developing practice in Dallas, Texas. Late in September 1873, Dr. John Henry Holliday bid good-bye to his Southern home, his family and his friends. Young Holliday did not know that he had taken his first step toward becoming a frontier legend and would never again live in his beloved Georgia.

Young John Henry Holliday was an award-winning dentist. According to the *Dallas Weekly Herald* of October 9, 1873, Doc won three premium prizes at the North Texas Agriculture, Mechanical and Blood Stock Association Fair at Dallas. Those awards were for the "best set of gold teeth," "the best vulcanized rubber dentures" and "the best set of artificial teeth." If only these specimens still existed, they would make a great tourist attraction and a historical curiosity.

Sometime after this location to Reconstruction-era Texas, Holliday discovered that he had contracted pulmonary tuberculosis (the disease later advanced into the military tuberculosis that killed him). He now had a second reason to remain in the drier climate of the southwest. The Seegar–Holliday partnership lasted for about six months because Doc had discovered gambling. Even on the frontier, this "hobby" was not socially conducive to a professional image.

John Holliday left Dallas for Denison to try an independent dental practice, while making short train trips back to Dallas for the enjoyment and excitement of cards and dice. Doc continued to practice his dental profession to support his "hobby" until he became proficient enough to support himself as a "Knight of the Green Cloth" at the gaming tables. A successful professional gambler needed a competitive spirit, a remarkable memory, and above average mathematical ability. John Henry Holliday, late of Griffin, Georgia, exceeded that standard. At some point as Doc's disease developed, his eyesight weakened and he occasionally wore glasses to correct his vision. There exists a photograph of him wearing glasses.

On New Year's Day 1875, Doc and a saloonkeeper named "Champagne Charlie" Austin entertained themselves with at shooting contest, with each other as the target. The next day, the *Dallas Weekly Herald* told their readers about the comical shootout. A Dallas County grand jury indicted Holliday for assault with intent to commit murder, but at his trial the jury found him not guilty. Later, the judge fined him $10 for running gambling events. By early summer 1875, Doc Holliday was working in Fort Griffin, west of the Dallas–Fort Worth area.

On Saturday, June 12, 1875, the Shackelford County sheriff arrested 25-year-old "Dock Holladay" and Mike Lynch, charging them with "playing together & with others at a game of cards in which spirituous liquors were sold" and for "gaming in a saloon." Doc would later become reacquainted with some Fort Griffin gamblers in the new railroad town of Las Vegas, New Mexico. One of the women arrested in this Fort Griffin raid was named "Kate" and she was charged with "keeping a disorderly house" in the settlement of "shady ladies" on The Flats. Was this "working girl" also John H. Holliday's female companion Kate Elder?

Many historians believe that frontier legends Wyatt Earp and John Holliday first encountered each other at Fort Griffith, Texas, in the fall of 1877, but it is possible they had seen each other at Deadwood, Dakota Territory, in the fall of 1876.[5] At different times between 1872 and 1880 John Holliday would open a dental office in whatever town he cur-

John H. Holliday, DDS (courtesy Robert G. McCubbin Collection).

rently called home. One of these times was in early 1878 in Dodge City, Kansas. Doc's advertisement in the *Dodge City Times* said he would provide his professional services in room 24 at the Dodge House "during the summer." The ad ended by saying, "Where satisfaction is not given money will be refunded." I wonder how many Texas drovers spent some of their trail drive earnings utilizing Holliday's dental services that summer versus bucking his poker table skills?

Doc and "Mrs. Holliday" stayed in Dodge City until the late fall of 1878, and in one of her four recorded reminiscences, Kate said pointedly, "During the seven months that Doc and I lived in Dodge City, Wyatt Earp was just an acquaintance." This remark seems to be less than factual. In 1907, Bat Masterson commented on the Earp–Holliday friendship, writing, "His [Doc's] whole heart and soul were wrapped up in Wyatt Earp and he was always ready to stake his life in defense of any cause in which Wyatt was interested. Damon did no more for Pythias than Holliday did for Wyatt Earp."

John Holliday saved Wyatt Earp's life during "a scrimmage" with a drunken and rowdy contingent of Texas cattle drovers in Dodge City on Saturday evening, September 19, 1878. This event cemented the men's budding friendship and is likely the main reason why Wyatt Earp endured Holliday's moments of ill temper and hot-headedness. In August 1896, Wyatt wrote about that night in an article for the *San Francisco Examiner*: "On such incidents as that are built the friendships of the frontier."

It has been said that a friend is a brother that destiny forgot to give you. Alfred Henry Lewis caught the spirit of the Doc and Wyatt relationship in his 1905 novel, *The Sunset Trail*, when he wrote, "The brothers Earp and Mr. Holliday became friends at sight. It was as though a fourth [brother] had been born into the Earp family." Lewis was counting only the "Fighting Earp Brothers": Virgil, Wyatt and Morgan. Newton, James and Warren were secondary to the Fighting Earp brothers' gunfighter legend.

After living in Dodge City, Doc and Kate moved to northeastern New Mexico Territory. They lived in the infant railroad towns of Otero and New Town Las Vegas for a year before they joined Wyatt and James Earp and their families on an overland trip to Arizona Territory. Holliday and Kate stayed in the territorial capital city when the Earps, now including Virgil and his wife, Allie, left Prescott headed for Tombstone in late November 1879.

In February 1880, Doc Holliday did leave Prescott. He returned to Las Vegas, New Mexico, to keep an appointment for a hearing before the San Miguel County District Court. He also attended to some business concerning his investment in a sheep herd and to sell a saloon he owned in Meadows City. When Doc completed his business in Las Vegas, he took the railroad to New Albuquerque on the Rio Grande, opened another saloon and entered into a partnership in a hotel in Bernalillo, 10 miles north of Albuquerque. These events are discussed in detail in our book recounting Wyatt and Doc's adventures in New Mexico Territory.

After Doc Holliday left New Albuquerque in May, he returned to Prescott. He had resettled in the Arizona territorial capital before June 2, 1880, which is known because on that date the United States census lists him as a resident of a boardinghouse on Montezuma Street. One of Doc's two roommates was a 45-year-old bachelor named Richard E. Elliot. The Maine native was the owner of the Accidental Mine and a leader of the local temperance movement. The other roommate was a 39-year-old divorced man from Ohio named John J. Gosper, founder of the *Phoenix Herald* and owner of a thoroughbred hog farm in the Salt River Valley. The stately looking Gosper was secretary for the Arizona Territory and served as its acting governor during the prolonged absences of its territorial governor General John Charles Frémont. Holliday's friendship with the flamboyant, one-legged John Gosper, a fellow Methodist church member, was soon to play a part in the political war in Tombstone and Cochise County.

Author's Perspective: Richard Elliot, John Gosper and Doc Holliday were an odd trio. It would have been fun to have been a mouse in that boardinghouse and observe the free-wheeling discussion among a Yankee war veteran turned government bureaucrat, a hard-rock miner turned Republican capitalist, and a Southern-born aristocratic dentist turned saloon/hotel owner, shares owner in a sheep herd, and professional gambler.

Doc and his Hungarian-born gal pal Kate Elder seem to have reconnected in the late summer of 1880. In one of Kate's autobiographies, she mentions that Doc received a letter from Wyatt that fall telling him that Tombstone needed a dentist. The truth is less romantic. Wyatt needed a dealer for his new faro game at the glamorous Oriental Saloon and another stalwart of the eastern gamblers' brotherhood. A second inducement for relocating was that Prescott's two new gaming tax ordinances, enacted during Doc's spring sojourn in New Mexico, made the town a less desirable locale for an independent faro table operator. Doc Holliday decided to try his luck at the gaming tables in booming Tombstone and asked gal pal Kate to accompany him. But en route another one of their many "disagreements" caused Doc to arrive in Tombstone alone.

3

A Man Called Bat

To me he will always be Bat Masterson, the quick fighter, the square gambler, the staunch friend and the generous foe—the fastest of my frontier friends.—Wyatt S. Earp, "Wyatt Earp's Tribute to Bat Masterson, the Hero of 'Dobe Walls" *San Francisco Sunday Examiner*, 16 August 1896

Canadian-born Bartholomew "Bat" Masterson disliked his formal-sounding given name, so while still in his youth he changed Bartholomew to William Barclay. The family referred to him as Bart or Bat as a nickname. He was born November 26, 1853, at Henryville, Quebec, Canada. Masterson first met Wyatt Earp on the buffalo hunting range and later they worked together upholding the law in Ford County, Kansas. Young Masterson earned his reputation as a courageous and hard fighter during a five-day siege in June 1874 when buffalo hunters faced a massive war party of Comanche, Kiowa, and Cheyenne at Adobe Walls in the Texas panhandle.

On February 11, 1876, the *Jacksboro (TX) Frontier Echo* noted that a fiery-tempered corporal in the 4th Cavalry, stationed at the cantonment on the Sweetwater near the village of Mobeetie in the Texas panhandle, killed his "lady friend" in his attempt to shoot Bat on January 24. Masterson was wounded, yet he was able to kill Melvin King aka Anthony Cook.

Adelia Earp Edwards, the Earp brothers' sister, whom they lovingly called Deelie, fondly remembered Masterson during the family's stay in Dodge City. The then old lady recalled that all the young women in Dodge City "turned their heads at him." Bat was a "real dandy dresser and forever laughing and playing." She also said, "Why, one time at a dance he nearly danced my feet off" and her future husband, Bill Edwards, would not talk to her for a few days. Masterson held a reputation as a lady's man during his youthful years.

On Tuesday, February 8, 1881, Bat Masterson, by then the 28-year-old former sheriff of Ford County, Kansas, boarded the westbound Santa Fe at Dodge City seeking new adventure working for Wyatt Earp as a faro dealer in Tombstone, Arizona Territory. The former buffalo hunter and Indian fighter spent the next few days traveling across Kansas, Colorado and New Mexico. One of Masterson's fellow travelers was George Buffum, who would one day write *On Two Frontiers* and *Smith of Bear City*. Another passenger was William Henry Stilwell, an attorney from St. Lawrence County, New York.

President Rutherford B. Hayes had appointed Stilwell as an associate justice of the three-member Supreme Court of Arizona Territory and trial judge for the first district court located at Tombstone. Judge Stilwell would play an important role in Wyatt Earp's effort to combat the Cow-boy confederacy headquartered in the newly created Cochise County.

Unfortunately there is no known record of this Arizona-bound expedition to tell us what the former lawman and his fellow travelers did or saw as they sped across the plains. The trip over the newly built Santa Fe Railroad tracks took them through Trinidad, over Raton Pass to the meadowlands at New Las Vegas, on over Glorieta Pass through the Sangre de Cristo Mountains to New Albuquerque, and down the Rio Grande toward Rincon and west to the end-of-track. Here railway passengers took a stagecoach west to Deming, where westward bound travelers took another stagecoach to the Southern Pacific Railroad end-of-track to board a SPRR passenger car headed for Benson in Arizona Territory. The Southern Pacific and the Santa Fe joined rails at Deming on March 1, 1881. Masterson took a stagecoach for the ten-mile trip from Benson to Tombstone and a rendezvous with other former Kansas gamblers. In a mid–February 1881 issue, the *Dodge City Times* crowed like a proud mother hen: "The old Dodge boys are seeking fortune in the gold fields of Arizona."

The "Dodge City gang's" gambling operation, headquartered at the Alhambra Saloon owned by Joseph Mellgren and John Meagher with Wyatt as their silent partner, was situated on the north side of Allen Street in the middle of the block between Fourth and Fifth streets. In an 1896 interview in the *San Francisco Examiner,* Wyatt claimed that his "faro bank [operation] meant anything upwards of $1,000 a night." John Meagher would ride with Wyatt Earp's posse during the final raid against the Cow-boy leadership in the summer of 1882.

During his off hours, Bat was helping Wyatt cultivate local citizen support for Earp's effort to be a candidate for sheriff at the next election. For adventure, Masterson rode with the Earp brothers chasing stage mail robbers, but he did not get rich in Tombstone. He witnessed the notorious Allen Street gunfight between Luke Short and Charlie Storms and was a chief witness at the murder hearing that exonerated Short for killing in self defense.

The Tombstone chapter of Bat's life was short-lived. In mid–April 1881, he received a telegram requesting his immediate return to Dodge City because his brother Jim was in trouble. Bat said good-bye to Wyatt, and thereby to his place in Tombstone history. Masterson made the return trip to western Kansas as fast as the iron horse would carry him across New Mexico Territory. Bat's April 16 arrival in Dodge City on the 11:50 morning train signaled the start of the legendary "Battle of the Plaza" and ended with Bat's arrest, an eight-dollar fine, and an admonition to "get out of Dodge." Bat left town but returned many times over the next few years, especially in the summer of 1883 when Wyatt Earp returned to Dodge City to restore law and order to the community via famous Dodge City "peace commission."

Theodore Roosevelt wrote about Bat Masterson in his 1894 massive three-volume *The Winning of the West,* saying that Bat was a "noble spirit" who helped rid "the west of its murderers, of its bandits, and of its criminals and making it the garden spot of America." In 1905, President Roosevelt caused Bat's appointment as an office deputy, without assigned duties, in the United States marshal's office in New York City. Simultaneously, Bat wrote a weekly sports column for the *New York Morning Telegraph* and bet on a few athletic ventures. He died at his newspaper desk in 1921 and is buried in New York City.

Wyatt Earp must have been disappointed at Bat Masterson's early return to Dodge City. Masterson's sudden exit from Tombstone has provided historians with the "what if Masterson had stayed?" discussion concerning the future level of Cow-boy violence in Arizona. Would events have been different had Bat Masterson, and not the volatile Doc Holliday, been with the Earp brothers at the October 1881 streetfight? Would Bat have deserted Wyatt during the Iron Springs fight? Alas, history will never know the answer to these questions. However, we will examine Bat's post–Tombstone part in the Cow-boy campaign in a later chapter.

4.

Some First-Class Paladins

Paladin: a knightly defender.—World Book Dictionary

One of the guidelines George Washington established for his life concerned friendships: "Be courteous to all, but intimate with few; and let those few be well tried before you give them your confidence." Washington's adult life reflected that dictum.[1] Much the same quality could be said for Wyatt Earp. Some historians and western writers have questioned the composition of Wyatt's federal posse during the Cow-boy Campaign, claiming they were a band of questionable repute, little better than the men they were out to capture or kill. There is an old dictum in law enforcement: it takes tough men to hunt tough men. These posse men were known as hard and tough fighters in their day, but most important they were loyal to Wyatt Earp.

Who were the men who composed the battle-tested federal strike force of paladins led by deputy United States marshal Wyatt Earp? At different times Marshal Earp's posse included his youngest brother, Warren Baxter Earp, John Henry "Doc" Holliday, John O. "Texas Jack" Vermillion, John "Turkey Creek Jack" Johnson (John Blount), Sherman W. McMaster, Daniel G. "Big Tip" Tipton, and Origen Charles "Hair-lip Charlie" Smith. The sweeper, or cleanup, posse that closed the Cow-boy Campaign a few months later was composed of Lewis Watson "Lou" Cooley, John Meagher, Fred Dodge, Johnny "Crooked-Mouth" Green and O.C. Smith.

John O. "Texas Jack" Vermillion first met Wyatt Earp in Dodge City when he was a gambler with the nickname "Shoot-Your-Eye-Out-Jack," before he came to Arizona in search of a new future. Some historians have suggested that Vermillion worked as a carpenter and lived in a cave in the Dragoon Mountains before moving into Tombstone to serve as a special officer under city marshal Virgil Earp. Wyatt claimed that this fearless frontier fighter drowned in Lake Michigan in 1900 and has a final resting place in his native state. Peter Brand, Ben Traywick, and a number of other researchers are still seeking to provide a more accurate and complete portrait of this frontier shootist.

John "Turkey Creek Jack" Johnson was a heavy-set man from the lead-mining area of Missouri whose real name was John William Blount. He had a brother Wyatt helped to receive a pardon from prison. Using the name Johnson, Creek served as an officer in Newton, Nebraska, before going to Deadwood, Dakota Territory, where he first met Earp. According to Adelia Earp Edwards, "Bat (Masterson) and Creek were at our home most days when we were in Dodge City." Wyatt's sister also said Johnson was "that dandy, dancing" man who was "a real educated gentleman." In old age, Adelia fondly recalled, "he was sort of quiet and very dark and handsome."

The Spanish speaking Creek Johnson is believed to have gone to Arizona Territory as an undercover agent for a cattlemen's association and joined the Tombstone area Cow-boys to learn the methods of the area cattle rustlers. Johnson provided the Earps with valuable inside intelligence on the rustlers' activities and was such a successful thief that at one time he had a $2,500 reward posted for his arrest. Once, Virgil Earp, then Tombstone's chief of police, had to help him elude custody by faking an attempted arrest.

Wyatt Earp and Creek Johnson often saw each other after Tombstone when Wyatt was traveling the gambling circuit. Earp told novelist Walter Noble Burns that Johnson had been a Mason at some point and "was a bookkeeper and very well educated." No evidence has been found to support either assertion, but all the Blount brothers were members of the Independent Order of Odd Fellows. Just as they are with Vermillion, researchers continue efforts to bring this frontiersman out of the shadows.

Sherman Washington McMaster was a red-faced man about five feet eight inches tall, an Illinois native with a reddish-brown mustache and chin whiskers. He had light-brown close-cut hair, talked very quickly, and was fluent in Spanish. Like Wyatt, he loved fine horses. Sherman, called Mac by his friends, was a former Texas Ranger who had also infiltrated the Cow-boy organization and was a successful undercover operative for Wyatt Earp and possibly Wells Fargo Express Company. He was present in the Tombstone pool hall when Morgan Earp was assassinated. Paul Cool's research has enhanced our knowledge of this man, who as a child dined at the family table with the likes of Ralph Waldo Emerson and Horace Greeley. Cool even discovered the proper spelling of Sherman's last name: no "s" on the end of McMaster.

Daniel Gordon "Big Tip" Tipton was always an ally of the Earp brothers. Peter Brand, a new breed of Earp researcher from Australia, and the late Mark Dworkin, a Canadian, broke hard ground to bring Dan Tipton out of the shadows and give him depth. Tipton was a New Yorker by birth and a navy seaman before arriving in Arizona Territory. He was an honest gambler and a trustworthy friend. When ambushers assassinated Morgan Earp at Campbell & Hatch Saloon and Billiard Parlor, Dan Tipton, Sherm McMaster, and Wyatt were watching Morgan play pool. Tipton served as a trusted messenger between Wyatt and the Tombstone vigilantes and joined the posse during the final days of the hunt for the Cow-boys and the exile in New Mexico Territory and Colorado. Later, Dan Tipton was reputed to have been one of Wyatt Earp's enforcers during the Dodge City Peace Commission episode in the summer of 1883. In the 1890s, Tipton worked as a U.S. customs inspector in El Paso. He was arrested for helping to smuggle illegal Chinese laborers into the United States. He was found guilty and sentenced to 20 months in federal prison. In February 1898 he died of Bright's disease while in an Ohio prison. His grave is marked with a Civil War veteran's headstone arranged by Peter Brand and Mark Dworkin.

Origen Charles "Harelip Charlie" Smith also made part of the ride with the posse. Josie Earp liked Smith even if his parents had cursed him with a difficult moniker; Origen was for one of the early priestly leaders of the Catholic Church. He was called

"Harelip Charlie" because of his facial deformity caused by a cleft palate at birth. Smith was "a man of sterling quality, steadfast in his friendships and zealous in his duty." Wounded twice in action as an officer, he was fearless in a gunfight. The Connecticut-born Smith and Wyatt had been friends since their Fort Worth days in the 1870s. Smith was the only original strike force team member to join Wyatt on the return mission that killed Johnny Ringo. (In August 1887, Charlie Smith and Fred Dodge, then constables, accompanied Virgil Earp on a posse chasing train robbers near Fairbanks, Arizona. Dodge later recalled that Virgil was quite a sight with his boneless left arm flopping about as he rode.)

Lewis Watson "Lou" Cooley was a mysterious figure. He was born in Illinois in 1854 and ten years later moved with his parents to Fort Scott, Kansas. In 1873, Cooley went to Texas and worked in Dallas and Fort Worth until joining the westward movement of the railroad. He drove stage out of Fort Concho (San Angelo), Fort Davis and El Paso. In Arizona, Lou again worked as a stage driver in Yuma, Tucson, and finally in Tombstone. he was a Democrat and identified with the rowdy Southern-bred Cowboys, which, along with his tracking abilities, made him a useful undercover operative for Wells Fargo Express Company. Cooley counted among his backers E.B. Gage, N.K. Fairbanks, J.D. Kinnear, and Henry Hooker. He and Wyatt Earp associated with the same influential individuals. E.B. Gage would play a part in the quest to make Wyatt Earp the chief deputy sheriff of Colfax County, New Mexico Territory, in December 1884.

John Gregory Meagher was a Canadian born in 1843. John and his twin brother, Mike, were founders of Wichita, Kansas. John served as sheriff of Sedgwick County in 1872 and 1873, with the county seat at Wichita. When John's brother Mike was marshal of Wichita, Wyatt Earp was one of his toughest deputies. Mike was also a deputy U.S. marshal and a leader of the Kansas–Indian Territory Border Patrol and Wyatt Earp worked with him as a field deputy. John Meagher worked as a peace office in Caldwell, Kansas, before moving to Tombstone. John and his wife of six years divorced in 1879. Virginia was the daughter of trailblazer and scout Tom "Broken Hand" Fitzpatrick. Henry, the son of Virginia and John, rode with Teddy Roosevelt's Rough Riders in the 1898 war with Spain. In Tombstone John owned the Alhambra Saloon and Wyatt Earp was a gambling partner.

Fred Dodge was born in northern California in 1854 and as a youth joined his father in the mining business around Sacramento and later in Nevada. In late 1879, Dodge came to Tombstone and lived in southern Arizona until 1890. He operated saloons in Tombstone and Bisbee, served as a deputy sheriff and constable, and operated faro games. He ended his career serving 20 years as a distinguished investigator or special detective for Wells Fargo Express Company headquartered in Texas. He died at his ranch near Boerne, Texas, in December 1938. Josie Earp visited Fred, his wife, and his namesake son at the Dodge ranch after Wyatt's death. The journals and record books that Fred Dodge kept provided the framework for the book *Undercover for Wells Fargo*, edited by Caroline Lake, daughter of Wyatt Earp biographer Stuart N. Lake.

Author's Perspective: Some historians have claimed that there is no evidence, including existing Wells Fargo documents, that support Dodge's claim he was a deep-cover special agent of Wells Fargo, reporting only to the general superintendent, during the Earp era in Tombstone. The final judgment is still out on that claim, as new records are still being discovered.

John R. "Crooked-Mouthed" Green was a good man with a card deck or a pistol. He was nicknamed "Crooked-Mouthed" because he once had a bullet pass through his cheek and the healed wound distorted the appearance of his mouth. Green had also earned the moniker of "Cathouse Johnny" for being a protector of "Ladies of the Evening." When Wyatt Earp was the Pima County deputy sheriff stationed at Tombstone in 1880 he had cause to arrest Green. In July 1880 Green and his partner, John R. Adams, lost their saloon in Tombstone. Green and Earp became friends and in later years, they and their lady friends would be traveling companions on the gambling circuit. Green was with Wyatt in June 1883 as part of the Dodge City Peace Commission that restored law and order in the ole Kansas cowtown.

Author's Perspective: I believe that if Wyatt Earp had a traveling partner when he left Gunnison, Colorado, in July 1882 to lead a second strike force team against the Cow-boys, it was most likely Johnny Green and not Doc Holliday as some writers have claimed.

5

Some First-Class Jokers

Joker: A phrase or sentence hidden away in a law, contract or other document to defeat its apparent purpose; a bad-mannered or awkward person; in 1880s Tombstone an "honest rancher," or Cowboy.—Author's Dictionary, 2015

He was not a paladin, but there is no way to discuss the Earp brothers' Tombstone sojourn without mention of Johnny Behan. Contrary to movies, stories and fictional mythmakers, Behan did not arrive in Tombstone until 10 months after the Earp brothers had settled in the community. His quick social rise was due to his abundant charm and political connections.

John Harris Behan was born in Missouri in October 1845 and died of Bright's disease in June 1912. His grave in Tucson's Holy Hope Catholic Cemetery lay unmarked until 1990, when a group of western reenactors marked the site.

"Gentleman Johnny" Behan was of short-stature, a dandy, a self-proclaimed ladies' man, a lovable scoundrel, a consummate political opportunist who was always seeking a better government job, and a womanizing philanderer who contracted syphilis that contributed to his death. He was divorced in June 1875, four years after his "shotgun" marriage, for spousal abuse and adultery, and the court ordered Behan to pay $16.66 in monthly child support. He had a son and daughter. However, Behan's political friends had the divorce proceedings sealed during his lifetime. Victoria Zaff Behan remarried; "Gentleman Johnny" did not. He served a term as sheriff of Yavapai County (Prescott) and ran unsuccessfully for reelection in 1876. Two years later, he was unsuccessful in his bid to become the sheriff of Mohave County (Kingman).

In 1880, Behan moved to Tombstone and jointly operated the Dexter Livery Stable and blacksmith business with John Dunbar. Thomas Dunbar operated a ranch northeast of Benson, and, unlike his brother John and Behan, was a strong anti–Cow-boy advocate and supported the law and order faction in Cochise County. Johnny Behan even roomed with Cow-boy leader John Ringo. On October 3, 1879, Prescott's *Arizona Weekly Miner* reported how Behan had a dispute with a Chinese laundryman and was almost beat to death in the encounter. Johnny Behan knew how to hate, so in Tombstone he became a leader of the Non-Partisan Anti–Chinese League

In the 1881 session of the Arizona Territorial Legislative Assembly, John Dunbar's

brother Thomas introduced legislation to create
a new county out of the southwestern section of
Pima County. The bill passed and was signed by
the governor. The Dunbar brothers—natives of
Maine and friends of the state's powerful Republican politician James G. Blaine—and Behan used
their political friends to seek appointments to
head the new county government.

When the Democrat-controlled territorial legislature established Cochise County in heavily Democratic southeastern Arizona, John C. Frémont, the
Republican territorial governor, according to law
had to appoint the new county officials who would
serve until the next general election in November
1882. The new sheriff was the county's chief lawman
and also the county tax assessor and collector. The
job paid 10 percent of all the fees and assessed taxes
he collected. During the two years Behan held the
sheriff's post the job was worth about $25,000 a
year, or almost a million dollars in today's currency.
Governor Frémont earned $2,600 per year.

**John H. Behan, sheriff of Cochise
County, Arizona Territory, 1881–
1882 (author's collection).**

Behan and Earp were the candidates for appointment as the first sheriff of Cochise
County. Behan had the advantage because he had replaced Wyatt as the Pima County
deputy sheriff for the Tombstone area when Earp resigned in the fall of 1880 to support
Bob Paul's Republican candidacy for the sheriff's post against the Democratic incumbent.
So it was Behan, not Earp, who represented county law enforcement in the new county's
geographic area and the deputy sheriff was a longtime Missouri transplant who had served
in the Arizona legislature and still had political connections in Prescott. Wyatt Earp also
had law enforcement experience, but he was an Arizona newcomer, a Republican, and
had no political support for appointed office in a Democratic stronghold.

In January 1881, Johnny Behan and Wyatt Earp sat in Dave Cohen's Cigar Store, next
to the Crystal Palace Saloon on Allen Street, and discussed the bill in the Arizona Territorial General Assembly for creation of a new county from part of Pima County, with
Tombstone as the county seat. John Behan, always the slippery politician, conned Wyatt
Earp into a "gentleman's agreement" to make Wyatt his chief deputy, with a percentage
of the fees and taxes collected, if Earp would withdraw his candidacy for the sheriff's
office and support him. Earp understood that Maine's Senator James G. Blaine, secretary
of state designee under President-Elect James A. Garfield, had requested that Governor
Frémont appoint "Gentleman Johnny" as sheriff and John O. Dunbar as treasurer for the
new county. Wyatt agreed to the deal because he knew that a territorial governor was
appointed by the president but reported to the secretary of state. Frémont would do as
requested by his potential new boss. Holding true to his typical double-cross political
style, Behan selected another Democrat as his assistant after he received the sheriff's
appointment. This incident is the cornerstone for the county versus city and county versus
federal law enforcement mistrust overshadowing the new Cochise County government.

When Josephine Marcus, Behan's live-in mistress and nanny for his young son Albert, was added to the political mix Behan's world became explosive. First, "Gentleman Johnny" tricked her into financing a house, in his name, on Safford Street near the northeast corner of Seventh Street across from the new Catholic church building. Then, while Behan held up the wedding plans, he carried on an affair with his business partner's wife. Next, a lover's triangle enters into the equation when Wyatt and Josie, now split from Behan, had a chance meeting at the ice cream parlor and a simmering flirtation developed between them.

Long after Tombstone, Josie and Albert Behan remained friends and Wyatt grew to treat him like a son. Albert grew up to become a Border Patrol agent in Arizona.

In the final political accounting, Behan was unable to hang onto his lucrative prize and lost his own party's nomination for sheriff in 1882 and even faced five criminal charges for different acts of malfeasance in office. The charges were dismissed and Behan continued to run his livery stable. Next, he served two years as warden of the territorial prison before being fired. In his one act of courage he helped to break up a prison riot. For years he wandered Arizona, always seeking public approval and a public job. Legends have Johnny Behan serving as a manager in the Quartermaster Corps during the Spanish-American War of 1898 and as a "secret" government agent in China during the 1900 Boxer Rebellion. Yet researcher Lynn Bailey suggests that official records don't seem to support these claims.

Our friend Bob Alexander, a retired federal investigator turned college instructor and horse raiser, published a full-scale Behan biography and concluded his work by saying, "Johnny Behan's life history has been sacrificed to falsely embellish and perpetuate the Earp myth."

During the 1950s TV western craze, Walt Disney did his part to perpetuate the heroic saga of the heroic frontier peace officer with "Tales of Texas John Slaughter" on his weekly *Disneyland–Walt Disney Presents.* In all 17 hour-long episodes, tall handsome Tom Tryon portrayed Slaughter as a happy-go-lucky adventurer. Between 1958 and 1961, Disney Studios made a fortune in the overseas movie market with films composed of series episodes and at home with tie-in merchandise sales. Most of the "Texas John tales" were located in Tombstone as competition to other TV series depicting real-life Arizonans Wyatt Earp and Johnny Ringo or the fictional Sheriff Clay Hollister of *Tombstone Territory* and the fictional Frank Morgan of the contemporary *Sheriff of Cochise.*

The real John Horton Slaughter was a man of wiry short stature, had a sourpuss disposition and stuttering speech, was tubercular, asthmatic, and a cigar smoker, and possessed a less than heroic nature. In the spring of 1879, officers arrested Slaughter as a cattle thief in New Mexico Territory. The former Texas Ranger with a shady past dealing with other men's cattle knew his law and was able to convince local authorities they were mistaken about him and his cattle herd. Upon his release, Slaughter quickly relocated to what became Cochise County, Arizona Territory, and soon befriended the Cow-boy element. Many men like William Claiborne had previously worked for Slaughter in Texas or New Mexico and their supporters who brought their beef to his butcher shop in Charleston.

In October 1880, John Roberts, Slaughter's ranch foreman, posted a court appearance bond for Pete Spencer, a Cow-boy second-tier stalwart arrested on a grand larceny charge of stealing Mexican mules. In this arena, following the Earp era, Slaughter became a wealthy cattleman and was later twice elected, as a Democrat, Cochise County sheriff (1887–1890).

Charlie Siringo, a famous frontier-era Pinkerton detective later turned writer, told about a cattle-stealing case that sheds some light on the southeastern Arizona Cowboy cattle-stealing operations. Siringo wrote that his investigation determined that Lincoln County, New Mexico, rustlers composed of Billy the Kid and his friends stole some cattle in the Texas Panhandle and then sold them to a man named Slaughter, who drove the cattle to Arizona and resold them in Old Mexico. Siringo believed that Slaughter used his cattle-fencing profits to purchase Mexican cattle stolen by the Cow-boys; these "international" cattle became the foundation stock for his 230,000-acre border ranch in the southeastern corner of Cochise County near Guadalupe Canyon.

John Slaughter was a key figure in leveling suspicion that Doc Holliday was involved in the attempted Benson stage holdup in March 1881. He claimed to have seen Holliday returning to Tombstone from the direction of the attempted holdup. What was Slaughter's motive for the lie?

Today, John Slaughter's San Bernardino Ranch headquarters is a museum and public park. You can stand on the porch of the big ranch house and gaze across the manicured lawn into Mexico. Only a barbed wire fence serves as the designation line of the international border.

The loose-knit confederation of rough-riding daredevils called the Cow-boys had been roaming the southwest for years but had been held in check by the army's efforts to control the Apaches. Now in the late 1870s, miners had invaded the Indians' ancestral homelands in southeastern Arizona and found gold, silver, cooper and other minerals. New settlements were established for the support of these miners and the new community dwellers provided a fresh market for food supplies, with a high demand for beef. The Cow-boys had an open market to sell their questionable beef supply, at below the market price, to government supply agents for the army and the Indian reservations commissaries. A town butcher was not always too particular about the brand on the cattle he bought if in turn he could make a profit by selling his trimmed-out beef to eager housewives and restaurant owners in his community. This system worked very effectively if local police were not overly efficient in law enforcement.

Who where the hardworking "honest ranchers" of southeastern Arizona Territory in the late 1870s and early 1880s? Newman Haynes "Old Man" Clanton and his son Joseph Isaac "Ike" Clanton, William "Curly Bill" Brocius, and Johnny Ringo were the field captains of the Cow-boy confederation. The worker bees were Phineas "Fin" Clanton and William "Billy" Clanton, Robert Findley "Frank" McLaury and Thomas Clarke "Tom" McLaury, Eliott Larkin Ferguson alias Pete Spencer, Frank Stilwell, Johnny Barnes, Frederick "German Fries" Bode, Arthur Boucher alias William Grounds, Henry "Apache Hank" Swilling, Florentino "Indian Charley" Cruz, Joe Olney alias Joe Hill, Jim Hughes, Dick Gray, Billy Lang, Jack Gauze, Billy Allen, Charlie Thomas, Charlie "Bud" Snow, Zwing Hunt, Coley Finley, John Green and Charlie Green, Milt Hicks, Tall Bell, Len Redfield and Hank Redfield, Harry Ernshaw, Bill Leonard, Harry Head, Jim Crane, Dave Estes, Dick Lloyd, James Johnson, Jerry Alkinson, Charles T. "Pony Diehl" Ray, and William Floyd "Willie" or "Billy the Kid" Claiborne, "Babacomari Frank" Patterson, and Edward Collins.

PART TWO

"The Lion of Tombstone"

Up and down through the deserts he [Wyatt] raged like a lion ravenous for blood. He tracked down the assassins. He killed them cruelly without pity. There was no flinching in what he did, and no alibis or apologies afterward. He became his own law in a lawless land and atoned for the blood of his brothers with the blood of his brothers' murderers. Right or wrong, he believed with absolute faith in the righteousness of the justice he administered at the muzzle of a gun. For the men he slew in vengeance, Wyatt Earp had no regrets. No remorseful memories troubled him. No ghosts came back to haunt him.... Whatever else he may have been, he was brave. Not even his enemies have sought to deny his splendid courage.... What he did, he did. The record stands.—Walter Noble Burns, *Tombstone: An Iliad of the Southwest*, 1927

6

The Earp Brothers, Tombstone Businessmen

[Wyatt Earp] is now one of the wealthy men of Tombstone. He owns a large portion of the land on which the town is built, and some valuable mining property.—(*Dodge City*) *Ford County Globe*, 11 October 1881

The cornerstone of the Wyatt Earp legend is based upon the 877 days he spent in Arizona Territory during the early 1880s dealing with the Cow-boy troubles in the Tombstone area. Since the events of these 29 months have been told and retold in hundreds of thousands of print pages worldwide, we will not cover all of them here in detail. However, we will recap the major events that are pertinent to the focus of this work. In his 1927 historical saga, *Tombstone: An Iliad of the Southwest*, Chicago-based journalist and writer Walter Noble Burns wrote, "No man in Tombstone's history has been more bitterly maligned than Wyatt Earp."[1]

After leaving Dodge City, Kansas, Wyatt and James Earp and their families spent a short time in New Mexico Territory during the fall of 1879. It was not a protracted stay, since the gods of fate had ordained that Wyatt's destiny was awaiting him in a mesa-topped mining town called Tombstone. In fall 1879 Wyatt's adventures in the Land of Enchantment were still in his future. Those same fates that pulled at Earp had allowed Doctor and Mrs. John Henry Holliday to spend over a year in northeastern New Mexico before also marching into legend in Arizona Territory.

Pennsylvania-born Robert Jackways "Uncle Bob" Winders, a former Texas Ranger, was the owner of the Cattle Exchange Saloon in Fort Worth. He and his son-in-law Origen Charles "Hair-Lip Charlie" Smith, along with their families, left Cow Town in the summer of 1879 and settled in Tombstone. Contrary to Hollywood movies and Earp mythmakers, Winders' letters to James Earp convinced his bartender to roll the dice and stake his future in Arizona Territory. James convinced Wyatt to join him and Wyatt convinced Virgil to join in their adventure. The lure of wealth and family later brought Morgan, with his wife, and Warren to Tombstone.

On October 2, 1879, Tombstone's first newspaper, the *Weekly Nugget*, told readers, "No mining camp on the Pacific coast ever started to build with the great promise that Tombstone does today." The Earp brothers believed in the dream and had come to Arizona Territory to make their fortunes as entrepreneurs, not to work in law enforcement. Wyatt had first hoped to establish a stage line but quickly discovered that Tombstone didn't need another transportation system. The brothers prospected for ore-bearing rock and searched for a water source. They found both. The Earps had come to Tombstone with an economic fallback plan: saloon operation and gambling. The editor of Tucson's *Arizona Weekly Star* defined the "Knights of the Green Cloth" on March 3, 1881, when he wrote, "The profession of gambler is as honorable as members of any stock exchange in the world—and braver. Their word is as good as their bond."

Five decades after the event, Josie Marcus, Wyatt Earp's last wife, in her autobiography discussed Wyatt's entrance into Tombstone presaging historic events with an understatement. Her ghostwriter wrote, "It was [Monday] December 1 of 1879 and a chill wind whistled among the greasewood, lifting the horses' manes. A dip into a ravine, a long easy climb to an almost level, rocky hillside, and the Earps were in Tombstone." Allie Earp recalled her first sight of Tombstone, calling the village "a hodgepodge of shacks, adobe and tents."[2]

One of the first persons Wyatt Earp met in Tombstone was Andrew S. "Andy" Neff, his wife, Sarah, and their daughters. Neff, a veteran of an Iowa infantry regiment, operated the California Fruit and Produce Store at 324 Fremont Street and the Malcom Stage Station and Saloon about 2½ miles out of Tombstone on the road to Contention.[3] The stalwart Republican was also a limited partner of Tombstone's founder, Ed Schieffelin, in the Toughnut Mine. The Neff family had lived on a dairy farm near Prescott before coming to Tombstone in 1879 a few months before the Earps. It is unclear if Andy Neff had known Virgil Earp in Prescott, but in July 1881, when Virgil was Tombstone's chief of police, he made Neff one of his four special police officers with special responsibility for the safety of Fremont Street.

The Ohio native and Wyatt became friends and business partners. Andy and Sarah Neff, married at Fort Smith, Arkansas, became next door neighbors to Wyatt and Mattie Earp on the western extension of Fremont Street beyond First Street. Andy's oldest daughter, Wynona Leona (called "Nona" by friends and family), married a New Mexico peace officer named Abe Hixenbaugh in August 1890. The Hixenbaugh family played an important role in Wyatt and Josie's life in late 1884, and this is discussed in our book about Wyatt and Josie's adventures in New Mexico.

Nona Neff Hixenbaugh wrote the director of the Arizona Pioneers Historical Society a series of letters during 1935 and 1936 concerning events of her childhood in Tombstone and her friendship with Wyatt and Mattie Earp. She hoped to counteract some of

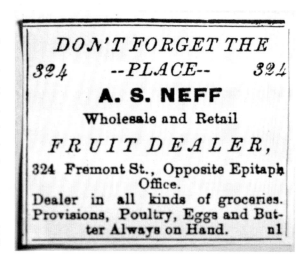

DON'T FORGET THE

324   --PLACE--   324

A. S. NEFF

Wholesale and Retail

FRUIT DEALER,

324 Fremont St., Opposite Epitaph Office.

Dealer in all kinds of groceries. Provisions, Poultry, Eggs and Butter Always on Hand.   n1

Advertisement for Andy Neff's Tombstone store published in the *Tombstone Daily Gossip* on March 29, 1881 (author's collection).

the anti–Earp information distributed by the society since the 1931 publication of Stuart Lake's Wyatt Earp biography. The historical society has never held a positive view of the Earp brothers or their actions in Tombstone, therefore much firsthand pro–Earp material in their care has remained elusive to researchers. In 1998, Nona Neff Hixenbaugh's long forgotten 1930s correspondence was, luckily, discovered by the author's friend and fellow Earp-era researcher Jeff Wheat.

"Wyatt Earp was almost a Father to me and I loved him and his wife [Mattie Blaylock] verry [sic] Dearly. We lived about 20 feet from his home in Tombstone. It seems as only yesterday I played in their yard," recalled Mrs. Hixenbaugh. Another time she wrote, "Don't think [it's true] or believe all [that] people tell you about the Earps for I was in their home every day and they loved children and dogs. Some good prinisable [principle]." The 60-plus-year-old woman remembered Wyatt as "one of the most tender-hearted men I ever met." She also recalled her preteen impression that Tombstone's "lawlessness of that day was a constant source of grief to him [Wyatt Earp]." She recalled how Wyatt would help her and her older sister with homework sessions and remembered the night she read an English composition from the stage of the Bird Cage Theater during a community assembly.

In another letter, Mrs. Hixenbaugh made her admiration for the Earps very clear: "Wyatt [Earp] was the one that always told the rest [of the Earp family] what to do and they always obeyed as well as every body else in Tombstone, but he was very kind and they [the Earp brothers] were all very honest although they all gambled. When they got into trouble it was always in upholding the law." (The Hixenbaughs visited Tombstone in the 1940s.)

In December 1882, Andy Neff sold his Tombstone grocery business to George W. Chapman, the city tax collector and a policeman, and moved his family to Colfax County, New Mexico Territory, to work for the Santa Fe Railroad and cultivate a small farm outside of Raton. The Neffs never forgot Wyatt Earp and named their youngest son Wyatt in honor of a man they loved and respected. The couple are buried in Raton's Fairmont Cemetery.

Some writers, led by the example of fiction writer Frank Waters, have tried to paint Virgil Earp as the big breadwinner for the brothers' families during their early months in Tombstone because he was a federal officer. Before leaving Tucson—on Thursday, November 27, 1879—Virgil took an oath to serve as a deputy United States marshal, but he did not earn his first arrest fee until almost four months later. The truth is the Earp family's early months in Tombstone were largely financed by Wyatt's gambling operation profits and his Wells Fargo Company duties. Virgil gambled some, but he mostly prospected. James received a military pension of $10 a month for wounds received during the Civil War, but his limited mobility still allowed him to earn a good living tending bar. He eventually established his own sampling room in the heart of Tombstone's business district.

None of the Earp family could be accused of suffering from ergophobia, a fear of work. It didn't take long before the Earp women were constructing a makeshift communal home, while the brothers and Bob Winders scouted a second nearby site for another mining claim. Wyatt had located a single-room, dirt-floor adobe house, for $40 per month, and had the wagons parked on each side. The canvas wagon covers were stretched over the space between the wagon and the cabin to form a covered area. Allie Earp recalled, "We cooked in the fireplace and used boxes for chairs." A few months later each family had their own house built upon their Mountain Maid Extension mining claim at the junction of First and Fremont streets. Allie recalled one time when Vigil was out of town and some drunken horsemen shot off some of the roof shingles on her nice new house.

The Earp women earned household funds by using Allie's sewing machine to produce custom sewing assignments at a penny per yard. Their largest job was constructing a large canvas tent for a saloon along Allen Street. Contrary to the vitriolic dark tales Frank Waters wrote about Wyatt, Allie Earp claimed in her real memoirs that it was Wyatt who convinced Virgil to let her bring the sewing machine to Tombstone. She claimed, "We made a lot of money with it." Mattie Blaylock, Wyatt's consort, was an accomplished seamstress and did special consignment work for local dressmakers.

During the months that "Uncle Bob" Winders had been in Tombstone before the Earp brothers arrived, he explored the local area for likely ore deposits. Winders and the Earp brothers filed a second mining claim on Wednesday, December 10, 1879, and called the discovery the *Earp* claim. The Earp brothers, singularly or in partnership, would file more mining claims within the next twelve months. The *Earp* claim was followed on January 14, 1880, by the 10-acre *Grasshopper* claim and in February by the *Dodge*, the *Mattie Blaylock*, the *Comstock* and the *Rocky Ridge*. The 30-arce *Long Branch* surface claim was recorded on April 20, before the brothers took time off from prospecting during the hot summer months. On November 4, 1880, Wyatt and two partners filed on the *Old Bull* and Virgil stacked out the *Red Star* claim, which proved to be the Earps last mining claim in the Tombstone District. Virgil Earp and his dog spent some time in early March 1881 hiking the country around Benson seeking likely mineral deposits. This was the last prospecting trip any of the Earp brothers was able to undertake before their law enforcement duties overwhelmed them.

In the early 1900s, Virgil Earp did some prospecting in Nevada along with Wyatt. After Tombstone, Wyatt and his final wife, Josie Marcus, prospected for gold and copper along both sides of the Colorado River, in Idaho, in Alaska, and near Kingman, Arizona. Wyatt was mildly successful with these ventures and with his Kern County, California, oil leases. In their last years, James Earp sometimes joined Wyatt to help him work his Happy Days lode claims near Earp, California. But as fast as Wyatt made money, Josie would find a way to lose it gambling.[4]

Morgan lived in Tombstone when Lou was with him, but during the periods when she was staying in California with his parents he made Bisbee or Benson, where his served as a special deputy sheriff for Johnny Behan, the base for his gambling efforts. When alone in Tombstone, Morgan sometimes shared a cabin with Fred Dodge, located on the site behind where the Bird Cage Theatre was later constructed. He also stayed in a cabin near the hoisting works on the Earp brothers' mining property near Hoptown.[5] Later, Warren Earp also used Benson as a base for his gambling ventures.

On March 30, 1880, the *Ford County Globe* updated Dodge City about the deeds of their former city marshal. The newspaper reported that Wyatt Earp and his Dodge City financial partner, Harry Finaty, had sold their *Copper Lode* mining claim for $30,000. Wyatt used his profit to become a silent partner in the Alhambra Saloon and

Gambling Hall operated by Wichita friend John Meagher, a former Kansas sheriff. Wyatt had served on the Wichita police force when Mike Meagher, John's twin brother, was the city marshal.

In addition to their mining and water rights claims, the Earp brothers owned a twenty-acre tract of agricultural land adjoining the Tombstone town site and an undetermined farm claim along the San Pedro River west of Tombstone tied up on title issues due to Mexican land grant issues. The Earp brothers also owned most of the residential property along both sides of the block of First Street running north between Fremont and Safford streets and about half of the block south toward Allen Street within the Tombstone town site. "US Deputy Marshal [Virgil] Earp and his brother Wyatt have been busy putting up dwelling houses during the past week," according to the October 22, 1880, *Tombstone Daily Nugget*. The brothers had added "landlord" to their resumes. Unfortunately, none of the three Earp brothers own residences have survived into this century. Virgil Earp's home burned on June 6, 1998.

In November 1880, the Earp investment team sold the underground mineral rights to the North Extension of the Mountain Maid claim. The brothers kept the surface rights for town lot investment. The land investment gamble was paying off. Each team member made money on his mining claims, land speculation, housing development, and gambling concession deals.

On Thursday, February 3, 1881, Wyatt Earp filed a water rights source claim for land on the east slope of the Huachuca Mountains. His investment combine, fellow gamblers, were Doc Holliday, Dick Clark and James Levy, who sold their water claim for $6,000 to the Sanborn Water Company to be developed as a water source for Tombstone. (Wyatt and Doc had to use their share of the profit to pay legal fees resulting from the street-fight hearing.)

The Oriental Saloon, located on the northeast corner of Allen and Fifth streets, was operated by Democrat powerhouse and Cow-boy sympathizer Milt Joice (Joyce) and his youthful California partner, William C. Parker. The two leased the gambling concession for their new establishment to four professional gamblers. *McKinney's Pacific Coast Directory for 1881* contains this listing: "Rickabaugh, Earp & Clark, Oriental Saloon, cor. Fifth and Allen." These three men were the portly Lou Rickabaugh and the tall and powerful Richard B. "Dick" Clark from San Francisco, and the tough Wyatt Earp, for his "peacekeeping abilities" with rowdy drunks and troublemakers. The pleasant-natured William H. "Sundown" Harris, from Dodge City, was a silent quarter-interest partner in the business. These men employed former Dodge City gamblers Luke Short, Doc Holliday and Bat Masterson to run their house games. The faro dealer's salary was $25 per six-hour session and an additional five dollars an hour if he worked extra hours. This compensation was considered a first-rate salary for that era when a day's wage was around a dollar.

The Earp brother's biggest learning curve was their unpreparedness for dealing with Arizona Territory's brand of business rings like the Cow-boy's crime confederacy; the 10-Percent Ring of corrupt Democrat politicians; the ethnic, cultural, social, and financial elites; and the black market economic stricture they faced in Tombstone. On May 30, 1882, the *San Francisco Examiner* published Virgil Earp's prospective on this subject. The former Tombstone chief of police was very blunt in his remarks: "The

Tombstone country is of a peculiar character, the community being unsettled and dangerous. Most of the business men there stayed simply to make money enough to live somewhere else comfortably, and of course the greatest object with them is to have as much money as possible spent in town and to get as much of it as they can, careless of the means of dispensation or the result of rough manners." Virgil Earp closed his perspective by recalling his law enforcement challenges in Tombstone: "Aside from the legitimate business men the bulk of the residents are idle or desperate characters, most of them coming into town broke and depending upon the gambling tables or criminal ventures to supply them with means of livelihood and dissipation."

On Monday evening, October 31, 1881, six-days after the streetfight between the Tombstone police and the Cow-boys, the Tombstone Common Council approved the 1882 tax roll assessment levied on all property located within the city limits. The mining and rent housing property of the Earp brothers, like many other property owners, saw an upward turn in taxable value. This type of value adjustment is normally viewed as a sign of financial success, but some Earp brothers detractors have used this tax assessment to allege the council was displeased with the brothers' police action and were punishing them. These detractors misunderstand the fact that it was Earp supporters, performing their duty as city council members, who increased the annual city property tax levy based upon the increased property values within their community.

A feature writer for the *Arizona Highway* magazine of July 1994 caught the truth of Wyatt Earp's focus in Tombstone when he wrote, "His work as a lawman, the centerpiece of the (Wyatt Earp) myth, was merely a sideline. In truth, Wyatt was a professional gambler and speculator whose primary motivation throughout his life was to get rich."

7

The Earp Brothers,
Law Enforcement Officers

"My experiences as an officer of the law are incidents of history, but
the modern writer does not seem willing to let it go at that."—Wyatt
Earp to Stuart N. Lake, 1928

What motivated the Earp brothers to become peace officers? A simple answer is
that their father, Nicolas Porter Earp, had often preached citizenship responsibility to
his sons: "Enforcement of the law is the duty of every man who asks for it protection."
In a new frontier community a peace officer interacted with all levels of society and
was an authority figure. He held the means for a steady paycheck and flexible hours
that allowed time for other business opportunities. Sometimes the Earp boys strayed
from the "narrow path," but they seem always to have found their way back. As Edward
R. Lyman has said, "Moral principle is a compass forever fixed and forever true."

Nicolas Earp and his sons—Newton, James, Virgil, Wyatt, Morgan, and Warren—
each wore a peace officer badge at some time during their lives. The Earps enforced the
law, sometimes with their own interpretation of it, first in Illinois, Iowa, and Missouri,
then later in Kansas, Indian Territory, Montana Territory, Idaho Territory, California,
Colorado, Nevada, District of Alaska, Arizona Territory and New Mexico Territory.

Wyatt Earp was born to be a frontier peace officer. He possessed a natural ability
to control men and was a master intimidator. He was a swift and strong pugilist in a
fight, and he was a quick and skilled functionary of weapons. He was cool under stress.
He was "courageous and bold" and was also considered one of the bravest men on the
frontier.

In most areas where the Earp brothers wore a badge, the peace officers' bond was
strong among the men who served at different levels of enforcement. In the Kansas
cowtowns, it was common for a man to carry authority on many levels; a town policeman could also be a deputy sheriff or constable. The Earps discovered that a mostly
noncooperative relationship prevailed in southeastern Arizona Territory. Here the sheriff's office, headed by Johnny Behan, actively protected the Cow-boys and assorted riff-
raff.

Unlike Kansas's seasonal itinerant drovers, these Arizona multicultural rowdies did not leave the area and return home at the end of the cattle drive season. These guys lived in the area year-round. On the economic front, the Arizona Cow-boys endeared themselves to local merchants by supplying needed trade goods, stolen in Mexico and smuggled across the border, at below the market wholesale prices, and thus had the support of most local businessmen.

The **United States marshal** has been annotated by fiction writers, dime novelists of the frontier era and modern radio, television and movie storytellers as the all-powerful law enforcement officer in this country. He had jurisdiction anywhere he went and his word was "the law" on all matters. In fact, a United States marshal has always had a very limited scope of authority and jurisdiction. He was paid no salary until the late 1890s or early 1900s.

The post of United States marshal was the first federal law enforcement position in the nation. The function of this peace officer has evolved since the Judiciary Act of 1789 established the office. The federal courts in his district were a United States marshal's chief client and the major focus of his service, but the president was his boss, as was to a lesser degree the precepts, written orders, of Congress. The marshal's primary duties were to serve the process of the federal courts—its warrants, summonses, and subpoenas—and enforce the lawful authority of the federal government. The marshals were the bailiffs of the federal court system and conducted the nine federal decennial censuses taken from 1790 through 1870.

It was not until President Ulysses S. Grant signed the Organization Act on June 22, 1870, creating the Department of Justice that the federal marshals had a direct boss, the attorney general, and an attempt to standardize federal law enforcement became a priority. Even a decade later the scope of the federal marshal's duty was fluid. This floating ambiguity provided Virgil and Wyatt Earp the broad ability they used to interpret their federal authority.

The president appoints a United States marshal, who serves at the chief executive's pleasure. For the first one hundred years of the republic, the United States marshal was the chief federal public relations person in his state or territory and oversaw the duty assignment of his deputies. U.S. marshals, like Arizona Territory's Crawley Dake, appointed deputies who served at the marshals' pleasure and were accountable only to the marshals. Many deputies looked upon the appointment as mostly a ceremonial position because it paid no salary, only process serving fees and mileage fees earned for serving orders of the federal court and making arrests for federal crimes.

Official records indicate that Virgil Earp came to Tombstone with a commission as a deputy United States marshal issued for the area around Prescott, which was altered later to make his service area centered around Tombstone. Later, Cow-boy partisans Johnny Behan and his civil deputy Billy Breckenridge would state that Wyatt was also a federal deputy sent to Tombstone to break up the Cow-boy confederation. Later actions seem to support their statements. It is worth noting that in the late 1800s, U.S. marshals were not required to maintain personal records concerning their deputies and Crawley Dake was not known for meticulous record keeping of any kind, especially financial. (It is a sorry fact, but many public records concerning Wyatt Earp once known to have existed can no longer be found. Now is not the occasion, nor does space allow, for a detailed discussion of this situation.)

Federal deputy marshals serving in the field could appoint assistant deputies, or "possemen," as needed to complete assignments, but they had to pay these temporary officers from their fee earnings or collected rewards. This procedure would play an important part in funding Wyatt Earp's notorious 1882 seek and destroy campaign against the Cow-boys.

The **sheriff** is chief law enforcement officer of county government in the United States. He is elected to office and can appoint a limited number of deputies, as specified by law, to assist him. In the 1880s, the sheriff also served as the county tax collector. He and his deputies earned no salary but were paid a fee according to the amount of taxes they collected and the number of county or justice court processes they served. Chasing stagecoach robbers, murderers, petty thieves, livestock thieves, and other criminals was not considered part of their "job description" by most sheriffs unless a court issued an arrest warrant for a suspect or a person or business posted a sizable reward. Today, sheriffs and deputies are paid a salary and benefits by the county government as prescribed by state law.

During 1882, the Cochise County sheriff earned $24,010.52 in fees. The reader can gain a better understanding of the fierce competition for the sheriff's post by computing the 1882 dollar value to the present-day value. A $24,000 income in 1882 would equate to $540,000 in today's money. An average salary for workers in 1882 was $600 to $1,200 per year.

A **marshal** or a **chief of police** was the administrative head of a municipal police force. The control of the Tombstone city government rested in a mayor and common council elected by the citizens. These city elections were strongly contested because the council enacted ordinances, set tax rates on property, and issued business licenses. The city government issued franchises for gas service, water service, and public printing. The council also controlled the city police force by appointment and salary and service fee payments of the chief and his policemen. These officers enforced the city ordinances. Tombstone paid its police chief $150 a month.

Under Arizona law, communities could elect a marshal who preformed limited law enforcement duties. Mostly he was a night watchman, within the limits of their community. He was paid by an established fee system for his services to the municipal court. A town marshal might also serve as the chief of police in an incorporated city or town but not always. This is a situation not always understood by historians, most fiction writers, and today's history buffs.

A **constable** is another local law enforcement officer. This individual is normally elected and serves as the enforcement arm of a justice of the peace court and has jurisdiction only in the precinct, a subdivision of a county, served by his court. In the prior-to-salary era, law enforcement officers earned performance fees, so another confusing situation is that any individual could serve simultaneously as a constable, town marshal, deputy sheriff, deputy game and fish warden, and other public law enforcement office and earn fees from *all* these offices.

8

The Cochise County Cow-boy War

Be it understood in this journal, cow-boy is a rustler, and rustler is synonym for desperado—bandit, outlaw and horse thief.—George Whitwell Parsons, *Private Journal*, 1 October 1880

Modern generations have had difficulty in understanding the evil nature that covered Arizona Territory during the 29 months the Earp brothers made that country their home. In his 1926 autobiography, *Scouting on Two Continents*, Major Fredrick Russell Burnham discussed his experience in Arizona during the Apache Wars and the Pleasant Valley Feud. Later, he became a decorated English officer in Great Britain's African Wars. The old warrior wrote, "In Arizona, my every turn was enmeshing me more completely in a network of rustlers, smugglers, and feudists. It was the twilight before the terrible night wherein stalk murderers, bandits, and all the grim underworld, which, once entered, grips a man in bonds that at first seem light as cobwebs, but later have the cruel strength of steel." Later, in 1908, Major Fredrick Russell Burnham was a founder, along with Sir Robert Baden-Powell, of the worldwide Boy Scout organization. He also took part in the Alaskan gold rush in the late 1890s and met Wyatt Earp in the "Last Frontier."

The area of Arizona that today is Cochise County was at first part of Pima County. In the early 1880s the region was enjoined in a divisive dispute over who owned the land upon which the village of Tombstone was founded. The dispute centered on a town-site development company of land speculators who claimed ownership of the land upon which Tombstone was being constructed and individuals who had bought their land or filed public land claims with the federal government. Historians call this conflict over clouded property titles "The Town Lot War." The Earp brothers and their friends sided with the individuals who held public land claim deeds because they held such property home sites and mining claims themselves.

One of the largest moneymaking operations in the developing community was the gambling concessions in the town's saloons. Gamblers from the Kansas cattle shipping towns and the Texas gaming circuit—called the "Easterners,"—had a turf conflict with the California and Nevada gold rush camp gamblers—called "the slopers"—for control of the disposable income in Tombstone. The Earps and their friends were a large influence in winning what was referred to as "The Gambler's War" for the Eastern Knights of the Green Cloth.

A third faction was the border Cow-boy confederation and their vast satellite empire of supporters. This group has been identified and discussed previously. The *Salt Lake City Tribune* of July 21, 1881, said, "The cowboy is a cross between vaquero and a highwayman, which intensifies the worst qualities of each type." A more pointed *Tucson Arizona Daily Star* editor said, "They are law-breakers of the most flagrant character." Meanwhile, the *Arizona Daily Citizen,* Tucson's other newspaper, continued the incrimination, saying anyone "who attempts to defend Arizona cowboys by restricting the term to its literal meaning of herder simply makes an ass of himself."

On another occasion the outspoken *Tucson Arizona Daily Star* editor wrote on February 13, 1881, "The stock industry is to-day paralyzed all through the section they [the Cow-boys] roam. The Cow-boys are outlaws, their hand is against the law-abiding people of the Territory, let them be dealt with accordingly. Let the public consider them outlaws, depredating upon the rights and property of the people, and wherever found let them be shot down like the Apache."

Everett B. Pomroy, United States attorney for Arizona Territory, in a June 23, 1881, situation report to Attorney General Wayne MacVeigh dealt with the misdeeds of the "Cow-boy" clan. He described these men in a blunt, bold and decisive manner: "The lawless element that exists along the border, who subsist by rapine plunder and highway robbery; and whose amusements are drunken orgies, and murder. The evil is one that feeding upon itself does not exhaust it, but causes it to thrive. It is now assuming alarming proportions. This element in certain isolated sections has long defied the local authorities, it now threatens to brave the constituted authority of the government itself." An article in *Harper's Monthly* added to the concern by calling the Cow-boys "terrorists" and "scourges of whole districts in Colorado, New Mexico, and Arizona."

A groundbreaking study of violence in southeastern Arizona and southwestern New Mexico conducted by researcher Paul Cool and published in the August 2014 issue of the *Wild West History Association Journal* proves that the many 1880–1882 tales of murders and depredations attributed to the Cow-boy confederation during these years were very real. In fact, Cool's study proves that the Cow-boy Crime Era would rank high even on the chart of modern-day murders and other major crimes. This study is a welcome addition to research on outlaw-lawman history.

As stated before, this is not a forum for an in-depth review of the Tombstone saga. On March 15, 1927, Wyatt Earp wrote an 11-page letter to author Walter Noble Burns in answer to his request for information about Tombstone. In his letter Earp wrote, "Now here is your story and I will give you facts as near right as I know. And I think you are getting the right thing. You know yourself, that every and each man you talk to, all have a different tale to tell." A wise man once said, "We all have chapters we would rather keep unpublished." This maxim is especially true concerning the Tombstone Saga.

It was not easy to fit all the pieces of the Tombstone Saga into a chronological sequence. This is my best attempt, but I don't insist on the correctness of every detail. I do hope the outline provides a concise way for the reader to grasp the flow of events that set in motion Wyatt Earp's Cow-boy Campaign in the spring of 1882. When I deemed it appropriate for clarity or background data, I made personal comments under a heading called "Author's Perspective."

Our timeline contains atmospheric data seldom ever mentioned in standard works on Tombstone or the Earps that details the day's weather conditions so as to set the stage for each event. The weather—and alcohol—often played a vital role, even if that has seldom been discussed, in the events taking place, or not taking place, on a given day.[1]

1879

On **Monday, January 6, 1879**, Arizona Territorial Governor John Charles Frémont wrote a letter to his boss, Carl Schurz, President Rutherford B. Hayes's secretary of the interior, concerning reported troubles with raiders along the border with the Mexican State of Sonora. The old frontier explorer wrote, "This statement greatly surprises me. Except for the occasional crime, relative to a border situation, no mention has come to me of any disturbances on the frontier. The authorities on our side have vigorously followed up every outrage, and General Mariscal, the Governor of Sonora, has shown every disposition to cooperate effectively with us in maintaining good order and a friendly understanding." The archives of the United States Department of the Interior contain many documents that demonstrate Governor John C. Frémont's detachment from the reality of daily life in Arizona. He spent most of his time in public office living outside of the territory. When he was in the territory he lived in Tucson, not in the capital city of Prescott.

Tombstone, Arizona Territory, "The Town to a Tough to Die," 1881.

Early April 1879 saw the birth of the "magic city of the desert," the silver mining camp on Goose Flats that became famous as Tombstone, "The Town Too Tough to Die." The discovery of the town site is credited to veteran prospector Ed Schieffelin.

Late September 1879, Pima County sheriff Charles Shibell took the first census of the population of the new village of Tombstone. He listed 474 individuals, which rose to over a 1,000 before year's end. A year later, the town had 10,000 people living in the area. By comparison, the old pueblo of Tucson had about 7,000 people; Prescott, the territorial capital of Arizona, had 2,074; and in Phoenix there were only 1,800 people.

Thursday, October 2, 1879, was a typical fall day in a settlement becoming a village.

The *Tombstone Weekly Nugget,* first published on this day, was a strong supporter of the Democratic Party in the southeastern section of vast Pima County. Months later the newspaper would befriend the Cow-boys and was not always friendly toward the Earp brothers. The newspaper's office was located midway between Allen and Toughnut streets on the east side of Fourth Street next to the rear of the Occidental Hotel and Saloon. The *Weekly Nugget*'s major competition would become the Republican-leaning *Tombstone Weekly Epitaph.*

George W. Parsons, Tombstone mining man and diarist (author's collection).

Sunday, October 26, 1879, was a cool fall day.

That day, Mrs. Henry (Melissa) Fuller, wife of a blacksmith-freighter, gave birth to a daughter. The baby, Inez, was the first child born in Tombstone and she joined her older brother, Wesley. Wes became a member of the Cow-boys. The *Tucson Arizona Daily Star,* October 31, reported on the birth saying, "The whole city got drunk over the news."

On **Monday, December 1, 1879,** "a chill wind whistled among the greasewood," around the nascent village of Tombstone, recalled an elderly Josie Marcus Earp.

This was the day Wyatt Earp first rode into the silver mining camp called Tombstone. His brothers James and Virgil, along with the women and children of the family, arrived with the wagons and remuda a few days later. Wyatt brought transportation-style wagons and a large working remuda to Tombstone. He intended to establish a stage line working out of the new silver mining camp, only to discover that the growing village already had two stage companies. Earp sold his work horses and wagons to the Tombstone Stage Line, owned by John D. Kinnear. During the November 1881 hearing concerning the events surrounding the Tombstone streetfight the previous month, Wyatt Earp testified that he had one of his race horses stolen from him "a few days after I came to Tombstone." Months later, he retrieved the animal from Billy Clanton, who had the animal stabled in Charleston.[2]

Within days of his arrival, James Earp accepted a bartender's post at a saloon—on Allen Street, Tombstone's main business street—operated by James Vogan and James Flynn. Months later, when Virgil Earp became Tombstone's chief of police, he selected James Flynn to serve as one of his night duty officers.

Friday, December 5, 1879, was windy and the cool air from the mountains gave a clear sign that winter was not far in the future.

A letter published in the *Chicago Tribune* on this day gave a clear explanation of what the newspaper called the "Gospel According to St. Gosper." The gospel was described as "the most suitable and eloquent sermon ever addressed to that class of human vermin [the Cow-boys]. The substance of it, as posted up in good print at the Post Office, is that the Hon. Mr. [John] Gosper, Acting Governor of Arizona, offers a reward of $500 to any person who kills a highway robber. To this, Wells & Fargo [Express Company] add an offer of $300 for the arrest and conviction of robbers of their express matter, but the Governor's proclamation is the one to win."

Saturday, December 6, 1879, was a nice winter weekend day around Tombstone.

Virgil and James Earp had arrived in Tombstone a couple of days earlier to discover that their brother Wyatt and Bob Winders, James's former boss in Fort Worth who had convinced the brothers to come to the mining camp, had located a mining claim site they called the *Northern Extension of the Mountain Maid Mine*. The day's land office filing included the underground mineral rights and the 17-acre surface area including all town lots located west of the junction of Fremont Street and First Street north of the road to Benson. The Earps built their houses here.

Sunday, December 7, 1879, had storm clouds in the mountains, but no snow fell.

A 25-year-old California-born gambler named Fred Dodge arrived in Tombstone on a stage driven by Lou Cooley. In later years, Fred Dodge would claim to have been a special undercover agent of the Wells Fargo Express Company, reporting directly to John J. Valentine, the general superintendent, assigned to be the company's eyes and ears in the mining camp.

Dodge soon became acquainted with the Earp brothers and when Morgan arrived in town a few months later he roomed with Dodge in a small cabin near the corner of Sixth and Allen streets, location of the Bird Cage Theatre. Many people thought Dodge resembled the Earp brothers so much he could have been a brother to them. Fred Dodge, Lou Cooley, and Superintendent Valentine would each play a major role in Wyatt Earp's final campaign to destroy the Cow-boy confederation in southeastern Arizona Territory.

Tuesday, December 9, 1879, was a wind-swept day in the high country.

At a saloon in Safford, north of Tombstone, on this day Johnny Ringo shot Louis Hancock, a cowhand working for his brother-in-law at a nearby ranch. On December 14, the *Tucson Arizona Daily Star* reporter clipped, "Moral—when you drank with a man that is on a shoot, and he says whiskey, don't say beer." Ringo's bullet tore through Hancock's lower left ear and the fleshy part of his neck—"a half inch more in the neck, would have killed him." Ringo was arrested by a Pima County officer but was released on bond to appear before the grand jury at Tucson in March 1880. Contrary to some fictional accounts by current "historians," Hancock survived his painful wound and continued to work at Safford.

Tuesday, December 16, 1879, was another wintery day in Montana Territory.

According to the minutes of the city council at Butte City, Montana Territory, Morgan Earp was appointed a policeman for the rough and tumble city. He and his female companion, Louisa Alice Houston, enjoyed the excitement of the Rocky Mountain copper mining town that straddled the continental divide. Louisa would later recall these months in Butte as her happiest time together with Morgan.

Tuesday, December 23, 1879, brought snow in the mountains around Tombstone.

The Tombstone village council adopted Ordinance #1, Annual Tax on Property, at that night's meeting. The village now had a procedure to collect a 1 percent tax on taxable property. Eight more ordinances were adopted and printed in the *Tombstone Weekly Nugget* on April 15, 1880. Ordinance #8 established the duties of the village marshal, while Ordinance #9 forbid carrying concealed weapons and the degrees of punishments or fines for breaking the law. Later, Ordinance #10 defined the Red Light District and occupational standards for the residents.

1880

In **January 1880** Wells Fargo Express Company employed Wyatt Earp as a messenger to guard company express shipments on routes originating in Tombstone. Earp would later become a special agent for the express company's detective force. In late December 1879, James Bunyan Hume, head of Wells Fargo Express Company's detective service, had visited Tombstone and met Wyatt Earp. The two men began a professional and private relationship that would last for decades.

Tuesday, January 6, 1880, was a nice winter local election day in Tombstone.

Alder Randall was elected Tombstone's second mayor and Fred White was reelected as the village's marshal.

Saturday, January 17, 1880, was, according to George Parsons, the young mining broker, "another delightful day" in southern Arizona Territory.

The *Tucson Arizona Daily Star* noted, "Tombstone is probably one of the most cosmopolitan camps this coast affords. Creed, color, and condition are not considered."

In **early February 1880**, Miss Lucas opened the first public school, in a single room with an earth floor. A year later, the community spent $3,000 to build a 30 × 50-foot two-room adobe building on a lot near the corner of Allen and Fourth streets next to a saddle shop. Eighty-five students attended basic grades during 1881–1882. A private school was opened in late 1879.

Tuesday, February, 17, 1880, was a pleasant day in Tombstone, with a very windy evening, according to George Parsons.

George Whitwell Parsons, a 29-year-old native of Washington, D.C., reached Tombstone. He had come to the new community seeking to become rich in the area's mining industry and would become somewhat successful. His private daily journal is a bedrock for study of the Earp era in Tombstone. The former divinity student and lawyer candidate turned bookkeeper and accountant had already experienced mining success in Florida and California. He became a friend of Wyatt Earp and decades later, in August 1900, while in Nome, Alaska, he wrote of Earp that it was "well to be known as his friend." Parsons wrote in his journal for February 17: "Shooting [in] the A.M. and two fellows in afternoon attempted to go for one another with guns and six shooters.... No law other than Miner's and that doesn't sit and deliberate, but acts at once."

Sunday, February 22, 1880, was a gloomy day of worship during the daylight hours and capped by a rainy evening, according to Tombstone diarist George Parsons.

Starting that day, the high desert mining village of Tombstone reached a milestone in its community development. Via a delivery subcontract, the 2,000 residents in the area received daily United States Mail service from the county seat of Tucson. (On June 4, 1880, John P. Clum was appointed postmaster of a fully operational post office. The last section of telegraph wire into Tombstone was installed on the rainy Tuesday evening of July 13, 1880, and the first coded message was received a short time later. Business leaders started discussing creating a telephone company for Tombstone in the spring of 1881.)

In **early March 1880**, John Doling, a Maine native, acquired enough land along the Contention–Tombstone road, in the vicinity of Watervale, to construct a horse racetrack. The first event was a three-day card held that summer. The Tombstone Driving Park racetrack became a popular sporting arena for Tombstone and the site was home to Tombstone's baseball team. Virgil and Wyatt Earp and John Behan enjoyed racing their thoroughbred horses at this track, one of the many competitive activities that developed between the men.

On **Wednesday, March 3, 1880,** George Parsons noted there was a "hard wind all day."

Johnny Ringo wrote Sheriff Charles Shibell that he could not attend the March session of the Pima County Grand Jury because he had been shot in the foot and could not travel. According to Pima County court records, District Attorney Hugh Farley requested that Ringo's bond be revoked, and on March 11 a capias warrant was issued for Ringo's arrest.

Sunday, March 7, 1880, was a clear cool day following the lengthy, hard wind-driven rain of the day before.

George Parsons told his journal that he was overjoyed to have acquired a cat, one of the most valuable assets in Tombstone, which he named Puss. The feline was needed to combat the mass invasion of rats and mice, smaller creatures that encouraged the presence of larger carnivores dangerous to man and beast.

Wednesday, March 10, 1880, George Parsons remembered it rained that night and now that it was daylight there were still rain clouds were in the sky. His sleep had been interrupted during the night and predawn by his cat running over him chasing mice.

The minutes of the city council at Butte City, Montana, contains the acceptance of Morgan Earp's resignation as policeman in the city. Records indicate that he was an effective officer and well liked in the community. Morgan Earp and his wife were headed for California to visit the senior Earps and then travel on to Tombstone.

Thursday, March 18, 1880, had a clear sky but strong, dusty winds.

The *Tombstone Daily Nugget* reported that "U.S. Deputy Marshal Urp [*sic*]" arrested C.S. Hogan of Tombstone for attempting a scheme to counterfeit American trade dollars. A trade dollar was the coin used to settle debts owed to businesses in foreign countries and was seldom used within the United States. This was Virgil Earp's first arrest as a federal officer. At Hogan's hearing, Hogan was granted a $5,000 bail bond to appear at his trial at the next session of court. He quickly skipped town, leaving behind his coin minting dies, which Virgil Earp turned over to the United States Secret Service, which took over jurisdiction in the case.

Friday, April 2, 1880, was an agreeable spring day in the mountain border region.

According to Grant County, New Mexico land deed records, Johnny Ringo and his partner were in the mining town of Shakespeare to sell a two-thirds interest in the Blakely Mine Claim, located in the San Simon Mining District, to John E. Price. Five days later, Ringo was involved in another mining venture with Mr. Price. He conveyed to Price a six-month power of attorney to broker the sale of the Sydney Johnson Mine, also in the San Simon Mining District, for no less than $2,000. Price's profit was to be any amount over the agreed sale price.

On **Saturday, May 1, 1880**, George Parsons, a mining developer and accountant, told his journal, "Fine day for a starter. Rough windlassing—so warm."

The first issue of the *Tombstone Weekly Epitaph* was sold on the streets of the rapidly growing mining camp. Editor John P. Clum wrote, "Tombstone is a city set upon a hill, promising to vie with ancient Rome upon her seven hills, in a fame different in charter but no less in importance." The new newspaper championed the Republican Party and the law and order movement but opposed to the town lot company's method of operation. The newspaper's office would be built on the north side of Fremont Street, but now a big tent served the staff.

On this date, Tombstone experienced the first of a number of fires that threatened the community in the early 1880s. The Dexter Corral and Stables, located on the south side of Allen Street midway between Forth and Fifth streets, burned, but the facility was quickly rebuilt.

Tuesday, May 4, 1880, was "warm," according to George Parsons, the northern-raised young man who loved the Southwest's sunny climate.

A young Texan named Arthur Boucher, alias William Grounds, wrote home to tell his mother how he was doing in the Arizona Territory: "I bought one [a horse] the other day and paid $65.00 for him. I got him from John Ringo...." Ringo was well known in Texas and held a reputation as a hard man. The horse must have been of high quality for such a price, which was about a month's wages for a day laborer/miner. By the end of summer, Boucher/Grounds had become a Cow-boy nicknamed "Curly Bill's Kid" and was suspected of rustling mules and cattle. He died after a gunfight with lawmen in April 1882.

By **Monday, May 10, 1880,** most people noted it was getting warmer each day.

George Parsons noted in his journal the physical labor he completed that day. He also recalled, "Bad state of feeling in town tonight and throughout day. Shooting and rows of various kinds. Lots being jumped—the trouble." The town-lot gang was up to their old manner of business operations and the marshal's office seemed powerless to act. A week later, Parsons bought a half interest in two corner lots at Safford and Second streets. He built rental houses on the property, so now he had a dog in the hunt.

Wednesday, May 19, 1880, the weather had become summer "hot."

George Parsons' journal contains this entry for the 19th: "Another Indian scare on hand and people somewhat excited. Victorio [an Apache war leader] is an ubiquitous piece of humanity." Two days later on Friday, Parsons added a follow-up concern about the local Native Americans: "Indian scare increasing. Dragoon [mountain] people coming in. Much excitement on San Pedro and Gila [rivers]." The concern and excitement grew over the weekend as there was considerable saloon talk about a raid by "savages" on the mining camp.

Saturday, May 22, 1880, was another warm day in the Tombstone region.

Indians shot at miners near Dos Cabezas, 40 miles from Tombstone, and caused some excitement in the area. George Parsons notes, "Some few [people] went out tonight all heeled in response to a call I suppose. No outbreak at San Carlos [Apache Reservation] as reported and nothing to fear here at least." Parsons must have believed what he wrote, because he and a friend attended the opening of Miss J's Ice Saloon that night. Parsons commented, "Fair frozen custard." On Sunday, he noted in his journal, "No Indian news tonight."

In early June 1880, newcomer Wells Spicer and two partners created a new-platted settlement on the eastern edge of Tombstone. They called the place New Boston and advertised that the community would have no government organization, taxes, or law enforcement. The effort died a slow death, as most people just ignored the whole idea. Spicer turned his attention toward his private law practice, his duties as justice and federal commissioner, and his stringer assignments with the *Tucson Arizona Star* and the *Arizona Quarterly Illustrated.* He was a suspected suicide in 1887.

Also during the first week of June 1880, the federal government conducted its ninth-decade count of persons living in the United States. James, Virgil and Wyatt Earp, with their families, are listed as living in Tombstone, while John Holliday is recorded as being in Prescott. New York City became the first American community to reach a population of one million people. (Today, with over eight million people, it remains the nation's largest city.)

Tuesday, June 8, 1880, was "fearfully hot," according to George Parsons.

George Parsons noted in his journal the truth of life in a mining camp: "Have a bad dysentery to fight against. Good rest, tarantulas, centipedes, scorpions and rattlesnakes to the contrary." A few weeks before he wrote, "Sleep well on floor [of his tent] nights. Its [*sic*] all well enough—if tarantulas, scorpions, centipedes or snakes don't walk over me."

Sunday, June 13 to Saturday, June 19, 1880, was a typical summer week. George Parsons recorded the outdoor working conditions for the laboring man. Sunday: "Weather last few days more bracing. Much wind. Knocked tent flat [the] other day." Monday: "Hot day. Sun came down today ... without mercy." Tuesday: "Another very hot day. Said to be 120 degrees in town. Terrible day." Wednesday: "Another scorcher today." Thursday: "Same." Friday: "Another scorcher in A.M. Slight sprinkling this afternoon and agreeable change in atmosphere." Saturday: "Cloudy—sprinkly day with first hard rain of the season tonight. I understand it begins about now and lasts till September."

During this time frame Johnny Ringo, Ike Clanton, Joe Hill, and George Turner delivered a herd of cattle, via New Mexico without paying a tax, to the San Carlos Apache Indian Reservation to sell to the meat contactor for $2,000. The sale was consummated at a sub-par rate, and the Cow-boys rode to Maxie and later to Safford for a celebration. The damage caused by this "rejoicing" was substantial. Pima County authorities made no arrests and the debt for the damage was uncollected. This quickly became a Cow-boy modus operandi.

Tuesday, June 29, 1880, was a nice summer day in Southern California.

The Tenth United States Census was enumerated in Temescal Township in San Bernardino County, California. Morgan Earp, 29, and his wife, Louisa Alice Houston, 25, are counted along with his father, mother, and younger brother Warren. Morgan is listed as a "farmer." The family entry also contained a 14-year-old young lady "visitor" from Utah who may have been a boarder or a domestic working for the family.

Wednesday, July 21, 1880, was a clear and pleasant summer day in Tombstone.

Three men, later identified by William Breakenridge, a Tombstone pioneer, as Cow-boy leader Curly Bill Brocius, along with friends Zwing Hunt, and Billy Grounds, stole six army pack mules from the military's Camp Rucker, located east of Tombstone in the Chiricahua Mountains at some point that day. Also, Lou Rickabaugh, Dick Clark, and W.H. Harris reached a lease agreement with Milt Joyce to operate the gambling concessions at the Oriental Saloon on the northeast corner of Fifth and Allen streets. The *Tombstone Weekly Epitaph* called the newly built facility "the most elegantly furnished saloon ... this side of the favored city of the Golden Gate."

Sunday, July 25, 1880, in Tombstone was a day covered by heavy rain clouds, with a "blinding rain in the late afternoon," as recalled by George Parsons' journal.

In this rainy weather, deputy United States marshal Virgil Earp, with his brothers Wyatt and Morgan, rode with a squad of soldiers from Camp Rucker led by Lt. Joseph H. Hurst seeking missing army mules. The animals were believed to have been stolen by the Cow-boys. Located by the Earp brothers at the McLaury brothers' ranch, the mules were being rebranded and held for resale. Lt. Hurst, misjudging the integrity of the McLaurys, made a deal with the Cow-boys to return the mules to the army camp in a few days when the weather might be better, then he would withdraw his complaint and not have the marshals arrest the brothers. The McLaurys agreed to Hurst's deal, but they never returned the mules.

Five days later, Hurst offered a small reward for the government mules and the arrest and conviction of the thieves. The army officer named Frank McLaury as one of the rancher accomplices to the theft, so the cocky New York native published a notice in the November 5, 1880, issue of the *Tombstone Weekly Nugget* claiming Hurst had really stolen the mules and called the officer a "coward, a vagabond, a rascal and a malicious liar." Hurst was a man who had been honored with the brevet rank of captain for heroic service during the Civil War. None of the posted reward money was ever paid and the mules were never recovered.

The Earps and the Cow-boys had experienced their first law enforcement encounter with each other and the rustlers claimed the bragging rights. The result was that the Cow-boys seem to have misjudged the Earp brothers as "milk-toast" officers they could push around or ignore.

Tuesday, July 27, 1880, was another day full of massive thunderstorms. George Parsons complained to his journal that the mosquito population had drastically increased in Tombstone.

Pima County Sheriff Charles Shibell was in Tombstone to assess conditions first-hand. The sheriff visited with Wyatt Earp, who was highly recommended by Wells Fargo's home office, about being a deputy sheriff for the new mining district. Newton Babcock, the current deputy, had been an active officer, but now he was in ill health and unsuited for active field work. The *Tombstone Daily Epitaph* of July 30, 1880, noted that Sheriff Shibell departed for Tucson on Thursday carrying an oath of office for his new deputy: "Wyatt [Earp] has filled various positions in which bravery and determination were requisites, and in every instance proved himself the right man in the right place." Wyatt Earp's deputy commission and oath, taken before Justice Mike Gray, were both dated the 27th. Over the next 15 weeks, according to court records and newspaper accounts, Earp proved to be a very active deputy sheriff for southeastern Pima County.

Wyatt Earp resigned his position as a Wells Fargo express guard in favor of his brother Morgan, and the *Tombstone Weekly Nugget* and the *Tombstone Weekly Epitaph* each reported his deputy sheriff's appointment with high praise. Wyatt's last Wells Fargo express guard paycheck, $95.82, was for his service during July. He had been being paid $125 per month for the past six months. Morgan Earp earned $45.83 for his first month as a Wells Fargo guard.

On **Wednesday, July 28, 1880,** George Parsons noted that mosquitoes were thick and all the roads around Tombstone were muddy yet passable if they had a caliche base.

Wyatt Earp, on his second day as a Pima County deputy sheriff, escorted accused murderer E.T. Bradshaw to the county jail at Tucson to await the action of the court.

Friday, July 30, 1880, was another sunny day in southwest Arizona Territory.

The *Tucson Arizona Weekly Miner* told readers how some Tombstone members of the Anti–Chinese League had tried to drive the local Asian population out of town and Virgil Earp, as a federal officer, had taken a hand in the altercation. In 1880, Tombstone had 110 Chinese natives who lived in a westside enclave called "Hoptown" and ruled by their feudal class system of fealty to religion and culture enforced by China Mary. The Earps lived a block west of Tombstone's Chinatown.

The Chinese underground opium and gambling dens and the sex cribs where a woman's body could be enjoyed for fifty cents were major factors in the city's seedier life style. When a strong wind blew from the west, the sweet smell of opium drifted across Hoptown to the east-side business section. In Tombstone's growing Sixth Street bordello district, Mexican girls earned a quarter per customer, French women charged six bits, and "American" gals collected a dollar. Top-tier "women of joy," regardless of their race, could command up to $15 for their individual entertainment routine. It has been estimated that 20 men a day were arriving in Tombstone and each one was seeking a job and some form of social interaction.

Stable owner and future Cochise County sheriff John H. Behan was a vocal member of the Tombstone Non-partisan Anti–Chinese League. The group met twice before Virgil Earp's action prevented future trouble. At first, the *Epitaph*'s editor, John Clum, used his newspaper to act as a cheerleader for the anti–Chinese movement, but he later toned down his fervor. In May 1882, Congress, reacting to nationwide pressure, overrode President Chester A. Arthur's veto to enact the Chinese Exclusion Act that forbid these hard-working, underpaid laborers entry into the United States for 10 years. This racist exclusion law was extended for another decade in 1892.

Saturday, July 31, 1880, was another day of the extended heat wave that gripped the Tombstone area. This was the type of weather that brought flies, ticks, scorpions, Gila monsters, and rattlesnakes seeking shelter from the desert sun and they often encountered man.

Deputy Sheriff Wyatt Earp took custody of Roger King, the anti–Chinese agitator who headed the movement to drive the small Asian population out of Tombstone, for the murder of his cabinmate Tom Wilson. The killing took place about daybreak on Friday outside the Headquarters Saloon on Allen Street. Roger King claimed self defense. Since Tombstone had no jail at this time, Deputy Sheriff Earp held his prisoners, under guard, in a rented room of the San Jose House on the northwest corner of Fremont and Fifth streets.

On **Sunday, August 1, 1880,** George Parsons noted in his journal, "The flies were terrible today and combined with the heat rendered this the most and in fact only uncomfortable day in Arizona thus far for me."

Wyatt Earp arrested John J. Pace for forgery and attempted jail break. Pace, a fellow anti–Chinese crusader, tried to bluff Deputy Babcock with a fake telegram from Sheriff Charlie Shibell ordering the release of King to Pace. Earp smelled a rat and said no to the release and two days later, the *Tombstone Daily Epitaph* trumpeted, "The frustration of the plan is entirely due to the judgment and good sense displayed by officer Earp." At court on Tuesday morning, Pace posted a $500 bond to appear before the next grand jury.

Tuesday, August 3, 1880, George Parsons noted, was rainy, with very hard rain in the evening. The rain did keep the temperature at a moderate level for summer.

Acting upon a formal complaint by the Mexican woman whom Diego Meindies was living with, Deputy Sheriff Wyatt Earp arrested in the afternoon and charged him with brutally beating her. According to the *Tombstone Daily Epitaph*, the Mexican posted a $500 bond to appear in Judge Mike Gray's court. Assaulting women was a low-life crime on the frontier.

The *Daily Epitaph* recorded that Mrs. Allie Earp, Virgil's wife, left the mining camp "for a visit to her old family home in San Bernardino. We wish her a pleasant trip and a speedy return." She stayed with the senior Earps and met Morgan's 25-year-old wife, Louisa Alice "Lou" Houston, for the first time.

Wednesday, August 4, 1880, was considered a "hot day" by George Parsons.

The *Daily Epitaph* of Thursday would report that Pima County Deputy Sheriff Wyatt Earp, accompanied by his younger brother Morgan serving as a posseman, investigated a murder at Watervale on the 4th. They discovered that a transient teamster had killed an old resident of the area named Captain Malcom. After interviewing all parties involved, an arrest was made on August 25 and Special Officer Morgan Earp escorted the suspect during the 12-hour stage trip to the county jail at Tucson.

Friday, August 6, 1880, was a "cloudy day. Rain tonight. Hard of course," noted George Parsons in his day journal.

The *Daily Epitaph* reported that Ike Clanton had arrived in Tombstone from the Cow-boy country around San Simon with "fifty head of beef cattle for the Tombstone market." Northern Mexico ranchos had recently suffered from Cow-boy raids.

Monday, August 9, 1880, was another hot late-summer day in Tombstone and the surrounding countryside.

George Parsons told his journal, "Tombstone is getting a pretty hard name. Men killed, shot—stabbed, suiciding [*sic*], etc., every day or two. This thing must be stopped."

Wednesday, August 11, 1880, was part of what George Parsons called "delightful weather.... delightful rains generally at night" in southeastern Arizona Territory. The rain helped to reduce the heat index and made being outside more enjoyable.

That night, Tombstone miners held a mass meeting at William N. Ritchie's Hall on Fifth Street to discuss organizing a miner's labor union. Owners of the largest mines presented a document to the meeting pointing out the fact that they already paid a higher than normal wage. They added that all the area mine foemen had orders not to employ any union miner. The owners promised the miners that they would close their mines before they would deal with a union. The union movement died before it was born, but years later would rise again.

Saturday, August 14, 1880, was a typical mid-summer day in southeastern Arizona.

Deputy Sheriff Wyatt Earp's posseman Morgan Earp, acting upon a warrant for the murder of Mike Killeen, arrested George Perine at Richmond, just north of Tombstone.

On **Monday, August 16, 1880,** George Parsons recorded in his private journal that he considered the day a very pleasant one, with a beautiful moonlit night.

Pima County Deputy Sheriff Wyatt Earp, with brothers Virgil and Morgan as a posse, pursued four suspected horse thieves and located one at Charleston. He was arrested.

Tuesday, August 17, 1880, saw another pleasant late-summer day that ended with a moonlit night comfortable for sleeping.

While serving as a court bailiff, Deputy Sheriff Wyatt Earp became involved in a legal dispute between justice of the peace James Reilly and attorney Harry B. Jones. Reilly and Jones threw a few blows before Deputy Sheriff Earp intervened and arrested both men for disorderly conduct in a public place. Earp took Jones to justice of the peace Mike Gray's court to face the disorderly conduct charge. Gray released Jones on his own recognizance. When Justice Reilly finished his day's court schedule, Earp took him before Justice Gray. Reilly was also released on his own recognizance.

Also that day, justice of the peace James Reilly fined Harry B. Jones, a Tombstone councilman, $25 and a day in the county jail for contempt of court. This action is what led to the fistfight. Deputy Sheriff Earp was ordered to take Jones into custody and convey him to Tucson for incarceration in the Pima County jail. After Reilly was taken before Justice Gray, Reilly ordered Earp to appear in his court in the morning to explain why he should not be held in contempt of court. Deputy Sheriff Earp reminded the justice he could not be in his court in the morning because the justice had already ordered him to take Harry B. Jones to Tucson that evening. Earp's truthfulness earned him a fiery enemy in James Reilly.

So justice of the peace James Reilly had fined Harry B. Jones, a Tombstone councilman, $25 and ordered a day in the county jail for contempt of court. Deputy Sheriff Earp was ordered to take Jones into custody and convey him to Tucson for incarceration in the Pima County jail. Deputy Sheriff Wyatt Earp and his brother Virgil, his posseman, escorted Harry Jones to Tucson on the evening stage. Earp was acting upon orders of

Justice James Reilly that Jones serve a day in the county jail for contempt of Reilly's court.

Local newspapers had a field day expounding upon Reilly's behavior from the bench and citizens of Tombstone saw the pettiness, incompetence, and naivety of Justice Reilly. Over 100 residents signed a petition demanding Justice Reilly resign his post due to his disgraceful conduct. Among the petition signers were Wyatt and Morgan Earp. The hot-tempered Justice Reilly did not seek reelection in the fall and resigned his office after the county election so his successor might take office early. James Reilly disliked Wyatt Earp after their confrontation and his own public embarrassment by being arrested by the peace officer.

On **Wednesday, August 18, 1880**, George Parsons recorded an unusual atmospheric phenomenon: "Strange sight tonight. A rainbow in the dark. There was a complete arch of white light in the west—a veritable rainbow in the night."

Deputy Sheriff Wyatt Earp escorted Harry B. Jones to see John Wood, the district court judge in Tucson, for a habeas corpus herring on the Tombstone attorney's ordered jail confinement. Judge Wood released Jones, citing Justice Reilly's lack of authority to order Jones to jail, and dismissed the contempt charge, fine, and sentence. The district court was displeased with James Reilly's mismanagement of his court.

The Earp brothers returned to Tombstone late on Friday, August 20. They had attended to some personal business and checked out the poker games in Tucson.

On **Friday, August 27, 1880,** the region surrounding Tombstone was recovering from the massive thunderstorm that hit the area the day before.

Deputy Sheriff Wyatt Earp escorted George Perine to Tucson on the night stage. Perine was bound for a hearing before the Pima County grand jury on a charge of murdering Mike Killeen. Perine was freed from custody in October.

The *Daily Epitaph* noted that Deputy Sheriff Wyatt Earp had arrested Dr. Henry Hatch a few days earlier for a dispute with a man named Welch. The charge was brandishing a firearm in a rude, angry, threatening manner. Justice James Reilly fined the doctor $100 and court costs. Hatch had been involved in a similar incident earlier in May.

Thursday, September 9, 1880, was a warm fall day in Tombstone, but rain clouds developed in the evening.

Many of Tombstone's leading citizens gathered in Kelly's Wine Rooms that evening and organized a volunteer firefighting unit. The original sixteen members named it the Tombstone Hose Company No. 1. Harry B. Jones was elected the president of the group, Wyatt Earp was selected as the secretary, and Leslie F. Blackburn was selected as the foreman of the firefighter team according to the *Daily Epitaph*'s report. Milton Joyce, Fred White, Marshall Williams, John H. Behan, and Artemus Fay were elected to the board. A fundraising committee was organized to acquire the money for firefighting equipment and a fire station. (The fire station is a Tombstone tourist attraction today.)

The Grand Hotel, with a bar and restaurant, opened for business. The facility became a business and social meeting place for Cow-boys when they visited in town.

Saturday, September 11, 1880, was a day of unseasonable on-off-on rain and warm fall weather for the Tombstone area that weekend.

The *Daily Epitaph* justly praised the recent action of Morgan Earp, Wells Fargo's shotgun messenger for the stage run between Tombstone and Benson. At some point during the trip, Earp discovered that the canvas cover for the storage boot on the back of the stage had come untied and that two bars of silver had fallen out of the storage compartment. He had the driver backtrack their route and they discovered the two silver bars in the middle of the road. The complete shipment arrived safely at the Wells Fargo Company Express office and was deposited on the next train.

On **Tuesday, September 14, 1880,** the streets of Tombstone were still muddy as a result of Monday's heavy rain.

John Harris Behan, the lifetime political opportunist, two-time legislator, restaurant and hotel operator, and former sheriff at Prescott, arrived in Tombstone along with his young son. He found a job as a bartender at the Grand Hotel's fancy saloon, home base of the Cow-boys. He soon persuaded Josephine Sarah Marcus, his young Jewish lover, to join him in the mining camp. Her money was used by Behan to fund the house he bought at the northeast corner of Seventh and Safford in a new Tombstone housing development.

Monday, September 27, 1880, was a nice day for working outdoors around Tombstone.

James, Wyatt, and Morgan Earp and John H. Holliday (recently arrived in Tombstone from Prescott) signed the Great Register of Pima County, Arizona Territory, to vote in Precinct 17 (Tombstone). Virgil Earp had registered to vote on January 20, 1880.

On **Monday, October 4, 1880,** the smell of an early winter was heavy upon the air, but the nights were still pleasant. Storm clouds were building over the mountains.

Pima County Deputy Sheriff Wyatt Earp arrested James Henry upon a complaint by his wife accusing him of beating her. The *Daily Epitaph* noted that Justice Gray fined Mr. Henry $7.50 and ordered a $200 bond for him to keep domestic peace in his home. Tuesday was payday for the Tombstone miners, so this family quarrel might have been over money problems.

Saturday, October 10, 1880, was a "pleasant day" after Friday's gloomy heavy rain.

A few weeks earlier, Wyatt Earp had "eighty-sixed," or ejected, Johnny Tyler, a West Coast gambler, from the Oriental Saloon. Newly arrived to town Doc Holliday taunted Tyler: fight or leave the camp. For once, Tyler used his head and left. Later, Milton E. Joyce took up Tyler's case with Holliday, according to Tuesday's *Tombstone Daily Nugget.*

Doc Holliday shot Milton E. Joyce, owner of the Oriental Saloon and member of the new county board of supervisors, in the hand and his youthful bartender William Parker in the left toe during an altercation. The massive Joyce beat Holliday with his pistol before city marshal Fred White broke up the fight by arresting Holliday. The three wounded men spent Sunday in bed recovering. On Monday, Justice James Reilly fined Doc $20 for "assault with a deadly weapon" and charged the dentist-gambler $11.30 in court fees. There was some concern that Joyce might lose his hand or his life, but he survived to nurse a hatred of John H. Holliday.

Deputy Sheriff Wyatt Earp, and his brother Morgan acting as a posseman, traveled to Charleston to assist Deputy Sheriff Milton McDowell in bringing three prisoners to Tombstone and then delivering them to the county jail at Tucson. The men were fined $150 by Justice James Burnett for their part in a near riot when they had attempted to assist their friend Jerry Barton following his killing of E.C. Merrill. The young bartender was able to post his bond, via friends Frank Stilwell and John Campbell, and thus escape jail time.

On **Friday, October 15, 1880,** George Parsons told his private journal, "Warm spell on us at present."

Since October 8, Deputy Sheriff Wyatt Earp had been around Tombstone serving 32 court papers for attachment of property. These legal papers were served upon orders issued by Justice James Reilly for past due accounts. Wyatt Earp earned $29 in service fees, according to Justice Reilly's court records.

On **Saturday, October 23, 1880,** George Parsons noted the day was a rainy one that ended with a "very unpleasant night." He also noted that coyotes were thick, packs roaming close to town seeking food.

Pima County Deputy Sheriff Wyatt Earp arrested Pete Spenser, a saloon operator in Charleston and a known associate of the Cow-boys, on a warrant for mule stealing. Spenser later lived in a rented house on the same street intersection where the Earp brothers had their houses so he could spy on the brothers' movements. Spenser's wife and the Earp women were friendly.

Monday, October 25, 1880, George Parsons recalled it was "cloudy today. More of the good rain."

Another milestone in professional athletics occurred in Tombstone as a Frenchman and one of the town's night constables engaged in a three-round wrestling match. The match was staged at the Opera House on Sixth Street to a standing room only crowd. The winner's prize was $500 and any side bets. Constable J.W. Bennett won two of the three rounds and the money.

Thursday, October 28, 1880, proved to be a pleasant day, according to George Parsons.

The *Daily Epitaph* carried the following notice: "Attention is called to the announcement of V.W. Earp for Constable of the Seventeenth Precinct. Mr. Earp promises all the qualifications necessary for the position and if elected will no doubt fill the office satisfactorily."

During the first hour of the day, Fred White, Tombstone's first city marshal, having been elected on November 28, 1879, and reelected on September 10, 1880, was fatally shot and his assailant, Cow-boy leader Curly Bill Brocius, was quickly buffaloed and arrested by Deputy Sheriff Wyatt Earp. Marshal White had encountered Curly Bill in the small alley in front of White's home. The ally runs east-west between Fifth and Sixth streets, cutting Block 5 between Allen and Toughnut streets in half. White's house was the second house west of the intersection located on the north side of the alley near the corner at Sixth Street.

Pima County Deputy Sheriff Wyatt Earp and his friends manhandled and arrested other Cow-boys who were disturbing the peace shooting at the stars in the clear morning sky. The celebrants were in vacant lots west of White's home. Among the Cow-boys involved with Curly Bill in the attempt to "tree" Tombstone and kill the marshal were Ike and Billy Clanton, Frank and Tom McLaury, Charles T. "Pony Diehl" Ray, Dick Lloyd, James Johnson and Jerry Atkinson. Wyatt Earp, as deputy sheriff, placed a strong guard around the small Tombstone jail to prevent any attempt to free the incarcerated

Cow-boys by their supporters or a lynching attempt by Marshal White's legion of friends.

During **Friday, October 29, 1880**, many people in Tombstone were excited to enjoy the nice fall weather on the high desert region of southeastern Arizona.

At a special meeting, Mayor Randall and the Tombstone Common Council appointed deputy United States marshal Virgil Earp as the assistant town marshal, at a salary of a $100 per month, to serve as leader of the police while Marshal Fred White was incapacitated.

The *Daily Epitaph* reported "some dissatisfaction was manifested this morning" because it was learned that Deputy Sheriff Wyatt Earp had released Jerry Atkinson from jail, until they learned that Justice Mike Gray had ordered his release upon posting a bond. A short time later, Atkinson's body was found near Groton Springs on the Southern Pacific Railroad line and the money he was known to be carrying was missing. It is believed he was working a deal with some of the San Simon Cow-boys at the time of his death.

Marshal Fred White died from his painful wound after he gave a statement, under oath, concerning his shooting by Curly Bill. White said the incident had been an accident and that he believed that the Cow-boy leader had not intended to harm him. Many residents believed that the Cow-boys had been hired to assassinate the youthful village marshal by the Town Lot gang. The location of the shooting adds to this belief.

Later in the day, Pima County Deputy Sheriff Wyatt Earp and his posseman George "Shotgun" Collins, later a constable at Wilcox, escorted Curly Bill to Tucson for placement in the Pima County jail to await his hearing. The jail log shows he remained in custody until December 27, 1880.

Saturday, October 30, 1880, was another nice fall day to be working outdoors.

Mayor Randall and the council appointed Virgil Earp the acting marshal of Tombstone until a special election could be held on November 12, 1880. This election would select a town marshal to serve until the regular town election to be held on January 4, 1881. Virgil withdrew his name as a candidate for Precinct 17 constable because he hoped to receive the voters' public approval—at the special election—of the town council's action in naming him the community's acting marshal.

Sunday, October 31, 1880, had "a little rain this A.M. early," according to George Parsons' journal of his life in Tombstone.

"Immense demonstration this afternoon at White's funeral," wrote Parsons, as an estimated 2,000 mourners participated in the burial march to the cemetery. The 31-year-old New York–born lawman's funeral was held in the hall of the Grid Block on Fremont Street. George Parsons felt the eulogy of the fallen Marshal White by the Rev. Joseph McIntyre "hit some of the people hard licks."

In the evening Deputy Sheriff Wyatt Earp earned praise for his quick and decisive action in arresting a Nevada murder fugitive named James "Red Mike" Langdon located loafing in front of the Bank Exchange Saloon. However, when notified of the arrest, the Silver State's governor wanted nothing to do with the fugitive from justice and refused to issue extradition papers for his return to Nevada or to pay any reward money for his capture. Thus, the Bowie knife killer and troublemaker was released from Cochise County custody and quickly left town.

Tuesday, November 2, 1880, was another nice fall day in Tombstone.

This was National Election Day in America. In Tombstone, 819 votes were cast for territorial officers. Nationally, James A. Garfield of Ohio earned 6,564 more popular votes (less than one tenth of 1 percent margin of the total vote)and won 19 of 38 states for 214 electoral college votes (out of 369 votes) to become the 20th President of the United States. Garfield's opponent was General Winfield Scott Hancock of Pennsylvania, a Civil War hero who had been the favorite to win the general election and regain the White House for the Democrat Party for the first time since 1856.

On **Thursday, November 4, 1880,** the weather was still trying to make up its mind if it wanted to be in winter mood yet.

Artemus Fay, editor of the *Daily Nugget*, gave praise to Virgil Earp by calling him "a fearless and efficient officer" and continued by saying he would "serve the city faithfully if elected." Three days later, Fay explained, "The Marshalship for the next two months will be a profitable office, as he will collect the city taxes."

John P. Clum, later a staunch backer of the Earp brothers, now used his newspaper, the *Daily Epitaph*, to support Ben Sippy for the town marshal's job. This support seems odd in light of Clum's fight against the Town Lot Company and lot jumpers. Clum may not have known that Sippy, along with over a dozen other miner-fortune hunters, was currently squatting on town lot surface property claimed by the Vizina Consolidated Mining Company.

Saturday, November 6, 1880, was a nice day and pleasant evening.

The citizens of Tombstone held a large evening bonfire meeting at the corner of Fifth and Allen streets to confront Mayor Alder Randall concerning his schemes to defraud the town in his dealings with the Town Lot Company. Again lynch talk was heard, but acting village marshal Virgil Earp was at the public meeting to maintain order. George Parsons recalled, "Determined men spoke determined words."

Sunday, November 7, 1880, was again a pleasant day in Tombstone.

The cold ashes of Saturday night's massive bonfire meeting were visible as a number of private meetings were held on Sunday afternoon and evening. These men conspired to develop an action plan for winning control of the mayor's office and town council at the January elections and, second, how to curb the profiteering of Randall and his Town Lot coconspirators. Tombstone's mayor learned of the meetings and sought refuge with friends in Tucson.

Monday, November 8, 1880, was a mild fall day in the mountains of southeastern Arizona Territory.

Professional prize fighting came to Tombstone that night as a hard-glove lightweight fight "according to the rules of the prize ring" was staged in the Arcade Saloon, according to the *Daily Nugget*. The purse was $500 and any wager winnings. The fight ended with a knockout in the 12th round. Village Marshal Virgil Earp was present to maintain order.

On **Tuesday, November 9, 1880**, according to George Parsons' private journal, the "weather [was] getting cold" around Tombstone.

Wyatt Earp resigned as a deputy sheriff of Pima County. "Wyatt Earp's resignation as deputy sheriff was heard of by his many friends with regret," reported the *Daily Nugget* on November 12. "During the time he held office he has been active and prompt in the discharge of all duties and every citizen had the consciousness that his life and property were as well protected as they could be by any single officer."

Earp was now free to assist his friend Bob Paul, of Tucson, in his challenge to the accepted vote count in three precincts for Pima County sheriff. Now, Wyatt made a deal with Curly Bill to provide the inside tale of how the election was stolen by the Cow-boys in return for Earp's positive testimony at his hearing for killing Marshal White. The deal was made and during Curly Bill's hearing, Earp was a major defense witness, claiming that Bill's pistol was defective and even gave a demonstration to the jury to prove his point. The Cow-boy chieftain was released, but he never forgave Wyatt Earp for buffaloing him in front of his fellow raiders.

Curly Bill indicated that the Cow-boys, led by Ike Clanton, had rigged the 1880 Pima County sheriff's election. The voter fraud case was heard in the District Court at Tucson in January 1881, and the court ruled that Paul had won the election by 65 votes when the suspect votes were discarded. On April 12, 1881, the Arizona Territorial Supreme Court dismissed Shibell's appeal and Paul quickly took office as the rightfully elected sheriff of Pima County.

The high-court ruling had a major effect in the Tombstone area, since the three suspect precincts had become part of the new Cochise County by the time legal challenges were exhausted. The Cow-boys still held their political influence in the countryside around Tombstone, with their 10-Percent Ring friends firmly in control of the new county government centered at Tombstone.

Thursday, November 11, 1880, showed all the signs that Mother Nature had finally decided it was time for summer to do its magic in the Southern Hemisphere and that winter's fury would soon arrive in Tombstone, Cochise County, Arizona Territory.

Tombstone Mayor Alder Randall conveyed 2,200 town lots to the Tombstone Town Lot Company owned by Randall and his partners. This action caused a firestorm on the streets and in court as lot ownership was challenged.

Friday, November 12, 1880, was a cool damp winter day on the Tombstone mesa.

Tombstone, now calling itself a town, held a special election to select a person to be their marshal for three and a half weeks until the town held regular elections for the town's officials. A popular 30-year-old Pennsylvania-born miner named Benjamin Sippy received 311 votes to 259 ballots cast for Virgil Earp, acting town marshal. The Earp brothers felt all their law enforcement efforts had meant nothing to the people they had tried to serve. The *Daily Nugget* reported that Jim Flynn withdrew from the marshal's election. The newspaper said, "Both the gentlemen who remain in the field are well qualified for the office and the city can have the assurance in the event of either's election of having an efficient officer." Saturday's *Daily Epitaph* congratulated Ben Sippy and said he "should receive the support and assistance of all good citizens."

Pima County Sheriff Charles Shibell appointed former Yavapai County sheriff Johnny H. Behan, a Tombstone stable owner and bartender, as deputy sheriff to replace Wyatt Earp. On November 24, Sheriff Shibell would also appoint Leslie F. Blackburn, a strong political supporter, as a deputy sheriff in Tombstone. Since Behan had a reputation for misplacing public funds, Blackburn's principle duty was to handle the tax collection function and serve as a bill collector.

That evening an enthusiastic mass outdoor community meeting, attended by miners, tradesmen, day laborers, and some of the town's business leaders, was held at John Vickers' Hall on Fremont Street. The meeting's purpose was to once again protest the misconduct of Mayor Alder Randall and his town lot sales scam. Lynch talk was an open conversation. The Earp brothers took no part in this assembly.

Saturday, November 13, 1880, noted George Parsons, was a cold raw day in Tombstone, with rain in the early evening hours. It was certainly not a pleasant day for working outdoors.

The mining survey for the First Northern Extensions of the Mountain Maid mining claim was conducted by the owners. Bob Winders, aided by Thomas Kelly, carried the measuring chain while Wyatt Earp served as the flagman. George Meley and Doctor John H. Holliday served as witnesses that the job had been completed as required by law and stated in the official paperwork attested to by Henry G. Howe, the deputy U.S. mineral surveyor. The certificate was filed in the Pima County Recorder's Office testifying to $500 worth of mining claim improvements completed by the owners.

The town marshal, Ben Sippy, arrested John Scott and George "Shotgun" Collins for target practice. Justice Mike Gray fined the men $10 each, according to the *Daily Nugget*. A few days later, the marshal raided an eight-man vagrants' camp. Four men made their escape, while the other four appeared before Justice Mike Gray. They were freed and ordered to get a job or get out of town.

Monday, November 15, 1880, was "cool—but [a] pleasant day" in the Tombstone Mining District, according to George Parsons.

During the town council meeting, Virgil Earp resigned as the assistant town marshal of Tombstone. Earp and Mayor Randall maintained a philosophical disagreement over the legality of the police being required to serve eviction notices to town lot owners until the court challenge had been settled. The town council authorized a $54.83 payment to Virgil for his police services. With Earp out of the way, the Cow-boys were back in business working as eviction enforcers for the Town Lot Company.

John Behan, the self-declared debonair bonvivant and Casanova about town, arrested his first men as a peace officer in Pima County. The new deputy sheriff took James Ryan into custody for suspected burglarizing of miners' cabins. According to the *Daily Epitaph* of November 16, Marshal Ben Sippy arrested five offenders of the fast-driving ordinance; one of these men was George Collins.

Saturday, November 20, 1880, continued the cold days and colder nights.

The *Daily Epitaph* said, "Our new marshal is too much for you; so make up your mind to keep out of his clutches by keeping inside the law." On Friday, Marshal Sippy had arrested three more men for fast-driving within the city limits.

Monday, November 22, 1880, was another cold and cloudless day and a colder night.

George Parsons noted in his journal, "Town quiet these days." Earlier that Monday, four dissatisfied members of the rustler confederacy shot Robert "Bob" "Dutch" Martin in the head during a heated discussion at their camp in Stein's Pass. Martin's death made Curly Bill, currently in the Tucson jail, the unchallenged leader of the San Simon Valley Cow-boys. The incident was reported in the *Tucson Arizona Weekly Star* on December 2.

Friday, November 26, 1880, was a pleasant day in Tombstone, as had been yesterday, a day of thanksgiving across the nation.

Cienega is Spanish for "marshy place" or "a water source," and *Animas perdidas* means "souls lost in hell." Cow-boy leaders Ike Clanton and John Ringo filed a land use and water rights location notice in Grant County, New Mexico. The land claim for 320 acres to be used for cattle grazing and hay farming in the Animas Valley—along the continental divide about 28 miles north of Guadalupe Canyon in the extremely remote Peloncillo Mountains in New Mexico's Bootheel section—is on file in the county clerk's office in Silver City. The land claim first called the Alfalfa or Cienega Rancho later became the San Simon Cienega. Some historians have also referred to the acreage as the Joe Hill Ranch, since Hill once tried to jump the Clanton–Ringo claim and start his own rustling operation. (In this century, the Clanton–Ringo land is part of the world's largest private nature conservation reserve.)

By the spring of 1881, the Cow-boys had a well-organized operation covering the border region of southeastern Arizona and southwestern New Mexico. "Old Man" Clanton's sons lived at the Arizona homestead, about 12 miles from Tombstone on the San Pedro River, which was a mountaintop adobe fortress affording an unobstructed view in all directions and thus providing a secure sanctuary at the end of the rustler trail. Clanton friends brothers Robert Findley "Frank" and Thomas Clark McLaury, settled near Soldier's Hole in the Sulphur Springs Valley and this place became a stop on the trail from Mexico. The Animas Valley hay farm in New Mexico became the first safe stop after the Cow-boys concluded a raid into Old Mexico.

Some Arizona historians suggest that Virgil Earp once led a small federal posse into southwestern New Mexico Territory during the manhunt for Cochise County Cow-boys. The posse might have searched the high, lonesome country of the Animas Valley in New Mexico's boot heel. The hunt may have been just an overnight campout or no more than a few days in the mountains. Federal marshals during this era often crossed back and forth between New Mexico and Arizona seeking outlaws in the rugged and ill-defined mountain regions between the two territories. One of the illegal trade corridors was an isolated pass called Guadalupe Canyon. Virgil Earp's posse would most likely have centered their Cow-boy search around the Cloverdale store because Newman Haynes Clanton, commonly called "Old Man" Clanton, was the rustlers' spiritual leader and mentor. He had recently

John and Mary Clum. John was the mayor of Tombstone and editor of the *Tombstone Epitaph*, 1881 (Public Domain/National Postal Museum).

settled at the hay ranch in Clanton Draw and different members of the Cow-boys were known to use Clanton's two adobe ranch buildings as a hideout and staging area for their raids into Old Mexico.

In **December 1880**, Wyatt Earp retrieved his stolen race horse, Dick Naylor, from Billy Clanton at a Charleston livery stable owned by Frank Stilwell. Clanton vowed to steal another of Wyatt's horses. Sherman McMaster, Earp's undercover man among the Cow-boys, had tipped him to the horse's location. Tombstone had a half-mile racetrack north of town near Watervale, where Wyatt was often seen with his thoroughbreds. The Earp brothers had built a stable near their houses at the corner of First and Fremont streets to house their horses.

On **Saturday, December 4, 1880**, George Parsons noted, "The Zephyrs are upon us."

John Clum, editor of the *Daily Epitaph*, filed a request for an injunction with the district court to keep the Tombstone Town Lot Company from selling or evicting any individual from their property. The territorial court granted injunction held until February 17, 1882, when the case was settled.

Early in the morning Marshal Sippy, according to George Parsons, was "compelled to take off his coat and show he meant business" when he ordered some town site men to return a house they had removed from a disputed lot on Fremont Street. The *Daily Epitaph* reported the event on Sunday, saying, "Marshal Sippy made many firm friends yesterday by his prompt and efficient action. He demonstrated the fact that he is in sympathy with law and order and that he is not afraid to assume a little responsibility." John Clum's newspaper also trumpeted that the town lot company "cannot make Marshal Sippy their tool."

On **Sunday, December 5, 1880**, the weather was less windy but getting much cooler.

There were no "blue laws" in Tombstone, so intoxicated men gathered in small and large groups generating "lynch law" talk against Mayor Alder Randall and his town lot partners. The protest was widespread on the streets of Tombstone this day of Christian worship.

Tuesday, December 7, 1880, exhibited signs that winter was on its way.

The *Daily Nugget* on Thursday noted that Marshal Sippy arrested Henry Hooker on this date, owner of the vast Sierra Bonita Ranch in northern Pima County (soon to be located in the southern part of the new Graham County), for fast-driving his buggy to show off his thoroughbred horses. Hooker was fined $7.50 for his crime and the marshal was lauded by the newspaper: "Stick to 'em, Sippy. You'll break it [speeding] up after a while."

About 9:00 o'clock in the evening, Marshal Ben Sippy was called to Allen Street to settle trouble between George C. "Shotgun" Collins and John A. "Scotty" Scott. George Parsons noted the event in his journal: "Some pleasantries exchanged on street tonight.... None of the bullets took effect." Justice Michael Gray fined each man $10 and court costs for "discharging firearms in the public streets." Collins would be arrested by Sippy for being drunk and disorderly on December 12 and Justice A.J. Felter ordered him to pay a $15 fine and costs.

Saturday, December 11, 1880, was "gloomy" weather to start off the weekend.

The *Tucson Arizona Citizen* carried a small display ad on this day for the "Parsons & Redfern Mining and General Agents" in Tombstone. George Parsons and his Washington, D.C., partner J.L. Redfern were always eliciting new clients for their fledgling location and development mining enterprise. The young mining developer and community leader counted California mining magnet George Hearst, General William T. Sherman, and U.S. Grant, Jr., among his friends and major clients.

Saturday, December 18, 1880, according to George Parsons, was "fine weather."

Mary "Mollie" Dennison Ware Clum, 27-year-old wife of the *Daily Epitaph* editor and town postmaster, died on this afternoon at her home in the aftermath of childbirth. She was the niece of prominent Ohio politician William Dennison, Jr. Her granddaughter, Marjorie Clum Parker, described her as "ambitious, big-eyed and full lipped, beautiful and moody." The young woman left behind for her husband's care a two-year-old son, Woodworth "Woodie," and a daughter, Elizabeth "Bessie," who was a week old. George Parsons wrote in his journal: "Half of the present female population or more could be better spared than she."[3]

Mary Clum was buried Sunday afternoon with a Presbyterian church funeral in the new community graveyard, today called Boothill Cemetery. Little Bessie died on July 7, 1881. Mrs. Parker recalled, "Time and desert wind erased the markers of that famous last resting place of the frontier and neither her husband or her son later could identify her grave."

Wednesday, December 22, 1880, was a "clear and bright day" for winter weather.

George Parsons noted, "Shootists [were] again on the rampage. 'Red Mike' shot last night and another man reported killed tonight." A few weeks earlier, Sippy had arrested one of his own deputies for loudly arguing in a saloon.

Saturday, December 25, 1880, was, George Parsons noted, "[A] Fine day. Grand weather."

The Tombstone Driving Park held a Christmas Day double event horse racing card. In the $100-purse trotting match Virgil Earp entered "Old Doc," Wyatt Earp ran "Sorrel Reuben" and their friend James Vogan rode "Prince." In the second event, a mile-long race, the event pitted two horses against each other.

1881

On **Tuesday, January 4, 1881**, the weather seemed to cooperate for Tombstone's municipal election.

The recently widowed newspaper editor/postmaster, John P. Clum, is elected Tombstone's third mayor and Ben Sippy is reelected town marshal by defeating Howard K. Lee, a pawn of the town lot company, 556 to 125 votes. The council candidates who ran with Clum to represent the town's four wards also won, thus causing George Parsons, who served as chair of the executive committee of the Protective Party, to be very happy with the election results: "Grand glorious victory and overwhelming defeat to the opposition." Clum was elected by a 367-vote majority. George Parsons noted that a number of "bombs," fireworks, were exploded in celebration, while Mayor Randall was scared that a mob was coming for him.

Author Perspective: John Clum in later years would recall, "This ticket met with opposition from the gambling and saloon element, but was strongly supported by the miners." Clum conveniently forgot that the Earp brothers were gamblers and saloonmen when he later claimed to have always strongly supported the Earp brothers' law enforcement efforts. He also forgot that the pages of his own newspaper, during 1880, do not support his later assertions.

Saturday, January 8, 1881, was a typical winter day in the mountain country, clear days and cold nights.

Curly Bill Brocius and his Cow-boy confederates raided Charleston in celebration of their leader's escaping murder charges for killing Tombstone town marshal Fred White by hurrahing the San Pedro River town. The Cow-boy revelers disrupted a religious meeting and made the preacher "dance" to the tune of their bullets. George Parsons said the Cow-boys "played the devil generally."

Sunday, January 9, 1881, Tombstone weather remained "cold," according to diarist George Parsons.

Bored with the burg of Charleston, the drunken Cow-boys, led by Curly Bill, rode the ten miles over to Tombstone to continue their rambunctious celebration because there were more party girls in the larger town. These celebrants quickly commenced shooting up the interior of the Alhambra Saloon and then held an impromptu horse race up and down Allen Street. Meanwhile, other Cow-boys were randomly shooting at whatever drew their attention. Marshal Ben Sippy and his police force were hard to locate during this merriment.

Friday, January 14, 1881, was a cold clear day in southeastern Arizona Territory.

George McKelvey, Charleston's youthful precinct constable, arrested 20-year-old Michael "Johnny-Behind-the-Duce" O'Rourke for killing a mining engineer named Philip Schneider. A local miner's mob threatened to lynch the youthful gambler, so McKelvey started to Tombstone with his prisoner. Their wagon, pulled by a team of mules, chased closely by a horseback group. On the road outside of Tombstone, the Charleston constable was joined by deputy United States marshal Virgil Earp, who was in the country inspecting the improvement work being done on the Earp brothers' "Last Chance" mining claim. Earp pulled the light-weight O'Rourke up behind him and headed Wyatt's race horse Dick Naylor on a two-and-a-half mile run to Tombstone. When they reached town, Virgil sought refuge in Vogal's Saloon, where James Earp was the bartender. Virgil sent a messenger to locate Wyatt and Morgan.

Someone at the Charleston Mill used the company telephone and called their Tombstone headquarters with the news of Schneider's death and O'Rourke's escape. Monday's *Daily Epitaph*, January 17, reported that "in a few minutes Allen Street was jammed with an excited crowd, rapidly augmented by scores from all directions." Marshal Sippy, backed by "a strong posse well armed," was able to get the prisoner safely out of town. "Marshal Sippy's sound judgment prevented any such outbreak [a lynching] as would have been the certain result, and cool as an iceberg he held the crowd in check. No one who was a witness of yesterday's proceedings can doubt that but for his presence, blood would have flown freely." More research into the incident suggests that the newspaper misinformed the public concerning some facts.

The *Tucson Arizona Citizen* of January 22, 1881, said, "The Citizen now learns that to Deputy United States Marshal Virgil Earp and his companions (including his brothers Wyatt and Morgan) the credit of saving the young man from the fury of the miners is due." In later years, in spite of past loyalties, Billy Breakenridge agreed with George Parsons, Fred Dodge, and John Clum that, contrary to the original misinformation in Clum's newspaper, the Earp brothers had played a leading role in maintaining law and order during the O'Rourke drama. Witnesses said that town marshal Ben Sippy and Deputy Sheriff John Behan had stood by and watched the action. This incident is a major event in the legend of the Earp brothers.

> **Author's Perspective:** One fact is undisputed: a lynching was prevented and the prisoner was spirited out of Tombstone and taken to the county jail at Tucson to await a hearing. However, contrary to Tombstone myth, Johnny-Behind-The-Duce was not freed at his trial; in fact, he never faced a court. On April 19, 1881, Tucson's *Arizona Citizen* reported that Michael O'Rourke escaped custody by scaling a 16-foot wall at the Pima County jail, disappearing from Arizona history.

There was only one injury during the O'Rourke affair. In one of the journals he kept during his long life on the frontier, Fred Dodge claimed that when he was assisting the Earp-led posse to quickly move O'Rourke from Vogal's headed down Allen Street to the corral for the wagon and team to convey the gambler to Tucson, he tripped over the toppled shoe-shine stand on the boardwalk in front of the saloon. Dodge received a deep gash, just above his right ankle, from the iron footrest on the stand. The wound needed medical care and the boot needed repair.

In this day's journal entry George Parsons noted, "The law must be carried out by the Citizens or should be when it fails in its performance as it has lately done. Tonight I was requested to attend a strictly private gathering and went." This may have been the first occasion where the dissatisfaction with Marshal Sippy's job performance was discussed by town leaders.

Shortly after the Duce incident, Tombstone business leaders who had been expressing disappointment with their marshal and police force, in spite of the public facade offered in the local press, organized a Citizen's Safety Committee to support or supplant, if necessary, the city police in maintaining the peace and order of the rapidly developing community. This group was also behind a future clandestine change in the leadership of the Tombstone police force.

On **Tuesday, February 1, 1881**, the new county, with Tombstone as the county seat, recently created by Arizona territorial lawmakers out of the southeastern section of Pima County, came into being. The county was first named Huachuca, but the name was changed to honor the Apache chieftain Cochise before Governor John C. Frémont signed the creation bill into law. For political reasons, this Republican governor appointed only Democrats to all the new county's administrative offices to serve until the next regular general election in 1882.

Thursday, February 10, 1881, was a day of "high winds and dust" around Tombstone.

There was a "run" on the Safford, Hudson and Company Bank as false rumors flew about town that the bank was not solvent. The tales were quickly disproved and at day's end the bank had posted more deposits then withdrawals. George Parsons helped the bank staff handle the customer concerns and that night wrote in his journal, "Much excitement today."

Another milestone in the relationship between the Earp brothers and the political grifters in Tombstone was reached when John H. Behan was appointed Cochise County's first sheriff on this date. John Behan's first action as sheriff was to renege on his "understanding" with Wyatt Earp to name him his undersheriff or chief deputy in exchange for Earp's support of Behan's appointment as sheriff. Wyatt Earp was a Republican. Harry Wood, a 10-Per-Center, Democrat and editor of the *Daily Nugget*, received the lucrative opportunities. The broken trust between Behan and the Earps was never repaired and this breach played a major role in the future of law enforcement in Tombstone and Cochise County. Milton Joyce, another Earp antagonist, was named one of the four county supervisors.

Tuesday, February 15, 1881, was a "fine day," according to George Parsons.

John H. Behan took his oath of office and served his first day as sheriff of Cochise County. He set up his office at his livery stable since the new county had no courthouse yet.

On **Monday, February 21, 1881,** Arizona's eleventh territorial legislature upgraded Tombstone's town charter to city class; the community had the second largest population in the territory. Under this government charter the newly elected Tombstone Common Council, led by Mayor John Clum, amended Ordinance No. 3 to change the marshal's position to that of chief of police and head of a police department with regular and special police officers recommended by the chief but approved by a board of police commissioners and the city council.

On **Friday, February 25, 1881,** George Parsons noted that it was "grand weather" for this time of the year in the Tombstone area.

Bandits made history by conducting the first stage holdup in Cochise County. George Parsons made this entry in his journal on Saturday: "Stage stopped last evening three and a half miles from Contention, but only $135 in W.F. and Company's box it being the off night. Passengers undisturbed." No one was ever identified or prosecuted for this robbery.

This same night in Tombstone another incident in the gambler's war took front and center as Luke Short, a key member of the eastern gambler's cartel, killed Charlie Storms, a gladiator for the West Coast gamblers. The duel was staged on the street in front of the Oriental Saloon on Allen Street. During the inquest held concerning the shooting incident the jury declared that Storms had acted in self defense. Bat Masterson had been a witness to the incident and testified at the proceedings. The grand jury took no action concerning this killing.

On **Thursday, March 10, 1881**, George Parsons was basically an outdoorsman. He wrote in his journal, "Rain night before last and hail and wind last night and this A.M. early. Cold blustering day."

U.S. marshal Dake appointed Leslie F. Blackburn as a deputy federal marshal assigned to serve as the bailiff for the federal preliminary court at Tombstone operated by Wells Spicer in his capacity of United States commissioner in southeastern Arizona. In this post Spicer presided over internal revenue, import customs, and mining and public land cases. Mail robbery cases could also be reviewed by this court. The post was is in addition to Spicer's peace justice court duty.

Monday, March 14, 1881, was a warm day to work outdoors but the evening was cold.

Marshal Ben Sippy disarmed and arrested his deputy Joe Nichols for fighting. Sippy fired him and employed William Withrow, with the approval of the town council. A few days before, Marshal Sippy had arrested a robbery suspect.

On **Tuesday, March 15, 1881**, George Parsons' journal noted, "A strange and pretty sight this A.M. Just enough snow had fallen to whiten everything around and it looked very pretty. Would like to see a good snowstorm once more. Didn't last long." The astronomical records of the prestigious United States Naval Observatory at Washington, D.C., indicate the people in southern Arizona Territory were able to witness a full moon Monday evening that must have added to the spectacle.

Beside the weather conditions George Parsons took note of a more deadly event: "Excitement tonight. Out going stage attacked by robbers and driver and one passenger killed." Contemporary records indicate that a group of at least four highwaymen tried to capture the mail coach near Drew's Station between Tombstone and Benson. These men were unable to stop J.D. Kinnear's stagecoach, so they received no money from the passengers or the strongbox with six silver bars from the Contention Mill during the attack. Unfortunately, the bandits killed Kennear's driver Eli "Bud" Philpot and a Canadian miner named Peter Roerig, who was riding in the dickey seat behind the guard and driver. Wyatt Earp, in an August 9, 1896, feature in the *San Francisco Sunday Examiner*, said bitterly, "Such were the coyotes who kenneled in Tombstone during the early '80s. They did this thing deliberately. It was murder for murder's sake—for the mere satisfaction of emptying their Winchesters."

On **Wednesday, March 16, 1881**, snow was still on the ground and heavy snow clouds covered the sky in Tombstone country.

Sheriff John Behan and deputy U.S. marshal Virgil Earp organized a joint posse that left to track the attempted robbers of the Benson stage. Nearly forty cartridges were found at the attack site, and some Tombstone historians have proposed the idea that this was not a serious robbery attempt but rather an aborted attempt by the Cow-boys to murder Wells Fargo Express Company's shotgun messenger Massachusetts-born Robert Havlin Paul. The old California lawman was legally contesting his loss in the recent election for Pima County sheriff. The Cow-boys did not want Paul as sheriff in their territory because he looked unfavorably toward their activities.

Bat Masterson, who had arrived in Tombstone from Dodge City earlier in the year, was one of the nine possemen that rode with the joint posse. He stayed with the Earps when the sheriff's team turned back to Tombstone and was part of a monumental sixteen-day, 300-mile manhunt for the would-be Benson stage robbers. Wyatt remarked in 1896 that "manhunting meant nothing more than hard work and cold lead."

Forrestine Hooker recalled how Wyatt had found a section of a dime novel at a Cow-boy hideout and followed a trail of ripped-out pages to another Cow-boy safe house. Here, at the Redfield Ranch, the Earp part of the joint posse caught Luther King. King confessed to having been the man who held the horses while his partners Jim Crane, Bill Leonard, and Harry Head attempted the holdup. King, now a federal prisoner, was sent back to Tombstone under the guard of Sheriff John Behan and Wells Fargo's Tombstone station agent Marshall Williams. The posse escorting King to Tombstone arrived on March 21. The rest of the sheriff's posse soon also gave up the chase and returned to Tombstone.

Meanwhile, the federal possemen continued on the trail until Bob Paul's mount died, and both Bat Masterson and Wyatt Earp's horses became worn out during the long hunt. Paul was able to acquire a new horse and continued on the hunt with Virgil and Morgan. Since Sheriff Behan had neglected to send replacement horses to a rendezvous point as he had promised, Wyatt Earp and Bat Masterson, carrying their saddles, trail gear and weapons, were forced to walk 18 miles back to Tombstone.

Upon reaching Tombstone, Wyatt Earp learned that their only prisoner had "escaped" from Sheriff Johnny Behan's jail. This event, coupled with Behan's other broken promises, played a key role in the Earps' mounting mistrust of Cochise County's chief law enforcement officer. The three remaining suspected stage robber–murderers escaped capture only to face death for committing other crimes.[4]

Saturday, March 19, 1881, the snow had melted, but the weather was still cool during the day followed by a cold night.

The politically motivated mud tossing continued against Earp supporters in that day's issue of the *Daily Nugget.* The Cow-boy newspaper published false rumors suggesting that John H. Holliday, DDS, was the mysterious "fifth" stage robber present at Drew's Station on Tuesday night.

> **Author's Perspective:** History has shown that the "fifth bandit" was a fabricated individual created by a writer at the *Tucson Star* as a "red herring" to publicly discredit the Earps' efforts to curb the activities of the Cow-boy range riders via Wyatt Earp's known association/friendship with the temperamental gambler and brawler. This innuendo rumor mill was a well-crafted maneuver of media deceptive suggestion and misdirection and continues to color public opinion concerning the law and order campaign to combat the Cow-boys.
>
> In my full disclosure mode, I should note that Wyatt Earp's friends Fred Dodge and John Clum in later years each claimed he had always suspected that Doc Holliday had helped the bandits plan the Drew's Station holdup along with Billy Leonard. Dodge even added that Johnny Barnes, as a sixth bandit, was in hiding along the roadside.

The Kenner Stage Lines had difficulty employing any new stage drivers as a result of the recent killings on the Tombstone–Benson route. Fred Dodge and Morgan Earp would drive the route for a few runs before Jimmie Harrington, a good driver and fearless coachman, arrived in Tombstone to take the reins full time.

On **Monday, March 21, 1881,** the residents of Tombstone awoke to see the snow in the lowlands gone and a warmer day developing.

According to the *Daily Epitaph* of March 22, Warren Earp, youngest of the Earp brothers, was fined $25 in Tombstone's Police Court by City Recorder O.C. Wallace for discharging a firearm within the Tombstone city limits. Warren had arrived in the mining community from the Earp family homestead in southern California while his older brothers, except for James, were out of town hunting stage robbers. The troubled young man had a history of being unable to hold his liquor and seemed to always be in trouble when his brothers were not around to oversee his actions. His propensity for picking barroom fights and a quick temper triggered by liquor contributed to Warren Earp's death in 1900.

Monday, March 28, 1881, was a warm day in Cochise County, Arizona Territory. At about 7:30 p.m. on this spring evening, confessed Benson stagecoach robber

Luther King escaped the custody of Cochise County under-sheriff Harry Wood, who was also the editor of the *Daily Nugget*; John O. Dunbar, county treasurer, business partner with Sheriff Johnny Behan and operator of Dunbar's Corral on Fifth Street near Fremont Street; and Harry Jones, a deputy sheriff and Tombstone lawyer. Wood, Dunbar and Jones were in Dunbar's office in his corral, which also doubled as Johnny Behan's sheriff's office, to conduct a horse sale between King and Dunbar.

The *Tombstone Evening Gossip* reported the next day that King took Deputy Sheriff Campbell's pistol as he slipped out a back door of the stable office and made his getaway on a horse saddled and waiting by the door. Wood's own *Daily Nugget* reported the King escape happened in "a single unguarded moment" and "every effort possible will be made to secure his capture." John Clum's *Daily Epitaph* caught the gravity of the escape, saying Luther King knew vital information concerning the attempted stage holdup and murder but also had knowledge concerning "the extensive stock stealing now being perpetrated in Southern Arizona." The *Tucson Arizona Weekly Star* of April 7 noted that Luther King was the fifth Cochise County prisoner to have escaped "from the jail and officers in the past few months." The new county was just two months old, but Behan was an experienced sheriff, having served a term as Yavapai County sheriff at Prescott.

The *Evening Gossip*, a diminutive 8-by-11-inch, four-page newspaper, was the only local news source that mentioned that James B. Hume, Wells Fargo's chief detective, who was in town helping coordinate the search for the hold-up men for his employer, had warned the sheriff's office that afternoon he understood an attempt would be made that evening to liberate King from custody and requested that Sheriff Behan increase his guard at the Sixth Street county jail. The *Evening Gossip* ended its account by naively saying, "We do not know where the blame lies, but suppose it will be made known shortly." George Parsons stated his feelings very bluntly for his diary: "Some of our county officials should be hanged. They're a bad lot."

Friday, April 1, 1881, was still "fine weather" in Cochise County, Arizona Territory.

On this April Fool's Day, deputy United States marshal Virgil Earp and his brother Morgan returned to Tombstone. The brothers were the last members of a 9-man joint county and federal posse that had left the city on March 16 to investigate the robbery and trail the four accused Benson stage robbers. Sheriff Behan and his men had quickly abandoned the hunt to the federal officers. These men ran out of food and water and rode three horses to death in the pursuit.

Tuesday, April 5, 1881, caused no concern among weather watchers.

The *Daily Epitaph* reported that a group of "Chinamen" laborers accused Deputy Marshal William Withrow of extorting money from them. They refused to pay, so Withrow and another deputy locked them in the city jail. Marshal Sippy released the Chinese laborers when he found no evidence to support their arrests. Withrow resigned the police force and left town. Marshal Sippy seemed to backhandedly condone his deputy's actions when he told the *Daily Epitaph*, "I do know that police service in Tombstone is a dangerous and arduous service." He added, "The best police service is secured by rewards." Tombstone police court records show that during April and May 1881, the local officers made over 20 arrests ranging from fast-driving and disturbing the pace to saloon brawling and burglary.

Sunday, April 10, 1881, was another windy spring day for Tombstone citizens, but worship service attendance was still respectable for a Palm Sunday.

Sheriff Behan and his deputies were unable to curb the county's influx of horse stealing in the mining sites around Tombstone. A couple of days later, Tombstone police posted a few undesirables out of the city. It is interesting to note that Johnny Ringo left Arizona about this time headed to Texas. According to the *Austin Daily Statesman* of May 3, city marshal Ben Thompson had arrested Ringo the evening before for carrying a pistol and disturbing the peace. He was fined five dollars and cost for the pistol and $25 and costs for breaking the peace of Austin: "He settled with the city and left a wiser if not sadder man."

Tucson's *Arizona Weekly Citizen* reported that an eight-mile-long telephone line hung between Tombstone and E.B. Gage's administrative office at the Grand Central Mine was in operation. Wyatt Earp, in his 1926 autobiography, claimed he used a telephone while working on the Benson stage robbery investigation in the spring of 1881. Gage and Earp were friends and the mining superintendent would play a role in Earp's being offered an under-sheriff's job in Colfax County, New Mexico Territory, during December 1884.

On **Saturday, April 16, 1881,** Bat Masterson arrived in Dodge City, Kansas, to assist his younger brother Jim, who was in political as well as business trouble. Bat had been summoned from Tombstone a few days earlier. As soon as Masterson stepped off the train on this date, he was embroiled in a gunfight with brothers-in-law Al Upergraff and A.J. Peacock. The battle of the Dodge City Plaza ended with Peacock being wounded, Bat being fined $8.00 for disturbing the peace and the Masterson brothers leaving town, via police orders.

Sunday, April 17, 1881, was a pleasant Easter Sunday in Tombstone.

People around Tombstone were able to attend a Catholic mass or a service at the Methodist-Episcopal Church–South or Presbyterian Church–South that morning. On Wednesday evening, the formation group for an Episcopal church held their first services in Tombstone. The mining community also had a small Jewish gathering that held a weekly Sabbath service and *Torah* study. They even established their own consecrated cemetery, which is still in use.

George Parsons had recently captured a Gila monster and was keeping him in his room. He enjoyed showing the reptile to his lady friends before sending the orange and black beadlike-scaled poisonous lizard East as a gift for friends. The *Daily Epitaph* printed a story about Mr. Parsons and his unusual pet, which many said resembled a small colorful alligator.

Monday, April 18, 1881, was a typical spring day in Tombstone.

The *Evening Gazette* of Reno, Nevada, published the following reprinted from the Tombstone newspaper exchange: "The DAILY NUGGET announces the arrival at Tombstone, Arizona of Tom Fitch and wife." The same newspaper, on February 9, 1881, had reported that Fitch "has made $1,000,000 in Arizona—not by the coinage of his tongue, but out of mining property." The new attorney would quickly make his mark on the history of Tombstone and within a few months he would play a role in the destiny of Wyatt Earp.

Tuesday, April 19, 1881, continued the nice spring weather and people enjoyed it because they knew that the hot summer was just around the bend.

Mayor John Clum and members of the Tombstone Common Council approved City Ordinance No. 9 concerning the carrying of firearms and other weapons within the confines of the municipality. Some felt this ordinance was not strong enough, while others felt it was too ambiguous to be effective. The overt in-your-face violation of this Tombstone ordinance by the Cow-boys was the direct cause of the streetfight with the city police in October 1881.

John Clum, his mother-in-law and his two small children boarded the evening stage to Benson. There they planned to connect with the railroad for their journey to Washington, D.C. The mayor was taking his infant son and baby daughter to be raised by his late wife's family. It was difficult for a single man to raise small children in a frontier mining town like Tombstone.

While in the East, the Tombstone mayor also visited a firefighting equipment dealership in Watertown, New York. John Clum was in town investigating the different types of equipment available within the budget he had to purchase and deliver the equipment to his growing city.

Thursday, April 21, 1881, was a typical spring day in southern Arizona.

George Parsons noted in his journal entry for this date, "Two men probably killed at Charleston for robbery and I'm glad of it. Time a lesson was taught the cowboys by...." The mining developer did not finish his sentence, but he could have been thinking of the vigilante action that had tamed other frontier areas. Parsons was one of Tombstone's business leaders who established the Citizen's Safety Committee and served on the executive committee.

Thursday, May 19, 1881, was very cool and windy for working all day outdoors according to George Parsons.

William "Curly Bill" Brocius was shot, in the jaw, the bullet exiting via his neck, at Galeyville by his friend Jim Wallace. Deputy Sheriff "Uncle Billy" Breakenridge, a friend of Curly Bill, arrested Wallace and took him to Tombstone. Brocius was laid up for a few weeks but lived. Wallace was freed at his hearing and quickly left for New Mexico. George Parsons, while traveling with the Tombstone posse hunting renegade Apaches, saw Curly Bill and two other Cow-boys on October 6, 1881, while the posse was resting at a ranch in the Sulphur Springs Valley. Virgil Earp and Curly Bill greeted each other with a handshake and some quiet conversation. According to George Parsons, Curly Bill didn't seem like he had fully recovered his health in the four-and-a-half months since he was wounded.

In **early June 1881**, the San Simon Valley rustlers gathered a "Cow-boy Militia" of about 70 raiders to avenge the death of four of their own at Fronteras, Mexico, on Friday, May 13, and headed south to seek their style of revenge. These events were reported in the *Daily Nugget* of June 9, 1881.

On **Thursday, June 2, 1881,** the weather had been in the triple digits for the past few days. George Parsons, who was working outdoors during these days, called it "sweltering."

Wyatt Earp, now working as a Wells Fargo "private man," had a quiet meeting with Cow-boy leader Ike Clanton in front of the Crystal Palace Saloon on the corner of Fifth and Allan streets. They discussed a mutually beneficial plan Wyatt had developed to capture the robbers of the Benson stagecoach in March. Wyatt explained that he would arrange for Clanton to receive the full $1,200 reward offered by Wells Fargo Express Company for the four robbers if Clanton would provide him with the information of where he could arrest the accused rogue Cow-boys. Ike Clanton needed time to think on the idea. Wyatt Earp coveted the glory of arresting the Benson stage bandits to enhance his outlaw hunting and law enforcement credentials in the Tombstone community for his future political campaigns. He knew that Ike Clanton, a dirt-farm boy from Callaway County, Missouri, was always looking for a quick dollar and that his Cow-boy friendships were secondary to amassing wealth.

The *Epitaph* on Saturday reported, "The Fire Company, at their meeting Thursday evening, elected the following named gentlemen honorary members: Judge A.O. Wallace, Mr. Pearce of the Empire [Mine], Prof. John A. Church of the Tombstone M & M Co., Wyatt Earp, J.R. Farrell of Sulphuret and Flora Morrison [Mines], Josiah White of Contention, Lyttleton Price, District Attorney, Judge Wells Spicer and C.H. Light, Esq. [a freighter]." Within days these men would all see more firefighting action than they ever dreamed about.

On **Monday, June 6, 1881,** the weather was becoming very hot in southern Arizona.

Ike Clanton sought out Wyatt Earp for an update on their proposed partnership. At the conference Clanton was accompanied by fellow Cow-boys Frank McLaury and Joe Hill. They asked Wyatt Earp if the Wells Fargo reward for Bill Leonard, Harry Head and Jim Crane was payable either alive or dead. Earp said he believed the answer was yes, but he would request an official answer from the express company and he would let Ike know as soon as he received a reply from the San Francisco office. Ike Clanton preferred the three men dead so they could not implicate the Cow-boy confederation leadership in the botched attempt to kill their enemy Bob Paul.

At a meeting that night of the Tombstone Common Council, the councilmen approved a two-week leave of absence request for chief of police Ben Sippy. Following an interview, the city trustees appointed Virgil Earp as the acting police chief during the leave period. Later circumstances, like a report contained in the July 19, 1881, issue of the *Daily Nugget*, seems to indicate this action was a public charade to conceal the fact that the city's business leaders paid Sippy to leave Tombstone and never return. Since Ben Sippy was the elected city marshal, the city council could not fire him. However, Sippy could voluntarily choose to vacate his elected office. The *Daily Nugget* article said that Sippy left owning the city $200 in collected fees and numerous outstanding debts to city merchants. In May, the marshal/chief of police had been reprimanded by the city council for release of some prisoners and for having been absent from duty without approval of the police committee, yet the city council granted Ben Sippy a $50 a month raise. The city council's dissatisfaction may have dated from January and Sippy's nonparticipation in the Johnny-Behind-the-Duce incident.

On **Tuesday, June 7, 1881,** the overnight rain made the day cooler and the night cold.

T.J. Cornelison, a Tombstone policeman, arrested Willie Claiborne for being drunk and disorderly and brought him before Justice A.O. Wallace. The "Billy-the-Kid" wannabe was fined $7.50 and court costs for his overindulgence.

Workmen had been working on the construction project for weeks and that night the Irish League held a dance in the newly completed Schieffelin Hall.

Wyatt Earp was given a decoded Wells Fargo telegram, received at 4:00 p.m. by

Marshall Williams, from L.F. Rowell, assistant to Wells Fargo's president, stating, "Yes we will pay rewards for them [the three Benson stage robbers] dead or alive." Wyatt showed the Rowell telegram to Ike Clanton and the two men agreed to the information deal offered by Earp.

> **Author's Perspective:** Some Cow-boy supporters have claimed that Wyatt Earp made up the story about a Wells Fargo telegram. In fact, the telegram was introduced as "Defense Exhibit A" and recorded in Ike Clanton's cross examination testimony during the hearing concerning the events of the October streetfight. Fate, however, chose to alter the agreement by having the three wanted suspects killed in other, unrelated incidents. Ike Clanton lost his "blood money" and Wyatt Earp lost the opportunity to advance his social and political standing.

Wednesday, June 8, 1881, was cool during the day but became cooler after dark and "cold nights very," according to Mr. Parsons.

Late Tuesday evening, Ike Clanton and a gambler named "Little Dan" Burns, also called McCann, engaged in a fistfight on Allen Street. Early that morning, the men were stopped from shooting each other by chief of police Virgil Earp and Constable Hugh Haggerty. The incidents were reported in the June 9 issue of the *Daily Nugget* as "Almost a Shooting."

Thursday, June 9, 1881, proved to be a pleasant outdoor workday, but as the sun set the evening became much cooler and a jacket was needed outdoors.

The Tombstone *Daily Nugget* made an editorial observation concerning past and present law enforcement activity in the community. The newspaper said, "The business before Judge Wallace (Tombstone police court) has been unusually dull for some weeks, but yesterday it began to look up again. Probably the [new] Chief of Police has something to do with the revival of business."

The Tombstone police report for June 1881 indicts that Virgil Earp's five-man police force made 48 arrests that month and the city police court collected $324.50 in fines. The nature of these arrests follows: two for assault with a deadly weapon; two for assault and battery; three for carrying concealed weapons; three for petty larceny; fourteen for fighting and disturbing the peace; eighteen for being drunk and disorderly; two for violation of City Ordinance 10 defining solicitation of prostitution conduct within or outside of the red-light district; one each for grand larceny, fast-driving, drawing a deadly weapon, and resisting arrest by an officer. This police report was double the arrest level of marshal and chief of police Sippy's last month in office.

Thursday, June 10, 1881, was another "fearfully hot" day in the mining camps around Tombstone.

According to an account published in the *Daily Epitaph* on June 12, the suspected Benson stage robbers and murderers Harry Head and Bill Leonard were killed on this date during an attempted robbery at Eureka, New Mexico, by Ike and Bill Haslet. Leonard was still suffering from the wound to the groin he received from Bob Paul's shotgun during the March stage robbery attempt near Drew's Station on the Benson–Contention City–Tombstone road. This attempted holdup ended with death of driver Eli "Bud" Philpot and passenger Peter Roerig, a Canadian miner.

The two Cow-boys Head and Leonard had been hiding at Bill Hick's Ranch, while Jim Crane had gone to Galeyville to be with friends. Bill Leonard and Doc Holliday, who both suffered from tuberculosis, were friends from their days in Las Vegas, New Mexico Territory.

Friday, June 11, 1880, was another "bracing" day and "much wind," according to George Parsons, who was working at a mining claim.

That night an almost total lunar eclipse was visible across the Southwest. The stars were very bright in the ink-black darkness.

Sunday, June 19, 1881, was very hot around Tombstone, according to George Parsons. The weather was so hot Parsons skipped church, did no work, and just rested in the shade on the porch of his house.

The *Daily Epitaph* told readers that the San Simon Valley Cow-boys raided Fronteras, Mexico. While in Mexico, the Cow-boys killed or wounded over 40 people in retaliation for recent Cow-boy deaths at the hands of Mexican vaqueros. With their mayhem mission in Mexico complete, the vengeful and rowdy San Simon Valley rustler "Cow-boy Militia" returned via New Mexico Territory and stopped at the isolated gold camp of Eureka for another revenge act. Here they found Ike and Billy Haslet and shot them to pieces in West McFadden's saloon along with a young German miner. Back home, the rootless rebels "treed" the little San Simon settlement and then amused themselves by taking potshots at a circus train as it passed the railroad depot.

Chief of police and acting city marshal Virgil Earp arrested his brother Wyatt for disturbing the peace and fighting. Wyatt Earp pleaded guilty in the Tombstone police court and was fined $25 and court costs.

Wednesday, June 22, 1881, was a typical summer day, with a faint northwestern breeze.

In the *Daily Epitaph* there were kind remarks about chief of police Virgil Earp: "Mr. Earp is well known as one of the most efficient officers the city has ever had. Being fearless and impartial in the discharge of his duty...." By the time the day was over the police chief proved the public praise was well justified.

In mid-afternoon on this Wednesday, a fire started in the Oriental Saloon and quickly spread until it consumed two blocks, between Allen and Fremont streets, in the heart of the Tombstone business district. When the fire was finally contained it had destroyed 66 businesses, with an estimated $175,000–$300,000 in property loss. Much of the loss was uninsured. The new volunteer fire company had quickly responded and made a valiant effort against the blaze, but the need for real firefighting equipment quickly became very obvious. Ironically, John Clum returned to Tombstone that evening from having purchased a fire engine and two hose carriages for the community's new fire department.

John Clum, in an article published in the April 1929 issue of the *Arizona Historical Review*, recalled, "On the train returning just east of Benson, we saw a great column of smoke rising over the hills to the south. I tried to make my fellow passengers believe we had a live volcano over there, but when I arrived at Benson I learned that Tombstone was burning."

George Parsons, one of the volunteer firefighters, was badly injured when a wall and roofing collapsed on him as he was fighting the fire. Parsons required months of medical care to fully recover from near-death injuries that scarred his face. An account of Parsons' recovery is contained in his daily journal and the local newspapers.

Wyatt Earp entered the burning Oriental Saloon and saved the money contained in the gambling concessions safe. The money he saved helped him to rebuild and continue some business operations. Later, in a second incident at a nearby hotel, Earp rescued a disabled lady and her daughter from the growing flames. The manner of Wyatt's unheralded act of bravery impressed a young woman bystander named Josephine Sarah Marcus so much that she gave Wyatt Earp a kiss for his bravery.

In a letter dated October 23, 1930, to Ira Rich Kent, Houghton Mifflin Company's editor of Stuart N. Lake's Wyatt Earp biography, Josephine Marcus, and Wyatt Earp's widow, requested that the book's publisher retain this heroic rescue incident in the biography because it was a special memory to her. The rescue story was edited out of Wyatt Earp's biography because of space limitations, but the incident remains unedited in the John Flood manuscript.

In the evening, Chief of Police Virgil Earp, coordinating with Sheriff John Behan and his deputies, organized round-the-clock patrols to protect life and property from looters and lot jumpers as the ashes of Tombstone's business district died out. On Friday, the *Daily Epitaph* complimented Virgil Earp's initiative as "just action on the part of the Marshal [that] acted like oil upon troubled waters and peace and order restored. The action of Marshal Earp cannot be too highly praised, for in all probability it saved much bad blood and possibly bloodshed." Among the special officers Virgil Earp placed on fire damage patrol were Fred Dodge, Texas Jack Vermillion, James Flynn, and Warren Earp. The *Daily Epitaph* praised all the officers, "who exerted themselves like veterans, both to preserve peace, prevent stealing and to fight the flames, between which they had no idle moments."

Thursday, June 23, 1881, was pleasant, but the air contained a strong smokey smell.

While Tombstone was still focused on the aftermath of its business district fire, Tucson's *Arizona Weekly Star* published a blistering editorial about the Cow-boys, saying, "The common enemy to all law-abiding citizens and to our Mexican neighbors must be wiped out, root and branch. They should be hunted down like reptiles, and made to answer the penalty of their crimes, without the law's delay. If the business is not settled soon, it will cost the government much treasure and many lives to redeem lost time."

Saturday, June 25, 1881, the air continued to have a smokey smell when the wind blew.

Sunday's *Daily Epitaph* noted, "There came near being a general mutiny, last evening (25th) over the jumping of a lot, in the upper part of the burnt district. The police force were promptly on hand and squelched the would be jumper."

On **Tuesday, June 28, 1881,** it was a hot day in Tombstone.

At that day's meeting of the Tombstone Common Council, chaired by Mayor Clum, they appointed Vigil Earp as chief of police with a $150 per month salary via the failure of Ben Sippy, the elected city marshal, to have returned from his approved leave to reclaim his job.

Wednesday, June 29, 1881, was a typically hot—even in the shade—summer day.

The horror of the fire the week before still resonated with city leaders as they gathered to organize a second firefighting company. The new group, called the Rescue Hook and Ladder Company, selected Justice A.O. Wallace as president. Milt Joyce, William Breakenridge, and Virgil Earp became members. Chief of Police Earp was a member of the finance committee to raise the funding for the needed equipment; even Wyatt Earp contributed $2.50 to the new company.

Virgil Earp filed a $5,000 performance bond for his duties as police chief to be guaranteed by James M. Vizina, a mine owner and a cofounder of Tombstone, and Charles R. Brown, owner of the Brown Hotel and co-owner of the Grand Hotel. The Grand Hotel was the Tombstone headquarters of the Cow-boys and their supporters.

Later, the common council requested that Virgil Earp post an additional performance bond to cover the duty of collecting the new city business license fees recently established by the common council. Chief of police Earp's friends posted the required new performance bond on Saturday, July 2, 1881.

Tuesday, July 5, 1881, was a cool day after the hard thunderstorm of Independence Day broke the heat wave at Tombstone.

"Big-Nose Kate" Elder, Doc Holliday's lady friend with benefits, was in Tombstone for a visit. They had an argument and in a drunken stupor she signed a written allegation accusing John H. Holliday of being one of the men who attempted to rob the Benton stagecoach in March. The document was prepared by Sheriff John Behan and his accomplice Mike Joyce.

Sheriff John Behan arrested John Holliday on the strength of Kate Elder's complaint, charging the gambler/dentist with attempted robbery and murder. Holliday had a hearing before Justice Wells Spicer for the charge of murdering Philpot and Roerig. Holliday had a second hearing before Spicer, now functioning as a U.S. commissioner, for attempting to rob the U.S. Mail sack. Holliday was granted release on both territorial and federal charges by posting a $5,000 appearance bail bond provided by John Meagher and Joseph Mellgren, owners of the Alhambra Saloon, and Wyatt Earp.

Wednesday, July 6, 1881, saw the nice weather in Tombstone still vacillating between hot and cool.

Kate Elder was arrested by chief of police Virgil Earp on a complaint made by Doc Holliday, charging her with being drunk and disorderly conduct. Earp held Elder until she sobered up, then took her before justice of the peace Andrew Jackson Felter's court. She was convicted and fined $12.50 plus court costs.

On **Thursday, July 7, 1881,** the weather was typical for a high-desert summer day in southeastern Arizona Territory.

Kate Elder was rearrested by police chief Virgil Earp and charged with making threats against life. Elder hired Wells Spicer to represent her in a habeas corpus hearing before Commissioner T.J. Drum in the First Judicial District Court in Tombstone. She was discharged due to the fact she had been "enraged and intoxicated" when she made threats against her lover. Kate Elder returned to Globe on the next stage. In old age she claimed that Johnny Ringo gave her the money to make the trip home to Globe. She operated a boardinghouse in the town.

Chief of police Virgil Earp recommended to Mayor John Clum and the city council that the Tombstone police force be reduced from eight to five officers, including the chief. The city officers were Virgil Earp, Jim Flynn, Alex Young, George E. Magee, and Andy Bronk. Three special policemen, unpaid by the city, were also appointed to patrol select areas; Ben Titus for Safford Street and the Hudson & Company Bank, M.F. Hogan for the Vizina Consolidated Mining properties, and Andy Neff for Fremont Street. On

August 1, 1881, chief of police Virgil Earp again requested the council to downsize the police force from five to three officers.

On **Saturday, July 9, 1881,** many Tombstone residents were ready for a little heat relief or a nice swift breeze.

Doc Holliday appeared at his 10:00 o'clock hearing before Justice Wells Spicer upon the charges of attempted stage robbery and murder. District attorney Lyttleton Price told Justice Spence he had "examined all the witnesses summoned for prosecution and from their statements he was satisfied that there was not the slightest evidence to show the guilt of the defendant; and not even amount to a suspicion of the guilt of the defendant." Price withdrew the criminal complaint against Doc Holliday, and Justice Spicer released him and his posted appearance bond. The *Daily Nugget* concluded its account of Holliday's hearing by saying, "Thus ended what at the time was supposed to be an important case."

> **Author's Perspective:** Wyatt Earp told writer Walter Noble Burns, in a letter dated March 15, 1927, that on the day of the stage robbery attempt and murders Doc Holliday rented a horse and rode out to visit his old Las Vegas, New Mexico, friend Bill Leonard, a fellow sufferer of consumption, at his cabin near the Wells. After a nice visit, John Holliday rode on to Charleston for a poker game that did not happen. He eat a late lunch and returned to Tombstone around 6:00 p.m. that evening riding on a tanker wagon driven by Henry Fuller, father of Wes Fuller, a second-string member of the Cow-boys. Henry was delivering a load of water to Tombstone. Holliday returned his rented horse to the stable and after supper, Holliday played faro at the Alhambra Saloon into the early hours of Wednesday morning, walked to his rented room after the game and went to bed.

Tuesday, July 12, 1881, continued the trend of "cloudy and showery weather," according to George Parsons.

Late that night another fire happened in Tombstone. It started in a dry goods store under a theatre building and fortunately was quickly squelched by quick action from people in the store. One man was badly burned.

The *Daily Nugget* reported that John Ringo had returned to Arizona Territory following a family and friends visit to Austin, Texas, and Liberty, Missouri. John Ringo was registered at the Grand Hotel in the heart of Tombstone on Allen Street.

Wednesday, July 13, 1881, was "a very oppressive day—sultry," according to Parsons.

That night, police chief Virgil Earp found a drunken Michael Ryan surrounded by three would-be muggers. Earp took the rescued intoxicated miner to the *Epitaph* office to have the reporter witness a search of Ryan and found $930 in his pocket. The man gave them an additional $300 to hold. Earp locked the money in a safe and escorted the Irishman home to sober up. Ryan did not stay home but went to the Crystal Palace Saloon, drank more, won $80 at faro, and got "quick-fingered" out of his funds. Ryan was now arrested for being drunk and disorderly. The police caught one of the suspected robbers of Ryan, but Justice O.A. Wallace freed him because of lack of evidence. A second one had escaped capture at Benson. Wallace fined Ryan $7.50 and Earp gave him his money. Thursday's *Daily Nugget* told about Virgil Earp's saving Ryan's money; "No doubt he is thankful … that Tombstone has a vigilant and honest Chief of Police."

Tuesday, July 26, 1881, was a day with "rain in torrents," according to George Parsons. "Toughnut Gulch a foaming torrent ten feet wide." There now had been two weeks of rainy days.

Chief of police Virgil Earp arrested two women for disturbing the peace fighting over a client. Justice A.C. Wallace assessed each a $33.50 fine and court costs, according to the *Daily Epitaph*.

About a week after these events, the *Daily Nugget* reported that on this date the Cow-boys, led by Old Man Clanton, raided a herd of Mexican beef in Sonora and drove them north to Clanton's ranch near Cloverdale, New Mexico. A Mexican posse gave chase and recovered their cattle. The stolen cattle were quickly rounded up and headed back toward Mexico by the vaqueros when they were counterattacked by the Cow-boys. The outlaws drove off the cattle's rightful owner and retrieved their stolen cattle herd. The diplomatic protests were fast and furious from south of the international border to the secretary of state in Washington.

Friday, July 29, 1881, was "another bright and pleasant though warm day," according to an entry in George Parsons' journal.

Mayor John Clum's *Daily Epitaph* took the city's court system to task for releasing two hard cases the police had arrested for burglary and carrying a concealed weapon. "If the police officers are not to be backed up in enforcing the city ordinances it would be well for the City Council at its next meeting to repeal them.... There would seem to be a chance for some one to make an explanation. If the 'gang' are to run the town it should be known at once."

In late **July 1881,** Josephine Marcus, who since April has been known in Tombstone as Mrs. John Behan, returned to Tombstone from a visit to her family in northern California and discovered her man in bed with her friend. Josie felt this was justification to break up with her womanizing lover. Historians have identified the other woman as Mrs. Ida "Kitty" Jones, wife of John Behan's friend and attorney, Harry B. Jones. Marcus remained in Tombstone for almost a year before she returned to San Francisco. Her employment during this period is unknown, but her friendship with Mrs. Addie Borland, a dressmaker on Fremont Street, and Sol Israel, owner of the Union News Depot, which sold newspapers and books, most likely provided her with an opportunity for employment at one or both of these places. It is believed that Josie Marcus met Wyatt Earp at Sol Israel's store.

Monday, August 1, 1881, following over two weeks of rain, the weather was still making outdoor work difficult and the downpours had caused many road washouts around Tombstone, thus delaying the mail delivery to the community by days.

At the monthly meeting of the Tombstone Common Council, chief of police Virgil Earp suggested that the town was under control and made a request to reduce the police force from five officers down to two policemen and the chief. Virgil Earp suggested that James Flynn and Andy Bronk be retained as night shift officers, while he handled the day duties, and to add Joseph Bowman as a fourth special policemen. The city council agreed, based upon the July 1881 police report indicating the officers made 60 arrests: thirty-eight for being drunk and disorderly; nine for fighting and disturbing the peace; one for receiving stolen goods; one for attempted murder; two for carrying concealed weapons; one for grand larceny; two for petty larceny; three for committing a nuisance; one for discharging a firearm; and one for fast-riding a horse within the city limits.

The August police report, 22 arrests, seemed to support Chief Earp's plan to reduce the size of the police force; the September police report contained 39 arrests.

On **Wednesday, August 3, 1881,** the heavy late summer rains of Monday had disappeared and the sun was once again shinning, but the rainy weather had damaged the streets and weakened the walls of Tombstone's adobe buildings.

The day's *Daily Epitaph* headlined a story "The Careless Use of Fire-Arms" and described how almost every evening recently the residents of the sparsely settled north Tombstone along Bruce and Fitch streets were experiencing the discharging of firearms: "Only a few days ago a spent ball dropped in front of a house and among several little children who were playing there at the time. Fortunately it did no harm, but that does not render the person who fired the shot any less censurable."

The *Daily Nugget* carried this story: "Wyatt Earp's Chain Gang Cleans Streets." The reporter told readers that "Chief of Police Wyatt Earp had the chain gang out yesterday, cleaning the streets. Chief Earp believes cleanliness is next to godliness, and is making the streets of Tombstone a model." Vigil Earp, as the city's health officer, had recently gotten the city council to authorize the use of prisoners to do public service while they were in the city's custody; this service also provided the prisoners with some healthy outdoor exercise. Deputy United States marshal Wyatt Earp was acting police chief of the city during Virgil's absence from Tombstone.

The *Daily Nugget* also reported that Bob Clark had discovered the remains of a smuggler train from Sonora in Skeleton Canyon that was rumored to have been attacked by the Cow-boys on Monday. Later, the *Daily Epitaph* said the Mexicans were killed while eating breakfast and the killers got away with $3,000 in cash.

On **Tuesday, August 9, 1881,** Tombstone experienced the first day of a monsoon.

According to the *Daily Nugget*, 30-year-old North Carolina–born chief deputy United States marshal Joseph W. Evens left Tombstone after conferring with Wyatt Earp and other leaders of the town's law and order element. Evens, who lost an arm during his Civil War service, had served as the general superintendent in Arizona Territory and special agent for Wells Fargo before becoming Marshal Dake's chief assistant in 1880.

Author's Perspective: Chief deputy United States marshal Evens had served as the general superintendent in Arizona Territory and was special agent for Wells Fargo before becoming Marshal Dake's chief assistant in 1880. I believe that during this visit to the mining camp deputy chief Evens replaced Virgil Earp, now the full-time chief of Tombstone's police department, as the lead federal marshal for the Tombstone district and elevated his brother Wyatt to the position via a request from former employers, the Wells Fargo Express Company and the Southern Pacific Railroad. This action was not a reproach to Virgil Earp's past federal service but a realistic recognition of the restriction his new city police job placed upon his mobility outside the limits of Tombstone. Virgil Earp still retained his federal commission, but he was no longer expected to lead federal posses. The operation procedures of the Tombstone City Council, led by Mayor John Clum, prohibited the chief of police from being absent from his city duties without prior consent of the council's police committee and approval of the city council, except for an emergency.

Thursday, August 11, 1881, was the third day of heavy rain in the Tombstone area and made working outdoors very unpleasant and added an extra difficulty factor. Most people limited their travel to extreme need only. Many of Tombstone's adobe buildings had their outer walls weakened by the continuous heavy rainy weather and some of these unreinforced walls were now collapsing. That evening the rear section of the Cochise County Recorder's Office, on Fremont Street, fell into its Grotto cellar.

Arizona's chief deputy United States marshal Joseph W. Evans briefed his boss, Crawley P. Dake, at their office in Prescott about his meeting with the Mexican government's consul in Tucson during his return trip from Tombstone. The one-armed chief deputy reported the Mexican diplomat expressed "great dissatisfaction at the seeming neglect of our Gov't [concerning the Cow-boy's crossing the border raiding] and threaten to take vengeance on all Americans in Sonora."

Saturday, August 13, 1881, George Parsons told his journal that it was "another rainy day" in Tombstone.

That day became a primary event marker in the history of law and order vs. the Cow-boys. Tombstone writers like Jack Ganzhorn, Wayne Montgomery, Glenn G. Boyer, Ben Traywick, Karen Holliday Tanner and Michael Hickey have claimed that Virgil, Wyatt, Morgan and Warren Earp, along with Doc Holliday, were at the peaceful and isolated Guadalupe Canyon in the predawn hours of this Saturday. It was raining 60 miles away in Tombstone.

The basic story these writers tell is that Virgil Earp's federal posse was cooperating with a detachment of Mexican federal police as they tried to "peacefully" arrest a group of cattle rustlers led by Newman Haynes "Old Man" Clanton. The arrest failed when the Cow-boys resisted arrest during the predawn assault on their camp.

The historic Guadalupe Canyon runs east-west across the New Mexico–Arizona border just a few yards north of the border with the Mexican state of Sonora located at the southern base of the Peloncillo Mountains. Modern Tombstone residents seem to confuse Guadalupe Canyon with neighboring Skeleton Canyon. This should not be surprising since within a year of the ambush the *Daily Epitaph* was referring to the site as Skull Canyon. The debate over the location of the ambush and the area's name continues among field historians as well as armchair history buffs.

Contemporary newspaper dispatches like the interview with Mexican army general Adalfe Dominquez on August 18, 1881, and the tale of a wounded Cow-boy survivor plainly state that Mexicans conducted the predawn assault. Harry Ernshaw, a second-tier outlaw who called himself a milk ranch operator, and Billy Byers, a ranch hand, took flight in a hail of bullets and escaped the attack. During this bloody melee "Old Man" Clanton, Dixie Lee Gray, Jim Crane, Charles "Bud" Snow, and William Lang died at the rustler's camp.

Clara Spalding Brown, the young Tombstone housewife and amateur journalist from New Hampshire, wrote about the Guadalupe Canyon killings in a letter published in the *San Diego Daily Union* on August 28, 1881. Mrs. Brown said, "While no one upholds the recent massacre those who think dispassionately about the matter realize that the Mexicans were not the first to inaugurate the present unhappy state of affairs along the border. They have suffered greatly from depredations of those outlaws who, under the guise of 'cowboys,' infest this county and pursue the evil tenor of their ways with no attempt at interference on the part of those whose duty it is to suppress crime."

In May 1881, Cow-boy raiders had massacred Mexicans near Fronteras, Sonora, and in July they struck again, killing another group of Mexicans. This time the deaths took place in Skeleton Canyon in Cochise County and the man charged with the suppression of all crime and tax collection in Cochise County was Sheriff John H. Behan. He took no action to antagonize his tax-paying, protection-paying Cow-boy friends, so others had to do his job for him.

On September 13, 1881, Ike Clanton sent a note and photograph of his father to ambush survivor Billy Byers. On the reverse side of the photograph Byers wrote, "Mr. Clanton Killed on Aug. 13–81 by Mexicans with 4 other Americans in Guadalupe Canon [sic], New Mexico." So, it would seem that six weeks before the Tombstone streetfight Ike Clanton had no reason to suspect the Earp brothers of any involvement in his father's death. It is doubtful that he ever seriously entertained such an idea in the few years remaining to him. Billy Byers died in Colorado in 1949. Jim Dullenty, a book dealer, wrote about the letter and photograph in 1996.

At one point in the subsequent investigation into the killings, high-level diplomats in both Washington and Mexico City became involved. Mexican army records indicate that a force of federal troops under the command of Captain Alfredo Carrillo was in the general area of the canyon with orders to capture or contain cross-border raiding American Cow-boys. The captain understood that if the rustlers were killed "resisting arrest," this would be an action acceptable to his chief, Commandante Felipe Neri, and Arizona's United States marshal Crawley Dake, who had a directive from John Gosper, acting territorial governor, to end the Cow-boys' reign of terror along the border region.

Within five days of the Cow-boy deaths in Guadalupe Canyon, General Jose Otero, the commander of all Mexican federal troops stationed in the northern sector of the State of Sonora, had his adjutant, General Adalfe Dominquez, in Phoenix conferring with acting governor Gosper concerning the border smugglers. When the dust finally settled and the international verbal war ended the canyon ambush incident of 1881 became just a footnote in the fight the United States and Mexico fought against the cattle raiders on both sides of the border. Flash forward a century and the struggle continues as illegal drugs have replaced cattle in the war with present-day border smugglers.

Author's Perspective: As stated above, Virgil Earp's duties as Tombstone's chief of police prohibited his active participation in this type of cooperative mission, so if any of the Earp brothers were present at the ambush it was Wyatt Earp, using his newly vested authority, who led the rain-soaked and muddy federal posse on the journey to Guadalupe Canyon.

A few years after the Guadalupe Canyon incident, special agents James B. Hume and John N. Thacker collaborated to produce a detailed report delineating the number of express office burglaries, stagecoach and train robberies committed against the Wells Fargo Express Company between 1875 and 1885. Their 2,000-page *Loss and Damage Ledger* listed the date and nature of each incident, the amount stolen, the amount recovered, the killing of drivers and messengers, and the names of outlaws killed "while resisting arrest." The information in this report has a direct bearing upon better understanding Wyatt Earp's Cow-boy Campaign. This *Loss and Damage Ledger*, June 13, 1882, entry, notes that Wells Fargo Express Company paid deputy

United States marshal Wyatt Earp a $1,200 bounty for killing Jim Crane in Guadalupe Canyon on August 13, 1881.

Tuesday, August 16, 1881, found George Parsons enjoying the pleasant morning weather, but he was sure it would rain again in the afternoon.

Chief of police Virgil Earp and his two-man police force had put a lid on the rowdy crowd living in or visiting Tombstone. The regular police patrolled the streets and special officers handled the major night spots. Most citizens enjoyed the new peace and safety this system provided, while a few businessmen bemoaned the loss of their "entertainment" revenue. The *Daily Epitaph* took note of this fact and used satire to remind citizens of what had been their recent past: "Cow-boys don't seem to visit our city very much. Don't they like the climate? We feel slighted."

On **Wednesday, August 17, 1881**, the Tombstone area was still deep in mud, with impassable roads all around the city. Flooding arroyos stopped stagecoaches and trains in the area. By this time it had been raining for nine days and nights.

George Parsons told his daily journal, "Bad trouble on the border and this time looks more serious than anything yet." In the predawn hours of this Wednesday, some Cow-boys had been killed as they returned to the United States from a raid into Mexico. Parsons felt, "in [his] mind," the Cow-boy deaths were "perfectly justified" because the men were known cattle thieves and murderers.

Thursday's *Daily Nugget* reported that on Wednesday evening policeman Jim Flynn arrested a man he charged in Judge Albert O. Wallace's court with being drunk and exhibiting disorderly conduct. The man was taken to jail for the night and Thursday morning was fined $5 and court costs before being released from custody.

On **Friday, August 19, 1881,** mining investor-prospector and safety committee member George Parsons commented on the rough weather around Tombstone in his journal: "Floods have been something terrible. Canons [sic] flooded and all roads and trails washed away—completely obliterated. Terrible storm tonight. Kept awake hours."

In Thursday's edition the *Daily Epitaph* editorialized, "There is altogether too much good feeling between the sheriff's office and the outlaws infesting this country."

Saturday, August 20, 1881, saw Tombstone's streets very muddy as a result of continued rainy days and nights.

The *Daily Nugget* reported that two men were creating a disturbance at "the well, if not favorably known crib of Mother McKenna" on Fremont Street. The two men were running away from the small house of prostitution in a joyous mood firing their pistols in the air when they spotted policeman Jim Flynn coming on the run toward them. Policeman Flynn gave a spirited chase after one of the two men, but according to the newspaper the man escaped as "a shot was sent after him" by the officer.

Sunday, August 21, 1881, was a pleasant day in the midst of a massive wave of rain.

Chief of police Virgil Earp arrested Mayor John Clum for riding his horse too fast within the city limits. Elm Eastman was arrested for using vulgar and obscene language in public, according to the *Daily Nugget*.

On **Tuesday, August 23, 1881,** George Parsons wrote "rain again and plenty of it tonight" in today's entry of his private journal.

Chief of police Virgil Earp and policemen Jim Flynn and Andy Bronk raided an opium den in Tombstone's Chinatown and arrested five opium-smoking Chinese, according to the August city police report.

On **Sunday, August 28, 1881**, some Tombstoners observed that the rains seemed to be subsiding in the volume of their downpour.

The *Tucson Citizen* published a loosely researched account of Ed Byrnes' gang of tinhorn gamblers and con men operating around the train depot at Benson. The article named Morgan Earp as a member of the group. This would seem to be a gross error since Morgan was in Tombstone at this time working as a special policeman. When he had been living in Benson he had served as a deputy sheriff under Johnny Behan and had in fact arrested Byrnes for other offenses. On May 24, 1882, following Morgan Earp's murder and Wyatt Earp's bloody Cow-boy campaign, the *Las Vegas (NM) Daily Optic* flatly denied any involvement of Morgan Earp with Byrnes' gang of "black-sheep" gamblers.

Thursday, September 8, 1881, George Parsons told his journal he believed the rainy season had run its course. Parsons was still recovering from the facial wounds he received while fighting Tombstone's June fire. Over the last couple of days the young mining investor-accountant had killed two tarantulas in his cabin that were most likely seeking shelter and safety from the weather.

The stagecoach between Tombstone and Bisbee was held up near Hereford. When news reached Tombstone, Sheriff Behan sent Undersheriff Harry Woods and deputy Billy Breakenridge to investigate. Wyatt Earp also led a federal marshal's posse composed of brother Morgan, and Wells Fargo Company's Marshall Williams and Fred Dodge. The bandits took $2,500 from a Wells Fargo express box and $608 and a watch from the two passengers. They rifled the mail sack.

Days later, after following a cold trail, the posses made two arrests. Wyatt Earp and Fred Dodge located T.C. "Frank" Stilwell, while Morgan Earp and Deputy Sheriff Dave Neagle arrested a second suspect named Peter Spencer (his real name was Elliott Larkin Ferguson). The prisoners were taken to Tombstone and charged with stage robbery and robbing the U.S. mail, the latter a federal charge. Justice of the peace/federal commissioner Wells Spicer set each man's bond at $2,000 for the stage robbery charge and an additional $5,000 for the mail robbery charge. The bond was posted by C.H. "Ham" Light, owner of the American Transportation Company, Billy Allen and Ike Clanton. The charges against Spenser were dismissed on September 16.

Frank Stilwell, no relation to the territorial district judge in Tombstone, was a Cochise County deputy sheriff under Sheriff Behan who operated a saloon in Charleston. Stilwell's father was the agent in Bisbee for the Tombstone-Bisbee Stage Company. Pete Spenser and Frank Stilwell had once been partners in a saloon and livery stable business in Bisbee.

Author's Perspective: It's a good bet that the Earp brothers now topped the "don't send him a Christmas card" list of Frank Stilwell and the embarrassed Sheriff John Behan.

Saturday, September 10, 1881, was a nice day for working outdoors.

On this date, as strange as it might seem to present-day readers, Marshall Williams and Virgil Earp jointly posted security for $25 worth of food supplies for Pete Spencer at P.W. Smith's Mercantile Store. The former Confederate soldier was destitute and needed supplies for himself, his new bride, and her mother. Spencer had a house across the street from the Earp family complex and his wife, Maria, had become friends with Virgil's wife Allie.

That evening, chief of police Virgil Earp attempted to arrest Sherman W. McMaster on a warrant for a stage robbery near Globe on June 11, 1881. According to the *Daily Nugget*, Chief Earp fired a few shots after McMaster as he left town after dark. Wyatt Earp later claimed that McMaster, a former Texas Ranger, was his undercover man among the Cow-boys and that Virgil had faked his attempt at an arrest. Charles T. (Pony Diehl) Ray, a second suspect in the Globe robbery, was captured but quickly escaped from the county jail.

Wednesday, September 14, 1881, was warmer than a normal fall day.

The *Daily Nugget* for Thursday reported the city's common council held a special meeting to evaluate two charges of misconduct brought against Andy Bronk. One charge concerned blackmail and the second was an accusation that Officer Bronk failed to arrest a man who fired a pistol within the city limits. Both charges were dismissed and Bronk continued performing his duties.

On **Thursday, September 15, 1881,** the weather was still warm for a fall day.

That night, the melodrama *The Ticket-of-Leave Man* became the first stage show at the new Schieffelin Hall, on the northeast corner of Fremont and Fourth streets, as a production of the Tombstone Dramatic Association. The Earp brothers and their wives attended.

Monday, September 26, 1881, was another workday for the range hands and miners that populated the country around Tombstone. The weather was still comfortable enough to work outdoors without a heavy jacket.

Both the *Daily Nugget* and the *Daily Epitaph* reported that Morgan Earp, a newly appointed special policeman, fired a harmless shot into the wall of a saloon to break up a four-man brawl over a monte game. The new officer quickly buffaloed the chief agitator and sent him off to jail in the custody of Officer Andy Bronk. The ramrod for the Total Wreck Mine was fined $10 and court costs Tuesday morning.

Saturday, October 1, 1881, was a rather nice fall day around Tombstone.

George Parsons recorded in his journal the popular definition of a cowboy: "Cow-boy is a rustler at times be it understood in this journal and rustler is a synonym for desperado—bandit, outlaw, and horse thief." Meanwhile, the *Daily Nugget* contained a brief account of Col. Richard C. Wood's recent cattle-buying trip in the Sulphur Springs Valley and his dealings with the Clanton and McLaury brothers. Wood was developing a ranch along the San Pedro River. The Cow-boy's newspaper trumpeted, "The Colonel speaks in the highest terms of the courtesy with which he was treated and the fair business dealings of the gentlemen mentioned. If they are types of the 'cowboys,' he asks no better luck than always to deal with such." R.C. Wood's father was a Tombstone businessman and banker and decades later the son would became president of the First National Bank at Fairbanks, Alaska.

Cow-boy rider Willie Claiborne shot and killed Jim Hickey during a brawl in Charleston's Queen Saloon. Hickey had been on a three-day drunk. A Cochise County grand jury indicted Willie Claiborne for felony murder on November 2 and bound him over to Judge William Stilwell's court for December 2 as Case 55.

Tuesday, October 4, 1881, was cool with storm clouds forming in the mountains.

About 1:30 in the morning, two pistol shots were fired near the Palace Saloon on Allen Street. Andy Bronk and Morgan Earp, Tombstone policemen, quickly responded to the shooting according to the *Daily Nugget*. The two officers found Dave Humphreys bleeding profusely from a nasty cut over his eye. He claimed to have been assaulted by an unknown person with "either a six-shooter or a cobble stone, he knew not which." Mr. Humphreys said he had fired the shots after the fleeing man who had attacked him.

Wednesday, October 5, 1881, had heavy continuous rain most of the day.

Far from Arizona, Gen. John C. Frémont resigned as governor of the territory. Since he had been appointed on June 8, 1878, by President Rutherford B. Hayes, Frémont had spent the majority of his time away from his desk in Prescott. John Gosper, the territorial secretary, had been serving as the acting governor since Frémont left the territory on an extended Eastern business trip in March 1881. President Arthur would need to appoint a new chief executive.

Around noon a well-armed posse, called the Tombstone Rangers, left the city under the leadership of Sheriff John Behan and chief of police Virgil Earp. The 40-man militia was seeking to capture or kill raiding Apaches in the mountains east of the city. The Apaches had left the San Carlos Reservation led by Geronimo and Natchez, son of the late Cochise, and were headed for the old Apache stronghold in the Dragoon Mountains.

Mayor John Clum, George Parsons, Marshall Williams, and Wyatt Earp were among the rangers who suffered from the rain and soft muddy roads. John Pittman Rankin, a black man, served the expedition as cook. Fred Dodge would have gone with the rangers except he was still recovering from a protracted case of mountain fever.

Thursday, October 6, 1881, was a damp day as the sun tried to dry out the countryside.

The bedraggled Tombstone Rangers continued the hunt for the missing Chiricahua Apaches. The men had spent Wednesday night at Edwin B. Frink's ranch and the next morning, minus many deserters, they moved on toward the Swisshelm Mountains. No Indians were sighted, so after a hot meal and some rest, the troop, riding under a hot sun and over a boggy landscape, recrossed the Sulphur Springs Valley to the ranch operated by the McLaury brothers.

Curly Bill and two other Cow-boys were at the ranch to greet the posse as they rode up to the ranch house. In a letter to Stuart Lake, dated November 6, 1928, George Parsons wrote that he and Virgil Earp had a friendly conversation with Curly Bill. Parsons noted, "The best of feeling did not exist between Wyatt Earp and Curly Bill and their recognition of each other was very hasty and at some distance. It was a rather tense situation."

Some more of the rangers decided to end their wilderness adventure and returned to Tombstone, while the remainder rode away from the McLaury place and headed to Soldiers' Hole. These few men spent the night encamped with the Buffalo Soldiers bivouacked at the site. George Parsons was impressed with the black troops and John Clum enjoyed his visit with some old friends among the Apache scouts.

Friday, October 7, 1881, was cool and damp from the past day's rain.

The remaining Behan–Earp posse, including the Earp brothers, now decided the

Apache threat was subsiding and made plans to return to Tombstone that morning. The last possemen reached town about 1:00 o'clock in the afternoon. Later, it was learned that about eighty San Carlos Reservation Apache fugitives had slipped into Old Mexico during the breakout.

Very quickly newspapers, like the *San Francisco Daily Examiner* and the *San Francisco Stock Report*, began to investigate the Arizona Apache conflict. "The Indians have been deliberately goaded into hostility in order that their property may be seized," said the *Stock Report*. Following his investigation, the adjutant general of the army's Department of the Pacific told the *Daily Examiner*, "The Apache war, as it is called, has been much exaggerated." The San Carlos Reservation held vast coal deposits needed by the Southern Pacific Railroad. Beef contractors, working with the Cow-boy rustlers, could sell large qualities of beef to the expanded army needed to fight the Apaches and also produce higher beef prices at civilian meat markets because local ranchers would have been frightened off their ranges.

Saturday, October 8, 1881, was a typical fall workday in the Tombstone region.

This Saturday evening five men set a dubious record by perpetrating the fifth stage robbery in eight months within Cochise County. The men ordered the driver of the Charleston stage to halt, but instead he jumped from the moving coach and escaped into the brush. The stage overturned and its eleven passengers were miraculously uninjured. The bandits, however, took about $800 from the passengers but "generously" gave each passenger five dollars for their trip expenses and rode off into the night, according to Sunday's *Tucson Daily Citizen*.

Thursday, October 13, 1881, was a cold day with a colder night in the mountains surrounding Tombstone.

George Parsons used the weather as an excuse to settle in by the fire and catch up on reading a new work, *Sunrise*, by the popular Scottish author William Black. Black's nineteenth published work was a gift he had received in the mail from an Eastern lady friend named Nathalie. To Parsons' delight the hero and heroine of this novel of international political intrigue were named George and Nathalie.

Deputy United States marshal Wyatt Earp, aided by his brother Morgan, arrested Frank Stilwell and Pete Spenser for having taken part in the Charleston robbery. This was the second verse of the same song. A few days later, in front of the Alhambra Saloon, Ike Clanton, Frank McLaury, Johnny Ringo, and Joe and Milt Hicks berated and threatened to kill Morgan Earp for arresting their friends again for stage robbery, according to information published in the *Daily Nugget* on November 17, 1881.

On **Monday, October 17, 1881,** the weather was cold, with frost in the evening.

The Tombstone Common Council approved a bill for $20 as payment to Morgan Earp for five days of service as a special policeman during September. During the council meeting, the Tombstone Police Commissioners, upon the request of chief of police Virgil Earp, approved appointment of Morgan Earp as a special city policeman who could be used as his services were needed. Morgan could now legally carry a firearm on the streets of Tombstone when he was on duty.

Wednesday, October 19, 1881, continued the cold weather in the region.

A special called meeting of the Tombstone City Common Council was held at 2:00 p.m. that afternoon to "investigate" undisclosed charges against policeman Andy Bronk.

This was the second hearing concerning Officer Bronk's performance in two months. He still held his job, according to the *Daily Epitaph*, the mayor's newspaper.

Thursday, October 20, 1881, was a cool day but enjoyable work weather.

Marshall Williams, Sheriff Johnny Behan and Virgil Earp left Tombstone to visit the annual San Augustin Feast and Fair in Tucson. Each man sought out the gambling concession area. Wyatt Earp was the acting police chief during Virgil's absence from the city.

Saturday, October 22, 1881, saw continued cooler weather heading into winter.

John Holliday returned to Tombstone from the San Augustin Feast and Fair in Tucson's Levin's Park. Morgan Earp had gone to Tucson to bring him back to confront the Ike Clanton problem. Kate Elder returned with Doc and stayed with him at his room in Fly's Boarding House on Fremont Street.

On **Monday, October 24, 1881**, it was still cool in the region around Tombstone.

The *Daily Epitaph* reported that deputy sheriff Billy Breakenridge had arrested Milt Hicks a few days before. Hicks had "in his possession and [was] fraudulently branding cattle belonging to a rancher" and not to him. That afternoon about five o'clock Hicks and two other prisoners overpowered assistant jailor Charles Mason and escaped from Sheriff Behan's jail. They ran south across Toughnut Street into the large, deep and overgrown arroyo called Tombstone Gulch at the base of the Tombstone Mountains. Sheriff Behan finally called on chief of police Virgil Earp to help organize a search for the escaped men. Chief Earp, with his deputies Andy Bronk and Lance Perkins, along with his brothers Wyatt and Morgan, joined Behan and Breakenridge; and "several others started in pursuit." Darkness ended the fruitless hunt. Milt Hicks joined his brother, who was already hiding in New Mexico Territory.

Tuesday, October 25, 1881, was topcoat weather for outdoor activities in and around Tombstone. A number of skunks, real and human, were about the town seeking food.

Many events that form the cornerstone of the Tombstone law and order streetfight legend happened on this day and the following day. The details of these events have already generated thousands of pages of information, so we will not recount them in detail as part of this outline.

On this date, Ike Clanton, Tom McLaury arrived in Tombstone. They had eaten breakfast with their brothers at the Chandler Milk Ranch. McLaury set up a bank account for his brother Frank with a $1,000 deposit from the receipts he received from a business transaction.

Fred Dodge was still suffering from the mountain, or intermittent, fever he had been fighting for a few weeks, so he was at his room resting. Late that evening a messenger brought word from J.B. Ayers, Wells Fargo's undercover man in Charleston, that Frank McLaury, Billy Clanton and Billy Claiborne were in town and planned to join Tom and Ike in Tombstone Wednesday afternoon. Dodge dressed and went looking for Virgil Earp. He found Morgan Earp, a special city officer, at the Alhambra Saloon and told him the news.

Ike Clanton had been drinking and causing trouble all afternoon and now after midnight he came into the Alhambra. A short time later, Doc Holliday arrived and engaged Clanton in a verbal war of profanity concerning Ike's claim Doc knew about Ike's "secret" scheme to betray the Benson stage robbers. Morgan Earp broke up the discussion just before Chief Virgil Earp and Wyatt Earp arrived. Wyatt sat at the lunch counter and made a sandwich. Ike went to the Grand Hotel. Chief Virgil Earp went across the street to the Occidental Saloon, while Holliday headed to the Oriental Saloon. After one more short conversation with Ike Clanton on Fifth Street, Wyatt told Ike to go home, "because there was no money in it." Wyatt closed his faro game at the Eagle Brewery and deposited his money in a safe, found Doc on Allen Street and walked with him on down the street toward their residences and their ladies. Morgan helped Dodge back to his room at Mrs. Young's Rooming House, where he roomed with his gambling partner Dan McCann.

Wednesday, October 26, 1881, dawned cool and crisp and turned windy, overcast, and cold by mid-afternoon. It snowed that evening in Tombstone.

In the early hours before dawn, Ike Clanton, Tom McLaury, Sheriff John Behan, chief of police Virgil Earp and another unnamed player sat down to a poker game in the back room of the Occidental Saloon. Ike Clanton was a big loser. Just before dawn, Virgil Earp collected his winnings, went home and crawled into a warm bed.

Before noon, a messenger awakened Wyatt Earp, and a deputy awakened Virgil Earp. Ike Clanton's visit to his rooming house awakened Doc Holliday. Each learned that Ike Clanton had proclaimed that "the ball will open today." He was going to kill the Earps and Holliday.

Around noon, chief of police Virgil Earp found Ike Clanton hiding in ambush and arrested him for carrying a weapon on the streets of Tombstone. In Police Court, Justice A.O. Wallace reviewed Cause No. 106 and heard Clanton's guilty plea. Clanton was fined $25 plus court costs and his weapon was confiscated and deposited at the Grand Hotel Bar until he was ready to leave town. A Tombstone butcher named Apollinar Bauer testified at the month-long hearing before Justice Wells Spicer that he saw Wyatt Earp, following the Clanton hearing, use his long-barreled Colt revolver to buffalo Tom McLaury outside of Justice Wallace's courtroom.

During the next couple of hours the tension around Ike Clanton's public conduct and blatant murder threats rose to a level of molten lava, engulfing his friends with him. Shortly after 2:00 p.m. the Tombstone streetfight started in a vacant lot on the south side of Fremont Street near the corner of Third Street. This was the *post hoc ergo propter hoc* moment that rose to the need for a federal strike force to bring about the destruction of the Cow-boy confederation. Hundreds of thousands of words have been written about this deadly streetfight, which today is famous as the misnamed "Gunfight at the O.K. Corral."

Frank and Tom McLaury, Cochise County ranchers—rustlers—illegal beef suppliers, died along with their friend Billy Clanton in an attempt to resist arrest by Tombstone peace officers. Three other Cow-boys—Ike Clanton, Billy Claiborne and Wes Fuller—ran away from the scene of the streetfight. Chief of police Virgil Earp and his posse members Morgan Earp and Doc Holliday were each wounded. Deputy United States marshal Wyatt Earp was the only peace officer combatant uninjured during the 20-second exchange of lead.

Wyatt Earp would later recall that the smoke and dust were so thick around the vacant lot where the fight began that he could only hear the men coming down Fremont Street toward him. His first thought was how he was to protect his wounded brothers from this "Cow-boy mob" with an empty pistol. He was very happy to see Mayor Clum and the other safety committee members coming to the aid of the police.

In later years, Marjorie Clum Parker, granddaughter of Mayor John Clum, wrote that her then three-year-old father was playing on the boardwalk and street in front of his father's *Daily Epitaph* office when the streetfight took place across Fremont Street and down the block near the southeast corner with Third Street: "Grandfather snatched his son indoors with admonition, [and] hastened after them [the town safety committee], mentally revising his editorial [for Thursday's newspaper]." Mrs. Parker was mistaken about her father's location on October 26, 1881, because his grandmother had taken him back East to live in late April 1881.

On **Thursday, October 27, 1881**, George Parsons noted that Tombstone had "snow in the morning. Windy and extremely cold and disagreeable" the rest of the day.

This day's issue of the *Daily Nugget*, chief newspaper voice of the Cow-boy confederation, tried to explain what caused the conflict between the Cow-boys and the city police: "The origin of the trouble dates back to the first arrest of [Frank] Stilwell and [Pete] Spencer for the robbery of the Bisbee stage. The co-operation of the Earps and the Sheriff and his deputies in the arrest caused a number of cowboys to, it is said, threaten the lives of all interested in the capture."

Luther H. Halstead, a freighter and livestock dealer who had relocated from Fort Worth in 1880, sent a telegram to Fort Worth informing William McLaury, the older surviving brother of Tom and Frank, about his brothers' deaths. Halstead had marketed the cattle sold by the McLaury brothers. The effort to canonize the fallen was started the moment Ike Clanton placed a sign in the hardware store window displaying the three open-faced caskets that proclaimed "Murdered in the Streets of Tombstone." The photograph of the three Cow-boys lifelessly staring back at their viewers from their ornate silver and black wooden caskets has become a western history classic.

Friday, October 28, 1881, was a cold clear day in Tombstone.

A "Buck Fanshaw"–style funeral for the three Cow-boys killed during the streetfight was held in Tombstone.[5] They were buried in the new cemetery, now called Boothill. The *San Diego Union* of November 3, 1881, commented on the McLaury–Clanton funeral: "Strangers viewing the funeral cortège, which was the largest ever seen in Tombstone would have thought that some person esteemed by the entire camp was being conveyed to his final resting place ... but such a public manifestation of sympathy from so large a portion of the residents of the camp seemed reprehensible when it is remembered that the deceased were nothing more or less then thieves. It is but a few weeks since all three were found to be implicated in the stealing of cattle and horses." Even today, resisting police arrest can result in justifiable homicide by officers.

The Cow-boys' funeral "was almost like a Fourth of July celebration," recalled Mrs. Virgil (Allie) Earp in her unaltered autobiography. "Hundreds of people came into town and got drunk. Everybody went, the band playing as usual, 'Where Was Moses When the Lights Went Out?'" The old spiritual was a frontier favorite, especially at funerals. Does the wording "everybody went" suggest that "Aunt Allie," and maybe the other Earp women, attended the "celebration" with other mourners? Most likely not. It is generally understood that none of the Earp family attended the Clanton or McLaury brothers' funerals, certainly not Virgil or Morgan, who were confined to bed due to their injuries.

The Earps could have heard and seen the funereal merriment from their residences, because the cemetery, now called Boothill Cemetery, is located a short distance from the site of the Earp homes on the road to Benson. Old Man Clanton was later reinterred on the rocky hillside. Today, all four graves are marked.

On this date the Cochise County coroner, Dr. H.M. Mathews, held an inquest concerning how the men who died during the streetfight were killed. The coroner called nine witnesses, but one refused to testify. The report, First District Court Document 48, of the 10-man jury failed to state whether the Cow-boys' deaths had been justifiable homicide or were murders.

The *Daily Epitaph* notified readers, in the "Local Splinters" column, "Morgan and Virgil Earp were doing as well last evening as could be expected from the nature of their wounds." That evening a "mystery woman" in black made a visit to the Earp home and frightened the wives. Some have claimed this was a failed assassination attempt on the wounded lawmen. Wyatt Earp asked his friends to help him protect his family.

Saturday, October 29, 1881, the weather was still cold in Cochise County.

Ike Clanton, the man who instigated the streetfight and then fled after it started, used the legal right accorded him by Arizona law to seek an arrest complaint against anyone he believed had committed a crime. Clanton charged the Earps and Holliday with killing his brother and friends during the streetfight. An arrest warrant for murder was issued for the four accused men and served by under-sheriff Harry Wood. Justice Spicer granted bond of $10,000 each for Wyatt and Doc. Virgil and Morgan were both confined to bed due to their wounds. The bail funds were quickly posted for Wyatt and Doc to appear at a preliminary hearing.

Following the attempted home attack on his family the day before, Wyatt Earp needed a safer facility for the protection of Virgil and Allie, James and Bessie, and Morgan and Lou. He arranged to move the families into the Cosmopolitan Hotel, where they were guarded by members of the Citizen's Safety Committee. Wyatt took this opportunity to send his sickly and laudanum-addicted Mattie to Cedar Rapids, Iowa, to visit her family and recuperate so he would not have to be concerned about her welfare while he was occupied with the family's medical and legal problems. Mattie Blaylock would not return to Tombstone until February 22, 1882, when she joined Wyatt at the Cosmopolitan.

Wyatt Earp's mining partner Carl Gustav Frederick Bilicke and his son owned the two-story Cosmopolitan Hotel, one of the city's first hotels, with a front verandah decorated with orange trees. It had a Steinway piano in the parlor and boasted one of the finest restaurants in the territory, later called the Maison Doree. Rooms were a dollar a night or $3 with board. There is some indication that the Earp brothers never paid for their extended stay. The Cosmopolitan Hotel burned in the great Tombstone fire of May 1882. After Tombstone, Gus and his son moved to Los Angeles and established the elegant Hollenback Hotel that Wyatt and his last wife, Josie, visited often in their golden years.

Monday, October 31, 1881, had weather that reflected the somber mood of the Tombstone community ... gray overcast and cold.

George Parsons wrote in his journal, "Met Wyatt Earp in [Cosmopolitan] hotel who took me in to see Virgil this evening, he's getting along well. Morgan too. Looks bad for them all thus far (the testimony at the streetfight inquest and filing of murder charges against them)."

At 3:00 p.m. 49-year-old Justice Wells Spicer, according to territorial law, convened an evidentiary hearing into the events of the streetfight. On this day the justice took testimony only from Dr. Matthews. The closed session was held in Spicer's private chambers

Tuesday, November 1, 1881, was a typical fall day in southeastern Arizona.

The streetfight hearing conducted by Justice of the Peace Wells Spicer began its first full-day session. The prosecution team was led by district attorney Lyttleton Price and he was ably assisted by Ike Clanton's private attorney, the renowned Texas-born Ben Goodrich. Thomas Fitch, an equally renowned attorney, served as Wyatt Earp's lawyer and leader of the defense team for the Earp brothers. He was an old friend of Mark Twain and had business connections with other "captains of industry." Doc Holliday was represented by Thomas J. Drum, who had his office on Fremont Street near Fifth Street a block east of the court. Wisely, John Holliday did not testify at the justice court hearing.

Friday, November 4, 1881, was a people-friendly weather day in Tombstone.

Thirty-seven-year-old William Rowland McLaury arrived in Tombstone. The Fort Worth attorney and former officer of an Iowa regiment during the War of the Rebellion asked to assist the prosecution, legally and financially, with its case against the men he felt had unjustly murdered his two brothers on Fremont Street. Justice Spicer agreed to Will McLaury's request. The faltering prosecution team thus acquired a new backbone.

That night, according to George Parsons, the executive committee of the Citizen's Safety Committee held a private meeting. A general members meeting was set for Tuesday evening.

Monday, November 7, 1881, was a nice day for being outdoors, but it was a cold night.

In a special hearing, Will McLaury caused the defendants' appearance bond to be revoked by Justice Spicer. Wyatt Earp and Doc Holliday were rearrested by Sheriff Behan. The defendants applied to Judge J.H. Lucas to grant writs of habeas corpus. The request was dismissed. At 3:00 p.m. Wyatt Earp and Doc Holliday were booked into the Cochise County jail as prisoners number 17 and 18.

Tombstone letter writer Clara Brown commented on the city's weather while Earp and Holliday were confined in the county lockup: "From a mild and lovely autumn we have been suddenly precipitated into a temperature of uncomfortable chilliness. The cold is not the worst part of the Tombstone winters, but the high winds and corresponding dirt." The Cochise County jail was a wooden structure 20 feet by 20 feet composed of two side-by-side walls constructed of 2-inch by 4-inch timbers nailed together, a single door connecting it to the jailer's office. The building was heated by a single wood-burning stove. The extended and intense cold snap provided the cause to increase the price of a cord of wood in Tombstone from $15 to $21, and since the jail was operated on a daily budgeted amount per prisoner there was minimal heat.

Tuesday, November 8, 1881, was another cold late fall day in Tombstone.

Sheriff John Behan made a show of posting extra guards at the county jail to guard Wyatt Earp and Doc Holliday. The *Daily Epitaph* joked with readers that Behan's action really was to protect "that insecure edifice to prevent anyone breaking in." Then the point was placed before the public: "If the Sheriff had been as active in preventing prisoners' [sic] breaking out, there would have been three more gentlemen for the courts to pass upon at the next term." For two weeks during these bitter cold nights, members of the Tombstone Citizen's Safety Committee kept watch over the tiny jail to protect Earp and Holliday from an attack by the Cow-boys or unwarranted assault from the sheriff's special guard force.

Wednesday, November 9, 1881, was another cool day with a biting cold night.

Ike Clanton was the third prosecution witness called before Justice Spicer's hearing. Clanton's testimony was not completed when court adjourned for the day.

Thursday, November 10, 1881, was a "very cold and disagreeable day. It snowed quite heavily part of the day and the mountains looked very pretty...."

At 9:00 a.m. Ike Clanton again took the witness stand in Justice Spicer's court.

Friday, November 11, 1881, was a day of continued overcoat weather.

The prosecution team told Justice Spicer that Ike Clanton was ill and unable to attend the day's session of court. Saturday's edition of the *Daily Nugget* reported that Clanton suffered from a bout of "neuralgia of the head." In the 1880s, doctors prescribed a solution of cocaine and water as a treatment for Ike Clanton's type of ailment.

Saturday, November 12, 1881, was another cold day in Cochise County.

A "hyped up" Ike Clanton resumed his testimony, then faced a lengthy defense cross examination, a short prosecution re-direct and defense re-cross before adjournment. During his sworn testimony, Ike Clanton admitted that he stated publicly, about 10:00 a.m. on October 26, 1881, that he intended to start a fight with the Earp brothers, Tombstone peace officers, as soon as he saw them that morning.

Monday, November 14, 1881, was yet another cold windy day.

The re-cross examination of Ike Clanton continued. Clanton continued to paint the Earps and Holliday as the bad guys and himself as the street-fight hero who, unarmed, had tried to stop Wyatt Earp from killing his brother, his friends and himself.

When court adjourned that afternoon Ike Clanton and Sheriff John Behan walked down to the L.M. Jacobs Mercantile to apply for a $500 loan from Mr. Jacobs. Behan had taken out a personal loan for $500 from Jacobs on November 1, and then the next day Behan and his jailer Billy Soule, who also testified for the prosecution in the street-fight hearing, borrowed an additional $200 from Jacobs. It is possible that these loans were used to finance the attorneys who were assisting the district attorney with his murder case against the Earps and Holliday. Ike Clanton repaid his loan on November 25, 1881.

Tuesday, November 15, 1881, was a cold day outside, but there was hot air in the courtroom.

Ike Clanton continued his wild tales under intensive and extensive examination by Tom Fitch and the defense team. During this examination Ike Clanton single-handedly dismantled a strong circumstantial case against the defendants. The prosecution quickly rested their case. Sensing disarray in the prosecution's case, the defense asked for a delay in presenting their case until Wednesday's session. The request was approved.

Wednesday, November 16, 1881, continued the norm in Tombstone, as the weather remained chilly during the day and cold that night.

Wyatt Earp was the first witness for the defense. Tom Fitch used a new provision in territorial law, enacted in February (Section 133 of the Laws of 1881, revised from 1877), that allowed the accused in a preliminary hearing to make a statement and not have to face cross-examination from the prosecution, as would happen during a trial. The prosecution objected to this new means of testimony, but Spicer ruled the procedure was legal under Arizona law. Justice Spicer allowed Wyatt Earp to read his presentation and the accompanying notarized written character testimonials from the city officials and prominent citizens of Wichita and Dodge City, Kansas, supporting his good citizenship and job performance as a peace officer in his former communities. Tom Fitch may have helped Wyatt, as the chief defense witness, compose the lengthy, methodical, and detailed narrative he read to the court.

During his lengthy presentation, Earp three times stated his conviction that under the precepts of "Common Law" he had a legal right to shoot the Cow-boys who had openly threatened to kill him and his brothers on sight: "I believe I would have been legally and morally justified in shooting any of them (Clantons and McLaurys) on sight." Wyatt maintained that as a lawman he had no duty to retreat. Wyatt Earp's presentation was the only testimony heard. The *Daily Nugget* published the two testimonials on Friday, November 18, 1881.

Thursday, November 17, 1881, could be called a "more moderate" day for late fall.

Will McLaury wrote his sister Margaret Appelgate saying he felt that Wyatt Earp and Doc Holliday's only hope of avoiding a death sentence "is in escape and should they escape from jail, their bones will bleach in the mountains…. I find a large number of my Texas friends here who are ready and willing to stand by me and with Winchesters if necessary. The only thing now is to keep my friends quiet—their [sic] came near being a general killing here last night which had it not been prevented would have closed my business here. I am trying to punish these men through the courts of the country first. If that fails—then we may submit." Most readers would view these statements as a developing disposition toward murder.

Shortly after McLaury's letter was received in Iowa, Margaret Appelgate's son Charles, a recent Iowa law school graduate, arrived in Tombstone to assist his Uncle Will in probating Tom and Frank's estate. Young Charles might have been sent to be the family's eyes and ears in Tombstone concerning Will McLaury's mental and physical health. The young attorney found time to enjoy the Tombstone night life and earned the nickname "Good Time Charlie."

Thursday, November 24, 1881, was still ruled by approaching winter weather.

This national Thanksgiving Day was special for Wyatt Earp and Doc Holliday, as they were released from the Cochise County jail on a habeas corpus writ and a new set of appearance bonds was provided. Tom Fitch had used the power of Wyatt Earp's presentation, strongly counteracting the prosecution's murder charges, to seek bond for Earp and Holliday.

Monday, November 28, 1881, was another winter day on the high desert.

The *Los Angles Herald* reported on December 1 an incident that happened on this date in San Bernardino. According to the newspaper, Nicholas Earp, inebriated patriarch of the clan, engaged in a verbal altercation with an employee of the Exchange Bank concerning his sons. Bryon Waters finally "knocked" the old man down and the village marshal took Earp home.

John Gosper, acting governor of Arizona Territory, wrote to United States marshal Crawley P. Dake: "Now, as to the remedy to be applied, I would suggest that the Department of Justice in which you are serving be requested to furnish you with funds sufficient to enable you to employ a man of well known courage and charter of cool sound judgment, which your good judgment can secure, who, with a suitable posse of men, can first fully comprehend the true nature of the situation and then with proper direction and courage, go forward with firm and steady hand, bringing as rapidly as possible the leading spirits of this lawless class to a severe and speedy punishment."

> **Author's Perspective:** As later events would prove, Marshal Dake already had the right man on the job, and he was currently defending his, and that of his brothers, tough and strict law enforcement actions at a preliminary hearing in preparation for a possible murder trial.

Tuesday, November 29, 1881, saw yet another winter day with cool temperatures.

Justice Wells Spicer issued his opinion of the hearing testimony and ordered the release of the Earp brothers and Doc Holliday, saying the evidence provided by the prosecution team did not support an order to hold the defendants on a charge of murder. As fate would have it, Ike Clanton, the key witness for the prosecution, proved by his erratic statements to be a strong defense witness. Clanton had even been supported in his "wild tales" by Sheriff Johnny Behan and Cow-boy friends Wes Fuller, Billy Claiborne, and Billy Allen. However, Virgil Earp and non–Earp partisan Tombstone seamstress Addie Borland and visiting Santa Fe railroad man H.F. Sills had added additional support to Wyatt Earp's well-defined defense narrative.

> **Author's Perspective:** Following Justice Spicer's ruling, Will McLaury was no longer interested in justice; he wanted revenge and as future events would prove he was willing to pay for it. Will's brother Tom was wearing a money belt containing nearly $3,000 when he died. There were rumors that someone had removed another belt containing $1,600 from his body while Tom lay dying. Tom also had deposit slips for nearly $5,000 from the Cochise County Bank. He had placed the money, payment for a cattle delivery to a local butcher, in the bank on Thursday, October 20, 1881.
>
> Following the month-long Spicer Hearing, Will McLaury wrote his family that he would still avenge his brothers' deaths, even if he had to kill the Earps himself. Will McLaury's son Findley wrote in 1963 that his father paid Ike Clanton $1,000 to have Cow-boy assassins murder the Earp brothers and others after he lost the legal battle to bring the lawmen to trial. Did Will McLaury really pay men to commit murder? Three major attacks were launched; one target was killed, one crippled, and one badly intimidated. The collateral damage was massive.
>
> Nearly $8,000 from his brothers' estate could have been the money that Will McLaury used to conduct his vengeance pursuit of the Tombstone city marshals. How had the brothers earned such a large sum of money? Was this money the profit from fencing stolen cattle to local butchers or winnings from a game of chance? Were they liquidating their assets so that they could leave the Tombstone area and return to Iowa as some Tombstone historians have claimed?

Thursday, December 1, 1881, was just one more winter day.

As a visible sign that he intended to stay in Tombstone as a businessman and remain active in the growing community, Wyatt Earp signed the *Great Register for*

Cochise County to verify his official residence in the mining camp. He was now eligible to vote in the next election. Wyatt Earp listed his main occupation as saloon keeper.

Often overlooked in the grand scope of events, is the fact that John H. Holliday, DDS, was arrested on this date for discharging a firearm on a Tombstone street. The establishment couldn't railroad him for murder, so in an act of humiliation Holliday, a noncommissioned police officer, was forced to pay a $25 fine and court costs, and was released with a warning about using firearms.

Friday, December 2, 1881, was just like the day before as far as the weather went.

A newspaper dispatch was sent from Tombstone saying, "The Cowboy faction accepts the [Spicer Hearing] verdict with bad grace and a smoldering fire exists which is liable to break forth at any moment. It is well known that several prominent residents of Tombstone have been marked for death by the rustlers." This Cow-boy "hit list" comprised Virgil, Wyatt, and Morgan Earp, John H. Holliday, Mayor John P. Clum, justice of the peace Wells Spicer, Wells Fargo's Tombstone agent Marshall Williams, Wyatt Earp's attorney Tom Fitch, and Dave Rickabaugh, leader of the Eastern gamblers.

On **Tuesday, December 6, 1881,** President Chester A. Arthur delivered his first State of the Union message to a joint session of Congress. James Abram Garfield of Ohio had been inaugurated on March 4, 1881, shot by an assassin on July 2, and died from the bullet wound and bronchopneumonia shortly before midnight on September 19. Vice President Chester Alan Arthur of New York took the presidential oath of office at his home in New York City at 2:15 a.m. on September 20, 1881.

Part of the new President's communication concerned the Cow-boy problem in Arizona Territory: "A band of armed desperados known as 'cow-boys' probably numbering from fifty to one hundred men, have been engaged for months in committing acts of lawlessness and brutality which the local authorities have been unable to repress." The president told the lawmakers that this trouble was affecting relationships with the Republic of Mexico. "I am embarrassed by lack of authority to deal with the [the Cow-boys] effectively," President Arthur continued. "The punishment of crimes committed within Arizona should ordinarily, of course, be left to the Territorial authorities." The *New York Times*, under the title "The Lawless Cowboys of Arizona" on February 9, 1882, printed President Arthur's follow-up special message to Congress concerning the use of military force in the Cow-boy disturbance. The president noted that the Cochise County sheriff's office (John Behan) was not taking sufficient action and that trouble along "the Mexican line" was reaching a flash point. The presidential message explained that Sheriff Behan "from personal motives ... desires to curry favor with the disorderly element of society.... It is, therefore, suggested whether it would not be expedient and proper that authority should be conferred by law upon the [Territorial] Governor ... to remove or suspend a Sheriff for neglect of duty and appoint a person in his place [who will uphold the law]."[6]

The Posse Comitatus Act of 18 June 1878 prohibited using the army or navy to assist civil peace officers in maintaining law and order. This federal legislation—a major part of the compromise that settled the disputed presidential election of 1876—originally designed to forbid the use of federal troops for routine police duties in communities of the former rebellious Southern states now applied to all areas of the nation. The president still had authority to use the military to suppress rebellions, riots, or civil disorder under the Insurrection Act of 1807. The *Reno (NV) Evening News* on April 14 and May 2, 1882, reported that President Arthur had discussed the Cow-boy troubles with his attorney general and during a couple of sessions of his entire cabinet. He had even weighed the idea of requesting Congress to amend the posse comitatus law so he could use the army in this special situation. In the end, the chief executive settled for a strongly worded presidential proclamation against lawlessness in Arizona Territory and issued the threat of declaring martial law. Under provisions of the Insurrection Act of 1807, a declaration of martial law would allow the president to dispatch federal troops to suppress the "Cowboy rebellion." This action was not required, because a deputy United States marshal named Wyatt Earp was about to settle the dustup.

Friday, December 9, 1881, George Parsons enjoyed the current Indian Summer as he was still recovering from the injuries he received fighting the Tombstone fire of June 22, 1881.

In his journal today, George Parsons wrote, "Another bad time tonight. The terrible word fire rang out on the night air late in the evening and rushing out on the balcony was saw the flames rushing towards back of Grand (Hotel). Fire was controlled before hotel caught and city saved." The new Rescue Hook and Ladder Company fought the fire that started in a 12-room boardinghouse on Toughnut Street.

Wednesday, December 14, 1881, George Parsons wrote in his journal that the weather was becoming colder and snow was in the air. He also mentioned that a friend had helped repel an attack on the Benson stage a few miles from Tombstone: "Duke emptied his revolver at them and they got away." In an interview with a *Washington Post* reporter, published October 30, 1882, John Clum recalled the day as "bitter cold," with snow in the evening.

As fate would have it, John P. Clum, muffled in a heavy overcoat, and four other men boarded the six-horse hitch stagecoach headed for Benson to connect with the Southern Pacific and Santa Fe railroad systems. The retiring Tombstone mayor was on a year-end holiday journey to Washington, D.C., for a Christmas and New Year's visit with his motherless young son and other family members who lived on the East Coast. Following behind the stage, "Whistling Dick" Harrington drove an empty ore wagon he was returning to Benson. Just beyond Malcolm's Water Station, four miles from Tombstone, the night sounds were disrupted by a cry of "Hold!" followed by a volley of gunshots.

A half-century after that eventful trip John Clum returned to the dying mining camp for a nostalgic visit. He told a reporter from his old newspaper, "There were nine of us [vigilante leaders and the Earp brothers] who were not supposed to get out of Tombstone alive. We received warnings written in blood." Clum dramatically continued, "We didn't pay a lot of attention to them [the Cow-boys] at first, but after a few months it became most unbearable."

The *Butte Miner*, in far-off Montana Territory, told its readers on Christmas Day about the attempt to kill John Clum: "At Tombstone, Arizona, great excitement prevails over the attempt to assassinate Mayor Clum. It is said Sheriff Behan claims he is powerless, as the Cowboys seem too strong a band." The newspaper added, "Saloon keepers and liquor merchants say that most of their trade comes from the [Cowboy] gang." About two dozen of the top Cow-boy shooters had attacked the stage. Clum left the conveyance, after the driver stopped to cut the harness of a wounded horse, and was quickly on the escape path. It was not discovered that the mayor was missing until the stage and the ore wagon reached Contention City. Word was sent to Sheriff Johnny Behan and at daylight a posse was sent in search of the mayor.

Walking cross-country, Clum finally reached the Grand Central Quartz Mill, rested for a short time and then borrowed a horse to ride on to Benson. Word was sent to Tombstone of his safety. John Clum continued on his eastward journey.[7]

Thursday, December 15, 1881, Committee of Safety member George Parsons noted in his journal that it was "cold now days."

Deputy United States marshal Virgil Earp, normally a happy jovial individual, and Milt Joyce, a hothead, had a confrontation in the Oriental Saloon. According to the *Daily Nugget* the two men had been discussing yesterday's holdup attempt when "Joyce laughingly remarked he had been expecting something of the sort ever since they (the Earps) had been liberated from jail." The insult earned Joyce a quick slap in the face. Joyce left the saloon with one more insult— about Virgil Earp not being able to shoot him in the back.

Friday, December 16, 1881, was a cold day with storm clouds gathering in the evening.

Milt Joyce continued his disagreement with Virgil Earp. Back in his saloon, Joyce pointed two pistols at the officer while hurling expletives at him. For once, Sheriff Behan acted quickly and grabbed Joyce from behind, disarmed him, and possibly saved someone's life. Charged with disturbing the peace, the county supervisor was fined $15 and released. Sheriff Behan's process sever "Uncle Billy" Breakenridge would later claim this incident caused enmity between former friends Johnny Behan and Milt Joyce.

The Tombstone weather did not keep the Cochise County Grand Jury from concluding their review of the findings of Justice Wells Spicer's hearings concerning the October streetfight. The grand jury refused to consider further investigation based upon the evidence given at the recently concluded hearing that found no grounds for criminal charges.[8]

Arizona territorial law allowed a district attorney to convene a grand jury to investigate any crime committed within its jurisdiction. In early December 1881, following release of Justice Wells Spicer's judgment, district attorney Lyttleton Price asked the Cochise County Grand Jury, already having done their duty, if it wished to review the Spicer Hearing evidence, hear additional evidence, or reconsider the justice's no-cause verdict. This review was one of many potential cases the panel had a chance to examine during their winter session. William H. Stilwell—the newly appointed judge of Arizona's First Judicial District was a native New Yorker in his early 30s who was intimidated by no one—gave the grand jury a strong directive to do their civic duty. This same session of the grand jury did, however, return four murder indictments; one of these was against Billy Claiborne, a second-tier Cow-boy who had left the street-fight scene as the shooting started. The grand jury issued fifteen indictments for grand larceny, one of which was against Cow-boy leader Curly Bill Brocius; and eight indictments for robbery, one of which was against Cow-boy leader John Ringo. Eight other indictments were for assault with a deadly weapon, one for perjury and one for forgery. The grand jury expressed its frustration over being unable to sustain indictments in "numerous charges of cattle stealing" because of wholesale intimidation of witnesses. "Such a state of feeling is deplorable in any community," the grand jury members reported, "when truth is awed into silence by terror of outlawry."

Most of the Cochise County legal system agreed that the process of justice as pre-scribed by territorial law was complete when a sitting grand jury refused to indict any-one involved in the streetfight. The grand jury accepted the conclusions of the evidentiary hearing by saying the city police had legally preformed their duty. Cochise County district attorney Lyttleton Price and district judge William Stilwell each decided not to further pursue a case against the former Tombstone peace officers.

Saturday, December 17, 1881, was "cold and rainy this morning."

The *Daily Epitaph* carried a pointed editorial: "The time has come when the Bible injunction, 'Choose ye this day whom ye will serve,' applies with particular force. There can be no halfway business in this matter. He who is not for law and order is against it, and such sentiments as appeared in the Nugget yesterday morning cannot be con-strued otherwise than an endorsement of the lawlessness that begot the attempted assassination of the mayor of Tombstone last Wednesday night. The people are not fools. They will mark these things down on the tablets of the memories where they cannot be erased by sophistical tongues of aspiring politicians. The next vote polled in what is Cochise county will be on the principles of safety to life and protection to prop-erty."

A few days earlier, Justice Wells Spicer had received a letter signed "A Miner" that made a death threat against the jurist. The *Daily Epitaph* printed the letter on this date and on Monday the newspaper published the flaming reply from Justice Spicer: "There is a rabble in our City who would be proud to be called cow-boys, if people would give them that distinction.... [T]hey are low-bred arrant cowards...." There was a foreboding of violence in the air.

Monday, December 19, 1881, was a nice day but cool.

The *Daily Epitaph* told readers that the most recent news from Contention City was that carpenters had started to build the new train depot and the Arizona and New Mexico Railroad was expected to provide service to the village within a few days. This station was to be Tombstone's railroad connection for the next two decades.

The Sandy Bob Stage Line announced new times for the run from Tombstone to the new railroad connection. The stage to catch eastbound trains would leave town at 5:00 a.m. and westbound connections would leave at noon each day.

Tuesday, December 20, 1881, was another cool day, but no rain was expected.

The ladies of the new Episcopal church congregation held a Christmas season fair that evening at Schieffelin Hall. The occasion was so successful that people were still claiming their prizes on Wednesday evening. George Parsons was among the men who helped with the set-up and the subsequent cleanup on Thursday. In his journal he noted, "Quite a financial and social success." A few days later he remarked that the profit, above expenses, was over $600 for the church fund.

Friday, December 23, 1881, was a cool day with storm clouds gathering in the west.

The Bird Cage Amusement Center opened a couple of lots west on the south side of Allen Street, near the southwest intersection with Sixth Street. Theatrical performers and managers William and Lottie Hutchinson owned what became one of the town's signature facilities. Contrary to popular legend, it is unclear if any Earp brother had the time to visit the Bird Cage during their remaining twelve weeks in Tombstone.

Saturday, December 24, 1881, was a still, windless, cool day with rain in the late afternoon and evening.

The Children's Christmas Tree and School Program took place at 2:00 p.m. in Schieffelin Hall. The teacher had decorated the hall Friday evening and the students' parents and community were welcome to attended the program of music and recitals along with distributing presents for the children. Wyatt Earp attended the afternoon party to watch his neighbor friend Nora Neff recite a Christmas poem.

On this Christmas Eve a select group of citizens gathered in the Mining Exchange Building to form the People's Independent Party and select a slate of candidates for the municipal elections in January 1882. The party pledged to clean up the town lot problem and bring fiscal responsibility to city government. John Carr, a blacksmith, ran for mayor and deputy sheriff Dave Neagle ran for marshal/chief of police.

Sunday, December 25, 1881, was a nice winter day this Sunday as the residents in Tombstone held a community Christmas Day worship service in the morning in the same courtroom where Wells Spicer had held the street-fight hearing in November.

The post office in Tombstone was open for business as usual in the afternoon and all the saloons in the city held wild evening celebrations that lasted until dawn. Allie Earp would recall in old age that the Earp families, still living in the Cosmopolitan Hotel, had a nice Christmas dinner that day. Days later the Earps were still eating nuts and peppermint candy from the celebration.

Wednesday, December 28, 1881, was a clear cloudless day in Tombstone.

At about 11:30 p.m. that evening, Doctor George E. Goodfellow and his friend George Parsons headed home after having shared a late supper. The men passed deputy U.S. marshal Virgil Earp near the corner of Fifth and Allen streets just moments before buckshot from shotguns almost killed him. The next day's issue of the *Reno (NV) Evening Gazette* reported the incident: "Nineteen buckshot struck Earp, inflicting dangerous and perhaps mortal wounds. The assault is undoubtedly the outgrowth of the recent fight with the Cow-boys in which Earp was engaged. The gang since threatened the lives of Earp and his supporters. The citizens are greatly excited."

Later, witnesses testified that Frank Stilwell (Virgil saw him enter the ambush site), Hank Swilling, Ike Clanton (his hat was found at the ambush site), Johnny Barnes and Johnny Ringo were the would-be assassins and lookouts, while Pete Spencer had held the Cow-boys' horses. George Parsons, and others, felt that Will McLaury (who, as of Monday, was en route to Fort Worth and his children via a visit to his family in Iowa) had paid the "blood money" for the ambush attack upon Virgil Earp.[9]

Two of acting chief of police Jim Flynn's policemen, Alex Young and W.W. Fly, had been standing near the entrance to the Oriental Saloon, directly across Allen Street from the construction site where Virgil's attackers fired their shotguns from, yet both later claimed they saw nothing of the assault and failed to give chase as the shooters ran away. Neither policeman offered assistance to the wounded federal officer as he stumbled down the street. Policeman Young had once worked for Virgil Earp but was dismissed during a force downsizing. Policeman Fly was the younger brother of the famous photographer and future Cochise County sheriff whose portrait studio and boardinghouse's walls formed the eastern boundary of the storage lot where the October streetfight with the Cow-boys began.

Tuesday, December 29, 1881, was a magnificent cool day in Tombstone.

Deputy U.S. marshal Virgil Earp had been carried across Allen Street to his room in the Cosmopolitan Hotel for medical care. Dr. Goodfellow quickly arrived on the scene and felt Virgil might die from the shotgun wounds he had received a few hours earlier. In an attempt to save Earp's life in the predawn hours of this day, the doctor removed the elbow joint and some bone splitters from Virgil's shattered left arm. George Parsons recorded in his journal that Virgil joked to his wife Allie, "Never mind, I've got one arm left to hug you with."

(Parsons recorded in his daily journal that Dr. Goodfellow kept Virgil's elbow joint and some of the shattered bone in his office. What happened to these Earp artifacts over time?)

On **Friday, December 30, 1881**, George Parsons noted in his *Private Journal* it was "beautiful weather again."

In the afternoon, the bedridden Virgil Earp, who, since being cleared of a murder charge nearly a month ago had resumed his former duties as the senior federal marshal in the Tombstone district, administered a new federal oath to his brother to replace the field commission Wyatt had received months earlier from chief deputy United States marshal Joseph Evans. United States marshal Crawley Dake, via a telegram, reaffirmed that authority and again granted Wyatt full power to appoint deputies and posse members. The *Phoenix Arizona Gazette* said Marshal Dake instructed Wyatt Earp "to spare no pains or expense in discovering the perpetrators of the deed" of wounding deputy United States marshal Virgil Earp. The *Daily Nugget*, at the time of the streetfight, had mentioned that Wyatt was a federal officer and a special Tombstone city officer. He had in fact been the acting city marshal in Virgil's absence (he was in Tucson) just a few days before the streetfight.

In late December 1882, Wyatt Earp started to prepare for an extended fight against the Cow-boys. He sold a mining claim to P.T. Colby et al., and conveyed a second quit-claim deed to the Intervener Mining Company to cover his recent legal fees. Meanwhile, he was also busy equipping and organizing his federal posse into a rapid response strike force. In early January 1882, the *Daily Nugget* reported that Wyatt Earp sold his gambling concession interest in the Oriental Saloon.

> **Author's Perspective:** I believe that Wyatt Earp had two reasons for selling his management interest in the Oriental Saloon gambling operation. First, he needed to devote his full time and energy to the campaign he was planning against the Cowboys and, second, just in case he was killed—or wounded like Virgil—Mattie would have money to take care of herself and him, if needed.

1882

New Year's Day was on a Sunday in 1882 and George Parsons noted in his journal, "Year ushered in by fine weather."

Tombstone's volunteer firefighters held a uniformed parade in downtown to welcome in the new year. A pensive George Parsons closed his daily journal entry with, "What? This year." No one could have foreseen the bloody mayhem of the next six months and the many changes for the Earp family, Tombstone, and the Cow-boy confederation.

Monday, January 2, 1882, was a nice winter day.

The Grand Uniformed Ball of the Tombstone Rescue Hook and Ladder Company was held that night at Schieffelin Hall. Tickets where two dollars per couple. Virgil Earp was to have been one of the reception committee to greet guests for the evening's festivities; instead he lay badly wounded in his bed at the Cosmopolitan Hotel.

Tuesday, January 3, 1882, was a mild day in Tombstone, Arizona Territory.

Tombstone residents went to the polls and selected a new mayor, four members of the common council, and a chief of police. David Neagle, Sheriff John Behan's deputy, was elected police chief and John Carr, a blacksmith, was elected mayor to replace John Clum. George Parsons told his journal that his choices had been "beaten by the ring and other crowd." The People's Independent ticket logged 830 votes while the Citizen's ticket tallied 298 votes.

Justice Wells Spicer filed with the clerk of the Cochise County Superior Court Fred Craig's massive handwritten transcript of the witness testimony taken during the preliminary hearing concerning the October 1881 streetfight. The transcript, *Territory–Vs–Morgan Earp, et al.*, became court Document 94. While in session, the county grand jury had access to this transcript as well as the testimony taken at the coroner's inquest.[10]

The evening's stagecoach brought George Hearst to Tombstone. He was a renowned California mining investor known across the West and he was looking at the Tombstone region for possible investment opportunities. Hearst was cognizant of the Cow-boy menace in the area so he consulted his friend and sometime mining investment partner Lloyd Tevis concerning the problem. Tevis, president of Wells Fargo Express Company, recommended Hearst employ Wyatt Earp as a bodyguard and guide while he investigated investment opportunities in the Tombstone Mining District. For a few days Wyatt Earp took a break from his official duties to undertake a private job to acquire some quick money and develop political friendships.

Wednesday, January 4, 1882, brought a nice day with signs of cold weather coming.

George Parsons confided to his journal: "Met George Hearst this morning and had quite a talk. He seems to like the camp." Following a number of "look-sees" and broker discussions, the financial magnate choose not to become a player in the area's development. He seemed to sense that the boom was headed downhill due to the additional expense owners would need to overcome the developing water seepage problem in the mines.[11] (Lloyd Tevis and his multimillionaire law partner James Ben Ali Haggin did invest in Tombstone's San Pedro Mining Company.)

A few days later, Senator Hearst returned to California. He paid Wyatt Earp a respectable fee for his bodyguard and guide services and also presented him with a fancy gold watch and matching chain. A few years later, a pickpocket "borrowed" the watch while Wyatt and his wife were visiting Old Mexico. Over a decade later, Wyatt Earp again performed some protective duties for the Hearst family, this time when he was working in California.

Friday, January 6, 1882, was a another cold day and night in Tombstone and Cochise County.

Now that the Earp faction was out of office in Tombstone and the Cow-boys had nothing to fear from Cochise County lawmen they were back in action. About 3:00 a.m. the W.W. Hubbard & Company stagecoach running between Tombstone and Bisbee was attacked and robbed. W.S. Waite was the driver and Charley Bartholomew was the Wells Fargo express guard; they lost $6,500 in the strongbox and a coach horse was killed. Curly Bill was later seen carrying Bartholomew's shotgun and Johnny Ringo was suspected of being one of the three bandits.

Saturday/Sunday, January 7/8, 1882, was a very cold moonlit night in Cochise County.

Around 1:00 a.m. two highwaymen halted the Sandy Bob stagecoach running between Contention and Tombstone. The black-masked bandits accosted all the passengers before sending them on their way. New York–born James Bunyan Hume was one these unfortunate night travelers and he lost a pair of custom .45 Colts and $75 to the outlaws. Hume, as the chief of the Wells Fargo Express Company's detective and protective services, had an awesome reputation as a fugitive tracker and apprehender of men who preyed upon society. The pistols were missed by their owner, but loss to Hume's pride and professional reputation was more disastrous. The *San Francisco Exchange* lampooned the detective: "A man of Hume's reputation and supposed 'sand,' armed to the teeth as he was, should have been able to take care of the two highwaymen." The express company offered a $300 reward for the bandits' arrest. Hume believed he knew the offenders, but he was not able to develop the needed evidence to make the arrest. Curly Bill was later seen wearing Jim Hume's fancy revolvers.

Tuesday, January 17, 1882, was a cold day, with a sprinkling of light snow during the afternoon. This was not the most enjoyable kind of weather for working outdoors or traveling cross-country.

George Parsons told his journal, "Much blood in the air this afternoon. Ringo and Doc Holliday came nearly having it with pistols." This incident occurred on Allen Street in front of the Occidental Saloon. Retiring police chief James Flynn arrested the two men before real trouble broke out. Wyatt Earp was in the crowd standing by watching the verbal sparring between Holliday and Ringo and was arrested by the city police for carrying a weapon on a public street. Doc Holliday and Johnny Ringo were each fined $30 by the police court justice, A.O. Wallace, but Wallace released Wyatt Earp, admonishing the city police about making false arrests and reminding them that a federal marshal had legal authority to be armed at all times.

On Wednesday, the *Daily Epitaph* noted, "Chief of Police yesterday, in the gentle zephyrs that occurred on Allen Street, by his prompt action, gave unmistaken proof that he thoroughly understands his business and is fearless in its execution."

Wednesday, January 18, 1882, was another cold day in southern Arizona.

Because of Johnny Ringo's court appearance on a weapons charge, Justice Wallace decided to reassess the charge that Ringo had robbed a poker game at Galeyville in August 1881. Wallace also reviewed Ringo's $3,000 bail bond on that charge. Ringo was out of jail pending the calling of his robbery case before the court. Wallace revoked the appearance bond and issued a bench warrant for Johnny Ringo's arrest on the robbery charge.

Friday, January 20, 1882, was a pleasant day in Tombstone.

Johnny Ringo was arrested upon a new bench warrant and jailed to await a court appearance on Monday morning.

Crawley P. Dake, the United States marshal for Arizona Territory, arrived in the city to check on Virgil Earp's health and to give Wyatt orders to use any methods needed to "stop the Cow-boy raids." Dake arranged with Wells Fargo's home office in San Francisco to borrow $3,000 as advance money to finance a federal field posse to conduct operations against the Cow-boy confederation. The loan was to be repaid when Marshal Dake's expense accounting was approved and paid by the Justice Department auditor in Washington, D.C.

Marshal Dake deposited all but fifteen dollars of the $3,000 loan money at the Hudson & Company Bank, next door to the Oriental Saloon on Fifth Street in Tombstone. Arizona's chief federal marshal claimed the fifteen dollars to cover his "expenses" in arranging the money for the Earp posse and spent an additional $340 of the loan on a saloon party—political glad-handing—to celebrate his field deputy's planned assault upon the Cow-boys. It is very unlikely that Wyatt Earp, a known teetotaler, accompanied Dake on his saloon rounds.

Before Marshal Dake returned to his Prescott office he "borrowed" an additional $100 from Wyatt Earp for his expenses during the trip. Dake had helped himself to $355 of the special campaign account and $100 in a "kick-back" request from his embattled deputy.

Saturday, January 21, 1881, was, according to George Parsons, "pleasant as can be."

The *Daily Epitaph* noted that the county coroner's inquest held on the 13th had adjourned for eight days so Sheriff Behan could serve 17 subpoenas for witnesses who were already present at the hearing. The accused murderers escaped during the hearing recess. Meanwhile, two more men were killed in the same railroad construction camp, according to Tucson newspapers. The *Tombstone Daily Epitaph*'s story contained an editorial comment suggesting these botched murder investigations were "criminal negligence of a ten-per-cent sheriff" more interested in collecting service fees then in seeking justice.

Wells Fargo Detective John Thacker,[12] who was in Tombstone, informed Wyatt Earp of his company's loan to fund the campaign to destroy the Cow-boys and took him to the Hudson & Company Bank to verify Marshal Earp's authority to draw against these funds. Wyatt Earp carefully selected his posse and equipped them for duty. Fiscal records indicate that deputy United States marshal Earp spent only $536.65 of the money in the special account. These funds provided for the strike force's field equipment and horses.

Monday, January 23, 1882, was a cloudless day in which a topcoat was needed outdoors and while riding.

Marshal Wyatt Earp left Tombstone with his eight-man posse, a federal marshal's strike force, headed toward the outlaw hangout of Charleston seeking Cow-boys he wanted to arrest on previously unprocessed warrants.

Sheriff Behan released Johnny Ringo from the county jail only to find out the justice court had not yet accepted his new bond. James Earp had seen Ringo ride out of Tombstone headed up the Charleston road, so he filed a citizen's complaint with the district court alleging that Johnny Ringo was a fugitive from justice, having escaped jail. A bench warrant was issued for Ringo's arrest. District court judge William H. Stilwell authorized two citizen posses, without proper police authority, to take custody of the Cow-boy leader and return him to the county jail because the judge knew the sheriff's office would do nothing to recapture John Ringo.

Tuesday, January 24, 1882, was another clear cool day and cold windy night in the Tombstone region.

Tombstone's new mayor issued a proclamation explaining that Marshal Wyatt Earp's posse, which had left town Monday, was authorized by First Distinct Court judge W.H. Stilwell to serve federal warrants on various persons charged with crimes. Mayor John Carr, the Irish blacksmith, requested that the public assist the federal posse with its mission in any manner requested by the officers.

Wednesday, January 25, 1882, was very much a typical winter "dark-dismal day" in the Tombstone area, according to George Parsons.

Tombstone community leader Parsons wrote in his diary, "The Earps are out too [in addition to two citizen posses headed to Charleston to return Johnny Ringo for jumping his bail] on U.S. business and lively times are anticipated. Our salvation I think is near at hand. It looks like business now when the U.S. Marshal Dake takes a hand under special orders." Marshal Wyatt Earp was determined to end the Cow-boys' criminal reign and now took the lead role for federal law enforcement in southeastern Arizona.

Wyatt Earp and his men conducted a door-to-door canvass of Charleston searching for Cow-boys and their supporters. The Cow-boy supporter local media quickly dubbed this procedure a "siege" by thugs with federal badges.

Friday, January 27, 1882, was a "gloomy" day, according to George Parsons' daily journal.

The *Daily Nugget* published a satire, "A Pestiferous Posse," about Wyatt Earp's campaign. The Cow-boy newspaper felt that Earp was an annoying pest or nuisance chasing after these fun-loving businessmen and accused the federal marshal of being a thug persecuting honest Democrat ranchers so he could enhance his law enforcement credentials to seek the sheriff's job as a law and order Republican candidate in the fall election.

Meanwhile, the *Daily Epitaph* reminded readers that Sheriff Johnny Behan held "bench warrants, unexecuted, in his hands against men charged with crime, who frequently parade our streets in the most unconcerned manner." The newspaper said a recent coroner's inquest could not reach a conclusion in a murder case at San Simon because Sheriff Behan had "been derelict in his duties" by not serving subpoenas in the Cow-boy controlled village. The war for public opinion, fought with paper and ink, was in full combat mode.

Johnny Ringo quietly had a preliminary hearing on his grand jury indictment for robbery and the court ordered him held to appear at the noon session of court on Tuesday.

Saturday's *Daily Nugget* noted that former city policeman T.J. Cornelison was released from jail that day by order of the district attorney because, as the *Daily Nugget* said, there was "no evidence to warrant a continuance of the case." Now out of jail, Cornelison took every occasion to accuse Virgil Earp of extortion while he worked for him.

Few people in Tombstone, at the time, put any credit in the former policeman's tale, but present-day haters still dredge up the mudslinging of the nineteenth century and quote it as fact.

On **Saturday, January 28, 1882**, the ground was covered with snow, and the cold made outdoor activates unpleasant. George Parsons called it a "disagreeable day."

Crawley Dake was in Tombstone, having come to town from Phoenix. As he made the rounds of the mining camp's saloons buying drinks for the local barflies, the United States marshal for Arizona Territory confidently proclaimed that his federal forces would soon stop the Cow-boy problem. George Parsons noted in his journal, "Met Dake U.S. Marshal tonight."

Arizona Territory's acting governor, John J. Gosper, also visited Tombstone for a firsthand assessment of the reported law enforcement–Cow-boy problem. It is unclear if Doc Holliday met or spent time with his one-time Phoenix roommate during Gosper's visit, but the acting governor returned to the capital convinced that the lawless situation called for strong action. Gosper condemned the lack of cooperation between Sheriff Johnny Behan and the seriously wounded Virgil Earp. Arizona's acting governor, believing the truthfulness of the *Daily Nugget*'s anti–Earp propaganda campaign, issued a harshly worded statement concerning Wyatt Earp's recent use of forceful tactics against the "innocent citizens" of Charleston. Regrettably, Gosper never spoke with Wyatt Earp during his stay in Tombstone.

> **Author's Perspective:** Strange how the passage of time can change one's perspective of events to suit a new personal agenda or to belatedly provide justification for a past misjudgment. Consider the March 25, 1911, letter John J. Gosper wrote to Miss Sharlot Hall, territorial historian for Arizona, explaining his unpublicized, now-it-can-be-told law and order mission behind his January 1882 trip to Tombstone. Gosper confided, "I secretly placed a vigilant committee into existence at Tombstone" because the Cochise County Cow-boys wanted "to prevent his [Wyatt Earp] becoming a candidate for sheriff in connection with Johnny Behan who was known to be friendly toward the Cow-boys."
>
> In one of his letters, John Gosper also mentioned that he had kept a "journal" while he was in public office, but historians have not been able to locate it. If found this journal might provide valuable insight into the acting governor's thinking at the time. Sadly, this courageous and once wealthy mining operator and Arizona territorial leader would die, in 1913, penniless and unattended in the Los Angeles County Hospital.

Monday, January 30, 1882, was a day filled with snow, ice, and cold winds.

Wyatt Earp and his men searched the area around Charleston on Friday, Saturday and Sunday. To get out of the miserable weather, the posse stayed at the small Pick 'Em Up Hotel, a few miles from Tombstone on the Charleston road, on Sunday night.

Early in the day, Cochise County deputy sheriff Dave Neagle arrived at the hotel to serve an arrest warrant on Sherman McMaster for the old horse-stealing charge. Sheriff Johnny Behan had revived this charge as a means to embarrass Wyatt Earp by arresting one of his deputies, a la the arrest of Frank Stilwell. George Parsons encountered the Earp posse around 9:30 in the morning, on the Charleston road, heading back to Tombstone. Later in the day, Sherman McMaster posted a bond in Judge Felter's justice court, but for some reason this case never came to trial.

Shortly after arriving back in Tombstone, Wyatt Earp learned that Ike and Phineas Clanton were in town. They had surrendered to a citizen's posse led by Charles Bartholomew, a Wells Fargo employee acting under questionable legal authority, at about 2:30 that morning. The citizen's posse had been guided to the hiding place of the Clanton brothers by Pete Spencer. Ike Clanton later expressed concern that he felt that Wyatt Earp intended to kill him and his brother if he got custody of them, so he surrendered to Charlie Bartholomew's ad hoc civilian posse as a matter of safety for himself.

That afternoon, the Clanton brothers came into the Tombstone district courtroom believing they were wanted on stage robbery charges, and they and their lawyer were surprised to learn the brothers were also wanted for assisting in the attack on Virgil Earp. The attempted murder warrant was quickly served by John H. Jackson, believed to be a civilian process server. Ike Clanton's attorney Ben Goodrich argued before district court judge William Stilwell that John Jackson had acted without legal authority in serving the attempted murder warrants. (In the fall of 2004 researcher Woody Campbell discovered John Jackson's appointment notice as a deputy United States marshal filed in the National Archives. The appointment was dated 27 January 1882, and was endorsed by Judge Stilwell, but it took a week for it to become public knowledge.) Judge Stilwell overruled attorney Goodrich's objection but then granted the two Clanton brothers a $1,500 bail bond each and released them to appear in his court Thursday morning for their formal hearing.

Also on this date, Sheriff Johnny Behan was arrested upon a complaint filed by Sylvester B. Comstock, a leading Tombstone citizen, charging the sheriff had committed perjury when he submitted a false expense account claim to the Cochise County board of supervisors. Comstock believed that Behan had falsified his records and charged Cochise County taxpayers twice for a $365 bill. Ironically, Comstock was the co-owner of the Grand Hotel, the Cow-boy's Tombstone headquarters, and the Mount Hood Saloon, a Cow-boy favorite, as well as being the chairman of Tombstone's Democratic Party. The businessman had served on Tombstone's first common council in 1879.

Tuesday, January 31, 1882, saw snow still on the ground and winds made the air cold.

The Clanton brothers faced stage robbery charges in Judge William H. Stilwell's court. Defense attorneys Alexander Campbell and Ben Goodrich produced seven Cow-boy witnesses who claimed the defendants were in Charleston at the time of the stage robbery. In spite of the testimony of prosecution witnesses the defendants' alibis were upheld and Ike and Finn Clanton were discharged.

Following the Ike Clanton case, Judge Stilwell convened a preliminary hearing for the perjury case lodged against Sheriff John Behan by Sylvester B. Comstock on Monday. When Sheriff Behan was asked to enter a plea on the charge, James B. Southard, the sheriff's attorney, used the "lack of statutory violation" defense, a legal technicality, to obtain Sheriff Behan's freedom from prosecution on the perjury charge.

A "citizen's committee" composed of the city's Republican Party leaders, including George Parsons and John Clum, gathered that evening to select candidates to recommend to Marshal Dake as replacements for the Earp brothers as federal marshals in the Tombstone area. The meeting was chaired by Justice A.O. Wallace, party chairman.

Author's Perspective: This open rejection by their party leadership and by men who they had believed to be their friends was a hard smack in the face and a deep blow to the Earp brothers' pride. This is most likely the incident that caused the brothers to make plans to sell out and leave Tombstone. They now had two questions to answer: when to leave and where to go.

On **Wednesday, February 1, 1882,** the weather was cold and snowy in Tombstone.

Smarting from the court's recent treatment of their cases against the Cow-boys, acting governor Gosper's rebuke of Wyatt Earp's forceful pursuit of Virgil's attackers and the results of the "community meeting" held the night before, the Earp brothers took the first step toward leaving Tombstone. Wyatt and Virgil Earp gave Arizona's United States marshal Crawley P. Dake their resignations as deputy United States marshals. Step two was to find some interested real estate buyers.

Dake, a former army major in the Civil War, was staying at the Grand Hotel, the Cow-boys' Tombstone headquarters. It is unclear if Wyatt Earp personally delivered the resignation letter or sent it via a messenger. The brothers said that they would "remain subject to your orders in the performance of any duties which may be assigned to us, only until our successors are appointed." If United States marshal Dake ever wrote a formal reply, accepting or rejecting their resignations, to the Earp brothers that message has been lost.

Next, Wyatt Earp continued his unexpected actions and exploded a second public-relations bomb on this fateful Wednesday. Researcher Paul Johnson uncovered the details of Wyatt Earp's peace offer to the Cow-boys as reported in the *Daily Nugget.* The newspaper said Earp notified Ike Clanton he wished a status quo ante understanding between them, that he "wished to interview with him with a view of reconciling their differences and obliterating the animosity that exists between them."

Author's Perspective: I believe, as do some other historians, that privately Marshal Crawley Dake instructed Wyatt Earp to remain on duty and complete his mission. He may even have suggested that he step up his relentless operation against the Cow-boys. As was predictable, Ike Clanton, the less-than-lightbulb-bright braggart rustler Cow-boy chief, vocally and publicly declined the peace offer and placed the Cow-boys on the wrong side of public opinion. This Ike Clanton misstep, like his actions before the streetfight, set in motion a new bloody campaign that would finally topple the Arizona Cow-boy confederation.

Thursday, February 2, 1882, was a cloudy, cool day and cold night in Tombstone. It seemed the winds might bring some snow to the area.

Today the general public was notified that John Henry "Jack" Jackson, a Canadian-born miner working in Tombstone who was already bailiff in federal commissioner's court presided over by Wells Spicer, had been requested by Crawley Dake to expand his duties and do the field work Virgil Earp had previously undertaken. Jackson and his wife were active members of the new Episcopal church along with John Clum and George Parsons. Disappointingly, Jackson took little action against the Cow-boys until May 1882, when he and his Tombstone rangers rode along the Mexican border for a few days, and upon their return hid from a possible Indian raid on Tombstone. Jackson had left Arizona Territory in disgrace by the end of June 1882. He went to Oregon, hunted gold in Alaska, and finally settled in California.

The pile-on continued for the Earp brothers this Thursday as Judge Stilwell held the preliminary hearing for the attempted murder charges made against Ike and Finn Clanton for their part in the assault upon Virgil Earp. The district judge was forced to release both suspects due to alibis provided by their Cow-boy associates.

Monday, February 6, 1882, was a "gray day," according to Endicott Peabody, Tombstone's new Episcopal church rector. "High wind blowing & much dust."

On this date President Chester A. Arthur appointed Frederick A Tritle as the sixth governor of the Arizona Territory. Tritle was confirmed by the Senate on March 8. The Pennsylvania native had been living in Tucson since 1880 and working in the mining industry in that region. According to the *Phoenix Gazette*, March 4, 1882, Tritle told a gathering at the Bank Exchange Hotel that had come to hear him speak that he would continue to live in Tucson and come to Phoenix when territorial business needed his attention. The new governor received a warm greeting from those gathered to see him.

Tuesday, February 7, 1882, was "cold & bit uncomfortable tho' fine," according to Endicott Peabody.

United States marshal Crawley Dake secretly withdrew the remaining $2,108.35 from Wyatt Earp's Cow-boy campaign account held at Tombstone's Hudson & Company Bank. Dake deposited the dedicated funds into his personal bank account in Prescott. Because of Dake's habit of playing fast and lose with public funds and his known kickback schemes with his deputies, prominent Tombstone law and order men (not to be confused with the Republican Party leadership) supported Wyatt Earp with their own money. Years later, William Herring, a prominent Tombstone attorney, testified to federal investigators that these community leaders supported Wyatt Earp's posse because they "had gotten tired of waiting on the [federal] authorities [to provide the funding for a posse] & had taken the matter in their own hands."

Thursday, February 9, 1882, was a "fine day" according to Pastor Peabody's diary.

The United States Army upgraded their facility in the Huachuca Mountains from a "camp" to a "fort." The facility is still a functioning military post.

Ike Clanton filed murder charges against the Earp brothers and Doc Holliday in the justice of the peace court in Contention City. Clanton charged the men with the Cow-boy deaths during the Tombstone streetfight. Justice James B. Smith issued arrest warrants based upon the same Arizona law Clanton used during the Tombstone hearing. The arrest warrants were given to Sheriff Johnny Behan with the directive to "bring them [the Earps] forthwith before me at my office on Main Street of the Village of Contention."

Author's Perspective: Once more the Earp brothers' business plans had been sidetracked by one of Ike Clanton's stupid reckless moves. Because of Wyatt Earp's attempt at peace a week earlier and Ike's current release by the court, Ike Clanton felt the Earp brothers were weakening and he was now in the "catbird's seat." In his mind, Wyatt Earp and his brothers were "on the run" from the struggle. Ike Clanton had the financial and legal support of Will McLaury and his money, which bought good will among area businessmen and Tombstone barflies. Ike Clanton also knew his dealings with Sheriff Johnny Behan's "graft-machine" shielded him from arrest by Cochise County officers or the new Tombstone city police officers. The plain truth was that the Cow-boys wanted the confrontation to continue until the Earp brothers were dead or had moved out the Arizona Territory. A legal hanging would also be acceptable.

As executor of his brothers' estates, Will McLaury sold or exchanged a portion of his late brother's Sulphur Springs Valley ranch to Ben and Briggs Goodrich as attorney fees. The Texas-born brothers were the lawyers for the Cow-boy faction and they had assisted the county's prosecution team during the street-fight hearing before Justice Wells Spicer.

In June 1882, the Goodrich brothers sold the McLaury ranch at Soldiers' Hole to Albert Thomas Jones, who was the Cochise County recorder and a member of Johnny Behan's grifter ring. The rewards kept coming. Ben Goodrich became Cochise County district attorney, and later a member of the territorial legislature and owner of the new Tombstone water company, while his brother was appointed the attorney general for Arizona Territory in 1887.

On **Friday, February 10, 1882,** Endicott Peabody saw the day as "dark & gloomy." Dark and gloomy was the same feeling Wyatt and Morgan Earp and Doc Holliday must have had that day when they were arrested by Sheriff John Behan based upon a murder warrant issued by peace justice James B. Smith at Contention City. Virgil Earp was not arrested, since he was still confined to his sick bed at the Cosmopolitan Hotel.

These three arrests received mixed comments from the general population on the streets of Tombstone. The legal community expressed concerns about double jeopardy issues. These arrests also drew a quick rebuke from Wells Fargo's chief special agent, James Hume, who accused Sheriff Johnny Behan of being in league with the Cow-boy element. Hume's remarks appeared in the *National Police Gazette* and the *San Jose Times* and were reprinted in the *San Francisco Exchange* on February 16, 1882.

On **Saturday, February 11, 1882**, Parson Endicott Peabody considered the weather a "fine (day) with occasional slight showers."

Wyatt Earp's attorney Tom Fitch was out of Tombstone on business, so Earp contacted William Herring,[13] a member of the Citizens' Safety Committee, to represent him and his brothers. The attorney filed a writ of habeas corpus before probate court judge John Henry Lucas, the only district-level judge currently in Tombstone able to hear this appeal to dismiss the arrest warrant. Judge Lucas, a member of Tombstone's Debating and Literary Club, didn't address the merits of the murder charge or the double jeopardy issue but ruled that the Contention City peace justice had the legal authority to issue such an arrest order. The 1880 federal census enumerated 149 people in the village of Contention City.

Monday, February 13, 1882, was a day of "bad weather again," according to Parsons.

Justice Wells Spicer issued arrest warrants, upon a statement of fact from Wells Fargo express guard Charlie Bartholomew, for Charles T. "Pony Diehl" Ray, Al Tiebot, and Charles Haws, as reported in the *Daily Nugget* of February 28. The men were charged with the theft of $6,500 from the stage robbery of January 6, 1882. Some present-day historians claim that these three men were in jail in Cisco, Texas, at the time.

Tuesday, February 14, 1882, was a gloomy St. Valentine's Day in Tombstone and Contention. In this day's diary entry, Endicott Peabody called it a special day for lovers and a "wretched day. Wet & disagreeable."

George Parsons noted in his journal that Sheriff Behan escorted the Earps and Holliday to Contention City for their court appearance: "Quite a posse went out. Many of Earp's friends accompanied armed to the teeth, they came back later in the day, the good people below beseeching them to leave and try case here. A bad time is expected again in town at any time. Blood will surely come. Hope no innocents will be killed."

The leaders of the Citizens' Safety Committee had feared that Clanton and the Cow-boys would use the 10-mile trip from Tombstone to Contention as an opportunity to ambush the Earps and kill them. The safety committee circumvented the supposed plan by sending a dozen armed men to accompany the federal lawmen/prisoners to their noon hearing. Sheriff John Behan was surprised to see the armed posse gather for the trip. Because of the inclement weather, William Herring, Wyatt Earp's attorney, drove his covered buggy accompanied by his teenage daughter and his Winchester. The mass of armed men quickly caused Justice Smith to adjourn the court proceedings and remand the hearing to a larger Tombstone courtroom, proceedings to reconvene there at 10 o'clock Wednesday morning.

On **Wednesday, February 15, 1882**, in Tombstone the "weather [was] rainy and very disagreeable," according to George Parsons' journal.

The *Daily Epitaph* said, "The weather thus far this winter re-establishes the faith in the two rainy seasons of southern Arizona. We have, up to date, been favored with an abundance, and at this writing, eleven o'clock p.m., Feb.14th, the gentle rain is coming down upon the plains, while in the mountains snow is being deposited for an abundant summer supply for the Huachuca water company." (A century and some decades later, the water system from the Huachuca Mountains is still supplying Tombstone.)

The *Daily Epitaph* also reported that Briggs Goodrich, Ike Clanton's attorney, withdrew himself from participation in the new murder case Ike Clanton had filed against the Earp brothers and Doc Holliday in Contention City, "believing, as it is reported, that the present case is mere persecution" of men who had already been cleared of the same charges in a previous preliminary hearing in Arizona Territory.

Contention City peace justice James B. Smith opened his hearing at 10 o'clock in the morning and quickly triggered a series of legal maneuvers between the prosecution and defense attorneys. Since Justice Smith had left the official charge document in his Contention City office the hearing was recessed until Thursday. Probate judge John Lucas now heard the habeas corpus plea made by the defendants and determined that Ike Clanton had no legal cause to reopen his case against the defendants unless he could produce new evidence to be considered. The Earps and Holliday were ordered released from custody. There were no more legal actions taken concerning the streetfight.

The weather was not the only disagreeable thing in Tombstone as the "Gambler's War" raised its ugly head again. Dan Tipton and saloon owner Benjamin Maynard had "fisticuffs" and Tipton received a cut over his eye. The brawl was stopped by a quick-acting policeman before further harm took place. Maynard and Tipton's friend Lou Rickabaugh had tried to kick each other's lungs out on January 17, the same day Ringo and Holliday had words.

As an elderly man, Cochise County deputy sheriff Billy Breakenridge recalled that on a rainy night he had encountered his friend Frank Stilwell lurking in a Tombstone alley. The former deputy said he was waiting to ambush someone. Breakenridge ordered the Cow-boy home immediately, telling him he had already caused enough trouble for awhile: stage robbery, mail robbery, and attempted murder of a federal officer. A few moments after Stilwell left the area, Doc Holliday passed Breakenridge headed home to his apartment and Breakenridge felt he had inadvertently saved the gambler's life. Stilwell would use another stormy night a few weeks later to try once more to kill a member of Wyatt Earp's posse.

Wednesday, February 22, 1882, was Ash Wednesday and, according to Pastor Endicott Peabody's diary entry, "charming, like a spring day in its brightness & warmth," in the Tombstone area.

Celia Ann "Mattie" Blaylock, Mrs. Wyatt Earp, returned to Tombstone following her extended stay with family in Iowa. She checked into the Cosmopolitan Hotel with Wyatt. Two weeks earlier, Morgan Earp had sent his wife Louisa to California to his parents' home for medical treatment and rest. She is believed to have suffered from heart trouble and what today is known as fibromyalgia. She died in 1894.

Tuesday, February 28, 1882, was "even finer than yesterday," according to Endicott Peabody. The eastern-born preacher wrote in his diary that he felt Monday had been a "beautiful day spring like perfect." George Parsons told his journal that he had found Monday to be "windy and drizzly" in the morning. Two people, two opinions on the weather.

The *Daily Nugget* published a dispatch taken from the *Prescott Miner* explaining that United States marshal Crawley P. Dake had authorized Wyatt Earp and his posse to continue patrolling along the Mexican border looking for Cow-boy raiders. However, the *Daily Nugget* claimed that their newspaper had received a telegram from Marshal Dake stating he had no knowledge of Marshal Wyatt Earp's movements, "but supposed they desired to serve some old warrants." On the same page the newspaper carried an exchange from the *Prescott Democrat*: "We are informed by Marshal Dake that the resignation of the Earps, as Deputy United States Marshals, has yet to be accepted, owing to the fact that their accounts have not yet been straightened up. As soon as that is done, they will step out." Dake's funding accounts were frozen by the Department of Justice in 1881 for failure to balance his office financial records. These accounts were still unsettled when Dake died in March 1890.

Monday, March 6, 1882, was "very cold weather. Worst yet," according to the entry in George Parsons' journal.

Tombstone police department records show that city police made an arrest for petty larceny and another man was taken into custody for carrying a concealed weapon.

Tuesday, March 7, 1882, the *Daily Epitaph* said, "The thermometer at sunrise this morning stood at 13 degrees above zero, thus showing 19 degrees of frost."

The *Epitaph* also noted, "John H. Jackson, United States deputy marshal, went to Benson this morning on business connected with the seizure of 600 gallons of untaxed spirits." Meanwhile, Les Blackburn, Tombstone's other federal deputy marshal and Cochise County deputy sheriff, was busy guarding the community's federal courtroom and collecting import duty on Mexican shipments. City chief of police Dave Neagle arrested a man for carrying a concealed weapon; the man was fined $5 and court costs.

Under the headline, "Harpers [Weekly] and the Cow-boys" the *Daily Epitaph* editorialized about a recent article the national magazine published concerning acting governor Gosper's recommendations of how to deal with the Cow-boy depredations: "That our affairs are now in a better condition than formally is not due to any wise and decisive action on his (Gosper) part, but only by the firmness of [Federal District] Judge Stilwell and U.S. Marshal Dake, whose actions have clearly demonstrated that no interference whatever is needed from the military arm of the government."

Friday, March 10, 1882, according to Episcopal rector Endicott Peabody, was a "fine" day to play baseball in Tombstone, while George Parsons found the day "pleasant and delightful" to be working at one of his mining properties.

Tucson's *Arizona Daily Star* noted that Sheriff John Behan was on the westbound train headed to San Francisco on business. This may have been one of his trips to receive medical treatment for his sexually transmitted disease. The disease contributed to his death in June 1912.

The rumors of late February that made the rounds in Tombstone concerning a possible Apache raid and a scare about a smallpox outbreak in Arizona were proved false, but many people, including George Parsons, still took the smallpox vaccination.

Monday, March 13, 1882, Pastor Peabody noted, was "fine but high wind & so much dust" in Tombstone.

The *San Diego Union* published its regular communication from Tombstone resident Mrs. Clara Brown: "The turbulent condition of affairs which was prevailing at the time of my last letter has been for some time subdued, though exactly in what manner I cannot say, as the movements of the posses sent from here almost daily at that time were secret." In a closing statement Mrs. Brown said, "There is a lull in cowboy criminality (which we hope is something more than temporary), and the Indians apparently having left Dragoon Tombstone people have been obliged to look to other causes of excitement."

9

One for Morg ... Another for Morg ... and Another ...

Deputy Marshal [Wyatt] Earp was very active in his efforts to suppress this "quasi" insurrection and prevent the violation of United States laws. Deputy Marshal Earp and his band killed quite a number of these cow-boys, and a regular vendetta war ensued....—United States District Attorney James A. Zabriskie, in a report to United States attorney general Benjamin Harris Brewster, 22 January 1885

In spite of Wyatt Earp's efforts the Cow-boy depredations continued to disrupt daily life of Cochise County residents. Marshal Dake was under constant pressure to fire Earp, but for once he kept his projected path. Theodore Roosevelt expressed this "stick-to-it" idea when he wrote, "The best executive is the one who has sense enough to pick good men to do what he wants done, and self-restraint enough to keep from meddling with them while they do it." The powder-keg events in Cochise County were having a wider effect. The cauldron of violence had reached the temperature to boil over into southern New Mexico Territory and the Mexican state of Sonora.

Special Tombstone correspondent Clara Spalding Brown wrote to the *San Diego Daily Union*, published March 31, 1882, sharing with readers her nonpartisan on-the-ground observations: "The calm of the last two months was but the precursor of a storm such as we hope will never again visit the camp of Tombstone." The "storm" was Wyatt Earp taking the gloves off and answering the Cow-boy's final midnight atrocity with his version of a shock and awl campaign—1882 style.

On **Saturday, March 18, 1882,** as the day ended the Pale Horseman of the Apocalypse was unleashed. George Parsons remarked in his diary that it was a "very disagreeable day. Rainy and windy. Stormy and disagreeable night." Episcopal priest Endicott Peabody confided to his diary, "Hard rain all day—Very unusual for this time of the year in these parts."

The *Daily Epitaph* reported that the "city council will hereafter require the Chief of Police to act as janitor of the city hall. Perhaps the city attorney or some other official pet will get additional pay for these extra services on the part of the chief."

During the day, Wyatt Earp chanced to encounter Briggs Goodrich, an attorney favored by the Cow-boys, who told Earp he felt his clients were seeking further trouble with his family. The lawyer claimed he had no specific knowledge of impending trouble, but he encouraged the Earps to be on their guard. He also delivered a personal message from Johnny Ringo to Wyatt that Ringo would be no party to any future trouble between the Cow-boys and the Earps. Goodrich repeated his general warning to the Earps later that night at the theater and again at Morgan's inquest hearing on Sunday.

The *Daily Epitaph* advised readers, "The Lingards to-night. This will be the most enjoyable entertainment of the season, and not one who loves good acting and a laughable farce should miss the show." On this evening, Doc Holliday, Morgan Earp and Dan Tipton took Wyatt Earp, who enjoyed the theater, to Schieffelin Hall as a birthday night out, and the guys laughed through *Stolen Kisses* preformed by the Lingard Troupe.

Following the Lingard entertainment, the three men walked south on Fourth Street to Allen Street. As they turned the corner east onto Allen Street, Morgan and Tipton said they were not ready for bed and wanted to go by Campbell and Hatch's Saloon to see the other posse members and play a game of pool. The posse members now gathered there as an unofficial headquarters since Wyatt had sold his interest in the Oriental Saloon. Wyatt told them he intended to stop at the Alhambra Saloon and check on his faro bank before going to bed early, so the men parted in front of the saloon.

Morgan and Tipton saw Allie Earp walking back to the Cosmopolitan Hotel, where the Earp family had been living since the streetfight. She had gone out on this rainy night to get Virgil some candy for his sweet tooth. Tipton went on to Hatch's while Morgan escorted his sister-in-law back to the hotel. Later, Allie would say that Morgan told her he wished Virgil was well enough so the family could all leave Tombstone: "I'd like to get away from here, tonight."

Morgan Earp challenged Bob Hatch to a late-night pool game. Sherman McMaster and Dan Tipton were among the onlookers. Wyatt Earp later told Forrestine Hooker that as he was readying for bed he had a premonition all was not right, so he got dressed again and went to check in on the pool game. Doc Holliday's actions that night are unknown, but it is believed he had gone to bed. Under the headline "The Deadly Bullet," Monday's issue of the *Daily Epitaph* described what transpired next.

While playing pool with his friend Bob Hatch at about 10:50 p.m. Morgan Seth Earp was assassinated by a shot fired through a glass panel in the back door of the Campbell and Hatch Saloon and Billiard Parlor. The lethal piece of pistol lead entered Morgan's back to the left of his spinal column, ripped through his left kidney and liver, and exited near the gall bladder on his right side before coming to rest in the thigh of Maine native George Augustine Byron Berry, a prominent mining investor who had been observing the spirited game while warming himself near the stove. The assassins fired a second shot that missed Wyatt, who was sitting along the wall watching his kid brother's game, and drilled into the wallpapered panel behind him. Just like Vigil's ambushers, Morgan's killers escaped into the mud-dark rainy night.

Dr. William S. Miller quickly arrived to attend the fallen lawman. He was soon joined by doctors George E. Goodfellow and Henry M. Matthews, the county coroner, who tried to help the suffering young man. According to Stuart Lake's research notes, Morgan had survived a wound from a gunfight in Miles City, Montana, but still carried the bullet in his body. He had also survived a serious multiple shoulder wound received during the recent October streetfight. Unfortunately, Tombstone's doctors agreed he would not survive this time due to the damage to his internal organs. It was difficult for Wyatt to watch as the Death Angel claimed his favorite brother. Morgan Earp was just over a month short of his 31st birthday when death claimed him.

Allie and Virgil's doctor helped him get out of his sick bed at the Cosmopolitan Hotel, assisted him in getting dressed, and then accompanied him next door to Campbell and Hatch's place to see his mortally wounded brother. The Earp women—Bessie, Allie and Mattie—changed to street clothing and came with Virgil to say good-bye to their brother-in-law. They all set and cried quietly amidst the gloomy scene of loss and despair.

At some point, Doc Holliday learned of Morgan's shooting and joined the final watch for his friend. Some of Earp's other friends arrived for the death vigil while Wyatt's standing posse stood guard against additional trouble. Meanwhile, the killers were racing through the night to establish alibis in Tucson in Pima County.

Endicott Peabody mentioned the murder of Morgan Earp in a letter to a friend. The pastor said he understood Morgan's last words concerned not being able to again play pool. The young preacher expressed his Victorian aristocratic and Episcopalian judgment of a man he did not know: "Fancy a man saying such a thing at such a time. It may seem a certain daring but it argues a sad want of any kind of religious feeling or unsaid human feeling for his wife & family that are in California." Peabody did know Wyatt Earp and supported his Cow-boy campaign.

Morgan Earp was raised in the Methodist church but became a believer in spiritualism as he grew older. The brothers often discussed the meaning of Job 14:14: "If a man die, shall he live again?" In later years, Wyatt Earp claimed that Morgan's spirit guided his actions during his Cow-boy campaign and twice alerted him of danger in time to save his life. Deathbed witnesses claimed that Morgan asked Wyatt to get the men who killed him but warned, "Don't let them get you, brother." Resolutely, Wyatt Earp promised his brother, "I will get them." At that moment academic law enforcement become very personal. Some called it retribution.

Morgan's big greyhound was brought to the pool hall so the dying young man could say good-bye to his dog. The *Daily Nugget* reported that the dog "howled and moaned" and "when the body was taken to the hotel, no sadder lot followed than that of the faithful dog." One source mentioned that James took the greyhound along with the casket to California. It is unclear what happened to Virgil's dog or Wyatt's racehorse when they left Tombstone.

On **Sunday, March 19, 1882,** Endicott Peabody could not have asked for a more "fine day" to preach to his growing congregation. It was Wyatt Earp's 34th birthday.

The *Daily Epitaph* of March 22, 1881, reprinted an account from Tucson, saying, "(Frank) Stilwell arrived here (Tucson) Sunday morning to appear before the Grand Jury (Monday) on a charge of stage robbery near Bisbee last November." An alibi was established.

Meanwhile, early Sunday morning Wyatt sent a telegram to Colton notifying his parents and Louisa Alice Houston of Morgan's murder. Adelia Edwards recalled that her sister-in-law collapsed on the floor of the senior Earps' home in grief at the news of Morgan's death "and sobbed and sobbed." Adelia also said that Louisa "went off to Arizona to bring his body back to Colton." Morgan Earp researcher Kenny Vail discovered it was possible that Louisa took an express train from Colton and was able to rendezvous with James, who was accompanying Morgan's body, at Yuma. The *Yuma Times* made note of deputy United States marshal Morgan Earp's casket passing through their community on its way to its final resting place in San Bernardino, California.

Wyatt made undertaking arrangements for his brother and planned a public viewing in the parlor of the Cosmopolitan Hotel on Sunday morning. He had Morgan dressed in one of Doc Holliday's best blue suits. At some point that morning, Wyatt had received a telegram from his father requesting that Morgan not be buried in Arizona Territory but asking that he be shipped to California for interment. Wyatt had the casket prepared for transport. There would be no large public parade down Allen Street led by the town band or the body displayed in a store window. This was to be a private affair with friends and family.

"The funeral cortege started away from the Cosmopolitan Hotel about 12:30 yesterday with the fire bells tolling its solemn peels of Earth to earth, dust to dust," noted the *Daily Epitaph* on March 20. Wyatt and his well-armed posse escorted Morgan's body to the railroad station at Contention. James Earp escorted his brother's casket west on the evening Southern Pacific train and Wyatt and his escort returned to Tombstone. Tuesday's *Los Angles Times* reported that James Earp had arrived in that city Monday evening.

Dr. Henry M. Matthews conducted a coroner's inquest for Morgan Earp on Sunday afternoon. The panel heard testimony from Bob Hatch, Dan Tipton, Sherman McMaster, Dr. Goodfellow, Briggs Goodrich, and Marietta Duarte Spence, sifted the evidence and then named some suspects in Morgan's assassination. Matthews' report—Cochise County District Court Document 68, Coroner's Inquest: Morgan Earp—was presented to William H. Stilwell, judge of the First District Court of Cochise County, who issued murder warrants for the arrest of the suspects on Monday.

Author's Perspective: Some amateur psychologists have suggested that Morgan's death was the final straw that set Wyatt on a fast track to a nervous breakdown. It seems more logical to me that Morgan's murder awakened the sleeping lion within Wyatt Earp and the vision of his brother's dead body steeled his resolve for personal justice; he was about to become the deadly sword of *lex talionis*, the ancient Law of Retaliation, and would extract "an eye for an eye." But first, Wyatt Earp had family matters that needed his undivided attention.

At the family meeting Sunday morning, Wyatt told his brothers he planned to go on the attack against the Cow-boys. Priority one was for James to escort Morgan's body to California. The second priority was to keep Virgil safe, and if he stayed in Tombstone he would be a liability to Wyatt's plan. Wyatt told Virgil that he needed him to get ready to take Allie to Colton on Monday because Wyatt could not both protect him and chase Cow-boys. Virgil agreed, since he was still recovering from debilitating wounds received in the attempt upon his life in December 1881. In fact, Virgil had barely been able to leave his bed only a few days before Morgan's death and understood that he was in no condition to physically help Wyatt track down Morgan's killers. Wyatt and some of his men would see that Virgil and Allie got out of Tombstone safely. Priority three was for Warren to safeguard Bessie and Mattie as they undertook the task of closing up the families' homes; when James returned in a few days he would escort them to safety in California. Warren would then join Wyatt's seek and destroy mission against the Cow-boy confederation.

Wyatt Earp burned with a righteous anger. The Greek philosopher Aristotle once made a noteworthy pronouncement concerning anger: "Anybody can become angry, that is easy; but to be angry with the right person, and to the right degree, at the right time, and for the right purpose, and in the right way, that is not within everybody's power. That is not easy." Anger is one letter short of danger. Wyatt Earp was angry and dangerous.

Alice Earp Wells, Newton Earp's daughter, told researcher Jack Burrows that her father, Wyatt's older half-brother, along with her Uncle Jimmy and Grandfather Nicholas, were packed and in readiness and daily awaiting Wyatt's summons to join his strike force and help kill Cow-boys; but Wyatt's clear thinking forestalled a possible bloody family feud. Deputy United States marshal Wyatt Earp kept the public focus of his raids on neutralizing the Cow-boys and not on his family's loss.

Was Marshal Wyatt Earp a commando-style strike force leader in his campaign against the Cow-boys? He most certainly did not think of himself in that manner. However, an unbiased evaluation of his actions and strategies suggest that he did in fact conduct his Cow-boy Campaign like a present-day raider strike force operating within enemy territory supported by local assistance.

United States Marines who complete the rigorous training to become members of the Corps' elite Force Recon (motto: *celer, silens, mortailis*—swift, silent, deadly) learn combat principles that have roots dating back to tactics established by Benjamin Church during the numerous Indian campaigns of the colonial era. Colonel Church is the great-grandfather of America's Special Forces and his manual of ranger tactics was further developed by Major Robert Rodgers, leader of Rodgers' Rangers, during the French and Indian War, by General Francis "the Swamp Fox" Marion of the Continental Army during the American Revolutionary War, and by Colonel John Singleton "the Gray Ghost" Mosby of the Southern Confederacy during the War Between the States. Modern-day special forces were developed during World War II, and these skills were honed during the protracted conflict in Vietnam.

In the mid–1750s, Major Rodgers wrote a list of twenty-eight fighting techniques, methods and tactics for his Rangers. It is unlikely that Wyatt Earp ever read these "Ranging Rules," but he was a natural leader of men and understood human nature and the basic principle of combat with fists or weapons. There is an old dictum among special operations forces: strike fast, strike hard, no safe haven, and go violent and ugly early.

The first of Rodgers' rules Wyatt Earp used was: "If the enemy pursues your rear, take a circle till you come to your own tracks and there form an ambush to receive them, and give them the first fire." Deputy Marshal Earp used this concept when he faced Sheriff Behan's Cow-boy posse at Riley Hill on Hooker's Ranch.

The second article used by Deputy Marshal Earp was just as basic: "If your number be small, march in a single file, keeping at such a distance from each other as to prevent one shot from killing two men." This edict is what saved Wyatt Earp and his strike force team as they approached the secluded Iron Springs location.

A third principle was simple logic: "If you are obliged to retreat, let the front of our whole party fire and fall back, till the rear hath done the same, making for the best ground you can." Like Church, Rodgers, Marion, and Mosby before him, Wyatt Earp often retreated so he and his team could live to fight another day. Hit and run, hide, hit and run....

On **Monday, March 20, 1882,** Parson Peabody said it was an "almost perfect day—barely a cloud & temperature just right," while George Parsons recalled the weather was a "little cool again." The *Daily Epitaph* noted, "Spring came to-day at 12 o'clock in the most genial possible manner."

The *Tucson Weekly Citizen* recapped for their readers, on May 14, 1882, the Cowboys' bloody new modus operandi: "The Cowboys fearing that they might share the same fate [as their confederates who died in the Tombstone streetfight] in case they refused peaceable obedience to laws, determined to rid themselves of the only officers—be they good, bad or indifferent—who ever had nerve to enforce the law against them and commenced a war of assassination."

> **Author's Perspective:** Up to this point, Arizona Territory's judicial system had not favored Wyatt Earp's effort to fight the Cow-boys. By the time of Morgan's death, Wyatt had come to feel that local judges were corrupt and would, upon hearing their false alibis, release the Cow-boys. In his Wyatt Earp biography, Stuart N. Lake provides a dramatic conversation between Judge W.H. Stilwell and Wyatt after the jurist supplied Marshal Earp with federal arrest warrants for the Cow-boys on Monday: "If I were serving these warrants, Wyatt, I'd leave my prisoners in the mesquite where alibis don't count." As recorded, the judge's suggestion might be fact or it might be fiction, but evidence suggests that Wyatt Earp determined that this time his antagonists would not be required to appear in a court but before the Supreme Judge of the Universe. In Job 38:12–13, God asked his beleaguered servant this question: "Have you ever commanded the day to break, assigned the dawn its place, so that it seizes the corners of the earth and shakes the wicked out of it?" Wyatt Earp was going do some earth shaking.

Under the "Local Personals" column in the *Daily Epitaph* the newspaper reported, "V.W. Earp and his wife left for his parents' home, at Colton, California, to-day. He was accompanied to Contention by his brothers and several personal friends." This report gave an accurate summation of Wyatt Earp's original plan, but plans change.

The day's weather made little difference to Wyatt Earp and his posse as they escorted the wounded Virgil and his wife, Allie, to the New Mexico & Arizona Railroad branch line train station at Contention City and on to Benson to connect with the westbound Southern Pacific Railroad for the fifty-mile trip to Tucson. Wyatt told Walter Noble Burns that he and Doc Holliday decided at the last moment that they would accompany Virgil and Allie on to Tucson and see them safely onto the westbound train that evening. The rest of the posse stayed in Benson to await Wyatt and Doc's return. When the party arrived in Tucson, Doc Holliday deposited his and Wyatt's shotguns in the Wells Fargo Express Company office at the depot. He then joined the Earps in the dining room at the Porter Hotel, next to the depot, for supper.

Wyatt's campaign plan changed quickly at about 7:15 that evening as darkness settled around the Tucson railroad station. The Earp party had finished eating supper at Porter's Hotel and were boarding Virgil and Allie for their trip when Wyatt suddenly spotted Frank Stilwell as he crossed the track in front of the train. (There is one report that says before Wyatt Earp saw Frank Stilwell someone had taken a shot at Virgil and Allie as they sat in the train coach awaiting their departure.) Wyatt took his shotgun from Doc as he told him to get Virgil and Allie settled in the train's passenger coach, then to follow him. Wyatt ran into the darkness after Frank Stilwell and his friends.

Deputy United States marshal Wyatt Earp found Frank Stilwell cowering in the rail yard and used his double-barreled shotgun to present the former deputy sheriff with a one-way express ticket to meet St. Peter. Stilwell's fellow assassins, Ike Clanton and Apache Hank Swilling, narrowly escaped their own lethal summons as they ran from a confrontation with Wyatt Earp's shotgun. About 100 yards west down the track from the depot, Doc Holliday found his friend standing over Stilwell's dead body. Some historians believe that it was Holliday who provided the bulk of the post-mortem wounds that Pima County coroner Dexter Lyford found on Stilwell's corpse. Following the death inquest, Frank Stilwell's mangled body was buried in Tucson with one unidentified mourner present for the occasion.[1]

As the westbound train pulled out of the Tucson station, gunshots were heard in the distance and, according to Kate Elder's memories, many people assumed it was a celebration in Old Tucson because the town was lighted by a modern gaslight system for the first time that evening. Virgil and Allie soon learned differently. As the train moved past Wyatt's position, he ran alongside their passenger coach and told them, "I got one for Morg." Allie Earp later recalled, "We rested more easy after that but for two things. We kept worryin' about Wyatt. The second was different." Virgil had knocked over the baking power tin of salve for his wounds during the shooting excitement and the contents got all over the couples' clothing. As the speeding train moved across southern Arizona that evening, Allie wore Virgil's cartridge belt and his pistol so her husband could quickly reach his weapon with his good hand if circumstances dictated.

Author's Perspective: Wyatt Earp's implied promise to his older brother as they waved good-bye in the Tucson rail yard was that there would be more shootings in the days to come. Tombstone diarist George Parsons wrote in his *Private Journal*, "A quick vengeance and a bad character sent to hell where he will be the chief attraction until a few more accompany him."

Deputy U.S. marshal Wyatt Earp's "dance-card" contained the names of Ike Clanton, Frank Stilwell, "Apache Hank" Swilling, Florentino "Indian Charley" Cruz, William "Curly Bill" Brocius, Johnny Ringo, Pete Spencer (Eliott Larkin Ferguson), Johnny Barnes, and Frederick "German Fries" Bodie, who worked as a faro dealer for Johnny Behan's gambling layout. Will McLaury and Sheriff Behan were secondary candidates, but if Wyatt could locate them, or any other Cow-boy, in a convenient situation he would not hesitate to "dance" with them. Frank Stilwell had become the first name removed from Wyatt Earp's most wanted list. Earp would discover a few days later that he had also been named to a most wanted list.

An often overlooked piece of pertinent information is contained in the Wells Fargo Express Company's huge *Loss and Damage Ledger*, compiled in 1885, and is relevant to this discussion. For nearly a century, the express company claimed that its Tombstone office records perished in the San Francisco earthquake and fire of 1906, until Dr. Robert J. Chandler, Wells Fargo Company historian, located some of those missing records in the old office vault. Almost lost among hundreds of other entries in the 2,000-page *Loss and Damage Ledger* is a small notation that the express company paid $150 to Wyatt Earp for killing Frank Stilwell.

Tuesday, March 21, 1882, Endicott Peabody wrote in his daily diary that the weather was "fine like yesterday only [a] trifle windier," while George Parsons called it a "fine day. Summer."

In the predawn hours, Wyatt Earp and Doc Holliday left Tucson and walked to the Papago railroad siding outside Tucson where they flagged down an eastbound Southern Pacific freight train headed to Benson. Here they rejoined the rest of the strike force team and told them about the events in the Tucson train yard. Later, the men took the next train for the short-line trip down to Contention City, where the federal officers reclaimed their stabled mounts and buggy to return to Tombstone. The federal posse arrived in the mining camp late in the afternoon in time to read the day's edition of the *Daily Epitaph*, which published a "Special Dispatch to the Epitaph" from Tucson. The bulletin was headlined "Another Assassination, Frank Stilwell Found Dead This Morning, Being Another Chapter in the Earp–Clanton Tragedy."

In the newspaper dispatch from Tucson two theories concerning the wayward deputy sheriff's death were presented: "One is that the comrades of Stilwell, fearing that he might turn state's evidence have silenced him." The second viewpoint was that the Earp posse had killed him. "In either case his taking off verifies the saying that 'the way of the transgressor is hard.'"

Tuesday evening about 8:00 p.m. Sheriff John Behan, backed by a small posse including David Neagle, Tombstone's chief of police, confronted Wyatt Earp and his friends as they were leaving the Cosmopolitan Hotel. Behan had received a telegram from Tucson, not an arrest warrant as some have claimed, requesting Wyatt Earp's detention for questioning. The *Los Angles Times*, on March 28, informed readers about Sheriff Behan telling deputy U.S. marshal Earp, "I want to see you." Wyatt Earp's reply was recorded as, "Behan, I don't want to see you; I have seen you once too often. If you're not careful you'll see me once too often." The Cochise County sheriff received the underlying message and did not press for the requested conference. Later, Behan claimed that Earp's posse drew their weapons on him and to avoid a fight on the streets of Tombstone he let the fugitives escape and then planned to pursue them in the daylight. Few people in Tombstone believed that fairy tale.

Wyatt and Warren Earp, Doc Holliday, Sherman McMaster, Jack Johnson, and John Vermillion carried their personal gear and weapons as they walked west on Allen Street toward Philip William Smith's corral on the corner with Third Street to get their horses. Along the way banker Hyman Solomon, who had quarters in the P.W. Smith General Mercantile building on the corner of Fourth Street, noted that Holliday did not have a rifle, so he went into the store and got a new Winchester from the store's gun rack for him. Charlie Smith and Dan Tipton were waiting at the corral with the horses ready to travel and the posse rode slowly out of Tombstone without further interference from the sheriff or his deputies.

As late as December 13, 1896, the *Tombstone Prospector* reported that the Pima County grand jury criminal indictment against Wyatt Earp for the murder of Frank Stilwell was still valid and available to be served against the former federal marshal. It would also appear that the murder warrant just finally disappeared from the court docket.

Author's Perspective: In that day's *Daily Epitaph* "Local Personals" column appeared this notice: "J.N. Thacker, Esq. of San Francisco, is at the Cosmopolitan (Hotel)." Thacker was a special agent (detective) for Wells Fargo Express Company who reported to chief special agent Jim Hume. Had Wells Fargo's point man been sent to Tombstone to assess the situation in the mining camp and Wyatt Earp's mental state after his brother's brutal murder? Had he come to assist Wyatt Earp with the logistics to launch a murderous counterattack against the Cow-boys?

Both Wyatt Earp and John N. Thacker had rooms at the Cosmopolitan Hotel, so it is possible that after some much needed sleep and something to eat Earp held an early-evening war council with Thacker. The two men could have discussed Wells Fargo Express Company's willingness to make a pledge of the company's public support and financial assistance for the deputy federal marshal's new seek and destroy mission.

That day the spring weather in southern California cooperated so that the grieving Earp family could bury Morgan's remains in what is now called the Old City Cemetery in Colton. The graveside service was a simple family affair. Louisa Alice Houston cried for her lost love.

Thursday's *Los Angles Times* reported that Virgil Earp "was in town Tuesday evening and was interviewed by a TIMES reporter, but the best efforts failed to elicit any information. He said he was non-committal." The wounded officer, having come directly from his younger brother's funeral, was most likely in town for a medical appointment.

Author's Perspective: A decade after he was laid to rest Morgan Earp was reinterred on November 29, 1892, in the new Hermosa Gardens Cemetery due to the original grave site's being in the pathway of new railroad tracks. The current grave site is marked, but some present-day researchers question if Morgan's body was properly identified and suggest that he may really rest under the railroad. A grave site misidentification seems unlikely since Earp family members lived in Colton at the time of the reburial and they made no such misidentification claim.

Wednesday, March 22, 1882, dawned "cool and clear" around Tombstone.

Shortly before daylight, Wyatt Earp and his posse broke their camp at Watervale, a few miles northwest of Tombstone near the present location Ed Schieffelin's grave site monument, and headed their horses toward the Dragoon Mountains.

Cochise County sheriff Johnny Behan swore out an arrest warrant for Wyatt and Warren Earp, Jack Johnson, Sherm McMaster, Dan Tipton, O.C. Smith, Texas Jack, and John Holliday for resisting arrest Tuesday night. Justice A.J. Felter issued the warrant. Now Behan organized a sheriff's posse of "honest ranchers" and sent them to locate and arrest—and kill if they could—Wyatt Earp and his federal posse, such action justified by the recently arrived Pima County murder warrant for killing Frank Stilwell in Tucson or the resisting arrest warrant just issued in Tombstone. George Parsons noted in his journal, "The Cow-boy element is backing him (Behan) strongly." At different times over the next 10 days, Sheriff Behan authorized posses led by Curly Bill or Johnny Ringo, based in Charleston, to take the field in search of Wyatt Earp and his posse.

The standard pay for members of a sheriff's posse was five dollars a day and an extra three dollars if a posseman used his own horse. Behan gladly provided rental horses from his own stable for the day rate and after Gentleman Johnny finally recalled all his posses he submitted a whopping $2,593.65 to the Cochise County taxpayers for his "cat and mouse" junkets.[2]

Wednesday evening, Endicott Peabody told his diary, "Word came that Earps had killed 1 of the Indians guilty of murdering Morgan Earp." Florentino "Indian Charlie" Cruz aka Filomeno Sais had received his midday trial before Wyatt Earp's gun at Pete Spencer's wood camp located in the hills near the eastern entrance to South Pass on the Chiricahua Road, a few miles from the Doyle Ranch on the sloops of the Dragoon Mountains. The coroner's inquest determined that the posse members had added their own coupe de grace to the body. George Parsons wrote in his diary, "More killing by Earp party. Hope they'll keep it up." Thursday's *Daily Epitaph* headlined the story, "Still Another Killing."

Deputy United States marshal Wyatt Earp had hoped to find Pete Spencer at his wood camp, but he did not know that his former Tombstone neighbor was in Sheriff Johnny Behan's jail seeking protective custody after learning about Frank Stilwell's sudden death in Tucson. Upon learning of Earp's killing of Stilwell and Cruz, Hank Swelling surrendered at Charleston to deputy sheriff William Bell, and Frederick "German Fries" Bodie gave up to deputy sheriff Frank Hereford. These three Cow-boys wanted Sheriff Behan's protection from Wyatt Earp's deadly shotgun. The game had changed and they didn't like the new rules.

In the classic style of the early 1900s novelist, Bat Masterson's friend Alfred Henry Lewis wrote in *Sundown Trail*, his 1905 novel featuring Masterson as the hero, about Wyatt's bloody action: "They [the Earp posse] invaded the [outlaw hide-outs in the] San Simon [Valley] and blotted out the Mexican Florentino. This was light work, like killing a jackrabbit. There should be braver game in the San Simon [Valley]." Mr. Cruz was number two on Wyatt Earp's deadly dance card.

In San Bernardino, California, a grieving Louisa Alice Houston Earp mailed a copy of Morgan's printed funeral card and a personal message to her and Morgan's friend Budd Davis, a boardinghouse owner in Butte, Montana Territory, concerning her husband's murder. Lou wrote, "Oh Budd it is so hard to give up the dearest of all earth." Louisa remarried in 1885 and died in 1894 at age 39. The second marriage doesn't seem to have been a happy relationship.

Meanwhile, in an unprecedented move, top management of Wells Fargo held a press conference at their San Francisco headquarters office to declare the express company's unconditional approval of deputy United States marshal Wyatt Earp and his campaign against the Cow-boys in Arizona Territory. The express company's declaration of support was based upon the recommendation of John N. Thacker. The next day, one of the West's most widely read newspapers, the *San Francisco Examiner*, published a notice of Wells Fargo's action in a feature article detailing the background for the company's public advocacy. On May 27, 1882, the *Examiner*'s editors endorsed Wyatt Earp's bloody seek and destroy campaign as having been "sensational warfare against the cowboys."

Thursday, March 23, 1882, provided nice spring weather as Wyatt Earp and his men rested in their mountain camp awaiting information from the Citizen's Safety Committee regarding the safety of Earp's family still remaining in Tombstone.

According to the day's *Daily Epitaph*, Pima County sheriff Bob Paul came to town for firsthand assessment of Sheriff Behan's plans for dealing with Wyatt Earp and his men. Upon seeing the nature of the men the sheriff had selected for his posse he refused to join Behan's "honest ranchers" to hunt for the Earps. George Parsons wrote, "He is a true-brave man himself and will not join the murderous posse here."

George Hand noted in his diary, "The cow-boys, twenty or more, have been prowling around all morning [in Contention City]. They are well mounted, well armed and seem intent on biz. They are in search of the Earp party who took breakfast 2 miles above here this morning. 3 P.M.—they again came from the direction of Tombstone, watered their horses here and started again at double quick for Kinnear's ranch."

After lunch, Sheriff Behan and his 12-man posse made a quick trip to Contention City. Behan found no sign of the Earp posse in the mill town, so he returned to Tombstone. Around five o'clock that evening, the frustrated sheriff arrested Dan Tipton and Charlie Smith, who had returned to Tombstone for money, supplies, and information for Earp's federal strike force, as they were preparing to leave the city. The leadership of the Citizen's Safety Committee went into high gear to seek the release of Earp's two men.

Friday morning, the *Daily Nugget* claimed the arrests of Tipton and Smith were for "aiding and abetting the Earps." However, the court records show that Sheriff Behan claimed his double arrest was for "resisting an officer and conspiracy" stemming from the nonincident Tuesday evening at the Cosmopolitan Hotel in Tombstone.

> **Author's Perspective:** In a stroke of genius the Cow-boy public relations effort, led by the *Daily Nugget* and the *Tucson Star*, resurrected the myth of a feud between "peaceful rangehandes" and "a family clan of bulling town police" created during the hearing over the October streetfight. The plotters now restoked the fires as a smoke screen to discredit Wyatt Earp's new efforts to enforce law and order in southeastern Arizona Territory. "To put your enemy in the wrong," wrote American Revolutionary War patriot Samuel Adams, "and keep him so, is a wise maxim in politics, as well as in war." So successful was the Cow-boy's PR campaign that well into a second century after its birth, new gullible converts continue to parrot-cry the Earp vs. Cow-boy feud myth.

Friday, March 24, 1882, dawned as "a beautiful early summer day" in Tombstone, according to George Parsons' entry in his daily private journal. Meanwhile at Contention City, George Hand remembered a "fine morning" and also noted in his daily diary there had been "a light shower of rain and wind storm this afternoon."

Wyatt Earp was expecting Charlie Smith and Dan Tipton to return from Tombstone with news and money to continue his field campaign. However, Thursday evening, in an angry rage, Sheriff Johnny Behan had arrested Tipton and Smith as they were preparing to leave town. Once again someone had betrayed the federal officers to the Cowboy's champion.

This morning the Citizen's Safety Committee dispatched two new messengers, Tony Kraker and S.C. "Whistling Dick" Wright, to find the strike force while a bail hearing was arranged for Tipton and Smith. Some local businessmen including T.S. Harris, Virgil Earp's son-in-law, paid the required money for an appearance bond for Tipton and Smith. A judge later dismissed the charges and censured the sheriff for his actions. George Parsons wrote, "False charges. Behan will get it yet."

Meanwhile, that afternoon out in the chaparral an event that historians now record as the high-water mark of Wyatt Earp's Cow-boy Campaign transpired. Wyatt Earp's shotgun killed Cow-boy leader Curly Bill Brocius as the Cow-boy fought a face-to-face duel with the marshal at Iron Springs in the Whetstone Mountains. Earp's long-barreled pistol next wounded Milt Hicks and mortally wounded Johnny Barnes. Wyatt's courageous battle will be discussed later as we examine the Otero Letter sentence by sentence.

According to a report published in the *Silver City (NM) New Southwest and Grant County Herald* of April 29, 1882, some of the Cow-boys that survived the firefight at Iron Springs stole four mules from a Mexican herder near Calabasas, then for good measure took $200 and clothing from two Chinese cooks. The Cow-boys sent the naked Asian workers running for cover as they fired their pistols into the air. It is assumed the animals and money assisted the Cow-boys' escape to Old Mexico so they could elude a future encounter with deputy United States marshal Wyatt Earp and his strike force.

The day's *Daily Epitaph* told readers that Mrs. James Earp and Mrs. Wyatt Earp left the city to take a Southern Pacific Railroad passenger coach for Colton, California: "These ladies have the sympathy of all who knew them, and for that matter the entire community. Their trials for the last six months have been of the most severe nature." On Saturday, the *Los Angeles Herald* noted the two ladies had arrived safely at the home of the senior Earps in California.

Bessie Earp's 18-year-old daughter, Harriett "Hattie" Catchim, had married Thaddeus Stephens Harris, 26 years her senior, on February 3, 1881, so she remained in Tombstone with her husband. She would oversee that the Earp family's personal possessions were shipped to Colton or elsewhere if needed. Harris bought his father-in-law's interest in four Tombstone mining properties for $1,000 in gold coin on April 29 when it was clear that James Earp no longer intended to return to Tombstone. Hattie and her husband divorced after nine years. Hattie Catchim remarried and enjoyed life on a ranch with her husband and daughter. Ann Collier, a new generation researcher, has done yeoman service in tracking the life of this frontier lady.

Frank Catchim, Bessie Earp's son, also remained in the Tombstone area. He worked on the Snake Ranch and also drove a freight wagon for Julius Durkee. The *Epitaph* of June 7, 1891, reported that Frank Catchim and his freighting companions Morgan Hudspeth and George Thompson were attacked by Apaches near the Oso Negro Mine in Arispe, Mexico. James Earp's 27-year-old stepson died during the fight.

On **Saturday, March 25, 1882,** George Parsons told his dairy that it was "a very disagreeable day indeed," while Endicott Peabody noted that the weather was "little of all kinds of weather, chiefly clouds & thunderstorms," and George Hand called the day "cold & cloudy." He also noted, "Rain & hail nearly all day."

On Thursday, Sheriff Behan had arrested Dan Tipton and Charlie Smith and on Friday they were released from jail on bond. On Saturday Col. William Herring, Wyatt's attorney, appeared in Justice Andrew Jackson Felter's court to challenge the legality of the arrest of the two federal officers as charged in the *Territory of Arizona vs. Wyatt Earp, et al.* Herring claimed that Sheriff Behan had no legal warrant to serve on Tuesday evening, thus the county officer had no right "to legally arrest and restrain the defendants of their liberty." The justice agreed that Behan did not acquire any warrant until Wednesday, thus dismissing the case because the sheriff had no authority to arrest them on the night in question. Bond money was returned and Dan Tipton remained in town as an information resource, while Charlie Smith rejoined the federal posse.

The *Daily Nugget* reported that Sheriff Behan and his posse of "honest ranchers" arrived at Contention City, west of Tombstone, at about 8 o'clock Saturday evening. George Hand said, "Raining so hard they put their horses in stable." A report of the Earp–Cow-boy firefight at Iron Springs reached the village that claimed that Wyatt Earp had been shot. Later, according to George Hand's diary, "A man came to town 10:30 this evening to get candles, says he saw the Earp party at Drew's ranch few miles [north] from here." Wyatt Earp and his men spent the night camped about six miles north of Tombstone at Sycamore Springs.

Forrestine Hooker, John Flood, and Stuart Lake each claimed that Wyatt Earp made a final visit to Tombstone for a summit with the leadership of the Citizens' Safety Committee that rainy evening two days before Frederick A. Tritle, the new territorial governor, was to visit Tombstone. This late-night conference was held in a mine powder house on the edge of town. Forty years after the meeting, Mrs. Hooker wrote that Jonathan N. Thacker, Wells Fargo chief special officer, was present and confirmed the company's full support of Earp's actions. An entry in the Wells Fargo & Company's Cash Book for April 1882 clearly shows that Thacker paid Wyatt Earp for his expenses in killing Frank Stilwell and Curly Bill Brocius.

During the core of the conference, Col. William Herring, Wyatt's attorney, advised Earp to suspend his Cow-boy Campaign. He suggested a two-part action plan. First, Wyatt would take his posse and leave Arizona Territory and allow the political furor to subside. Second, Wyatt's supporters would have time to assess Earp's legal options and devise strategy to keep him, and by extension his posse, out of jail or from execution if found guilty of murder. Following much discussion, Wyatt Earp reluctantly agreed to Herring's request with a big stipulation. He could use the time the conspirators needed to construct the escape plan and arrange asylum to conduct a final sweeping search for Cow-boys. This proviso was accepted and his supporters assured Wyatt that he and his posse would receive all the assistance they would need, including financial support, to reach a safe sanctuary.

Herring and other attorneys on the Citizen's Safety Committee set about reviewing the rule of common law and the territorial and federal statutes to design a plan to secure the continued freedom of Wyatt and his men. In 52 BC, the Roman lawyer and philosopher Marcus Tullius Cicero made a speech in a Roman court later printed as *Pro Milone*. In this defense brief, Cicero postulated the legal doctrine *inter arma enim silent leges*, translated "in times of war [insurrection], the law falls silent." In 1861, United States Supreme Court chief justice Roger Taney broadly ruled that Cicero's doctrine meant that in troubled times the safety of the people becomes the supreme law, thus trumping the written law. Cicero also set forth another legal principle still used in tort cases, *res ipsa loquiter*, interpreted to mean the court should let the facts speak for themselves. The lawyers had their justifiable foundation if Wyatt Earp was ever arrested and brought to trial.

The news would not reach Tombstone until Sunday, when George Parsons noted, "Another murder and this time of a most startling nature." About 8:30 p.m. on Saturday evening Martin Ruter Peel, a deputy U.S. mineral surveyor, was shot and killed by two men in his office in the Tombstone Mill and Mining Company facility located at Millville across the river from Charleston. Many believed the killing was a botched robbery attempt by Cow-boys seeking money to escape the wrath of Wyatt Earp. George Parsons, who knew Peel and attended his funeral and graveside services, believed it had been "possibly an attempt at theft and perhaps simply thirst for gore on account of [the] attitude of [his]company against the outlaw element." Judge Peel would later make a strong challenge for citizens to support the law and order faction in ridding the county of the criminal element that plagued the region

Martin Peel's father was an attorney and served as the first probate court judge for Cochise County. Judge Bryant L. Peel wrote an open letter "To the People of Tombstone" saying, " Perhaps I am not in a condition to express a clear, deliberate opinion, but I would like to say to the good people of Cochise County there is one of three things you have to do. There is a class of cut-throats among you and you can never convict them in court. You must combine and protect yourselves and wipe them out or you must give up the country to them, or you will be murdered one at a time, as my son has been."

The *Daily Epitaph* reported that John Henry Jackson, the miner so many Tombstone citizens wanted to be appointed deputy United States marshal for their area replacing the Earps, was still gold prospecting near Victorio, New Mexico Territory. He had been out of Tombstone since March 18 and was not expected to return anytime soon.

On **Sunday, March 26, 1882**, Endicott Peabody noted the day had "tremendous wind blowing the dust in fast bands & making it most uncomfortable" in Tombstone. George Hand called the day "very windy. Quite cold this evening."

Mrs. Clara Spalding Brown, a special correspondent writing from Tombstone, told readers of the Sunday edition of the *San Diego Daily Union* her impressions of Wyatt Earp's efforts. She was adamant in contradicting the Cow-boy propaganda about the Earp brothers' aggressions. Brown said she would "bear witness that it was not the Earps who first disturbed this quiet [in Tombstone], and that their criminal actions since have been from the determination to avenge the murder of a dearly beloved brother. I do not present this as sufficient excuse for their conduct, or approve any act contrary to law; but there are certainly extenuating circumstances to be taken into consideration."

In his diary recording life at Contention City, George Hand seems to provide additional data about that morning: "The sheriff party left, struck the trail of the Earp party a few miles below town, returning toward Tombstone and followed it." John Behan could not locate the Earp posse anywhere in Tombstone, but he found Pima County sheriff Bob Paul still in town continuing his investigation into the killing of Frank Stilwell.

After a short early-morning ride, Wyatt Earp's federal posse was joined by six prospectors headed for the Winchester District and they all shared a frugal breakfast. After they ate, the small group continued northward to Dragoon Summit Station along the railroad. The Tombstone miners continued on and the federal posse ate lunch and awaited the passenger train from the west. At about 1:00 p.m. Wyatt Earp told Conductor Smith that he wished to search the eastbound Southern Pacific passenger train stopped at the station. The *Los Angles Daily Times* of March 27 noted that "after passing through the cars [the posse] mounted their horses and started in the direction of the mountains." One of the posse wrote the *Daily Epitaph* that they had expected to find "a friendly messenger" on that train. Future events would suggest that deputy United States marshal Wyatt Earp might have expected to visit with a special envoy from the Wells Fargo Express Company corporate office.

Late Sunday afternoon, the Earp posse arrived at the Percy Ranch headquarters to rest their horses and request refreshments for man and beast. The federal posse left the ranch after dark when the moon had come up because Hugh and Jim Percy feared retaliation from the Cow-boys if the federal officers spent the night at their place. The Earp posse camped that cold night about a mile north of the Henderson Ranch in a grassy meadow.

Days later, Cochise County deputy sheriff Frank Hereford, who had hidden in a corncrib on the Percy Ranch while the federal officers were relaxing, told reporters that from his "vantage point" he saw that Wyatt exhibited visible signs of "a couple of ugly flesh wounds in the region of the breasts and shoulders." Many historians have questioned that "observation." George Parsons, in an entry dated August 9, 1881, in his daily journal, wrote, "Frank Hereford the fairy."

Take note that Benjamin Hereford, a Tucson attorney, was a brother-in-law and business associate of Governor Tritle. In 1882, Hereford's son Frank served as one of Sheriff Behan's deputies and hid from Wyatt Earp and his men during the Cow-boy Campaign. It is uncertain whether the governor and young Hereford saw each other during Tritle's fact-finding visit to Tombstone. Later, Frank Hereford became Tritle's personal secretary. Benjamin Hereford was a law partner with James Zabriskie. Wyatt recommended the law firm to Curly Bill Brocius after he arrested him for killing Fred White, Tombstone's town marshal, in October 1880.

On **Monday, March 27, 1882,** Endicott Peabody pronounced the day "well nigh perfect." Diarist George Parsons noted in his daily journal that it was "a pleasant day," while in his Contention City quarters, George Hand seemed to recall a different type of day in the San Pedro River valley: "Cold, clear morning. Cold all day."

Fredrick A. Tritle, the newly sworn territorial governor, arrived in Contention City via a train at 11:00 a.m. and took a stagecoach on to Tombstone for a personal on-site assessment of the "insurrection" in Cochise County. This visit was just nine days after Morgan Earp's ambush murder in Tombstone, seven days after Frank Stilwell's killing in Tucson, five days following Florentino Cruz's execution at South Pass, and three days after Curly Bill's bloody death and the wounding of other Cow-boys at Iron Springs.

William Murray, Governor Tritle's former business partner, and Milton Clapp, a wealthy Tombstone banker, escorted Governor Tritle around town to visit with town leaders and other citizens. Mr. Peabody commented to his diary, "Gov. pleasant but somewhat commonplace." Murray and Clapp were both leaders of the Citizens' Safety Committee and Earp supporters. The governor spent the night as Milton Clapp's houseguest. An enthusiastic public reception was held for the governor Tuesday night with much handshaking. George Parsons called this "muscle business" taking place. The ladies enjoyed the social event.

In the predawn light of this cold Monday, Wyatt's posse broke camp and rode northward towards Col. Henry Hooker's 800-square-mile Sierra Bonita Ranch. The headquarters was about 30 miles north of Wilcox a few miles inside Graham County. It is important to note that, while Wyatt Earp's federal posse had authority to function within Graham County, Sheriff John Behan possessed no authority to function in Graham County.

Marshal Earp and his federal posse reached the Sierra Bonita Ranch in the afternoon. Wyatt felt the ranch headquarters was a place safe from attack by the Cow-boys or a posse of "honest ranchers," so he and his men could relax for a few hours. Here their host provided some refreshments for the possemen and grain for their horses.

Henry Hooker was the leader of the regional livestock association, so Marshal Earp provided him a briefing of the posse's actions against the Cow-boys since his brother's murder. The *Daily Nugget* would later claim that during this meeting Hooker paid Wyatt bounty money from the local ranchers for killing Curly Bill, but the facts do not support the accusation. The reward payment claim has a hollow ring when it is recalled the newspaper always denied that Wyatt Earp killed their friend, who had been Johnny Behan's special deputy sheriff used for tax collecting duty among the Cow-boy confederation.

Wyatt Earp later said that while visiting with the cattle baron he took his first drink of hard liquor since his first wife and their baby's death in Missouri over a decade earlier.[3]

Around seven o'clock that evening, the rested Earp posse left the Hooker ranch with fresh, well-bred horses provided by the rancher from his breeding herd in exchange for their tired mounts. The posse made no effort to hide their trail and camped under the stars on Reiley Hill. The hill was a virtual fortress centered within a vast stretch of flat rangeland located about two miles from the Hooker ranch headquarters compound. A few years later, soldiers from Fort Grant used the hill as a signal corps post. Today, stone walls mark the campsite.

The *Daily Nugget* reported that Dan Tipton left the city on the 5:00 o'clock morning stage for Benson for connection with the train east headed to Wilcox. Tipton was planning to rejoin Wyatt Earp's federal strike force camped near Hooker's Ranch. He was carrying $1,000 from mining giant E.B. Gage to help cover the posse's expenses.

On **Tuesday, March 28, 1882,** Tombstone's Episcopal pastor was happy with the weather: "Like yesterday—only more so." George Parsons called the weather a "fine day." George Hand recalled this Tuesday as a "cold morning, clear & very pleasant" out in the Cochise County countryside.

Governor Frederick Tritle was in good spirits as he issued a strong statement of support for the overall effort to rid southeastern Arizona of the Cow-boy menace. Tritle sent a message to President Chester A. Arthur requesting more federal assistance in the effort against the Cow-boys. He next requested U.S. marshal Dake to send an additional federal marshal's posse out with orders to complete the job of rounding up the Cow-boys begun by Wyatt Earp and his men.

As an addendum to the main event, the *Daily Nugget* of May 10, 1882, published a letter to the editor from deputy U.S. marshal John H. Jackson, leader of the Tombstone rangers sent to clean up behind Wyatt Earp's posse, who had returned after weeks searching Cochise County for any sign of the Cow-boys or raiding Indians without any success. Jackson's posse found a peaceful countryside during its 400-mile ride and believed that the Cow-boys had fled the county or been killed by Wyatt Earp's federal marshal's strike force.

The *Los Angles Times* published a lengthy interview with James Earp. Wyatt's older brother claimed that in Tombstone "business is dull, and lots of men are idle." James compared Tombstone to Los Angeles—"like jumping from a coal pit into a parlor"— and said the only thing that had kept the brothers in Tombstone was their vast mining property claims. He told the reporter the brothers "have by hard work and close attention to business acquired many thousands dollars worth of property, having one claim next to the Bizner Mine, for which they refused an offer of $16,000." James also claimed Wyatt would "fight it out to the bitter end."

On this Tuesday morning, Sheriff Behan and his 21-member "posse of honest ranchers, including men like Johnny Ringo and Finn Clanton," road into Henry Hooker's Ranch demanding breakfast, refreshments for their horses, and directions to find the Earp posse. One source says that Hooker told Sheriff Behan the Earp posse was camped on Reiley Hill. Following a heated verbal exchange, the sheriff's group left Hooker's Ranch headed not toward Reiley Hill but north toward the army command at Fort Grant.

At Fort Grant, Sheriff John Behan, operating out of his jurisdiction in Graham County, offered to rent the services of Indian scouts to track Earp's federal posse and to rent a cannon and men to attack the federal posse's camp on Reiley Hill.

Author's Perspective: Strange that Sheriff Behan should have needed Indian scouts to find Wyatt Earp, yet knew exactly where he wanted the army to take its cannon. Sheriff Behan returned to Tombstone without his foe. Sol Israel, who operated Tombstone's largest news and book shop, knew both John Behan and Wyatt Earp and once expressed this assessment: "As to Johnnie Behan, he was afraid of his own shadow."

It is worth posing the question of Sheriff Behan's motive in requesting the Indian trackers. Had Behan hoped to force the federal marshals into firing upon the Indian scouts so he could later claim that Wyatt Earp had assaulted federal troops? Did Johnny Behan think he could use this "hostile" action as a provocation to force the United States Army into helping him capture the federal marshal's posse? These questions could be some good discussion topics for attendees at the annual Tombstone Territory Rendezvous held in the old mining camp.

On **Wednesday, March 29, 1882,** the Reverend Peabody found the day "as glorious a day as could be imagined." Countryside diarest George Hand called the day simply "cold."

The new Graham County sheriff, George H. Stevens, operating from his office in Safford, was informed that Wyatt Earp's federal posse was working in his jurisdiction, but he wisely exhibited no interest in interjecting himself into any effort to impede Marshal Earp's campaign against the Cow-boys. However, Sheriff Stevens was not happy with Sheriff Behan's invading his jurisdiction without notifying him or seeking his permission or assistance.

The record is vague concerning Wyatt Earp's action on Wednesday, but it would seem this is when they observed Behan's posse riding all around the area seeking a way to attack the federal officers without endangering themselves. Finally, the Cow-boy posse rode back south toward Tombstone.

On **Thursday, March 30, 1882,** George Parsons announced it was "beautiful weather now" and it was "still beautiful" in Tombstone, according to Endicott Peabody. George Hand noted this Thursday was a "fine morning—cool."

George Parsons wrote in his *Private Journal* this simple comment: "14 murders and assassinations in ten days." The mining man did not claim that all of these deaths should be credited to the actions of Wyatt Earp's posse, just that a large number of men had met a quick death in such a short time.

The Earp posse left the Reiley Hill site and moved north to within five miles of Eureka Springs, camped with a freighter named Barney Norton and enjoyed a good meal and pleasant company. Later, the posse stopped at the Cottonwood stage station for supplies. They now established a base camp along Cottonwood Creek in a canyon on the west side of the Graham Mountains about 10 miles north of the Sierra Bonita Ranch of Henry Hooker. The federal officers used this camp when they were not on an overnight raid seeking the Cow-boys in their Cochise County hideouts.

On **Friday, March 31, 1882,** the weather in Tombstone was "glorious—warmer, therm[ometer] must have been 80 in middle of day," according to the Reverend Peabody's diary entry for the day.

Within days of starting his bloody campaign against the Cow-boys, deputy U.S. marshal Wyatt Earp discovered that some of his top-tier quarry had escaped Arizona Territory to hide in Fronteras, in the State of Sonora, Mexico, until conditions were more favorable for their return. Wyatt contacted the Mexican federal police in Sonora to tell them to watch for Cow-boys in their area. "Apache Hank" Swilling (some contemporary accounts referred to him as a half-breed) was arrested on March 24. It is unclear how many days he was held in the Cochise County jail by Sheriff Behan, but he was given a 20-day sentence at his trial.

Tombstone historian Roy Young claims, citing accounts of the day, that Hank Swilling died near Fronteras, Mexico, while robbing a trading post; others have claimed he was killed while resisting arrest. In his May 14, 1893, interview given to a reporter for the *Denver Republican*, deputy marshal Wyatt Earp mentioned Swilling: "With a younger brother of mine [Warren], Doc Holliday and the others, I set out on horseback for a ranch, where I knew Apache Hank was staying. When we rode away from that ranch, Apache Hank was dead." Something similar happened to "Babacomari Frank" Patterson, a second-tier range rider whose ranch served as Curly Bill's final resting place.

In the day's issue of the *Los Angeles Express* a letter writer expressed this opinion: "It seems that the Earps believed that the sheriff and party were exceedingly friendly with the cowboys, and it is certain the sheriff made no effort to detect the murderers of (Morgan) Earp."

Also, the *Los Angles Herald* quoted a Tombstone visitor concerning Wyatt Earp and the report that he and his posse had left for Albuquerque: "This gentleman expressed the opinion that the Earps were 'blooded' and 'nervy' to the last degree. He rejected the idea of a retreat and thinks that the Earp brothers will fight the thing to the bitter end, and are likely to re-appear very suddenly in Tombstone, to the consternation of their enemies." The article noted that the only Cow-boy the Earp posse "held in high estimation is Ringgo [*sic*]." The account concluded: "Whatever else may be said of them (the Cow-boys), it cannot be charged that they are inactive for long periods."

In another section of the *Herald* it was noted that "Sheriff Paul, Tucson," had arrived in Los Angles on the Southern Pacific.

During the **first week of April 1882,** in Tombstone "the Moon was too full to sleep with comfort," while it was cool and windy during the day, according to George Parsons.

The Earp posse was so active during this period scholars may never be able to sort out the extent of this campaign. Official reports suggest that sometime during these first eight days of April the Arizona lawmen encountered Col. Albert Fountain and his New Mexico militiamen, who were also chasing the border Cow-boys in that territory. This is an area of the law enforcement campaign against the border Cow-boys that has yet to be fully explored by historians.

Sunday, April 2, 1882, was another night with a "moon too full to sleep with comfort," according to George Parsons. Parson Peabody noted that the Sunday afternoon temperature was in the 90s.

The *Los Angles Times* published a page two update on "The Arizona Troubles": "The recent outbreaks that have taken place, every one of a desperate and bloody nature, have given the city [of Tombstone] an unenviable notoriety abroad, and given the citizens over an immense stretch of country, a feeling of terror that is now bearing legitimate fruit in the prostration of business, driving away men of means and energy; turning back the tide of immigration of those who were seeking avenues for investment.... An appalling stream of blood has marked the course of these outlaws over a large portion of the country and their deeds of villainy have been heralded everywhere and is paralyzing all enterprise."

Monday, April 3, 1882, in Tombstone, the Reverend Peabody recalled was a cool and overcast day, while in the river valley George Hand said the day was "cold, cloudy, windy, dusty."

Murder charges against Pete Spencer for Morgan Earp's death were dismissed and Sheriff Johnny Behan released him from protective custody. Late in 1882, Spencer settled in Georgetown, New Mexico, where he served as a Grant County deputy sheriff until he killed a man and was sentenced to prison. On December 12, 1894, the *Silver City Eagle* reported, "Pete Spencer, who is well known in this section, was pardoned out of the Yuma penitentiary recently." He died of pneumonia in 1914.

Tuesday, April 4, 1882, was another cold day with a clear sky.

Many of the nation's larger newspapers carried press association dispatches and pictures concerned with the murder of Jesse James at his St. Joseph, Missouri, home the day before. The infamous bank and train robber had been killed by one of his own men seeking a promised gubernatorial pardon and state reward money.

It was noted by the *Albuquerque Evening Review*, on Wednesday, that none of the Arizona exchange newspapers had carried any account of "cow-boy murders" today. "The territory is evidently falling behind," it opined.

Wednesday, April 5, 1882, was "cold" in the countryside where the Earp posse was living, while in Tombstone it was "cool & clear."

When readers of the *Daily Epitaph* opened their newspaper they saw a letter from "One of them" in the Earp posse detailing the actions of the federal marshals since they left Tombstone on March 25. The letter was written on a couple of sheets of lined ledger paper and had been mailed from Wilcox on April 4. Some historians have given Doc Holliday credit for the composition due to his advanced education. However, I believe Wyatt Earp was very capable of having been the author. Earp was well read and certainly understood the subject, while Doc most likely contributed the jabbing humor.

Thursday, April 6, 1882, was a "cold morning. Windy, very dusty all day," according to George Hand's diary entry.

The *Albuquerque Evening Review* noted, "Affairs in Tombstone are in bad condition. A reign of terror exists; there are no competent officers and the citizens cowed are ridden over rough-shod by the lawless element."

Friday, April 7, 1882, was a cool day in Tombstone and "cold, windy & dusty" in the countryside, according to George Hand's personal diary. George Parsons noted in his private journal, "Killing business over for present."

The evening train from the East brought William T. Sherman, the commanding general of the United States Army, with his wife and General Orlando B. Wilcox, commander of the army's Department of Arizona, and other members of the official party to Benson. The group reached Contention City, via the spur railroad line from Benson, at 5:00 p.m. George Hand noted in his daily diary that General Sherman's party "remained only long enough for a few hand shakes and left for Tombstone" in a special stagecoach. Hand settled in for the evening to read the two issues of the *Spirit of the Times* sporting magazine he had received in the day's mail.

Saturday, April 8, 1882, was a very unpleasant day to be camped out in the mountains.

General Sherman visited privately with Tombstone's business leaders and that evening the Sherman party attended a public reception at Schieffelin Hall. George Parsons told his diary, "The toadying was sickening by many...." While the grownups hobnobbed, the youngsters enjoyed the huge bonfire built to welcome the general to Tombstone.

Tucson's *Arizona Daily Star* republished a report from the *Daily Nugget* from a man who had visited Wyatt Earp's camp in Graham County. The gentleman from Dos Cabesas said, "Wyatt Earp says if the Sheriff of Cochise county wants him he can always find him at his camp. They are represented as being well supplied with money and food, which is furnished by friends of the fugitives." He also noted, "They have chosen a position from which it would be extremely difficult to dislodge them, and have announced their intention of remaining there, for some time at least."

Easter Sunday, April 9, 1882, continued to be "cold, windy and dusty" in southeastern Arizona, according to the entry George Hand made in his diary.

In nature the mountain pine tree starts new growth about two weeks before Easter. By the time this celebration occurs most of the pines will have developed small yellow crosses on the tallest new shoots. Did Wyatt take notice of this Christian symbol of resurrection during his ride across Cochise County? Did he recall Morgan's fascination with spiritualism, the afterlife, and their many discussions on the subject?

United States marshal Crawley Dake had been asking the Department of Justice to provide him more funding so he could combat the Cow-boy troubles in southern Arizona. Unknown to anyone locally, special agent S.R. Martin of the Department of Justice, who was in Cochise County quietly investigating the depth of the Cow-boy problem, wrote his confidential report to attorney general Benjamin H. Brewster on this date. Martin wrote that deputy U.S. marshal Wyatt Earp and his small band of deputies had been very active for months and had killed a number of Cow-boys and were now working from a secret base in the mountains somewhere around Tombstone. From the style of his report, special agent Martin seems to have done his investigative job very well. He seems to have approved of the marshal's actions.

General Sherman left Tombstone in an army ambulance to travel to Fort Huachuca.

Endicott Peabody had 150 people at his Easter morning service held in the district courtroom and the chamber was decorated with many fresh cut flowers. The evening service was attended by 110 persons. George Parsons said, "Beautiful flowers and impressive services morning and evening. Best singing I've heard since leaving San Francisco. I had to go and get extra seats."

Monday, April 10, 1882, was a "fine day—cool & clear" in Tombstone, according to the diary entry made by Endicott Peabody. George Hand called the weather "cold, very windy & very dusty" in the remote countryside.

Further east, across the Sulphur Springs Valley, Wyatt and his posse were following a tip and were busy searching waterholes in the Swisshelms Mountains looking for Johnny Ringo. The outlaw slipped Earp's dragnet this time, but months later Wyatt returned to Arizona and finished the job. We'll discuss this in detail in a later chapter that examines the Otero Letter.

Wyatt Earp's fatigued strike force spent another cold night camped along Cottonwood Creek. The posse had been conducting their campaign for almost a month now and Earp knew that the mission's timeline was reaching a termination point.

On **Tuesday, April 11, 1882,** George Hand stayed in his cabin at Contention City all day, as he told his diary the day was "cold, windy." The Reverend Peabody noted the day as viewed from Tombstone had a "lovely sun set."

A messenger brought Wyatt Earp much needed money and directions from his supporters. They had devised a sanctuary plan that required Wyatt's federal posse to be in Deming, New Mexico. on Sunday afternoon to take the Santa Fe's evening train to Albuquerque. They also learned that Cow-boy supporters had spies stationed at Lordsburg searching for them, so the strike force needed to find a discreet way to circumvent that area.

General Sherman filed a report to attorney general Benjamin H. Brewster, in his official dispatch, giving the new head of the Department of Justice his support for Governor Tritle's plan to field a strong posse against the Cow-boys.

Wednesday, April 12, 1882, was "windy & rather cold" in the area around Tombstone, while the weather in southern Graham County was "cold. Quite windy & cold all day."

Deputy United States marshal Wyatt Earp and his fatigued posse left the Hooker Ranch and headed up-country to Fort Grant. Major General Orlando B. Wilcox, commander of the army's military Department of Arizona, had instructed his officers to supported United States marshal C.P. Dake's efforts to rid Arizona Territory of the Cow-boys and ordered his staff officers, with General W.T. Sherman's approval, to render necessary equipment, aid, supplies, or horses to Marshal Dake's federal deputies led by Wyatt Earp.

At the army encampment, Wyatt posted a letter to his sister Adelia Edwards in

California. This letter was sent to her so anyone who might be screening the mail would not suspect it was a letter from Wyatt. In his letter to his sister he enclosed a notarized deed-letter to his father. Wyatt used this means to deed his ten remaining mining claims, 12-town lots, 20 acres of farm land on the Babacomari River, and extensive water rights claims (water sold for three cents a gallon in Tombstone) to hold in trust. Wyatt was being a prudent businessman and may have also been apprehensive about his future— a murder trial, prison or death.

According to the *Daily Epitaph* of December 12, 1885, Nicholas Earp paid the taxes on the Earp brothers' investment property for a few years until the bottom dropped out of Tombstone's mining market, then the properties were confiscated for past due taxes. It would take two more decades before Wyatt's dream of financial success became a reality, but he had to journey to the "Last Frontier" in Alaska to accomplish this goal.

Earp conferred with Colonel James Biddle, who conveniently ignored the outstanding murder warrants for the federal officer and his posse. Biddle provided the posse with a hot meal and offered them fresh mounts before allowing them to slip away into the night as fugitives from Arizona justice. The posse spent a cold night camped a few miles east of the post. Biddle had already demonstrated a pro–Earp stance on March 28 when he refused Sheriff Behan's request to purchase the assistance of army Indian scouts to track the Earp posse or the use of a field artillery piece to blast the federal officers off of Reiley Hill on the Hooker Ranch.

> **Author's Perspective:** Without documentation it can only be speculation, but Wyatt Earp's action in divesting himself from ownership in his Tombstone properties could suggest he was taking legal precautions, suggested by his lawyer, against future action by bond holders and other creditors who might wish to claim his property as payment for a civil court judgment for his extralegal actions.
>
> Another possibility for the legal action with his property is that Wyatt was considering not reestablishing life with his estranged wife, Mattie, when his suspected legal battles had been concluded. Wyatt supported Mattie Blaylock for a period after she returned to Arizona to start a new life without him. Some Earp detractors claim the split between Wyatt and Mattie was spousal desertion on Wyatt's part when he did not go to California to claim her, Allie Earp claimed Mattie deserted Wyatt to join Kate Holliday in Globe.

On **Thursday, April 13, 1882**, around Tombstone the weather was "fine, cold. Much colder tonight," as noted by Endicott Peabody. Outside of the Tombstone area George Hand wrote that the weather was "cold, windy & dull." The Earp posse spent the day traveling northeast across country headed toward New Mexico. Due to mountain ranges, the men moved along river beds and canyons until they reached the drainage for Mule Creek, an entry through the mountains into the Land of Enchantment from the west. So great was the concern about the location of the Earp posse that on May 10, 1882, the *Weekly Nugget* was reporting that Wyatt had been seen near the Hooker Ranch "last week." Two weeks later, the paper's print facility was destroyed in the city's second major business district fire and the paper never published again.

When General William T. Sherman's train stopped in Colton, California, on this date the wounded Virgil Earp was one of the men who greeted him at the station. The *Los Angles Herald* of April 15 reported that during their short exchange Virgil requested that Sherman investigate the Cow-boy troubles in Tombstone during his visit in Arizona Territory and also ask the new president to continue supporting the effort to suppress the Cow-boys. Virgil told Sherman if he should need to visit with him in the future he would always be available. "For this the General thanked Earp, and said that it was his intention to look into the (Cow-boy) matter."

Friday, April 14, 1882, was highlighted by "high wind blowing & really uncomfortably cold" weather in Tombstone, according to Pastor Peabody. George Parsons wrote in his journal, "wind—very." George Hand felt the day was "cold & windy. Quite dusty day."

According to Saturday's issue of the *Daily Epitaph*, Wells Fargo's general superintendent John J. Valentine, traveling in his private coach on the Southern Pacific line, stopped on Friday at Benson to pick up the express company's special agent Lou Cooley, who also worked on the H.C. Hooker Ranch, for an update briefing on the action plan of the Earp posse. Valentine stopped at Wilcox to offload Cooley with expense money and a message for Earp. Valentine continued on east toward New Albuquerque and a projected meeting with Deputy Marshal Wyatt Earp. Sheriff Behan, who had been tipped about the Valentine–Cooley meeting in Benson, was personally in Wilcox to arrest Cooley "for aiding and abetting the Earps" and to collect arrest and mileage fees. Lou Cooley was escorted back to Tombstone by Sheriff Behan and his Wilcox deputy (more mileage fees) and jailed. Justice Wells Spicer heard the complaint and dismissed the charge since in the arrest warrant issued by Justice A.E. Fay Sheriff Behan did not

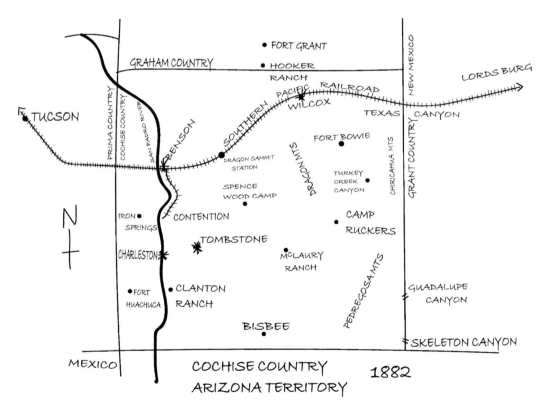

Map by Alexis Diaz.

specify the nature of the alleged aid Mr. Cooley provided. "Any man with a grain of common sense will see that the arrest and detention of American citizens upon such frivolous charges puts every man at the mercy of an officer who has any animosity or ill-will towards him," said the *Daily Epitaph*. Cooley eventually sued for his false detention and Sheriff Behan's misconduct became another barroom joke in Tombstone.

Meanwhile, late in the afternoon, Wyatt Earp's special strike force entered New Mexico Territory. The posse's extended hit-and-run campaign had badly crippled the loose-knit Cow-boy confederacy during what national newspapers and historians would soon be calling the Vendetta Ride. But Johnny Ringo still lived. In 1907, Bat Masterson wrote about the events of Wyatt Earp's bloody sortie but left his closing statement vague by saying, "This ended the Earp campaign in Arizona for the time being." It would seem that Mr. Masterson might have intentionally left a lot unsaid.

Author's Perspective: How many Cow-boys died during Deputy Marshal Wyatt Earp's 1882 spring campaign against the Cow-boys? The truth of that number may never be known, but two accounts published shortly after the events give the number as fewer than ten. On May 23, 1882, the *Ford County Globe* of Dodge City published a letter from Ed Colborn, an attorney friend of Wyatt's from Dodge City days, containing information learned in his "absorbing" conversations with Wyatt at Trinidad, Colorado. The judge wrote that since "the assassination of Morgan Earp they [Wyatt and his posse] have handed seven cow boys 'over to the majority.'" He went on to say, "From what I could learn, the Earps have killed all, or nearly all of the leaders of the element of cow boys, who number in all about 150, and the troubles in Arizona will so far as they are concerned, be over."

The *National Police Gazette* of July 21, 1883, reported on Wyatt's deadly Cow-boy cleanup saying, "In the terrible encounter which ensued he killed not less than eight of the assassins." In the year between these two published reports concerning the number of Cow-boys killed the count grew from seven to eight because the national magazine's total included John Ringo, who was killed two months after the Dodge City account was published.

A few points are clear about the deadly events that transpired during the spring 1882 Cow-boy campaign. First, deputy United States marshal Wyatt Earp was a determined and charismatic leader and he produced what Napoleon called "four o'clock in the morning courage" in his posse as they faced impossible odds. Second, the Cow-boys killed during the seek-and-destroy campaign died facing their executioner and not from a bullet in the back or from ambush during the cover of night. Third, his deeds would suggest that Wyatt Earp believed in *lex talionis*, a Latin term for the ancient "law of retaliation," even if he might have been unfamiliar with the legal phrase.

Wyatt made two statements concerning the seek-and-destroy mission he led against the Cow-boys. In one, using Shakespearean imagery, he defended the Cow-boy deaths: "We didn't kill none of the wrong men like Hamlet done to poor old Polonius." Wyatt's second comment is very revealing: "It takes a resolute man not to make mistakes when he gets to acting as his own law." It would seem that Wyatt Earp believed he made no mistakes.

Over a half-century after Wyatt Earp rode across Arizona Territory carrying his crusade into Cow-boy country, a real battlefield general expressed what Earp might have felt. "A good plan violently executed now is better than a perfect plan next week," wrote General George S. Patton, Jr., in his book *War as I Knew It*. It is unclear to this day whether Wyatt really developed a methodical assault on the Cow-boys or just rode out into the countryside counting on dumb luck. Either way, Wyatt Earp found his war and he made it swift, violent, terror-filled, and bloody.

<h1 style="text-align:center">10</h1>

Good-Bye, Tombstone

> For my handling of the situation at Tombstone, I have no regrets. Were it to be done over again, I would do exactly as I did at the time. If the outlaws and their friends and allies imagined that they could intimidate or exterminate the Earps by a process of assassination, and then hide behind alibis and technicalities of the law, they simply missed their guess.—*Wyatt Earp: Frontier Marshal*, Wyatt Earp as quoted by Stuart N. Lake, 1931

Josie Earp wrote in her memoirs about Tombstone: "Evil rises up out of the ground there." Even with that understanding, she had trouble accepting her husband's bloody deeds and in later years she tried to soften his killer image: "Wyatt was a nature that harbored no ill feeling toward anyone, even persons who had done him real injury." This belief became truer as the years added distance to the Tombstone saga. Josie wrote that Wyatt "had learned that revenge is NOT sweet. This attitude of his I could not at first understand but as the years passed I came to share the feeling to an increasing extent until today [the late 1930s] I do not find it in my heart to hate anyone." She may not have hated anyone, but she disliked a few people she felt mistreated her husband.

Whatever moral or tactical deficiencies Wyatt Earp's sanguinary campaign functioned under, it delivered an enormous psychological blow to the Cow-boys. The fallout would shadow Wyatt Earp for the next forty-seven years and lives today as part of his mystic legend.

Actus non facit reum, nisi mens sit rea

The Latin legal maxim *Actus non facit reum, nisi mens sit rea* means that the act is not criminal unless the intent of the act was criminal. Members of Wyatt Earp's posse believed their actions against the Cow-boys were justified under the unwritten Code of the West. They each believed that they would, if needed, receive a presidential pardon for their "extralegal" actions against the Cow-boys. Wyatt had told a reporter for the *Albuquerque Evening Review* of May 13, 1882, that he had come to town "to escape persecution while awaiting the results of an effort being made by Governor Tritle to secure their pardon from the president." Wyatt also mentioned a pardon to a *Gunnison Daily*

News-Democrat reporter in early June 1882. Doc Holliday had discussed his expected pardon deal in May while he was in a Denver jail awaiting an extradition hearing to return him to Arizona on a murder charge.

I have been unable to locate any official written documentation to support the concept that President Chester A. Arthur had agreed to pardon Wyatt Earp and his posse for any crime committed while operating as federal officers in a campaign to restore law and order in southeastern Arizona. Such an action, however, would not have been out of character for Chester Arthur. Such official proof may yet exist lying misfiled (just as Frank Warner Angel's special reports on the misconduct of the combatants during New Mexico's Lincoln County War did for decades) among some miscellaneous government department records. It is a historic tragedy, but about two weeks before his death from Bright's disease former President Arthur fell into a state of depression over his worsening health and ordered all of his private papers burned. There have been hours of discussion among historians speculating about what might have been lost with the destruction of Arthur's personal archives. In the context of this work we must ask if there was any information concerning the Earps or the Cow-boys in these lost papers.

For over three months deputy United States marshal Wyatt Earp had been campaigning against the Cow-boys. The last four weeks he conducted a series of raids on every known Cow-boy rendezvous site and camp in the Huachuca, the Whetstone, the Mule, the Dragoon, the Chiricahua, the Swisshelms, and the Peloncillo mountains. The Earp posse rode day and night across the San Simon Valley and the Sulphur Springs Valley and checked in on activities at Charleston, Galeyville, and San Simon. They killed or scattered the Cow-boys in a half a dozen firefights. Wyatt Earp and his men now suffered from battle fatigue. Nevertheless, the deputy federal marshal was prepared to shoulder the political fallout from his strike force raids, but his supporters were unwilling to let him stand alone. Some of these political and financial moguls spoke publicly in support of Wyatt Earp's extralegal actions, while others worked quietly behind the action front to protect the men who conducted the "black-ops" missions.

Among these conspirators were powerful leaders within the national Republican Party; the management of the Wells Fargo Express Company; the leadership of the Southern Pacific Railroad and the Atchison, Topeka and Santa Fe Railroad systems; and some major southwestern mining consortium investors. The governors of the State of Colorado, Arizona Territory, New Mexico Territory, and the Mexican state of Sonora were in accord to end the reign of the Cow-boy raiders. Circumstances seem to suggest that President Chester A. Arthur had a general knowledge of this cabal and supported the effort to rid the southwest territories of the Cow-boy menace by allowing the army to lend supplies to the effort.

In a footnote to chapter one of his enhanced version of Josie Marcus's autobiography, Glenn Boyer presents an intriguing idea. He suggests that by the end of March 1882 Wyatt had planned to end the Cow-boy hunt and slip over the border into New Mexico, making Silver City his headquarters "while the heat over his Arizona killings died down." Boyer also suggested that Wyatt planned to have Miss Marcus, his secret "girlfriend," join him in Silver City as soon as she could "leave Tombstone undetected, and, without leading his enemies to him."

The fly in this honey pot scenario was the bad timing of a renegade Apache raid out of Mexico aimed at encouraging Arizona's reservation Apaches to leave their confinement and join their brothers in killing Mexicans and Americanos. Border newspapers covered the raid as front-page stories. Boyer speculates that the Apache raid caused Josie to alter her plans after she left Tombstone. Instead of risking her life in attempting to cross the trail of the Apache raiders, Wyatt's conspirator put her on a train to her parents' home in California. Josie describes such an Apache raid in her manuscript, but untrue to historical fact she places the adventure in December 1879 as part of the Pauline Markham theatrical troupe's Prescott, Arizona, trip. Josie mentions meeting the famous army scout Al Sieber during the raid scare; army reports indicate that the scout was seeking Apache raiders along the Arizona–New Mexico border in the spring of 1882. It is also a fact that Sieber and Bob Paul were tracking three Mexican stage robbers in the Prescott area in December 1879.

To believe the Wyatt–Josie rendezvous idea one would first have to believe that Wyatt and Josie had developed more than a casual acquaintanceship during their stay in Tombstone. Disregarding the fictionalized work of Frank Waters and Glenn Boyer, none of the Earp women, including Virgil's wife, Allie, who was a close friend of Mattie Blaylock, or James' wife, Bessie, who traveled with Josie post–Tombstone, believed Josie had lived in the mining camp during the time they themselves were residents. Even in the age of Victorian moral standards, none of Wyatt Earp's family, business partners, or Tombstone friends ever publicly mentioned knowing of Josie Marcus's presence in Tombstone or an active liaison between her and Wyatt while they lived in the city. The one exception to this pronouncement is Doc Holliday's comment about Sheriff Behan's women to a Denver newspaper reporter. The Earp family, and some of Wyatt's close friends, understood that Mattie Blaylock had dissolved her relationship with Wyatt after Tombstone and returned to Arizona and that Josie Marcus eventually became Wyatt's helpmate.[1]

Friday, April 14, 1882: Mule Creek, New Mexico Territory

It was very windy and cold in the New Mexico mountains. After three days of hard trail riding, the eight-man Earp posse had traversed Arizona's eastern mountains and traveled through Mule Creek Canyon to cross the border and reach Mule Creek, a tiny farm and ranch settlement founded five years earlier by Dan McMillen, about six miles inside New Mexico Territory. Late Friday afternoon, April 14, 1882, following some needed rest, food, and water for the men and their horses, the posse continued its journey headed east along the Mule Creek trail until it reached a junction with the stage road heading south to Silver City.[2]

If Wyatt had been intent upon keeping the presence of his posse a secret during their 50-mile trip to Silver City, the men must have journeyed only at night after leaving the isolated Mile Creek settlement. They must have found this leg of their journey relaxing, because regional almanacs indicate the moon was in the third quarter cycle with a new moon arriving on April 17. It was light enough for the posse to move along the well-used road connecting the northern mining camps in the Mogollon Mountains and the commercial center of this mountainous region, yet dark enough for general concealment. Just west of their destination the saddle-worn group crossed the summit of the continental divide shortly after passing the present-day Gila National Forrest. The posse had reached the nearly 6,000-foot-high valley that sheltered Silver City.

Saturday, April 15, 1882:
Silver City, New Mexico Territory

In the early 1880s, Silver City, the county seat of Grant County, New Mexico Territory, had a population of around 3,500. In one of his many travelogue letters back home, Vermont newspaperman C.M. Chase wrote on November 27, 1881, that Silver City "is very rich, and possibilities are immense" due to the nearby copper and gold mines. The town "is really one of the pleasantest best ordered little cities in the territory, although situated in the midst of the wildest and most reckless surroundings." Chase believed the town was on the move and owed "Sheriff Whitehill and his deputies for its good order and safety as a place to abode." Chase concluded that the "locality is very rich, and possibilities are immense."

Around 10 p.m. on Saturday, April 15, eight well-armed men rode up to the Silver City Stage Line office in the room just east of the Exchange Hotel's main entrance. The hotel sat on the northwest corner of Broadway and Bullard, located in the heart of the town's business district. Louie Timmer, the proprietor of the Exchange Hotel, called his place the "Delmonico of the West" and the "Leading Hotel of the Southwest, the Most Stately Edifice in New Mexico."

A weary Wyatt Earp dismounted from his equally weary horse and went inside the office to confer with O.R. Smythe, the 41-year-old stage line superintendent. The native New Yorker had been awaiting the arrival of the marshal since early that afternoon when telegraph operator O.D. Stewart, a 23-year-old Ohio native, delivered an urgent message from Wells Fargo's home office. The express company requested a coach for a special run to Deming on Sunday morning if there was not enough passenger room for eight men on the regular six-horse run.

On Wednesday, March 23, 1882, the corporate management of Wells Fargo Company had made an unprecedented public endorsement of Wyatt Earp's actions in dealing with the outlaw troubles in Cochise County. The company leadership and their many business allies continued to support Wyatt Earp and his fugitive posse as they left Arizona Territory a few weeks later. The express company also continued to encourage a high level of support at the highest echelons of government. Letters on file in the National Archives written by Lloyd Tevis, Wells Fargo president, show that he corresponded with influential United States senators seeking their support for legislation granting the president authority to use federal troops to assist federal marshals in restoring peace and order in Arizona Territory. John J. Valentine, the general superintendent of Wells Fargo's western division, even arranged to confer personally with Wyatt Earp in Albuquerque. J.N. Thacker, the express company's special agent assigned to the case, was a strong public supporter of the Earp brothers' actions.

Smythe arranged to have a six-horse coach in front of the Max Schutz building on the corner of Main and Broadway at 7:30 Sunday morning. The federal officers boarded the coach for an eight-hour trip to Deming via the route to Hudson's Hot Springs. One of Smythe's best drivers, Sam Dicus, may have handled the ribbons for the Silver City–Deming run. The forty-seven-year-old Ohio native earned extra pay for the special Sunday trip, so he asked few questions concerning his passengers. All the stage line personnel were tradesmen with entrepreneurial tendencies, Republican Party political affiliations and respect for the might of Wells Fargo and Company requests.

With the stage trip schedule finalized, Earp led his men to the Elephant Corral livery stables, three blocks northeast of the Exchange Hotel near the town's outer limits, where they arranged to stable their mounts with Charley Bagsby. Now the men needed a safe place to spend the night, a place where they would attract little attention. A local newspaper provides one possible answer to the sleeping arrangements. The newspaper reported that the posse "put up at the Elephant Corral." This remark could simply mean this corral was where the posse stabled their horses. However, on the frontier large livery stables often had a small bunkroom attached where travelers could spread a bedroll on the floor for the night. There were no beds and no "honey buckets," but it was economical.

In April 1882, Silver City's *New Southwest and Grant County Herald* reported that the Earp posse had "slept in a private house up town" during their stay while in Silver City but did not name the residence. A fact to contemplate is that Wyatt's Tombstone neighbor and mining partner Andrew Neff had a relative who lived in Silver City named D.P. Neff. In 1882, Neff managed the branch store of the family mercantile business, headquartered in Trinidad, Colorado, and sold hardware, stoves and tinware. He lived on Bullard Street between Market and Yankee, a block north of the Exchange Hotel. Wyatt or some other members of the fugitive posse may have stayed with the Neff family in their "house up town." The senior partner, M.W. Neff, would play his part in this frontier drama a few weeks later in Trinidad.

Let us examine two other possibilities. Lottie Deno was a legendary faro dealer on the southwestern frontier gambling circuit. The Kentucky-born adventuress christened Carlotta J. Thompkins later married fellow adventurer-gambler Frank Thurmond and they lived their senior years as community leaders in Deming, New Mexico. In April 1882, Mr. and Mrs. Frank Thurmond lived in Silver City and she was the successful owner-operator of the lovely Broadway Restaurant, which had a second-story set of rooms available for overnight guests. The Broadway Hotel was one block west of the Exchange Hotel on the southwest corner of Broadway and Texas.

An alternative scenario to consider is that Frank Thurmond's brother Jim operated one of Silver City's houses of ill repute that was equipped with overnight accommodations. Wyatt and Doc had known Lottie Deno and the Thurmond brothers when they all worked the Texas gambling circuit in the late 1870s. It is very likely that the fugitive officers spent a few hours resting at one of these "private houses" during that short night.

Where did Wyatt Earp's fatigued posse spend the night of Saturday–Sunday April 15–16, 1882? Did they sleep on the floor of Silver City's White Elephant Corral? Was D.P. Neff's home used by the Arizona lawmen or was the "private house up town" that sheltered the posse a dwelling connected to one of the Thurmond brothers? These sleeping arrangements are one of those minor questions of the Vendetta Rides that remains unanswered.

Early Sunday morning April 16, 1882, the Earp posse, now somewhat rested, went to the Broadway Restaurant for breakfast. Mrs. Thurmond's establishment advertised "fresh oysters and fish and is prepared to serve them at all hours." All meals were 50 cents and a bottle of beer sold for twenty-five cents. Coffee came with the meal.

After breakfast, Wyatt set about trying to sell the posse's horses. The *New Southwest and Grant County Herald* reported that one Silver City corral operator became concerned that "one of the men, when asked his name, answered John Smith, and another Bill Snooks" when he was asked about purchasing six of the animals. He turned down the offer, later noting that the men were "well mounted and armed to the teeth." One can envision the personalities of Wyatt and Doc in the names Smith and Snooks. A week after the men had left town the local paper identified the mystery men as Wyatt Earp and his federal posse based upon stories published earlier that week in both the *Daily Nugget* and the *Daily Epitaph*.

Later Sunday morning, Earp sold six of the posse's horses to Levi Miller, a fifty-two-year-old blacksmith from Pennsylvania who wanted to start a new livery business in Silver City. Bagsby was unable to handle the six extra horses at his stable and Smythe had no need for saddle horses for the stage line, so they helped to arrange a quick deal with Miller for the purchase. The local paper editorialized that "the horses were worth much more" than the three hundred dollar price tag paid by Miller. Did this money fund the stage trip to Deming?

Charley Bagsby, at the White Elephant Corral, an undercover operative for the Well Fargo Express Company, was to care for two mounts and gear until he received orders for their disposition. The sale of five saddles and other tack was to cover the cost of caring for the two mounts Wyatt left. Their business in Silver City now completed, the fugitive federal officers were ready to take the special stage south to Deming.[3]

Author's Perspective: Had Wyatt unlawfully disposed of federal government property? Did any of these horses carry an army brand from Fort Grant? Did Wyatt have ownership papers on these horses or was he selling "stolen" property? Had Wyatt purchased this gear with the money given to him by Marshal Dake or had private funds provided for this equipment? More questions without answers.

It was at Silver City that O.C. "Hair-lip Charlie" Smith bid his comrades Godspeed and returned to Tombstone to make a report to the Citizen's Safety Committee. Wyatt and Warren Earp, Doc Holliday, Sherm McMaster, "Turkey Creek Jack" Johnson, "Texas Jack" Vermillion, and Dan Tipton boarded the stage to Deming and started their journey into seclusion in Albuquerque.

Ed Bartholomew quotes an unnamed Silver City newspaper dated April 15, 1882, in his *Wyatt Earp II* concerning the reported death of the Indiana-born outlaw chief Curly Bill Brocius: "A party is in town and reliably informed says Curly Bill is not dead as told here this week by the Earp party." Silver City was home to two weekly newspapers in April 1882. No known issues of the *Telegram* exist and the *New Southwest and Grant County Herald* does not contain any story about Wyatt Earp or his posse in its April 15, 1882, issue. Was this another false trail to discredit Earp's killing of Curly Bill? The question now becomes how any newspaper could have reported the Earp posse's presence in Silver City before their unexpected arrival and why men traveling undercover would talk openly about their identity or any past lethal actions they may have engaged in.

Tombstone's *Daily Epitaph* and *Daily Nugget* each reported to their readers on April

20 that the Earp posse had reached New Mexico Territory. Additionally, the *Daily Nugget* reported "the Earp party have been employed by the authorities of New Mexico" to continue the hunt for the Cow-boys who had taken refuse in that territory. The next day the *Daily Epitaph* expanded the speculation, saying the Earp posse—acting "in their capacity of detectives"—possessed "full knowledge of every person" involved in the Cow-boy operations and "decided to make an effort to bring the whole gang to justice." The newspaper also said the Earp posse was acting with "the knowledge of the [federal and territorial] authorities of New Mexico." The *Daily Epitaph* added these final remarks: "If the Earps have left the [Tombstone] country this is the most probable theory of the cause and their destination." One can only speculate whether Charley Smith was the source for the misdirected comment about Wyatt's new job as a New Mexico officer.

Since Silver City was the headquarters of the Grant County government, one might ask where Sheriff Harvey Howard Whitehill was on the weekend the Earp posse was in town. The *Santa Fe Daily New Mexican* noted that the sheriff was in Santa Fe and was "anxious to get back home." The Ohio-born Whitehill had come west as a twenty-year-old in search of adventure and served as sergeant-at-arms of the first legislature held in Colorado Territory before coming to New Mexico. After completing his eight years as Grant County's fourth sheriff (1875–1882), Whitehill served in the New Mexico Territorial General Assembly as Grant County's representative in the council, the upper chamber. He again served as sheriff in 1889 and 1890. Bob Alexander wrote his biography.

William Kilburn was the chief deputy sheriff in charge while his future father-in-law was out of the county. Kilburn was a stalwart officer who served as a constable and three terms as marshal of Silver City before dying in the line of duty in 1904. The chief deputy surely knew of the presence in Silver City's downtown business district of eight heavily armed men on a Sunday morning. The men had broken no laws and Wells Fargo Company was openly assisting them, so Kilburn had no reason to question these travelers or attempt to detain them.

Sunday, April 16, 1882: Deming, New Mexico Territory

Santa Fe Railroad gandy dancers brought the tracks to connect with the Southern Pacific line in early spring 1881. On the Tuesday afternoon of March 8, a few hardy souls had gathered in the railroad yards at Mimbres Junction, New Mexico Territory, to celebrate the "silver spike ceremony" that married the Southern Pacific and the Santa Fe Railroad tracks, and gave birth to the nation's second continental railroad route. A week later, the first through-train left Kansas City headed for California. Deming, the new name for the Mimbres Junction village, was on its way to becoming the transfer site for passenger and freight services of the two rail systems. Vermont newspaperman C.M. Chase, traveling around New Mexico in 1881, reported that Deming's "climate is delightful, the best out of doors."

Author's Perspective: Ed Bartholomew published an article entitled "Earp's Hide Out at Silver City," in the *Southwesterner* newspaper-magazine of April 1963 that claimed the "Earp gang" took "the stage to Fort Cummings" from Silver City. He was quoting from the April 25, 1882, issue of the *Las Vegas Daily Optic.* Bartholomew speculated that the posse then took another stage over the mountains to Rincon to catch the northbound train to Albuquerque. Ed claimed this was done so Earp could stay out of "the domain of officer Tucker at Deming." Later, in *Wyatt Earp II: The Man and The Myth*, published in 1964, Bartholomew wrote, "Because officer Tucker was stationed at Deming in March 1882, the Earp gang decided to bypass the rail stop, taking to horseback for their long ride and flight from justice in Arizona." It would seem that Ed could not make up his mind if Wyatt's posse took a stage or rode horseback to Fort Cummings. In fact, the Earp posse did neither.

Other historians have used a comment taken from Silver City's *New Southwest and Grant County Herald* stating that one of the possemen asked a corral operator about hiring a wagon and driver to take them to Fort Cummings and learned he could just as easily take a regularly scheduled stage to the recently reestablished cavalry post. Our friend Bob Alexander, a Dan Tucker biographer, spends the better part of four pages in his Tucker book trying to prove that the Earp posse took the stage to Fort Cummings. He later altered his belief to say the posse caught the Santa Fe train at Nutt Station located 18 miles east across the plains from the fort. The 1882 *New Mexico Blue Book*, published by the territorial secretary as a resource guide, lists no stage connections for Nutt Station or Fort Cummings. The *Blue Book* lists the infant town of Deming as Silver City's only railroad-stage connection.

Nutt Station, established in 1881 to honor the president of the Atlantic and Pacific Railroad at the time, H.C. Nutt, was the railroad junction for freighting supplies into the Black Range mining district and shipping out the silver ore from the camps of Lake Valley, Hillsboro and Kingston. The shipping point was 28 miles northeast from Deming. A 13-mile branch line built by the New Mexican Railroad Company connected Lake Valley to Nutt Station via a branch line constructed in the spring of 1884 and operated until 1934. In 1883, the Santa Fe Railroad added a freight stop between Deming and Nutt originally called Porter Station, now called Florida, which provided service to Fort Cummings until the military base was closed in 1886.

Had the Earp posse visited Fort Cummings, located on a plateau 4,750 feet above sea level, they would have found the post enclosed in a walled square with an arched entrance. They would also have found the 200-head dairy farm operated by a man named Lyon. He sold large quantities of butter to the area's miners but none to Wyatt Earp or any of his companions.

Bob Alexander is correct in his contention that contemporary evidence establishes Dan Tucker as a stalwart man in an era of strong men. In November 1881, C.M. Chase wrote that Deputy Tucker had already killed 11 men and "is still in harness, and promises to rid the locality [Deming] of the hateful element, before long." Tucker patrolled Deming with a cut-down 19½-inch double-barreled Richard shotgun imported from Belgium, and he depended upon his weapon and man-killer reputation to help keep order. This strategy did not always work, because Deputy Tucker still committed a few "justifiable homicides" during the months he patrolled Deming.

Fifty years after the events of early 1882, Dan Rose interviewed people who claimed to have known Tucker and wrote an article titled "Dan Tucker, the Killer" for the *Silver City Independent* of September 22, 1931. Rose wrote that during a three-day period

Tucker killed three men and wounded two others at Deming. It has been claimed that during these months he was bringing law and order to the infant railroad junction, Tucker also arrested 13 members of Curly Bill's Cow-boy gang from the San Simon Valley. This information would suggest that Tucker considered the Cow-boys to be outlaws in the same degree that deputy U.S. marshal Wyatt Earp considered these men beyond the law. Tucker was not always a straight arrow peace officer. In November 1881, he had not stopped the lynching of two prisoners while he was the law in Shakespeare, a mining town in Grant County.

Sherm McMaster knew Tucker from the time they rode together in a posse in January 1878 while working out of El Paso. McMaster may have told Wyatt about the deputy, because it is possible that Earp and Tucker had never had an occasion to meet each other. They may have known of each other only by reputation. Any person objectively evaluating a "what if" encounter between Wyatt Earp and Dan Tucker should consider five basic facts.

Fact number one: Wyatt Earp did not duck a possible encounter between the two men in Deming. The truth is simple: Wyatt and his posse were in Deming on Sunday, April 16, 1882. The *New Southwest and Grant County Herald* article recounting Earp's visit to Silver City reported the conveniently overlooked fact that Wyatt "made arrangements to leave the next morning on the Deming coach." This 53-mile trip was the fastest way for saddle-worn travelers to leave Silver City and reach the nearest train stop located at the 4,335-foot-high railroad junction at Deming. The chief Cow-boy defender in Tombstone, the *Daily Nugget*, reported on April 20, within days of the event, that the Earp posse had "been seen to board the train at Deming and go east."

Another source to consider is that Wyatt told Forrestine Hooker about the end of his Vendetta Ride and she wrote, in 1919/1920, "[T]hey went to Silver City, New Mexico; then Deming and Albuquerque." John Flood, Wyatt's secretary and the ghostwriter of his 1926 autobiography, wrote about the Earp posse's 1882 stay in Albuquerque: "Two weeks before, they had disposed of their animals at Silver City, New Mexico, at the end of a three day's trail. Then the stage to Deming, and on to Albuquerque by train." Based upon information Wyatt himself supplied, Walter Noble Burns wrote in his 1927 classic, *Tombstone: An Iliad of the Southwest*, that the Earp posse caught a train at the Deming station and headed north to find refuge in Colorado.

Fact number two: Deputy Sheriff Dan Tucker had no lawful reason to have accosted the Earp posse. There were no outstanding warrants for Earp or his men in New Mexico Territory. The Earp possemen were all sworn federal officers serving under a duly authorized deputy United States marshal with valid authority to be armed. Even so authorized, it is doubtful that the posse openly brandished their firearms. However, New Mexico territorial law in force in April 1882 permitted travelers to carry firearms while on their journey.

Fact number three: The seven men of the Earp posse were not vagrants; they were adequately dressed travelers possessing the necessary finances to purchase a railroad ticket, overnight lodging and food. There is some evidence, which we will discuss in more detail below, suggesting that Earp and his posse may not have been required to purchase tickets to travel on the Southern Pacific or Santa Fe Railroad lines during their campaign against the Cow-boys.

Fact number four: It is unclear where deputy sheriff Tucker was on Sunday, April 16, 1882. Newspaper listings show that Dan Tucker was often out of Deming on personal business during the period he was assigned to police the village. In fact, the *New Southwest and Grant County Herald* noted the week before the Earp posse reached Silver City that Deputy Tucker had been in California and was then currently in the county seat. It is possible that Tucker was in Silver City during the Earp posse's visit to Grant County. In late February 1882, the *New Southwest and Grant County Herald* said, "Deputy Sheriff Tucker is in town and reports everything quiet in Deming." It is very likely that Sheriff Whitehall honored Tucker's desire for reassignment to Silver City.

Fact number five: There is no reason to believe that Wyatt Earp would have kowtowed to Dan Tucker even if the deputy sheriff had unwisely tried to detain him. At least a half-dozen Arizona corpses could attest to Wyatt's willingness and ability to administer deadly force in his own defense or in defense of his friends. Six equally deadly men not keen on the idea of going to jail accompanied Earp. Also, consider that Wyatt Earp was an aggressive fighter who once offered to fight Ike Clanton in the rustler's own backyard at San Simon—*mano y mano.* In an unusual moment of common sense, Ike found the need to be in another place, doing anything but fighting with Wyatt. The editor of the *Dodge City Globe-Republican*, 10 December 1896, in a reflective assessment of Earp's performance as a city marshal recalled that Wyatt "was regarded as a man who feared nothing. He was generally liked by the citizens. He was cool and polite." I feel that had Tucker foolishly accosted Earp there would have been stern resistance, possibly an altercation, and had Tucker attempted to use weapons someone would have died.

A final, very important point to consider is that when Tucker was not performing his duties as a Grant County deputy sheriff he rode the stage between Silver City and Deming as a shotgun messenger for Wells Fargo. It would be hard to believe that Tucker was not aware of the publicly proclaimed support that Wells Fargo had given Wyatt Earp and the mission he and his posse had undertaken. Surely Tucker understood that Wells Fargo management expected all employees to support Earp or lose their jobs.

Judge Edward F. Colborn, Wyatt's attorney friend from Dodge City and Trinidad, told a reporter for the *Salt Lake City Herald* that the "Santa Fe (called the Southern Pacific Railroad in 1882) gave orders to its conductors to take the Earps on board whenever they desired" in a story published on December 12, 1896. Thirty years later, Wyatt made the same claim in his autobiography and added that if he needed to he could sleep in the caboose. The judge had been discussing Wyatt's campaign against the Arizona Cow-boys and ended his interview saying he believed Earp succeeded in his "Herculean task of establishing respect for the law."

After Sheriff Whitehill's defeat for reelection in November 1882, the loss of his deputy commission, and the final dismissal of murder charges against him in 1883, Tucker renewed his contacts with officials of the Southern Pacific and became a special officer for the railroad's police department.

Pima County Sheriff Bob Paul recounted an interesting side note to the Tucker–Earp nonevent at Deming. The sheriff told a Denver newspaperman that Tucker "had agreed to meet me in [Deming] New Mexico with a strong guard to travel as far in my company as I desired should I think additional guards necessary." Paul was describing his preparation plans to guarantee Doc Holliday's safe return to Tucson to stand trial for the killing of Frank Stilwell. Sheriff Paul mentioned nothing about trying to return Wyatt Earp or any of the other men who had been part of the federal posse to Arizona. Was Deputy Tucker just doing his civic duty or was he also part of the grand plan to protect Earp and Holliday?

For passengers coming from California on the Southern Pacific line seeking to connect with the Santa Fe route at Deming for points east, and likewise passengers from the east headed west, there was a two-hour layover. The engines and their accompanying passenger and freight cars had to be routed through the roundhouse so they could be turned around and refueled for the return trip. Train crews were changed and freight was unloaded and loaded. Another factor in the transfer delay was the regional time zones; west of the Rocky Mountains, the region operated on Pacific Slope railroad time and the Midwest operated on Topeka railroad time.[4]

Following a windy walk about Deming's growing business section and maybe a dollar supper at the depot restaurant or a 15-cent drink at a bar along Railroad Avenue, the Earp party finally boarded a green-painted Santa Fe Railroad express coach about eight o'clock Sunday evening and headed northeast toward the railroad junction at Thron (Rincon). Aboard the speeding passenger train, the weary federal posse began to relax a little from the tension of the past few weeks. A few hours later, the eastbound train arrived at Rincon and took on board the passengers who had arrived on the evening train from El Paso.

The conductor on all Santa Fe trains operating during this era had the authority to close the designated smoking car for public use and give it to large family groups for social occasions. It is unknown if this happened on the posse's 231-mile trip from Deming to Albuquerque. It is equally uncertain if the federal officers enjoyed the use of a Pullman sleeping car during their 14-hour journey or if they had to make do sleeping in the general passenger seats.

Sunday, April 16, 1882:
Thorn [Rincon], New Mexico Territory

El Rincon de Fray Diego was named to honor a 17th-century Franciscan priest who died in the settlement. However, when a post office was established in 1881 the government renamed the village Thorn in honor of an old pre–Civil War–era fort located a few miles north. The settlement became a major railroad junction for north-south and east-west trains; here the New Mexico Southern Pacific Railroad joined the Rio Grande, Mexico & Pacific Railway, the New Mexico subsidiary of the AT & SF RR. The village was also notable as being a haven for drifters, "holdups, footpads, and no goods" seeking a quick dollar.

In July 1881, the *Prescott Journal* published an editorial addressing crime in the new railroad towns: "In fact, there are a few points along the railroad in this Territory of New Mexico, where blacklegs [cardsharps, cheats] seem beyond the reach of law, where they openly and defiantly follow their infamous practices, and any stranger falling into their clutches must suffer. He has no law to protect him and no morality to defend him. That such a state of affairs exists anywhere is as sad as it is disgraceful." A good example of the hypocrisy in dealing with the outlaw situation in Arizona is shown in the fact that the *Tombstone Nugget,* the organ of the Cow-boy faction, reprinted the entire *Prescott Journal* article in its July 23 issue.

Federal investigator Frank Warner Angel referred to the men who made the Rincon locale their rendezvous site following their rustling sprees as "John Kinney and his murderous outfit of outlaws." Kinney was so brazen in his illegal business activities that he built his own packing plant near the railroad tracks at Thron to slaughter stolen cattle on site before shipping carloads of fresh dressed beef south to El Paso. At one point, the Massachusetts-born Kinney was the largest beef shipper in southern New Mexico. Locals even referred to the town as Kinneyville. In 1883, Major Albert Jennings Fountain led a company of Territorial Militia that finally ended Kinney's lawless rule of the region. The bandit leader relocated to Arizona after serving three years in New Mexico's territorial prison. He died at age 72 in 1919.

One of John Kinney's foot soldiers was Illinois-born Charles "Pony Diehl" Ray. He was one of the Cochise County Cow-boys who ran to Old Mexico instead of facing Wyatt Earp's rage. In late 1882, the Lincoln County War veteran returned to the Thron/Rincon area and worked with the Kinney Gang. In 1884, New Mexico authorities arrested Ray and convicted him of cattle stealing. As Prisoner #11, Ray earned five years in the newly constructed territorial penitentiary at Santa Fe.

The new community of Thron had no law enforcement officer, so Sam Armstrong, the local Santa Fe Railroad special agent, served as the de facto law. On Monday, March 6, 1882, three "holdups" tried to kill a judge stopping at the station. Armstrong and Judge Griffin returned fire and wounded one of the men, but all three escaped. Griffin then authorized Armstrong to organize and lead a vigilance committee to deal with the new rustler element arriving daily to escape Wyatt Earp's Cow-boy roundup in southern Arizona Territory.

John J. Valentine, general superintendent of the Well Fargo Express Company, was in Albuquerque on Sunday, April 16, 1882, when the Earp party left Silver City headed his way. That morning, Valentine dispatched Frank Stevens, a Wells Fargo special messenger stationed at Albuquerque, to assume the duties of director of operations at the company's Deming office. The regular messenger had recently suffered injuries in a massive train wreck at Thron.

The spacious two-story Thron express depot was visible for miles in all directions. The seven travel-worn man hunters had to change trains there. Stevens should have reached Thron in time to deliver Valentine's message to Wyatt Earp. The Wells Fargo chief was waiting in the Duke City to confer with Earp about current developments and to discuss a plan of action. After a short relief break and the updated message for Wyatt delivered by Stevens, the Earp posse was once again moving toward the promise of safety in New Albuquerque.

In 1883, following the collapse of the Kinney gang, Thorn once again became known as Rincon. The revitalized village thrived for many years, but over time their neighbor community of Hatch, located five miles east, eclipsed Rincon to become the agriculture center of the valley with their world-famous Southwest green chili.

Sunday, April 16, 1882:
San Marcial, New Mexico Territory

Upon leaving Rincon the passenger train moved through the night gaining speed along the lowlands on the east side of the Rio Grande. The next station stop was at New Town San Marcial, built in 1880 as the junction for connecting the Santa Fe tracks with the short line Rio Grande, Mexico & Pacific Railway from Thron/Rincon. French Catholic missionaries had named the original 1780s trading post on the east bank of the river La Mesa de San Marcial, for St. Martial of Limoges. The original site suffered a devastating flood in 1866.

In the spring of 1881 the Rio Grande floodwaters nearly destroyed the new railroad settlement and a July fire almost completed the job, but by recycling the usable timber and making new adobe bricks the people quickly rebuilt their village. In November, a Socorro newspaper noted the town contained five stores, the ancient adobe Catholic church, a post office, a hotel, a Harvey House, a freight depot, a telegraph office and an eight-engine railroad roundhouse. The skating rink and dance floor were the center for social gatherings along with the soda fountain. The two saloons handled the local needs of thirsty men. There was also a butcher shop, a mercantile store, lumberyard, and a Chinese laundry. The community had no school.

The new "end-of-track" settlement had its growing pains. Driven out of the New Town Las Vegas area by vigilantes, Dave Rudabaugh and a dozen or so of his misguided friends used the area as a hideout for a short time. In June 1881, an escaped felon named Ryan shot village marshal Charles Walker five times. Following the lead of other frontier settlements, a local vigilante group formed in San Marcial to help maintain law and order and took lethal action on September 6, 1882.

In 1882, San Marcial's village marshal was James H. Currie, who may have known Earp and Holliday from Dodge City. "Marshal Jim" had been an Indian fighter and had fought at Beecher's Island against Roman Nose's Cheyenne warriors. He had also worked as a Kansas peace officer, a railroad engineer in Tennessee, and a special agent for the Texas Pacific Railroad before settling in New Mexico Territory. His brother Andrew was the mayor of Shreveport, Louisiana, while Currie was considered a frontier man killer.

In March 1879 Currie picked a fight with some members of a traveling theatrical troupe. Before being restrained and locked in jail, Currie killed Benjamin C. Porter and wounded another actor in the Whitehouse Restaurant in Marshal, Texas. In June 1880 a Harrison County jury found Currie not guilty of murder because he had been drunk. The actor Currie had wounded was Maurice Barrymore, future father of entertainment legends Ethel, Lionel and John Barrymore and grandfather of Drew Barrymore. Jim Currie's reckless behavior finally caused his dismissal as an officer in Socorro County. He eventually drifted east into Lincoln County, where he killed his mining partner at White Oaks in the fall of 1888. This time the 47-year-old Irishman earned a six-year term as Prisoner #271 in the territorial prison at Santa Fe. Governor L. Bradford Prince pardoned Currie in March 1891 and he quickly vanished from the historical records.

It is very likely that most of the Earp posse slept through the mail, passenger, and equipment reshuffle before the trip north resumed on schedule. Since no copies of the

San Marcial Times for 1882 have survived into this century, it is hard to state whether the public knew of Wyatt Earp's short predawn sojourn in their village. Only a shadow of San Marcial remains since the devastating Rio Grande floods of 1929 and 1937 destroyed the village.

Monday, April 17, 1882:
Socorro, New Mexico Territory

Wyatt Earp's federal posse left Deming at about nine o'clock Sunday evening and, according to contemporary Santa Fe Railroad schedules, arrived at Socorro at about 3:30 on Monday morning. A short time later, after a crew change, the Santa Fe passenger train headed north again.

Nuestra Senora de Socorro (Our Lady of Aid) was one of the earliest Spanish settlements along the Rio Grande del Norte (Large River of the North). In his book *Wyatt Earp II: The Man and the Myth,* Ed Ellsworth Bartholomew claimed that the "Earp gang" entrained at Socorro and planned to hide out in the Oasis on the Rio Grande, at least, that is, until they discovered that the "dance hall element" was no longer welcome in the community by order of the Socorro vigilantes. The head of the local "citizen police" was Col. Ethan Eaton. In 1881 four men had received vigilante justice in Death's Ally and on October 1 the *Santa Fe New Mexican* reported that each corpse had a placard pinned on its back with the message, "This is the way Socorro Treats Horse Thieves and Footpads [muggers]."

Col. Eaton's great-granddaughter Grace LaFont Fullerton, who had married Elmer Fullerton, the son of the first captain of the New Mexico Territorial Mounted Police, told the author in the summer of 1995 that, according to family stories, her businessman ancestor held Wyatt Earp in high regard. To Mrs. Fullerton's knowledge, the two men never met personally, but Eaton admired Earp's forceful actions against the Cow-boys in Arizona Territory. He wished that Socorro County could have found a lawman of the same caliber during its troubled years, but what Socorro County got was a self-promoting windbag known to history as Elfego Baca. Albuquerque newspaperman George Fitzpatrick, who knew Baca in his later years, once wrote, "He [Baca] was something of an actor himself and he loved to dramatize incidents of his life in conversation with friends or interviewers."

In a December 29, 1876, feature article about Socorro an editor-reporter for the *Santa Fe Daily New Mexican* wrote, "Socorro is an important place for wool and wine." The community also produced firebrick and was the shipping point for the region's gold, silver, lead, and copper mines. One local farmer grew Louisiana cane to heights of 18 feet and sold the poles for fishing rods.

If Wyatt and Doc had visited the Socorro Plaza on their 1879 trip to Arizona Territory, they would have noted many changes in the community had they been able to view the town in the predawn glow of Monday, April 17, 1882. Miguel Otero, Jr., noted the differences three years had made in the growth of the town when he wrote, "Socorro was no longer a little adobe village; it was now a big mining center supporting two newspapers, train lines, and new office buildings."

In his book *Wyatt Earp II*, Bartholomew recounts a tall tale he claimed a Nebraska man named Dean Miller told him. According to Miller's story, it seems a man named Alexander "Shorty" Harris embarrassed Wyatt Earp during his stay in Socorro and caused him to leave the community quickly. The tale reports how Shorty "outdrew Earp time after time but didn't fire." Harris finally tired of the game and told Earp "if he ever saw him again he'd shoot him on sight."

Many questions surround this tall tale. Who was Alexander "Shorty" Harris? Where were the men of Earp's posse or Eaton's citizen police force during this "incident"? Bartholomew provides no reason for this imagined encounter, but even more lacking is a reason why Earp would continue to draw on this man or why Shorty would withhold his deadly fire and then threaten to shot Earp on sight next time the two men met. First, it was not in the nature of Wyatt Earp to play games with firearms. Second, lest we forget, at the time of this "incident," Wyatt was a deputy United States marshal sworn to uphold the law, not take part in barroom fights. Last, Bartholomew overlooked a poignant fact: Socorro was suffering from a major smallpox outbreak in early 1882, with 75 victims at one point, so it is very unlikely that any of the Earp posse set foot in Socorro. Wyatt never planned a stay in the town beyond a normal station stop.

Monday, April 17, 1882:
New Albuquerque, New Mexico Territory

The railroad telegraph operator at station 1416 (Socorro) sent a message to station 1340 (New Albuquerque) saying the northbound Santa Fe passenger train left on schedule at 3:50 on Monday morning, April 17, 1882. The morning train reached New Town Albuquerque's red-painted, two-story depot just as dawn was breaking over the Sandia and Manzano mountains.[5]

Twenty-one days earlier, on Tuesday, March 28, the *Albuquerque Morning Journal* had published a well-placed tip that Wyatt Earp and his fugitive federal posse would arrive in the area on the Atlantic and Pacific Railroad Express from Gallup at 6:18 that morning. The A&PRR was a subsidiary of the Santa Fe railway system. Obviously, Wyatt Earp and his federal posse were not on that train, but the trial balloon had generated no negative community reaction in New Mexico, so the sanctuary plan moved forward.

A road-weary Wyatt Earp finally arrived in New Albuquerque unheralded three weeks later. He was escorted by his equally weary posse of "Doc" John H. Holliday, John "Texas Jack" Vermillion, John "Turkey Creek Jack" Johnson, Sherman McMaster, Dan "Big Tip" Tipton, and Wyatt's youngest brother, Warren. These federal lawmen had been campaigning against the Cow-boys since January and had spent the last 28 days on an intense scout for outlaw camps. During the last month, the posse had served so many lead warrants on the Cow-boys that most people expected news of another strike any day.

Wyatt Earp's stealthy withdrawal from Arizona had been so well executed that on April 19, 1882, S.R. Martin—a special agent of the Justice Department writing from southern Arizona to update the acting attorney general, S.F. Phillips, in Washington

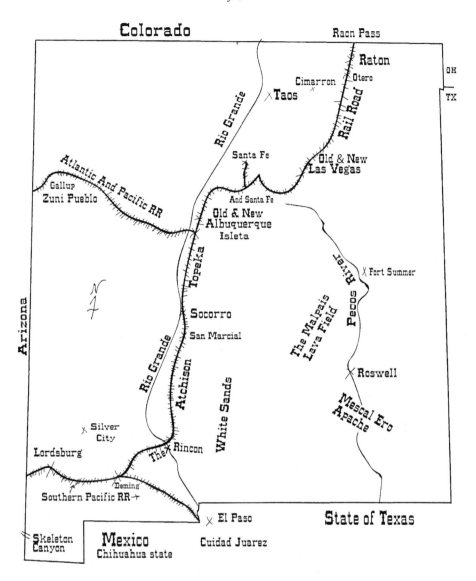

NEW MEXICO
Territory 1882

Map by Logan Wood.

concerning the progress of Marshal Crawley P. Dake's campaign to end the Cow-boy troubles—believed Earp's strike force was still operating within Arizona Territory. Martin reported that United States deputy Marshal Wyatt Earp, "who is now an outlaw [wanted by officers in Cochise and Pima Counties for murder] and others [his posse] are in hiding in the mountains awaiting their time for a big fight in Tombstone." In fact, Wyatt Earp and his federal marshal's strike force were sleeping in their warm beds in Albuquerque, New Mexico Territory.

PART THREE

The "Otero Letter"

All truth passes through three stages. First, it is ridiculed. Second, it is violently opposed. Third, it is accepted as being self-evident.— Arthur Schopenhauer, 19th century German philosopher

11

New Mexico's Campaign
Against the Cow-boys

Whenever any "Rustlers," "Cow Boys" or other desperadoes shall commit depredations upon the person or property of citizens, such commanding [militia] officers will at once pursue and capture such offenders at any cost, turning them over to the proper civil authority, and restore all stolen property to its owner.—Governor Lionel A. Sheldon, New Mexico Territorial Militia Commander-in-Chief, Executive Order No. 14, Point 4, issued to Territorial Adjutant-General Edward L. Bartlett

New Mexico territorial governor Lionel A. Sheldon concluded Executive Order No. 14 to adjutant general Edward L. Bartlett with a final point: "It is expected that this order will be executed with such promptness and vigor that bad men will take warning and avoid New Mexico as a field for carrying on their criminal occupations." The files of the Adjutant General's Office contain numerous reports detailing the actions of the territorial militia against the Cow-boys in New Mexico Territory.

Numerous acts of outrage committed along New Mexico's frontier during the 1870s and 1880s and at first laid at the door of hostile Indians were actually perpetrated by outlaw bands. These livestock raids were usually accomplished in such a manner as to give the impression Apaches had committed them. Indian raids were the original reason for the legislative assembly to create a territorial militia. Outlaw hunting was a secondary mission.

Traveling newspaper editor C.M. Chase, in a letter dated November 27, 1881, for publication in his Vermont newspaper, described the Cow-boy situation in southwestern New Mexico Territory to his readers back home: "The cow-boys, or roughs and thieves, are so numerous that no man ventures any distance from the village [of Deming] without his Winchester rifle, ready to repeat 12 or 16 times without reloading. With this element constantly on the watch for plunder, a man's life goes for naught."

In volume 17, *History of Arizona and New Mexico, 1530–1888*, of *The Works of Hubert Howe Bancroft*, published in 1889, the author reviews the career of Governor Lionel A. Sheldon. He summed up the man by saying, "During his career as governor he thoroughly cleared the territory of its lawless element, promoted industries and education, and brought peace and prosperity to the land." No official public records have been located to support the contention that Governor Sheldon was actively involved in any cabal to protect Wyatt Earp and his posse, but logic would tend to support that idea based solely upon events that took place during March–April 1882.

The *Raton Guard* published an interesting notice on April 28, 1882: "Governor Suttle [*sic*], of Arizona, has telegraphed to Governor Sheldon, of New Mexico, to meet him at Deming in order that both territories could arrange measures for protection." What kind of mutual protection were the two chief executives planning to discuss? Was this protection against the actions of the Cow-boy rustlers or protection from Apache raids or both? Was Wyatt Earp's Cow-boy Campaign on the agenda?

It is unclear if the two territorial governors held this proposed meeting because the two governors' movements are hard to pinpoint at this time. Few of Lionel Sheldon's personal or official public communications from his years as governor of New Mexico Territory have survived into this century. We do know, however, that Sheldon and territorial supreme court justice William T. Thornton, a future territorial governor, spend a few days in Socorro conferring with Socorro County citizens during late March, according to the *Santa Fe New Mexican* of March 28, 1882. The newspaper reported that the two men were assessing recent Apache raids and the Cow-boy rustler situation in the county that stretched from the Rio Grande to Arizona in south central New Mexico. We also know that in late March Arizona governor Frederick A. Tritle was in Tombstone receiving a firsthand review of the Cow-boy troubles and reports of a new wave of Apache raids. The railroad junction at Deming is a nice meeting point between Tombstone and Socorro for an uninterrupted afternoon chat in a private railroad car.

Tritle was appointed to succeed Governor John C. Frémont on March 8, 1882, via the governor's resignation of October 11, 1881. Frémont had been out of the territory since early spring and in the interim John J. Gosper continued his duties as territorial secretary and served as acting governor. Due to Frémont's numerous extended eastern trips, Gosper had conducted both duties about three-fourths of the span of Frémont's four-year tenure as governor. Frémont's federal salary was $26,000 per year.

The *Tombstone Daily Epitaph* of December 12, 1881, explained their point of view concerning the leader of Arizona's sister territory:

> Governor Sheldon of New Mexico is a man that deserves great credit for his unceasing exertions for the maintenance of peace and order within the boundaries of the territory over which he was appointed to rule. The Silver City *Mining Chronicle* says of him:
>
> Governor Shelton is visiting the southern view consulting with sheriffs as to the best way of putting down the rustlers along the Mexican border, and stopping cattle and horse stealing. There is a very promising field for the governor and sheriffs to operate in. The sheriff's could and would soon do work themselves were they allowed enough to pay them actual expenses while engaged in the pursuit. As the law now stands, they are not allowed enough to pay for the tobacco they would smoke (to say nothing about fluids) while chasing these thieves.
>
> Were the same energy displayed by our governor—we beg pardon, we have no governor to consult with our sheriffs, so amend by saying Pima, Pinal, Graham and Cochise counties consult among themselves, and co-operate with the sheriffs of New Mexico, they could soon rid this country of the cow-boy nuisance and earn the ever lasting gratitude of those who contribute to their support.

Lionel A. Sheldon, a native New Yorker, supported the effort to destroy the rustler gangs operating in New Mexico's southern tier of four counties. In his gubernatorial message to the Twenty-Fifth Territorial Legislative Assembly, which convened on Monday, January 2, 1882, Sheldon asked lawmakers to provide county sheriffs with financial incentives to combat the outlaw bands and rustler gangs. The governor stressed that "desperados and 'rustlers' are migratory in their operations" and the territorial government should encourage cross-county cooperation to restore law and order and continue that cooperation to maintain the peace.

The governor also reminded the public that territorial law provided an officer with a small mileage allowance and a one-dollar service fee to deliver an arrest warrant to a suspect. The service fee and mileage allowance was the same whether for a misdemeanor or felony arrest for racing a horse, murder, or livestock theft. Even the territory's cattle growers' association offered a standing reward for the arrest of cattle thieves, but it was seldom utilized because it was a small amount and hard to collect. The territory's outlaw-rustler problem lagged on unsettled until the Thirty-Sixth Territorial Legislative Assembly, held in 1905, created the New Mexico Mounted Police. Within a few years this small band of territorial rangers had the livestock-stealing problem under control.

On February 9, 1882, the *New York Times*, under the column heading "National Capitol News," carried a follow-up report from their Washington bureau concerning its recent account of President Chester Arthur's first annual message to Congress (today called the State of the Union address) and his request to have Congress amend the Posse Comitatus Act to allow the military to assist local law enforcement officers in the territories. The president buttressed his request with a message from secretary of the interior Samuel J. Kirkwood stating "that in New Mexico and Arizona a difficulty in the way of repressing the lawlessness arises from the fact that the Sheriffs are intimidated, or that from personal motives they desire to curry favor with the disorderly element of society. It is therefore suggested whether it would not be expedient and proper that authority be conferred by law upon the Governor of any territory to remove or suspend a Sheriff for neglect of duty and to appoint a person in his place."

No congressional action was taken at that time on the request to give territorial governors authority to remove public officials for neglect of duty. However, in New Mexico this authority was given to the governor, and Miguel Otero used this ability to appoint his cousin Perfecto Armijo as the replacement sheriff of Bernalillo County in 1905. In a related matter, Henry Teller of Colorado replaced Kirkwood, a disagreeable bureaucrat from Iowa, as interior secretary on April 17, 1882, the day Wyatt Earp and his posse reached New Albuquerque. Teller strongly supported settlement and business expansion in the West.

While Wyatt Earp was active in southeastern Arizona, Major Albert Jennings Fountain and his First Battalion of Volunteer Cavalry of the New Mexico Territorial Militia were in the field on New Mexico's western border, and many would-be bad men found they were no longer safe in either territory. In 1912, Ralph Emerson Twitchell wrote—in volume two of his multivolume *The Leading Facts of New Mexican History*, quoting from then available official government documents—that Governor Sheldon ordered Fountain to patrol the water holes in the troubled counties because he reasoned that the rustlers would need water for themselves and their stolen herds. On August 9, 1896, Wyatt Earp, via his ghostwriter, mentioned in the second installment of his *San Francisco Examiner* three-part human interest feature how "the gallant Major Fountain, at the head of his rangers," chased and killed the wayward Cow-boys Wyatt's own posse had forced out of Arizona Territory. Fountain's systematic checking of water holes is the same method Wyatt Earp employed during his own Cow-boy Campaign.

Lt. Col. Perfecto Armijo, sheriff of Bernalillo County, commanded a regiment of the territorial militia stationed in the northern section of the territory. Company F of this volunteer military force, headquartered at Albuquerque, was led by Captain John Borradaile, Armijo's real estate partner. Edger S. Howe, the militia company's first lieutenant, became marshal of New Albuquerque by appointment from Sheriff Armijo shortly after the Earp posse left the community. Howe's brother Henry was the pressroom supervisor of a daily newspaper called the *Albuquerque Evening Review.*

Contemporary reports state that the Albuquerque Guard, 36 enlisted men who wore colorful uniforms with plumed helmets furnished by the Jaffa Brothers Mercantile Store, were a well-drilled outfit and equipped for combat. Captain Borradaile placed Company F on alert in April 1882 for possible action against a hostile assault by a force of Arizona bounty hunters seeking to serve illegal warrants in New Mexico Territory, especially in the Albuquerque area.

Governor Sheldon was a friend of President James A. Garfield and used that relationship to control certain factions within the territory's Republican Party. Shortly after Garfield's death at the hands of an assassin's bullet, Sheldon begin having trouble with the Tom Catron–led wing of the territory's Grand Old Party. This open antagonism developed a gulf between the legislative assembly leadership and the chief executive that made the political climate of New Mexico unsettling as a long-term safe haven for Wyatt Earp and his posse.

New Mexico's frontier Jewish community had interlocking social, family, and business connections that were on a par with those in the deep-rooted Hispanic community. These early immigrants became merchants; livestock contract and commodities traders; real estate, mining and lumbering investors; banking directors; lawyers; and key movers in all levels of the territory's political arenas. The names of Gusdorf, Ilfeld, Jaffa, Spiegelberg, Seligman, Staab, Birnbaum, Goldberg, Salsbury, Schutz, Baer, Moise, Nordhaus, Solomon, Floersheim, and Zerkendorf, among others, dot the pages of New Mexico's history. Among the second tier of Jewish businessmen were William Rosenthal and Benjamin P. "Ben" Schuster, also spelled Shuster.

Rosenthal and Schuster were natives of Prussia, the largest of the Germanic states that would form the German Empire founded in 1871. These two opportunists developed the Spiegelberg–Staab beef monopoly, operating under government contracts, to feed the Arizona and New Mexico Indian reservations. Schuster did the leg work that cultivated a business relationship with an Ascencion, Chihuahua, rancher named Nicholas Hughes to buy Mexican beef to augment the short supply of local beef needed to execute the Spiegelberg–Staab food contracts. Members of the Cow-boy rustling confederation operating in southern Arizona and New Mexico delivered some of these South-of-the-Border cattle needed to uphold the Spiegelberg–Staab–backed contracts. Rosenthal, an ex officio member of the Santa Fe Ring, coordinated the legal local cattle buys and questionable purchases from places like the Chisum Ranch on the Pecos River.

William Spiegelberg was a "card-carrying" Santa Fe Ring member and in his capacity as cashier of the Second National Bank of New Mexico, headquartered in Santa Fe, provided the financial stability for Schuster and Rosenthal's beef transactions. Two additional facts help us to understand how this streamlined buy-sell operation really functioned. Rosenthal, as the assistant internal revenue collector for New Mexico Territory, was able to clear the way for quick entrance of his out-of-the-country beef into the United States; then to ensure that he encountered little interference with local law enforcement he also served as a deputy U.S. marshal under John Sherman. Rosenthal married into the politically powerful Jose Manuel Gallegos family in 1874 and lived with his in-laws. Following his death in 1880, the beef contract scheme he engineered quickly began to unravel.

Even the Jewish businessmen who sometimes bent the letter of the law understood the need for a stable and orderly society in which free commerce could develop and financial rewards be earned. To maintain a free-enterprise atmosphere on the American frontier, strong local law enforcement was mandatory but not always possible; so some business leaders like Henry Jaffa understood the need to provide aid and financial support to extralegal operatives like Wyatt Earp and his posse.

John Henry Tunstall, a young Lincoln County rancher, sent a letter to his father in England, dated April 27, 1877, explaining the reality of his life in America: "Everything in New Mexico that pays at all (you may say) is working by a 'ring.' There is the 'Indian ring,' the 'Army ring,' and 'legal ring,' the 'Roman ring,' the 'cattle ring,' the 'horse thieves ring,' the 'land ring,' and half a dozen other rings. Now 'to make things stick' to do any good it is necessary to either get into a ring or make one for yourself. I am work[ing] at present making a ring." (Tunstall's action to create his "ring" was the primary cause of his death. One of his range riders who avenged his death was a teenage William "Billy the Kid" Bonney.)

The Santa Fe Ring was a business octopus with tentacles reaching across the territory and beyond. This loose confederation received direction from the law office of Tom Catron in the "City of Holy Faith" and had loyal minions at all levels of government. The Santa Fe Ring's focus was the acquisition of Spanish/Mexican land grants and the development of these properties for the personal gain of the ring owners. A secondary focus was a monopoly of the territory's government supply contracts for military posts and Indian reservations. These ring men represented the new breed of Republican Party leadership and were willing to do whatever was necessary to accomplish their economic goals. The ring controlled its worker bees not with bribes and graft but with largess. The most popular form of favor was the "loan" of funds to support the minion's dream or needs. This loan obligated the receiver to assist the ring with its activities. The Santa Fe Ring's top leaders controlled the three branches of the territorial government and were supported by powerful federal officials. They were all, not incidentally, Free Masons, binding them further in a society of faith and a brotherhood of professional prosperity.

Among these Santa Fe Ring entrepreneurs were some of the Southwest's leading Republicans and businessmen. These men included United States Senate friends Jerome B. Chaffee of Colorado, future father-in-law of Ulysses S. Grant, Jr., Stephen B. Elkins of Ohio, and his former Santa Fe law partner Thomas B. Catron, New Mexico's United States district attorney and future United States senator. Mercantile giant and mining promoter Henry M. Porter of Cimarron, a friend of Cimarron hotel operator Henry Lambert, and Henry L. Waldo, a junior partner in the Catron–Elkins law office, were also Santa Fe Ring confederates. These five men were all invested in General William J. Palmer's railway empire, the Atchison, Topeka and Santa Fe Railroad system.

Collis P. Huntington, the Southern Pacific Railroad's Washington lobbyist, was one of New Mexico governor Samuel B. Axtell's best friends. Axtell had, as the congressman from the San Francisco Bay area, served on the powerful congressional Joint Pacific Railroad Committee. Here he helped the Southern Pacific Railroad receive a monopoly as the transcontinental railroad providing service into the state of California. Huntington wrote Gheral Colton, an investor friend, on October 29, 1877, concerning opportunities in New Mexico: "I saw Axtell and he said he thought that if we [the railroad investors] would send him such a bill [as the one Congress passed to benefit the Southern Pacific Railroad in California] as we wanted to have passed into law, he could get it passed with very little money; when, if we sent a man there, they would stick him for large amounts." In January–February 1878, the Twenty-Third New Mexico Territorial Legislative Assembly met in Santa Fe and passed Huntington's railroad legislation. The legislators had nicknamed the proposed legislation the California Bill.

President Rutherford B. Hayes dealt a near deathblow to the Santa Fe Ring when he removed Governor Axtell and other top territorial appointees from public office in 1878. The president based his action upon the findings of a youthful special investigator he had sent to the territory. Frank Warner Angel's secret mission was to discover the truth behind the violence and disorder in Colfax and Lincoln counties as well as the general disruption of peaceful trade along the Mexican border with both Arizona and New Mexico. Angel uncovered a massive web of conspiracy, which he detailed in his numerous reports to the secretaries of both the Justice and the Interior departments. Historians reference these findings as the Angel Reports.

Special Agent Angel uncovered a vast interlocking network of graft and corruption centered in Santa Fe and directed by the federal government's chief appointees. Angel described Governor Axtell as "a man of strong prejudices, impulsive, conceited and easily flattered—all of these make a man easily influenced and complete tool in the hands of designing men" like the leaders of the Santa Fe Ring. President Hayes acted quickly, removing Governor Axtell and attorney general William Breeden. Also fired were United States attorney and Santa Fe Ring leader Tom Catron. Even the territorial chief justice felt Hayes' sting. Now broken away from its power base, the Santa Fe Ring disbanded.

The president's actions set in motion a high-level cover-up, perpetrated by Washington friends of Catron and Elkins, to misfile, destroy, or bury deep in the archive files of the Justice and Interior departments some of Angel's most damning reports. This action kept the contemporary media and later historians from discovering for well over seven decades the true nature and influence of the Catron confederacy. Information gleaned from the Angel Reports is slowly finding its way into studies of life on the New Mexico frontier.

Independent facts substantiate all the allegations that special agent Angel investigated, but that is not as significant to present-day historians as the recorded attitude of the participants in the disputes. The findings of the special investigation in their totality describe a stranger social history then has been previously suspected, and the complete set of reports are deserving of a more detailed treatment than is possible in this work.

A new Santa Fe Ring was born when Thomas Benton Catron regrouped and quietly formed a new confederacy while he waited for a new president to take office. The political cooperative was reborn with some old faces, including Abraham Staab, Stephen Benton Elkins, Henry L. Waldo, and Samuel B. Axtell. Some historians add Frank Springer to this new list.

Four years after he was disgraced and fired as territorial governor by President Hayes, Axtell was back in New Mexico Territory. President Chester Arthur appointed Axtell as chief justice of the territorial supreme court in 1882 and the former governor was prepared to continue his reign of corruption. C.P. Huntington was ready to help Axtell and his friends achieve their financial goals.

Catron's men were out of office, but he had won the Lincoln County War for economic control of southeastern New Mexico and now focused upon the vast Maxwell Land Grant in Colfax County. Don Miguel A. Otero and his Democrat Party of native Mexican-American citizens had suffered a major political loss and an economic setback in the recent struggle, which saw Otero lose his bid to be the territorial delegate in the 1880 election. Otero's group of loyalists, however, held control over future railroad development within the territory and thus still held a strong hand in this high-stakes game of power and money. Otero knew he needed the new ring's assistance to expand his plans. The ring leadership begrudgingly accepted Otero because they needed him.

Abraham Staab's Santa Fe mansion was the center of social life in the territorial capital. He was a director of the First National Bank of Santa Fe, the first bank organized in the territory, financed by Lucian B. Maxwell with money he made from selling his massive land grant in Colfax County. He was also, incidentally, an investor in the Maxwell Land Grant development project. Staab organized and led Santa Fe's first chamber of commerce. He was a prime mover in the efforts to keep the seat of territorial government in the Ancient City and to build a territorial penitentiary in the community. He also worked tirelessly to bring a branch railroad into the capital city.

Henry L. Waldo was born in Jackson County, Missouri, in 1844. After the War Between the States, he migrated to New Mexico and settled in Santa Fe. He was a brilliant attorney, later becoming territorial attorney general, and he was a good friend of Steven Elkins and Tom Catron. Waldo was also a friend of Vermont-born railroad builder William Bartow Strong. In 1881 when Strong became president of the Santa Fe system he made Waldo his chief legal advisor concerning the company's interest in the New Mexico Territory. He was also the vice president of the Santa Fe–based land company developing New Town Albuquerque. The New Mexico Territorial Mounted Police rescued Waldo's grandson, Waldo Rodgers, from a kidnap plot in 1911.

Elkins and Catron were graduates of the University of Missouri's class of 1860. The brilliant and urbane Elkins became a Yankee, while the crusty, blunt, domineering Catron rode with the rebels. After the war, they reunited in New Mexico Territory and began to write their names boldly across the history of that land. They, too, were major investors in the Maxwell Land Grant enterprises.

12

Ockham's Razor: The "Otero Letter," Fact or Fiction?

What I aim to do is to confine my writings to actual facts and adhere strictly to the truth, let the chips fall where they may.—Miguel Antonio Otero, Preface, *My Life on the Frontier, 1882–1897* (1939)

The term Ockham's Razor is expressed in Latin as *lex parsimoniae* and translated as "the law of succinctness." Many credit a 14th-century English logician and Franciscan friar named William of Ockham as having been the first to postulate the principle. The priest said that the explanation of any phenomenon should make as few assumptions as possible—the simplest explanation that covers all the facts is usually the best. In the second Sherlock Holmes novel, *The Sign of the Four*, the young detective verbalized this axiom thus in 1890: "How often have I said to you when you have eliminated the impossible, whatever remains, however improbable, must be the truth?"

We embark upon a quest, over the next few chapters, to analyze a massive puzzle using the principle of Ockham's Razor as our guide. We will examine the revelations made within the Otero Letter and place these in historical context in light of established historical facts while seeking the most obvious explanation for their meaning.

Any discussion of the Otero Letter must deal with three major issues: the document's provenance, its authenticity, and its credibility. We will deal with provenance first.

On a sunny Sunday afternoon in July 2001, I accompanied my brother-in-law to the mammoth weekly public flea market that sprawled over acres of the south parking lot of the New Mexico State Fairgrounds in Albuquerque (the 236-acre complex was renamed Expo New Mexico in 2003). This turned out to be a huge community event where hundreds of sellers were offering their discarded "treasures" in individual "yard sale" spaces. At one such area, operated out of the back of an old pickup truck, I found some vintage western books and bought two of them. One book was a history of the southwest territories by Dr. Howard Roberts Lamar. The second book was the deluxe edition of the final volume of Miguel A. Otero's classic autobiographical trilogy that covers his nine years as territorial governor of New Mexico.

The elderly Mexican-American gentleman selling the books said that they came from his recently deceased grandmother's house, but that he knew nothing about them. He also said that he was selling her house in Albuquerque's south valley if I was interested. I thanked him for the offer, but I already owned property in the state. Later that evening, upon returning to our home away from home, I was thumbing through the deluxe edition of Governor Otero's classic I had bought and discovered an undated and unsigned letter carbon tucked into the end pages.

Upon reading the letter, I found it contained hitherto unknown information concerning the Earp posse's stay in Albuquerque and the events surrounding those hectic days in the spring of 1882. One of the revelations dealt with the cause of a disagreement between Wyatt and Doc during their stay in Albuquerque. I knew that my friend and Earp–era historian Gary Roberts was deep into researching his biography of Doc Holliday, so I phoned him and told him about the discovery. He was excited and volunteered to contact some other Tombstone-era researchers (Casey Tefertiller, Jeff Morey, Jeff Wheat and Mark Dworkin) and start a dialogue about the letter. The group's quick consensus was that if the letter was authentic it would be an important contemporary source document concerning personal and behind-the-scenes activities and feelings of the Earp posse. The letter contained an important revelation concerning the depth of the financial and political support provided to Wyatt Earp's effort to eradicate the border Cow-boys.

Author's Perspective: Except for the *True West* article in December 2001 announcing the discovery of the Otero Letter I was not publicly involved in the Internet debate concerning any aspect of the document. First, I was deeply involved in researching and writing my book *Fullerton's Rangers* chronicling the actions of the New Mexico Territorial Mounted Police. This massive project was published in 2005. Second, I was battling some health issues and don't want to waste my strength on mindless adversarial and personal character attacks that were prevalent on discussion boards during those years. I attended the group meeting at Las Vegas, New Mexico, in 2005 and brought the Otero Letter and my files to be viewed and examined.

I have a few Earp-era fact findings to my field research credit, having discovered Wyatt Earp's involvement in the 1884 Colfax County, New Mexico, troubles; Josie and Wyatt's Christmas holiday stay at the St. James Hotel in Cimarron, New Mexico; the 1884 description of Josie Earp in an Albuquerque newspaper; the only known issue of the *Otero (NM) Optic* (containing Doc Holliday's dentist office information); the only known issue of the *Tombstone Echo* (containing an account of Luther King's escape); records of Doc Holliday's many New Mexico business dealings and tax records; the Cipriano Baca–Wyatt Earp connection; and Doc Holliday's drink tab in a saloon ledger from Fort Griffin. I have shared all of these finds with other researchers.

What does the Otero Letter look like? The epistle in question is typed on standard-sized 8½ by 11 inch off-white paper commonly used in the 1930s and 1940s as a carbon copy back page to protect the typewriter's page roller from damage by over-pounding the keys. The message has some eraser-smeared words, and a few words even show signs of over-striking with some letters. The edges of the paper have some wear markings and a small piece is missing from the right edge at the centerfold. Located in the body of the letter is a tiny hole and a noticeable crease is visible across the middle where the paper was folded in half. The paper has a stain, maybe coffee or tea, on the back

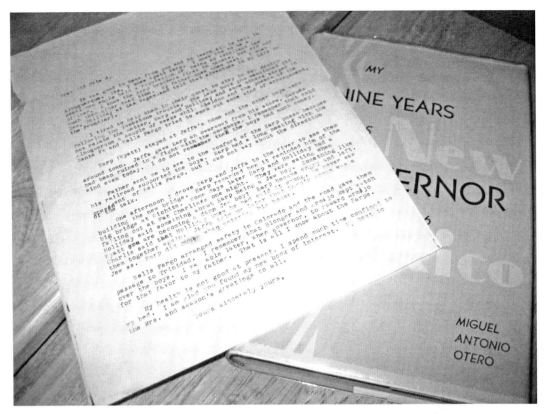

"Otero Letter" and Governor Miguel A. Otero's book that contained the letter (author's collection).

and shows signs of general color ageing. There is space left at the top for a formal letter heading found on printed business or personal stationary. Below is an annotated copy of the letter under discussion:

Dear Old Friend,

It was good to hear from you and to learn all is well in Albuquerque. Yes, I knew Wyatt Earp. I knew him to be a gentleman and he held a reputation of being an excellent law officer. I knew the Earp brothers first in Kansas, but did not [see] much [of] them after that time. My father knew them best. I knew Doc Holliday at Las Vegas and told that adventure in My Life on the Frontier [Vol.] I.

I tired [tried] to help them in their quest to stay in New Mexico following the Tombstone trouble. The Lake book you mentioned [*Wyatt Earp, Frontier Marshal*] did not relate the matter, Earp and Holliday and some others stayed in Albuquerque a couple of weeks while [New Mexico Territorial Governor] Sheldon and the powers of the Santa Fe [Railroad] and Wells Fargo tried to work out some kind of arrangement.

[Wyatt] Earp stayed at Jaffa's home and the other boys were around town. Jaffa gave Earp an overcoat from his store, Earp's had been ruined in a fight with the cow-boys. I remember that cold wind even today. I do not remember that the boys had much money.

Father sent me to see to the comfort of the Earp posse because his railroad supported the boys. Earp had a long meeting with the president of Wells Fargo, but I can not say about the direction of the talk.

One afternoon I drove Earp and Jaffa to the river to see them building the new bridge. Earp remarked how it reminded him of the big bridge at Wichita. Some days later, Earp and Holliday had a falling out at Fat Charlie's one night. They were eating when Holliday said something about

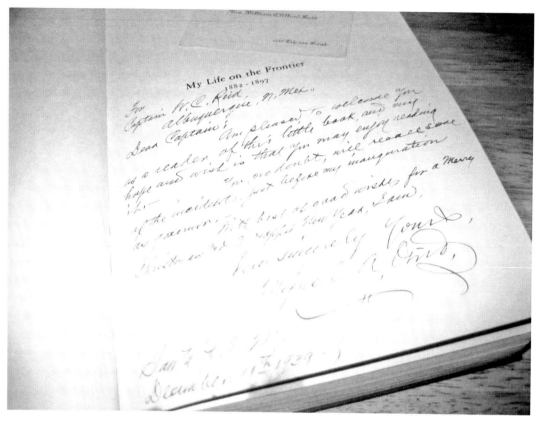

Governor Miguel A. Otero's book inscription to Captain W.C. Reid (author's collection).

Earp being a Jew boy. Something like Wyatt are you becoming a damn Jew boy? Earp became angry and left. Charlie said that Holliday knew he had said it wrong, he never saw them together again. Jaffa told me later that Earp's woman was a Jewess. Earp did mu ... [illegible] when entering his house.

Wells Fargo arranged safety in Colorado and the road [Santa Fe Railroad] gave passage to Trinidad. I remember that Blonger and Armijo kept watch over the boys. I was able later, when governor to reward Armijo for that favor to my father. That is all I know about the Earps.

My health is not good at present. I spend much time confined to my bed. I am glad you found my new book of interest. My best to the Mrs. and season's greetings to all.

Yours sincerely yours, [This draft is not signed.]

Author's Perspective: Since the letter contains some basic punctuation mistakes, it is my general impression that it is not the copy of a finished communication, but rather a copy of a working draft. Enhancing this idea is the fact that the letter contains no date, as if the writer was not yet ready to send the correspondence. Convenience gave the document the name "Otero Letter."

Dr. Gary Roberts, author of the acclaimed *Doc Holliday: The Life and Legend*, and I first divulged the discovery of the Otero Letter in our coauthored article for the December 2001 issue of *True West* magazine. We presented some internal and external evidence to start the debate on the merits of the letter, frankly stating, "Of course, further research must be done, not only on the substance of the claims in the letter, but also on the provenance of the letter itself before final conclusions can be drawn."

In July 2001, Mare Rosenbaum, associate editor of *True West*, explained why the magazine would publish new unverified material on the Old West: "[N]ew discoveries change our view of history—and for that reason alone, every tidbit that emerges is worth contemplating."

I have spent fifteen years seeking information to uncover the meaning and background of each sentence in the Otero Letter. The remainder of this book will be spent examining each sentence of the Otero Letter and evaluating the truth or falsehood of the statement.

A second issue concerning the Otero Letter is the authenticity of the document. Weeks after Gary Roberts and company began separate inquiries into all aspects of the "Otero Letter," I found time in September 2001 to make a special return trip to Albuquerque for a visit to the Center for Southwest Research at the University of New Mexico. The center is home to three generations of the Miguel Otero family's personal and business papers and archives. My mission was to examine the last 10 years of the "Letters Received" and "Letters Sent" files of the personal papers of Miguel A. Otero, Jr. I quickly discovered that Miguel Otero's "Letters Sent" files for the era in question contain numerous unsigned carbon copies of his letters, recorded upon thin yellow paper. This is another reason why I feel the document in question is a working draft and not a finished file carbon copy for a letter. The typewriter font style of the draft, aka the "Otero Letter," is consistent with the font style used in the late 1930s carbon copies of other carbon copy letters found in the Otero Collection.

During my detailed review of the Otero family correspondence archived in the Center for Southwest Research, I could not locate the original "question letter" or a file copy of the Watson Reed letter or a file copy of Miguel Otero's letter published in the *Tombstone Epitaph* in July 1936. In fact, I was unable to locate a file copy of any Miguel Otero communiqués related to the subject of Wyatt Earp or Doc Holliday.

In February 2005, I made a second trip to Albuquerque to examine the Otero Collection. This time I double-checked the letter files and reviewed Miguel Otero's personal research notebooks and draft manuscripts for his autobiographical books. The results of this search are discussed in another section.

Author's Perspective: I'm not sure why a letter writer, or their personal secretary, might have needed a copy of a working draft unless the letter writer had a habit of misplacing original drafts. It is possible the letter as originally drafted was never sent and the secretary thought the deleted content

Miguel A. Otero, governor of New Mexico Territory, 1897–1906 (author's New Mexico Mounted Police Collection).

of the draft held some personal revelation of significant interest worth preserving. The typist might have known or been related to someone mentioned in it.

Who might have authored the letter? Fortunately, the Otero Letter itself provides some authorship identity glues. We will next examine each of these to see what information they provide. *"Dear Old Friend"* suggests the author had enjoyed a long personal relationship with the individual he was addressing and further supports this belief by saying, *"It was good to hear from you and to learn all is well in Albuquerque."*

Internal content information would suggest that the letter's author could have been Miguel Antonio Otero, Jr., the former New Mexico territorial governor and territorial treasurer. This idea is bolstered by two statements made in the body of the letter. At one point the author wrote *"when governor"* and also noted that he had discussed Doc Holliday in one of his books, saying he *"told that adventure in My Life on the Frontier [Vol.] I."* Otero's autobiography for the years 1864–1882, published in 1935, was a mild success, resulting in a follow-up volume covering his pre-governor years of 1882–1896. In 1936, a deluxe edition of *My Life*, volume two, sold for $5.00 and a standard issue copy was retailed for $3.00. In 1940, a third autobiographical volume was published that covered Otero's nine years as governor.

The letter ends with another paragraph of personal data: *"My health is not good at present. I spend much time confined to my bed. I am glad you found my new book of interest. My best to the Mrs. and season's greetings to all."* Reason would suggest that the letter is circa December 1940. In the fall of that year Miguel "Gillie" Otero was ill much of the time and confined to bed in his Santa Fe residence at 354 Palace Avenue. Otero's correspondence from this time frequently mentions the declining state of his health.

From his catalogued correspondence, we learn that some of Miguel Otero's friends had asked him to complete his chronicles by writing another book covering his adventuresome years as territorial treasurer, United States marshal in the Canal Zone, and candidate for U.S. senator after leaving the governor's office in 1906. The elderly Otero said he was finished with his journalistic career. In 1927, he had completed a lengthy manuscript entitled "The Narrative of the Conquistadores of Spain and the Buccaneers of England, France and Holland." Two years later, he finished work on his "Ring Leaders in the Lincoln County War and Side-lights on Billy the Kid." Both of these manuscripts remain unpublished. An elderly Miguel Otero even refused attractive financial offers to write biographies of other celebrities he had known, much as he had done in his very limited-issue treatment of Billy the Kid. This 1936 biography was told from the *Nuevo Mexicano* point of view through ethnographic oral accounts and is still in print.

Miguel Otero had complained to an acquaintance that a new writing project was just too strenuous for him to undertake at this point in his life. He turned eighty-one years old on October 17, 1940, and his health was on its final downward spin. Before his death, the old political fighter and self-made historian had lost nearly half of his primetime weight, weighing less then ninety pounds when he started his "Long Sleep" on August 7, 1944. The old politician's final resting place is a single-plot grave site in Santa Fe's Fairview Cemetery.

Released on August 24, 1940, the final volume of Miguel Otero's autobiography concerning his nine-year stewardship as chief executive of New Mexico Territory during 1897–1906. The "Otero Letter" references *"season's greetings,"* which would seem to convey the former governor's wish of a happy yuletide season for his friend and his wife. This holiday reference seems to support the contention that the Otero Letter was composed in late December 1940.

When considering the authenticity and credibility of the Otero Letter a logical question to ask is who the intended recipient was. Who might have helped an aging and ill Miguel A. Otero prepare the communication? Among Otero's personal papers is a letter dated August 21, 1936, from the publishing house of Wilson-Erickson. This letter contains an up-to-date list of the people who had purchased a "Deluxe Edition" of *My Life on the Frontier* directly from the company. The printing was limited to 750 numbered copies, and this special edition anecdotal work sold 700 copies at six dollars each. A second "popular priced edition" sold for three dollars. The special edition subscription list contains two names of interest in any discussion about the recipient of the "Otero Letter." The first person of notice is "Miss. Clara H. Olsen" and the second is "Mr. W.C. Reid."

Miss Olsen served as Otero's personal secretary during his tenure as territorial governor and remained a close personal confidante after he left office in 1906. "Miss Clara" never married and after her retirement from government service (and working with over a dozen governors) she remained in Santa Fe (her family home was in Albuquerque). In later years, she did some of Otero's manuscript typing. Olsen was a member of the Archaeological Society of New Mexico and served on the society's Folk Lore Committee. This committee sought to preserve cultural tales of the social heritage of the new state. Would she have had an interest in preserving such information as that contained in the Otero Letter? Miguel Otero and his wife were also members of this society, even during the years they lived in the Panama Canal Zone. Eighty-two-year-old Clara H. Olsen died in 1953 and was buried in Section A of the Rosario Catholic Cemetery in Santa Fe.

Gillie Otero's friend William Clifford Reid was born in Indiana, studied law in Ohio, came to New Mexico Territory seeking adventure and settled in Las Vegas. The young lawyer and business manager of the *Las Vegas Daily Optic* served as chief clerk of the 1897 territorial house of representatives during Otero's first term as territorial governor. Otero selected Reid to lead one of New Mexico's volunteer companies during the 1898 war with Spain. After the war's end, Captain Reid joined the governor's party on a visit to President McKinley at the White House. In 1906, Governor Otero's successor, Herbert J. Hagerman, named Captain Reid as attorney general for the territory. Later, after his public service, W.C. Reid and James Hervey, another former attorney general, formed a law partnership in Roswell.

In 1915, Reid became chief legal counsel for the New Mexico division of the Atchison, Topeka and Santa Fe Railway (the company's name changed from "railroad" to "railway" in 1895), with his office in the Albuquerque headquarters complex. In 1927, Reid squired the building of Bluewater Dam and irrigation reservoir west of Grants (now the seat of Cibola County, created in 1981 as New Mexico's youngest county) as an agriculture support venture and a flood control effort to help prevent railroad track damage during seasonal floods. Today the lake and surrounding valley are New Mexico's

Bluewater Lake State Park. Reid bought a home at 1010 West Tijeras Avenue in Albuquerque's society section. He died of heart failure in November 1941. His wife Mabel died in 1945 and they are buried in Fairview Memorial Park in Albuquerque. They had one son, an attorney, who lived in Roswell.

I searched for over a decade to locate any personal papers belonging to Mr. Reid. I never located his correspondence but did discover that after Mrs. Reid's death her son consigned his father's book collection to an antiquarian in Albuquerque. Some of Reid's books ended up in Houston, Texas, in the library of a man who collected firsthand accounts of life on the American frontier. The collector's wife had worked at Carlsbad National Park before her marriage and loved the eastern New Mexico area. She and her husband vacationed all over New Mexico. The book collection was sold to a Houston bankruptcy attorney and antiquarian in an estate sale in the summer of 2014. The dealer offered these books for sale at an online auction in February 2015.

A copy of volume two of *My Life on the Frontier* once owned by W.C. Reid was one of the book offered at auction. I now own Captain W.C. Reid's book, signed by Miguel A. Otero. On the bottom half of the book's flyleaf the former governor wrote, "For Captain W.C. Reid, Albuquerque, N. Mex./ Dear Captain: Am pleased to welcome you as a reader of this little book and my hope and wish is that you may enjoy reading it./ You, no doubt, will recall some of the incidents, just before my inauguration as governor./ With best of good wishes for a Merry Christmas and a Happy New Year./ I am Very sincerely your, Miguel A. Otero/ Santa Fe, N.M. December 11th 1939." The "Otero Letter," written a year later, seems to echo the same literary style of this book inscription.

> **Author's Perspective:** I believe Miguel Otero may have typed the Otero Letter draft copy to his "Dear Friend" Captain Reid and given the draft to "Miss Clara" Olsen to type on letterhead for his signature. It might be that between the draft and the formal letter Otero reconsidered some statement he had made and decided it was too truthful or held potential embarrassment for his friend's former employer. Thus, the signature letter was sanitized and "Miss Clara" or some other yet unknown person saved the draft for its historical value. If my assumption is correct it would explain why a draft copy of the Otero Letter was produced.
>
> We still have a larger question, which is whether the signature letter, if it was typed and ever sent, still exists. Before a definitive answer concerning this question, or the legion of other questions generated by the Otero Letter, is possible, more research, and dumb luck, is required.

We next examine the credibility issue of the Otero Letter. The Otero Letter seems to be the response to a previous letter in which Otero's friend asked the former governor if he had known Wyatt Earp. The letter gives no indication as to what prompted the question.

On August 17, 1940, Miguel Otero sent a letter to a Denver, Colorado, resident named Watson Reed (not to be confused with William C. Reid) and discusses having known Wyatt Earp. This original letter is currently in the archives at Rutgers, the State University of New Jersey, where professional journalist Allen Barra, author of *Inventing Wyatt Earp: His Life and Many Legends*, discovered it in 1998. There is no carbon copy of the Watson Reed letter in Otero's "Letters Sent" files for 1940, nor is Reed's original letter to Otero contained in Otero's "Letters Received" files housed at the Center for Southwest Research. Does this mean that the Reed–Otero letter exchange did not happen? The answer is obvious, because the original Otero–Reed letter does exist. The only thing the missing letters prove is that there are some gaps in the Otero correspondence files or alternatively that these copies have been lost or misfiled.

Immediately upon publication of the discovery of the "Otero Letter," Allen Barra stated he felt the letter to be "dubious" and needed substantiation before it was taken seriously. Later, in an Internet post on *B.J.'s Tombstone History Discussion Forum*, May 16, 2005, Barra wrote, "Personally, I think it's a scam—and not a very good one." Barra never explained what he felt the scam might be. Gary Roberts addressed the "big elephant" in the room question: had I faked the document? "Chuck [accompanied by his brother-in-law] bought Miguel Otero's book in a flea market while he was visiting Albuquerque. He found the letter while leafing through it. The only way to get around that fact is call Chuck a fraud and me either a co-conspirator or dupe." Gary Roberts addressed the scam issue, saying he couldn't understand why someone would concoct as complicated a fraud as the "Otero Letter" and hide it in a book to be sold randomly at a flea market. "What would a hoaxer get out of this? Would someone go to this trouble for secret satisfaction or a private joke when it might never have surfaced? If this had been offered on eBay or was offered for sale in some similar manner, I would be more skeptical."[1]

By the time Barra made his scam comment the group of researchers mentioned above were in their fourth year seeking pro and con information. In fact, in July 2005 a small group of Earp researchers gathered in Las Vegas, New Mexico, and discussed the "Otero Letter," relevant research on it, and what this discovery could mean to the study of Tombstone. This was the first time the Otero Letter was displayed publicly for all to see up close and personal. Scott Johnson, the biographer of the Blonger brothers, summed up the meeting for most of us saying he felt not every incident described in the letter happened as written, but that these misremembered "facts" did not mean the letter was not genuine but "casts a long shadow over the authenticity of the Otero Letter." In an e-mail to the author, dated August 1, 2005, Roberts wrote, "I still do not believe this is a hoax, mainly because I do not see a hoax scenario that makes sense."

The discussion over the historical value of the Otero Letter reached a low point during 2009 when a discussion topic on a white supremacist organization's Web site contained a heated debate concerning Doc Holliday and the "Jew boy" remark. The truthfulness of the letter's content and the degree of the frontier dentist's anti–Semitic feelings took center stage. The discussion also questioned the manhood of Wyatt Earp concerning his supposed relationship with a Jewish whore and his friendship with an unreformed Georgia Rebel and Democrat.

Author's Perspective: In October 26, 2002, in a message post on *B.J.'s Tombstone Discussion Forum*, Gary Roberts summed up the discussion surrounding the news of the Otero Letter: "Already, the Otero letter has opened new doors for research that I—and others—had not considered before, if for no other reason than that, it has served a critical purpose." The day before he said, "If this letter is a fake, it is an extremely sophisticated one."

"Yes, I knew Wyatt Earp. I knew him to be a gentleman and he held a reputation of being an excellent law officer."

In the second sentence of the Otero Letter, the former governor answers the unrecorded question asked by his friend that caused the response letter. Gillie Otero made a similar remark concerning Wyatt's reputation in his 1940 letter to Watson Reed and in a July 1936 letter to the editor of the *Tombstone Epitaph*. In the *Epitaph* letter, the former governor stated that he had known both Wyatt Earp and Doc Holliday from his youthful days in Dodge City working for his father's mercantile company and did not mention anything about his later New Mexico associations with the men in Las Vegas or Albuquerque.

Some contemporary historians have suggested that if the Earp–Otero connection had been authentic, Otero would have included his knowledge of the posse's stay in Albuquerque in his own autobiography. They suggest that inclusion of the Earp–Holliday incident would have helped him sell his own books. To put this discussion in perspective, it should be remembered that Otero paid a professional editor to revise the first draft of his memoirs at the same time Stuart Lake was researching his Earp biography in the spring of 1928. Otero called this 1928 draft manuscript "my early recollections," but it has not survived as part of his personal papers, so it is impossible to say definitely that an aging Gillie Otero had not included the Albuquerque adventure in his earliest autobiographic manuscript.

"I tired [tried] to help them in their quest to stay in New Mexico following the Tombstone trouble. The Lake book you mentioned did not relate the matter."

During the summer 2005 Internet discussion concerning the "Otero Letter," some Tombstone era buffs claimed that the letter does not follow Otero's writing style. Others noted numerous similarities in syntax. In late 1940, Miguel Otero was a very ill man and it is possible that maturity had changed his style of communication. During his almost nine years as governor, Otero wrote annual reports on the state of the territory, and just a cursory reading of these tomes reveals a style of flowery Victorian prose. Later, Otero wrote the three volumes of his autobiography in a matter-of-fact style with long quotations from contemporary newspaper clippings and personal anecdotes favorable to him. He glories in fights with his political enemies. The two *My Life on the Frontier* books have a single purpose. Otero felt he needed to cover these years so he could justify the volume he saw as his real monument, a book on his tenure as territorial governor. Each set of Otero's writings convey a certain point of view during separate eras of his life. Otero wrote a friend concerning this subject: "I was writing 'My Memories,' and not attempting to write a story by some one else."

Over a period of months, Woody Campbell and Gary Roberts conducted a sentence and word analysis of syntax and style structure of the Otero Letter against confirmed Miguel Otero letters. The conclusion of this work was positive. "The patterns are consistent," wrote Roberts. "In fact, the similarities are too great to be coincidental. It is normal for us all to use similar expression when writing to others about a common subject." In a follow-up commentary Roberts wrote, "The importance of the Otero letter, if, as I believe, it is authentic can scarcely be overstated."

The discovery of the Otero Letter caused some to question, if the letter was authentic, why Miguel Otero had not revealed this blockbuster information in one of his books. In the 1940 Otero–Reed letter, the former governor writes that he had only recently read Stuart Lake's 1931 Wyatt Earp biography and had to telephone his friend who had loaned him the book to read to recall the author's name. This would tend to show that Otero had little or no knowledge concerning the Lake book's contents when he was writing his own memories of that frontier era in the mid–1930s.

It might be of value to note that Gillie Otero had a history of guarding his personal financial interests as a highly important daily activity. His successor as territorial governor, Herbert J. Hagerman, questioned Otero's personal financial ethics when he requested that the new chief executive pay him $177.32 as his 22-day share of the 1906 governor's office annual contingency expense account. This $3,000 fund was authorized by the territorial legislative assembly in addition to the governor's $3,000 annual salary and an office operational account of $8,700 (including the salary for his private secretary) provided by Congress. The territorial records indicate that Hagerman authorized payment of Otero's request in a letter dated March 6, 1906, but the new governor considered it as borderline graft by a public servant.

In 1933, Miguel Otero and his son the second Miguel III were dumped into a financial crisis when they lost their investments in the failure of the First National Bank in Albuquerque. In August, the former governor was even unable to assist his brother Page, living in California with his wife and children, who was gravely ill and financially strapped. Page died in September. The Great Depression was in high gear, so Gillie Otero took to writing to make extra money and lay claim to his place in New Mexico history.

Governor Otero did not include many personal moments of sorrow and joy within the covers of his three autobiographical works. One example of these omissions is how a Denver bunko artist swindled Otero's beloved father out of $2,550 a few weeks before the Earp posse arrived in Albuquerque and how Gillie tried to recoup the financial loss and jail the criminal.

Miguel Otero recounted at length his attraction to one young lady and his engagement to another, but he never mentioned his courtship of Caroline Virginia Emmett, daughter of a former chief justice of the Minnesota Supreme Court. The newly married Republican found his bride to be a political asset but gave only a matter-of-fact mention of their marriage in his biography. She is mentioned only as an addendum to his activities. Their first child, Miguel Antonio III, died after eight days, and Otero devotes a paragraph to the life and death of the child yet makes no mention of why his brother Page took his infant nephew's body to Denver for burial in the family plot. No mention of the birth, life or death of his seven-month-old daughter, Elizabeth, is recorded by Miguel Otero.

Otero does not mention his arrest for providing "intoxicating liquor" to minor-aged cadets attending the New Mexico Military Institute at Roswell nor does he discuss his persistent alcohol abuse that he hid from the public when he was chief executive. Governor Otero and his wife separated in early 1904 and divorced in October 1909, three years after his nine years as governor. From 1909 to 1911, Gillie served as territorial treasurer and invested in mining and real estate ventures, but he never was as financially secure as he had been as a young man.

The former governor remarried in 1913, wedding the widow of a political friend, and tried to regain his statewide political base but with no success. His second wife rated only a footnote mention in book three. In his three tales about himself, Otero glories in his near-death experiences with illnesses during his youth and his popularity as governor but never publicly expresses his personal emotions or inner feelings.

President Woodrow Wilson appointed the born-again Democrat as the United States marshal of the Panama Canal Zone in 1917 and he remained there until 1921. Upon his return to New Mexico he again tried to restart his political career but to no avail, so he became a senior statesman to other candidates and started his writing projects. His life-long alcohol abuse caused him to spend time in a sanatorium and became the main cause for Otero's spending his last three years mostly confined to his bed, where he died on Monday morning August 7, 1944.

Scott Johnson discovered, by reviewing copies of the *Las Vegas Daily Optic*, that Miguel Otero had altered the actual events of his life during the spring of 1882. In his book the former governor makes no mention of his father's fleecing by a bunko artist in Denver during April or his own presence in the Mile High City that month to rectify his father's financial loss. It would seem that Otero used social incidents copied verbatim and without attribution from the newspaper to convey the impression he had been in Las Vegas at the time.

Miguel Otero acknowledged he consulted the bound copies of the *Las Vegas Daily Optic*, then housed in the newspaper's office, to supply background color for his narrative and to refresh his memory concerning certain events. These file copies of the *Daily Optic* were used in the 1950s to microfilm the newspaper's collection. A comparison of the microfilm copy with hard copies in other collections reveal that stories concerning Don Miguel's Denver troubles were cut from the historic file copies. In a June 19, 2005, e-mail to the Otero Letter study group Johnson wrote, "Now, I won't insist that Otero tried to alter the 'first draft of history' by excising the *Optic* while writing *My Life on the Frontier*. But I think such a theory is consistent with the evidence, in a way that the Otero Letter is not consistent with his earlier writings."

Don Miguel A. Otero, congressional delegate from New Mexico Territory (Fred Lambert New Mexico Collection).

Some researchers have questioned why Miguel Otero didn't discuss Wyatt Earp, if he really knew him, in more detail in his book. It may come as a surprise that not everyone who ever had dealings with Wyatt Earp mentioned these events in their accounts of their own lives. Thomas Fitch, the attorney who defended Wyatt during the judicial hearing held concerning the streetfight in Tombstone, is a good example. This month-long court case, the so-called Spicer Hearing, was a watershed event in Earp's life and these events have a legion of fans today. Fitch, however, in his autobiography made no mention of Wyatt Earp, the Spicer Hearing, the Cow-boys' death threats he received for getting Wyatt acquitted or that he and James Earp were both in Nevada in the mid–1860s. Even at the time, Fitch considered the streetfight hearing of such minor importance that he took time off from his defense duties to prepare and deliver a public lecture on the subject of the "Invisible Police" to a Tombstone benefit to raise money for the organ fund of the town's Methodist-Episcopal church. Today, Tombstone has a street named in Fitch's honor.

Fitch and his wife were visiting with the Earps in the parlor of Denver's Tabor Hotel when Doc Holliday arrived looking for Wyatt. This late 1880s visit was the last meeting between the two living legends. Josie told of the event in her memoirs, but Fitch did not find the Earp–Holliday encounter important enough for his reflections.

People, in general, do not view the same events with the same degree of importance. Western author William R. Cox referred to the Tombstone streetfight as a "brouhaha," while others have portrayed it as the apex of the heroic fight to establish law and order on the frontier. Autobiographies exclude certain events for many different reasons. Sometimes it is a matter of length or editorial direction. One example is the two autobiographies of prizefighter Jack Dempsey. In the first, coauthored in 1960 with Bob Considine in the wake of the popularity of the Wyatt Earp television series, the fighter did not mention knowing Wyatt Earp. Seventeen years later, in 1977, Dempsey and his daughter Barbara produced a less flamboyant tale that included Dempsey's meeting Earp and his positive impression of the man.

A historic side-note to our discussion of incidents not mentioned concerns General George Armstrong Custer's wife, Libbie. In *Frontier I*, Otero mentioned that while at Sheridan, Wyoming, he met General Custer and General Sheridan when they escorted Grand Duke Alexis of Russia on his well-publicized buffalo hunt. During the seasons when Dodge City was the location for *The Life and Legend of Wyatt Earp*, one of the people who would occasionally visit television's version of the cowtown from nearby Fort Dodge and interact with "Marshal Earp" was Elizabeth Bacon Custer. The "reel" Libbie Custer and the "reel" Wyatt Earp were friends, but history does not record if the real Libbie Custer had even met the real Wyatt Earp.

Frederick Hazlitt Brennan, with Earp biographer Stuart N. Lake serving as his historical consultant, wrote 184 of the 226 episodes filmed for *The Life and Legend of Wyatt Earp* television series. Had Lake discovered some information about a genuine acquaintanceship between Wyatt Earp and the Custers? Did Lake have Brennan incorporate this Custer information into the scripts or was the multi-episode Earp–Custer storyline just another example of the legend part of the television series? Further research is required before a definitive statement can answer these questions.

The *Santa Fe Daily New Mexican*, on April 18, 1882, took note that "Mrs. General Custer, widow of the famous chieftain who met death at the hands of the Indians years ago, was in the city." The newspaper made no mention concerning the nature of her presence in the Ancient City. A few days later, Libbie Custer was a guest at the Montezuma Hot Springs resort likely having no idea about all the backdoor deals concerning Wyatt Earp. Las Vegas newspapers mentioned Mrs. Custer's presence in the city but did not interview her.

Gillie Otero did not chronicle Mrs. Custer's Las Vegas visit in his autobiography. He also omitted an earlier visit to Las Vegas by army chief of staff General William T. Sherman and once answered an inquiry concerning his relationship with Bat Masterson by saying, "I knew Bat Masterson very well." Yet, Otero wrote relatively little concerning Masterson personally nor did he chronicle any of their adventures together. Generally, Otero selected incidents that enhanced his central position in the event and would not place himself in a secondary role even to a national celebrity.

In fairness, we should note that, besides Generals Custer and Sheridan, Wyatt Earp, Bat Masterson, and Doc Holliday, former Governor Otero also claimed to have had adventures with Wild Bill Hickok, Calamity Jane, Buffalo Bill Cody, Jessie James, and Billy the Kid. Otero wrote that when he was a 9-year-old in Hays City, Kansas, in 1869 he witnessed Hickok kill a man. Later, Hickok introduced the young adventurer to Buffalo Bill, who took Otero and his brother on a buffalo hunt with him. Otero also played poker with Jesse James and Billy the Kid.

Otero could be very testy during his last years. Holding his personal honor very dear, he would not stand for anyone to question him on that point. Once a western history collector questioned his association with certain frontier personalities and got a brisk reply: "I was never an associate of criminals so please get me right." Otero seems to have forgotten he claimed friendship with Billy the Kid in a biography he wrote about the young killer. Otero also admonished the questioner, saying, "I am an authority and do not wish you to quote me in any of your books, except what you may find in my books, and I have written facts not fiction."

The manuscript of *My Life on the Frontier II*, contained in Miguel Otero's personal papers, has a notation written on page fourteen: "In summing up my work [on volume one], I find that a few facts were carelessly omitted." This is a telling comment when examined with the knowledge that written on page after page of the prepublication manuscript of *My Life on the Frontier II* is the word "omit" or the words "cut out." Some pages are only half sheets of paper with the top or bottom cut off, while in some cases whole pages are missing from the numbered sequence of the narrative. This book draft is a wonderful example of how a writer constructed a pre-computer era manuscript.

Author's Perspective: One last point to consider when assessing the authenticity of a historical document is the facts surrounding the document itself. One example to recall concerns a threatening letter sent to President Andrew Jackson in July 1835, reputedly by Junius Brutus Booth, a famous actor of his era. Jackson's secretary read the letter, thought it was a joke, and filed it among earlier threats made against the chief executive's life. This was an interesting action since an assassination attempt had been made against Jackson by a delusional housepainter on the steps of the Capitol just six months earlier. The would-be assassin's two pistols both misfired and a group of men walking with Jackson captured the man; one of these men was Congressman David Crockett. The Booth letter was viewed as a hoax or forgery until 2009.

Dan Feller and his research team from the University of Tennessee's Andrew Jackson Papers Project did some fact checking after reading the Booth letter. They discovered that Booth had been in Philadelphia appearing in a play during early July 1835 and had stayed at the Brown Hotel. The suspect letter was written on Brown Hotel stationary, dated July 4, 1835, and called Jackson a "damn'd old Scoundrel" and said, "I will cut your throat whilest you are sleeping." Future investigation uncovered that Booth had been drunk on July Fourth and did not appear in the play. Evidence indicates that Booth apologized to the theater's owner for his actions and mentioned that he had sent a malicious letter to a high government official. Handwriting comparison proved that Booth was in fact the letter's author. Booth never acted upon his threat against Jackson, but historians misjudged the veracity of the letter's author for almost 175 years. They also missed the larger historical implications, as the reader will recall that Junius Brutus Booth was the father of John Wilkes Booth, who, 30 years after his father threatened the life of a president, become the first man to kill an American president.

13

The Otero Family
of New Mexico

Mr. Otero, a political leader in New Mexico for over twenty years,
is intimately connected with the history of the Territory more than
any other living man.—*The Encyclopedia of the New West*, 1881 edition

An entry in the 1881 edition of *The Encyclopedia of the New West* places the influence of Don Miguel Antonio Otero, Sr., and his family into proper perspective. Don Miguel was following in the footsteps of his father, as had his brothers and sister. Now the grandchildren were becoming involved in the family businesses and public service. Ralph Emerson Twitchell, a highly respected New Mexico chronicler during his lifetime, recalled Don Miguel A. Otero, Sr., in his multivolume history of New Mexico: "He was a man of distinguished attainments, strong individuality, and a fine appreciation of the higher ethics of life. He was a conspicuous part in the development of the territory."

Don Miguel's father and mother, Don Vicente and Doña Gertrudis Aragón de Otero, came from Spain to make their home in Nuevo Espana in the early 1800s. In 1819, the vast area in the north along the Rio Grande del Norte became El Provincia de Nuevo Méjico of the new Mexican Republic. Don Vicente served as *alcalde* (mayor and judge) at the village of Valencia under both the Spanish and Mexican governments and became rich in land and livestock. Otero's hometown settlement became the seat of Valencia County after the United States territorial government established administrative regions in 1852. The county stretched from the western border of Texas to the Colorado River on the eastern border of the state of California.

Don Vicente and Doña Gertrudis had three sons and one daughter. The Otero brothers, Antonio Jose, Manuel Antonio, and Miguel Antonio, engaged in the mercantile business and later branched into banking, mining, livestock raising and land grant management. The oldest son, Antonio Jose, was named one of the first associate justices of the New Mexico Supreme Court. The boys' sister, Maria Candelaria Otero, married Ambrosio Armijo, a freighter and mercantile operator on the Plaza at Albuquerque, and had five children. The Armijos' son Perfecto Armijo played a part in the Earp posse's Albuquerque sojourn.

Don Miguel A. Otero, Sr., was born in Valencia, Valencia County, on June 21, 1829, in what was the Mexican El Provincia de Nuevo Méjico. He was a college Latin and Greek professor in Fishkill, New York, before becoming an attorney in Albuquerque. Don Miguel was a Democrat who had served as the private secretary to the territorial governor, served in the house of representatives section of the territorial legislative assembly and as the territory's attorney general before being elected to three terms as New Mexico's delegate to Congress in the 1850s. President Lincoln appointed Don Miguel as territorial secretary, disregarding his pro–Southern political leanings, so that he could return to New Mexico and attend to the family mercantile and banking business interests while still serving his country.

During the outbreak of the War Between the States, Otero was acting governor of the New Mexico Territory and prepared the territory to withstand an invasion of Confederate troops. Don Miguel understood the power of the governor either to take action or to turn a blind eye and not take action. Otero rallied Hispanic support to help to save New Mexico for the Union. In the 1870s, Don Miguel invested in land grant speculation, mining claim development, railroad expansion, and in the establishment of the San Miguel National Bank at Las Vegas.

Don Miguel married Mary Josephine Blackwood, daughter of a Charleston, South Carolina, judge. They had four children, the first two being daughters. The older girl, Gertrude Vincentia, died before Christmas 1876. She was 11 years old. Marie Josephine, born in 1868, married Henry O'Bryan at Las Vegas in 1888 and had two children. She served as the postmistress of Santa Fe prior to her death in an automobile accident in September 1928.

Page Blackwood Otero, Don Miguel and Mary's older son, was a unique individual on the western frontier. He was tough yet genial. He was an avid hunter and fisherman but also a dedicated conservationist and became New Mexico's first game and fish warden. He was an Indian hater but appreciated the Native American culture. Highly educated and a man of social status, he relished working in the field with crude hard-rock miners. Page was equally at home on a musical stage production, pitching at a baseball game or being a barroom pool hustler. He served as a New Mexico Territorial Mounted Police and a deputy United States marshal but had once been a boomtown vigilante. Page's youthful drunkenness turned into public alcohol abuse as he grew older and was the cause of his being fired from two public service posts. He could never overcome his disgrace and finally moved his family to California for a new start; but he died a tired, sick, and broken man who was deeply in debt and shunned by his own relatives.

The second son, Miguel A. Otero, Jr., was born on October 17, 1859, at the family home in St. Louis, Missouri. Beginning in the fall of 1866, Page and Miguel, called Gillie, attended a private boarding school in Topeka, Kansas, and later attended St. Louis University and, for a short time, Notre Dame. The Oteros were a close-knit family, with young Page being attached to his mother and Gillie to his father. The boys were pals during their youth and young manhood, but as the years passed political ambition and financial power caused a strain in their relationship following their father's death. Page remained a Democrat his whole life, while Gillie was an opportunist with his political views, enough to become a progressive Republican governor in between two lengthy stints in public service as a Democrat.

Fate has a way of making strange combinations. Within a 90-day span in early 1882 the death angel claimed the "three amigos": Don Manuel A. Otero, Don Ambrosio Armijo and Don Miguel A. Otero. These deaths turned the Otero family finances into an internal struggle among the cousins, a strain that was felt for decades. On May 18, 1882, the *Las Vegas Daily Gazette* published a "Notice" from Don Miguel Otero acknowledging that two weeks earlier, a day after Gillie returned to Las Vegas after his failure to reclaim his father's lost money from a Denver con artist, he had granted his attorney John F. Bostwick complete authority "to attend to and supervise all my interests and business affairs." Don Miguel died suddenly on May 30 ten days short of his 53rd birthday, and Page and Miguel Otero had to curb their playboy ways after the summer of 1882. Money and power took on a whole different meaning for the brothers.

"My father knew them best."

Don Miguel A. Otero, Sr., knew Wyatt Earp as a member of the Dodge City police force. Gillie Otero, who worked as a clerk in his father's mercantile store in the Kansas cowtown, would later recall assistant city marshal Wyatt Earp and Ford County sheriff Bat Masterson. The two lawmen were better educated, more widely read, more finely socially mannered, and politically better connected than many of their western counterparts. Father and son Otero were also acquainted with the Southern gentleman from Georgia—dentist, gambler, and saloon owner John Henry Holliday. Earp and Holliday both had business dealings with the Santa Fe Railroad.

14

Ten Days in New Albuquerque

The letter appears to clear up a mystery. One of the more curious elements of the storied Wyatt Earp–Doc Holliday friendship, a legendary relationship with a factual basis, has been the source of a quarrel between the two men in Albuquerque in 1882.—Mark Dworkin, "Henry Jaffa and Wyatt Earp," *Western-Outlaw Lawman History Association Journal*, Fall 2004

Walter Noble Burns' Tombstone book was the first published account to mention the New Mexico connection to the Cow-boy Campaign. Burns almost got the story right: "Sheriff Behan's pursuit ended in failure at the Arizona line. Wyatt Earp and his men passed into New Mexico, sold their horses at Silver City, and at Deming, took a train for Denver. The Colorado capital was their final destination." Burns' statement was half right, because at this stage of his Cow-boy Campaign Wyatt's only destination was the Duke City. The plan was to have the posse stay in New Albuquerque until arrangements could be finalized to establish a sanctuary from extradition back to Arizona Territory. Kansas, New Mexico, and Colorado were being explored as refuge locations, with Colorado finally being identified as the best choice.

Spanish governor Francisco Cuervo y Valdes led the thirty-five families that first settled the plaza of Albuquerque in the spring of 1706, seven decades before the formation of the United States of America. His villa was located on the eastern bank of the Rio Grande del Norte and named in honor of the Viceroy of New Spain, Don Francisco Fernandez de la Cueva Enriquez, the Duke of Alburquerque. The settlers in the new village eventually dropped the first "r" in the duke's title. The name Albuquerque had originated in southern Spain during the 1400s with the Islamic Moors and their word *Abu-al-Qurq*, meaning "the town of the Christians and Jews." The Spanish conquistadors brought the word to the New World.

New Albuquerque's clear dry mountain air assisted the land developers in marketing the location as a health center for persons suffering from chronic bronchitis and asthma. This may have been the initial reason for the consumptive Doc Holliday's first visit to the town. The Santa Fe Railway tracks reached the area on Saturday, April 10, 1880, and the new settlement along the tracks became a day and night pleasure playground. The new town retained its "end-of-track town" excitement even after the construction crews moved on following the Rio Grande Valley south toward the Mexican Republic.

William C. Hazeldine, Franz Huning and Elis Sleeper Stover formed the New Mexico Town Company, with Henry Waldo as the chief sales agent, and laid out over a hundred acres between the road connecting the Hispanic settlement of Barelas to the old adobe plaza of Albuquerque near the Rio Grande and the new railroad tracks on the flats. The *Las Vegas Daily Optic*, March 5, 1880, told readers, "Lots are selling and building going on rapidly." Meanwhile, the *Albuquerque Advance* was also boasting about the new town's progress: "Strangers coming in on the railroad will find the orchards, gardens and green grass on Railroad Avenue [present-day Central Avenue] a little different from anything at Santa Fe or Las Vegas."

One of the earliest boosters for New Town Albuquerque was the fiery, redheaded A.M. Conklin, who was the editor of the *Albuquerque Advance*. Conklin wrote on April 8, 1880, "All the leading business houses in the territory are turning their attention towards Albuquerque." Conklin's attention turned southward in July 1880 as the Ohio native relocated his publishing press to the rejuvenated Old Spanish plaza at Socorro and founded the *Socorro Sun*. Conklin was murdered in Socorro on Christmas Eve 1880 as he left a late-night church service.

C.M. Chase, editor of the *Vermont Union* published at Lyndon, Vermont, visited New Town Albuquerque on November 30, 1881. He wrote to the folks back home: "Set down in Vermont any of the business streets of Albuquerque for just one evening and the Governor, with all his staff and all the sheriffs, would take to the woods, under the impression that hell had broken loose, and that any attempt at legal restraint would be suicidal." Most of the large dance halls, called "terpsichorean temples," were still located in Old Town, but the new section had already developed its own saloon row along Railroad Avenue and was developing its own bordello area on North Third Street. Chase saw great potential in the New Town development and bought fifteen town lots at $200 each. A short time later, Mr. Chase visited Raton City, which was developing on the Colorado–New Mexico border, where he bought some lots in that village. The Vermont businessman made money on both of these town-lot investments.

New Albuquerque was still a growing community in the spring of 1882. It had over three miles of horse-drawn streetcar track down the center of Railroad Avenue, which ran from the railroad depot to the Old Town Plaza. A morning and evening newspaper kept the populace informed. The city had a telephone exchange and gas lighting in both the business district and the residential sections. A bank, a private academy, a foundry, a gristmill, a planing mill, four hotels, a few opium dens and at least two dozen saloons, along with other essential elements of civilization in the Victorian era, helped to define the new town. Five church groups and ten houses of prostitution provided for the spiritual and physical needs of the mostly male citizens. The largest New Town employer was the Santa Fe Railroad repair shop and yards, along with the locomotive roundhouse located near the tracks south of the depot area.

After the arrival of the Santa Fe Railroad's repair yard and engine roundhouse crew and the growth of the vice trade in the new community, the *Albuquerque Evening Review*'s editor, W.F. Saunders, started a crusade to remove the brothels and an opium den located on West Railroad Avenue. The editor wrote, "All western towns are vicious, but none of them flaunt their vice so openly in the face of strangers as does Albuquerque." The opium den disappeared within a few years, but the "red light district" remained a thriving commercial section until 1914, when a reform city council made the sex business illegal within the city limits.

"Father sent me to see to the comfort of the Earp posse because his railroad supported the boys."

Based upon newspaper accounts, personal papers, and the author's judgment, what follows is a possible scenario concerning how the arrangements were established to shelter the Earp federal posse in Albuquerque. It will be recalled that during the Saturday night conference, on March 25, 1882, at a powder storage facility in south Tombstone, Wyatt Earp agreed to have his supporters arrange safe retreat for him and his men while the legal process ran its course.

Don Miguel Otero was contacted about the plan and his assistance was requested. He made preliminary contacts in New Albuquerque with his friends and family to elicit their cooperation. The *Albuquerque Evening Review* of March 22, 1882, noted that Don Miguel's oldest son, Page, had arrived in New Albuquerque from his mining operations in the Magdalena Mountains northeast of Socorro. Don Miguel most likely asked Page to follow up on the informal arrangements and probably counted on Page to make sure all was in place at Albuquerque for the federal officers' arrival.

Over the next twelve days the *Albuquerque Evening Review* noted that Page and some of his mining friends were "batching in a tent" near Old Town "within handy distance of Rees and Loebner's Billiard Hall." He could have stayed at one of his uncle's homes in Old Town or even with his cousin, who was the sheriff, but Page enjoyed the outdoor life with his campmates.

During this period, the *Las Vegas Daily Optic* was reporting the speculation that billiard hall owners might try to arrange a match between Albuquerque's ace cue-man, Charlie Ronan, and Page Otero, also a deft handler of a pool stick. Ronan was a former New Las Vegas gambler known to Doc Holliday and other Easterner gamblers. Fate intervened in the proposed billiard match, but Charlie Ronan would play a later role in the Otero Letter saga.

On Tuesday morning, March 28, 1882, the *Albuquerque Morning Journal* reported, "Last night, at a late hour, a JOURNAL reporter learned that the famous Earp boys were headed for Albuquerque, and that they were on the Atlantic express which arrives in this city this morning at 6:18. In the party there are two of the Earps and five of their confederates." It is unclear if this notice was a leak in the ranks of the conspirators, miscommunication between Earp and his handlers, or a trial balloon, but the federal posse from Arizona was not on the train. Within days, the Cow-boy element knew that something was in the works that would change the conditions on the ground in Arizona Territory.

It is very possible that an inebriated Page Otero, playing a late-night billiard game, blabbed about the pending arrival of Wyatt Earp's posse in New Albuquerque and the discussion was overheard by a *Morning Journal* reporter. It is assumed that as soon as Don Miguel learned of the newspaper report that the telegraph or telephone wires conveyed his displeasure at this news leak. The *Albuquerque Evening Review* of April 3 1882, noted that Page Otero and his partying cadre of miners had returned to the Magdalena Mountains the day before and Gillie Otero had arrived in New Albuquerque, and added, "He managed to miss Page." Gillie Otero reestablished the sanctuary network and restarted the plan.

The *Santa Fe Daily New Mexican* carried the following item on page four of the Tuesday, April 4, 1882, issue: "Don Miguel A. Otero, of Las Vegas, came over to the capital yesterday and stopped at the Exchange hotel." On Wednesday, the paper explained that Otero had really made the 75-mile trip on Sunday and had "left for the south" on Tuesday. During his stay in Santa Fe, Don Miguel visited with old friends at the Germania, a private Jewish businessmen's social club. The wheels were back in motion to assist the Earp posse.

The Exchange Hotel had a commanding view of the plaza and was the oldest and most popular hotel in Santa Fe. Originally built as the U.S. Hotel in the mid–1840s it soon became the town's preeminent inn. The hotel sat on the southeast corner of the plaza, near the Seligman & Clever Mercantile Company, across the plaza from the offices of the territorial government. The Palace of the Governor was a rambling, block-long, one-story adobe structure with six-foot-thick walls that had housed the residence and office of New Mexico's governors since the colonial Spanish era and had also served as the territorial legislative assembly chambers since 1850. The centrally located Exchange Hotel advertised itself as the "headquarters for tourist, mining and commercial men," where rooms were four dollars a night. With the dawn of the 20th century, the hotel fell into disrepair and was a butcher shop in 1919 when it was demolished to make way for construction of the grand pueblo–style La Fonda Hotel of today.

When the *Santa Fe New Mexican* reported that Don Miguel was "going south" from Santa Fe, such an expression usually implied that the individual was journeying down to Albuquerque or Socorro or maybe El Paso. In this case, it is likely that Otero went to the Duke City to personally confer with his youngest son. The *Las Vegas Daily Optic*, April 8, 1882, reported that Gillie Otero left for Denver that day to handle a personal matter for his father. (Don Miguel's brother-in-law, Don Ambrosio Armijo, died at his home in Albuquerque on April 9, 1882. Don Miguel and the other family members attended the funeral.)

Young Miguel A. "Gillie" Otero (*My Nine Years as Governor of New Mexico,* **1940).**

On Monday, April 17, the day Wyatt Earp and his posse arrived in Albuquerque, Don Miguel A. Otero was at the Las Vegas Hot Springs. He gave a speech that day at the dedication ceremony of Montezuma Castle, a luxury resort hotel that was the first building in New Mexico Territory to be equipped with electric lighting. The hotel had a first-class restaurant, a casino, and an eleven-lane bowling alley housed inside the sprawling complex. The Castle became "the destination" for the era's rich and famous.

The Las Vegas Hot Springs resort closed in 1903 and the hotel later became a retreat for the Southern Convention of the Baptist Church. Even later, the old resort became a training center for Roman Catholic Jesuit priests. Since 1981, the century-old Montezuma Castle and the surrounding grounds have been the home of an international prep school called the United World College of the American West. Great Britain's industrialist-philanthropist Armand Hammer founded this renowned educational facility and HRH Prince Charles, the Prince of Wales and heir apparent to the British throne, headed the committee to dedicate the facility.

The Otero Letter does not mention who was physically present to welcome Wyatt Earp and his posse to New Albuquerque when they arrived in town on Monday morning, April 17, 1882. Had the well-known young Otero personally been in New Albuquerque his presence might have drawn unwanted notice. As fate would have it, family honor and business concerns required Gillie Otero's presence in Denver and thus he could not be in the Duke City to greet the posse. There is no evidence that any local dignitaries or officials greeted the federal lawmen. However, in Wyatt's 1926 autobiography, John Flood wrote a brief statement about the posse's short New Albuquerque stay saying, "At Albuquerque, Earp visited a friend." Flood did not name the friend or elaborate on the ten-day visit, so who was the friend that Wyatt Earp visited?

Houghton Mifflin Company published the first book-length Wyatt Earp biography in 1931. In the printed version of his manuscript, Stuart N. Lake made no mention of the vendetta posse's trip across New Mexico Territory or their stay in Albuquerque. However, Lake's research notes say that the tall, thin, mustached Michael Francis "Frank" McLean (McLain, McLane or McClain), Earp's Indiana-born friend from their days together on the Salt Fork buffalo range and the Dodge City gaming tables, met Wyatt Earp and his posse at the stately, two-story railroad station on the Monday morning of their arrival in New Albuquerque.

Stuart Lake wrote in *Frontier Marshal* that McLean served with Wyatt on the Dodge City police force, but no newspaper account or official city record has been located to support that assertion. However, in the summer of 1883, Wyatt and McLean did serve 10 days as special constables in Dodge City, so Lake might have confused this occasion with Wyatt's late 1870s service on the city's police force. Earp and McLean would become members of the "Peace Commission" formed by the Kansas attorney general in 1883 to restore law and order to Dodge City. Harry E. Gryden covered the commission's activities for the *National Police Gazette* and wrote that McLean had a record in Ari-

Wyatt Earp and Frank McLain, Dodge City, Kansas, 1883 (author's collection).

zona and along the Rio Grande "for wiping out Mexican ruffians." McLean received praise for being "cool and clear-headed" and possessed "great ability which he displayed in managing a [prize] fight has obtained for him the sobriquet of 'The General.'" (Researcher Jack DeMattos discovered that three months following the disbanding of the Dodge City Peace Commission, Frank McLean married a divorcee with five children. The couple settled in Fort Worth and McLean joined Luke Short as a partner in the White Elephant Saloon. The couple also lived in El Paso before settling in Chicago to raise their four daughters. When Frank's wife died he remarried. Frank McLean was 48 years old when he died in 1902.)

To the sleepy New Albuquerque depot crowd the meeting of these men would have appeared to be just a friend greeting some friends and did not attract the unwanted attention of a nosy newspaper reporter. Frank McLean, working on behalf of the Santa Fe Railroad, became the on-site contact for Wyatt while the posse stayed in the Duke City, and this does not negate the possibility that Frank McLean was implementing the arrangements previously established by the Otero father and son team. It is also safe to surmise that Frank McLean would have advised Wyatt Earp of the arrangements set for his conference with Superintendent Valentine later that morning.

Stuart Lake's research notes also contain information that Frank McLean provided Wyatt Earp with $2,000 for the federal officer's use while the strike force was in Albuquerque. The posse had been in the field about a month and "were paid five dollars per day for their service." Lake's notes are unclear as to whether this money was a personal loan from McLean or if it was "expense money" provided by Wyatt Earp's benefactors. In either case, Earp split the funds among his men and told them to spend it wisely because he believed there would be no more funding. He was wrong. Wyatt received a final $1,000 payment when the posse reached Raton City before entering Colorado.

"Earp had a long meeting with the president of Wells Fargo, but I can not say about the direction of the talk."

John J. Valentine was the general superintendent of the western division of Wells Fargo Express Company and Lloyd Tevis was the express company's president in 1882. Ten years later, in 1892, Valentine would succeed Tevis and serve as chief executive into the twentieth century. Valentine was an active on-site supervisor and the "man on the street" thought of him as the head of the express company. This on-site management style and his later long tenure functioning as company president could explain why in old age Otero refereed to Valentine as "president" of Wells Fargo in his 1940 letter.

Lloyd Tevis and his investment partners had a stake in stopping the wholesale cattle stealing from large ranches in Arizona and New Mexico during the spring and summer of 1881. They owned a large cattle and horse breeding ranch in Grant County, New Mexico Territory. These men possessed strong influence in capitalistic and political circles and certainly could have financed a covert operation designed to capture or kill the annoying cattle raiders who operated under the protection of the Cochise County sheriff and his lackeys.

Wyatt Earp, Wells Fargo's private man or special undercover agent in Tombstone, might have been just the right person to organize such a rustler hunt under the cloak of his deputy U.S. marshal's commission. Money and political support for future elections or business opportunities could have been two very strong motivations for the Earp brothers to undertake such an action.

A simple detective principle concerns properly connecting the small dots of the event with others so that they make understanding the big events easier. The marriage of Jim Hume's sister may have complicated his ability to focus his full attention on activities of the Cow-boys. Mary Hume married into the MacClaughry (McLaury) clan, making Wells Fargo's chief of detectives a second cousin once removed from Tom and Frank McLaury. The McLaury brothers were suspected of fencing cattle for the Cochise County Cow-boys and their place being a hideout for members who committed other crimes, like stage robbery. It would be interesting to discover the level of association these three men had during Hume's visits to the Tombstone area. The answer could hold the key to why Hume depended heavily upon the Earp brothers to investigate the Cochise County outlaw matters.

The reader should note that the Wells Fargo station agent in Tombstone, appointed in early 1880, was New York native Marshall Williams, who also used his express office location to sell cigars, tobacco, and stationery supplies. Williams was active in the Volunteer Fire Department and the Tombstone Republican Club. Hume was able to focus his concern about Williams' possible mishandling of his express office accounts. Williams may have suspected he was under suspicion of misconduct, so he suddenly departed Tombstone in early 1882, with a known prostitute as a companion. Hume's investigation showed Williams had been pilfering from Wells Fargo's freight charge funds. Tucson's *Arizona Daily Star* of February 9, 1882, noted that Williams "left about $8,000 of unpaid debts behind him as a kind of remembrance." Wyatt Earp debunkers point to Williams' misdeeds as part of a master plan of the "Earp Gang of Tombstone" to "pipe-off" Wells Fargo Express Company money shipments.

A definition for "pipe-off" is to steal a strongbox shipment before it leaves the express office and then stage a fake robbery to cover the misdeed. The facts are simple and very clear. The Wells Fargo Express Company always strongly supported Wyatt Earp and would not have done so had they suspected him of misconduct. Second, Wells Fargo Express Company's own shipping records refute the assertion that there was any misdirection of cargo originating from its Tombstone office—one more myth exposed to the light of truth.

John J. Valentine would have presented a commanding figure at a meeting with Wyatt Earp. His full beard and stylish suit, accented with highly polished boots, established the man. He was well read and lived his Episcopalian beliefs and personal creed, "Have faith in God and man," and was an active founder of the Young Men's Christian Association (YMCA) movement in Oakland. Superintendent Valentine projected an aura of bravery and trustworthiness and was always straightforward, scrupulously honest, and a taskmaster. His counsel was sought in many spheres of economic development and he wrote often for magazines like the *Overland Monthly* on subjects such as "The Natural Law of Money." He started employment with Wells Fargo in 1860 and was still working with the firm at his death in December 1901.

The *Albuquerque Evening Review* of April 17 noted that Valentine passed through Albuquerque "from San Francisco on his way to Kansas City." He and C.C. Wheeler, general manager of the Atchison, Topeka and Santa Fe Railroad, were both in Albuquerque on Sunday, April 16, 1882. They may well have taken this opportunity to have a drink together and candidly discuss the Arizona Cow-boy troubles and the ramifications to their business interests. This meeting might have produced the plan to shield Wyatt Earp and his posse behind the powerful influence of interlocking corporate interests. Wheeler had met with New Mexico governor Lionel Sheldon on Saturday, April 15, 1882, in Santa Fe. It is possible that the two men agreed that Wyatt Earp could not stay indefinitely in New Mexico due to the current political climate in the territory, but a short stopover was agreeable with the political leadership of both parties.

Denver was the Rocky Mountain regional hub for a consortium of financial power brokers who controlled both the legislative and executive branches of the Colorado state government. They also exercised strong influence within the court system most of the time. Many of the towns in the Centennial State owed their livelihoods to mining companies, thus causing local governments to comply with the wishes of these large corporate employers. Colorado seemed the safest area to sequester Earp and his men until the political shock waves waned and Arizona Territory returned to "normal."

Monday morning, April 17, 1882, is the only time that all the known facts allow for Superintendent Valentine, and possibly C.C. Wheeler, to have a face-to-face meeting with Wyatt Earp. If, as the Otero Letter claims, this meeting transpired, the men must have reached an agreement that Wyatt Earp would remain in Albuquerque, maintaining a low profile, until he received word to move his base of operations to Colorado. It is possible that Frank McLean also attended this conference. Later events suggest that additional funding for the posse may have been discussed. Meanwhile, arrangements to insure Wyatt Earp's protection from extradition to Arizona Territory were nearing finalization.

Although the following facts might be unconnected to the events under discussion, they are revealing. The *Santa Fe New Mexican* of April 21, 1882, reported that on Wednesday and Thursday, April 19 and 20, W.F. Smith, the general superintendent of the Atlantic and Pacific Railroad, a division of the Santa Fe railway system, was in town and staying at the Palace Hotel. A few days later, according to the *Las Vegas Daily Optic*, Smith was in New Las Vegas staying aboard his private railroad coach on Sunday, April 30, 1882. Wyatt Earp could have met with Smith at almost any time during his stay in Albuquerque, since Smith's residence was in the Duke City. At this date, it is unclear if Superintendent Smith played any part in Wyatt Earp's clandestine stay in Albuquerque or with his final strike force mission in July 1882.

"Earp stayed at Jaffa's home and the other boys were around town."

Who was this man Jaffa to whom the Otero Letter referred? The man in question was most likely Henry Naphtali Jaffa, one of three brothers who operated mercantile stores in New Mexico. Mark Dworkin and Scott Johnson did groundbreaking work in bringing this man into the spotlight of history. Henry was born September 15, 1845, in Hesse Kassel, Prussia, to Cantor Aron J. Jaffa (1800–1882) and his wife, Ellie Hahn-Jaffa (1810–1877). Four sons and three daughters composed the children in the family. Henry came to the United States in 1863 as a nineteen-year-old seeking to take advantage of the economic opportunities in the New World. By the time Henry Jaffa died on January 9, 1901, at age 56, he was known as a successful businessman, a chamber of commerce leader, a Free Mason, a leader of Albuquerque's Jewish community, and the city's first mayor under the American-style mayor and council system. Henry Naphtali Jaffa suffered from asthma, high blood pressure, and heart disease. He is buried in the consecrated Jewish Cemetery section within Fairview Memorial Cemetery located in the historic Southside area of Albuquerque.[1]

A Trinidad newspaper, then called the *Colorado Chieftain,* took notice of Henry

New Town Albuquerque, New Mexico Territory, "The Duke City," 1882 (author's collection).

N. Jaffa shortly after his arrival from Western Pennsylvania in the town of about 500 during the summer of 1870 and covered his activities over the next two decades. The deed records of Las Animas County show that Jaffa established a branch mercantile store for the popular H. Biernbaum & Company, under his management, in early July 1870. A short time later, the Jaffa brothers, Samuel and Henry, opened their own mercantile business in Trinidad on the northwest corner of Main and Commercial streets. In 1873, Amelia Jaffa, Joseph Jaffa, and Perry Jaffa joined Sam and Henry. Two years later, Sam Jaffa became the board secretary for the Trinidad Academy and helped to place the education institution on a stable financial foundation.

A year later, Sam was a key mover on the businessman's committee formed to bring the railroad to Trinidad and to keep the commercial center of the county in their town, not the new neighborhood of El Moro. Otero, Sellars and Company opened a business branch in the new settlement on the narrow-gage Denver and Rio Grande Railroad. Trinidad would win the fight when the Santa Fe laid track into that town. The *Daily Chieftain* of July 26, 1875, reported that the Jaffa family helped to establish the new synagogue in Trinidad. A few months later, on February 19, 1876, the *Las Vegas Gazette* noted, "Henry Jaffa, our enterprising townsman and merchant, started Monday on a trip to the States and to Europe (to visit family and bring the rest of the family to Colorado). A pleasant journey and a safe return."

Members of the Jaffa family were instrumental in building the opulent Jaffa Opera House in Trinidad, and it is today listed on the National Register of Historic Places. It was, incidentally, the site of a notable gunfight between two peace officers in 1882, George Goodell, a Trinidad policeman, and county undersheriff M.B. McGraw. McGraw

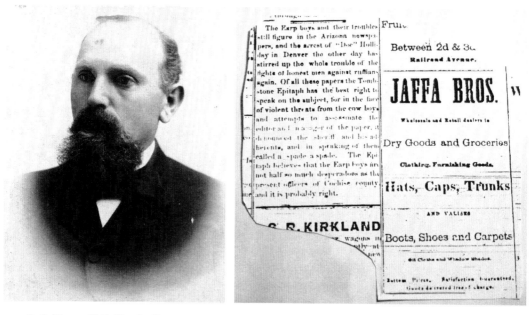

Left: Henry N. Jaffa, the first mayor of the City of Albuquerque, 1885 (Coda Memorial Collection, Center for Southwest Research, University of New Mexico, photograph # 000 119 0249).
Right: Jaffa Brothers Store advertisement juxtaposed with an account of the Earp brothers published in the *Albuquerque Evening Review*, April 20, 1882 (author's collection).

Jaffa Brothers Store in New Albuquerque, New Mexico Territory (Coda Memorial Collection, Center for Southwest Research, University of New Mexico, photograph # 000 119 0717).

had charged, in a letter to the editor of the local paper, that Goodell and his wife were, respectively, pimp and prostitute. Goodell killed McGraw, pumping six bullets into him.

It didn't take Henry N. Jaffa long to realize that successful business dealings in New Mexico Territory involved strong personal relationships that could not be segregated by ethnic or religious boundaries. In 1874, the three brothers opened a store on the old plaza in Las Vegas, followed in 1879 with a branch store in the new railroad town on the flatlands east across the Gallinas River. The next year, a temporary store opened on the Old Albuquerque Plaza with Willie Prager as the branch manager. Later, South Second Street became the location of a larger store in the new town development.

In 1886, Prager operated a mercantile store in Roswell in partnership with Nathan Jaffa, Henry Jaffa's nephew, and the men were very successful. Jaffa drilled the first artesian well in the Pecos River Valley and served as territorial secretary and acting governor in 1909. Prager would later serve on the Territorial Sheep Sanitary Board.

The *Albuquerque Daily Democrat* once commented, "Jaffa Bros. is the acknowledged headquarters for everything." The Jaffa Brothers' store stocked "all the knobby [fashionable, elegant] styles in ladies dress goods" in the women's ready-to-wear department. It carried "carpets of the latest styles and patterns, Brussels, three-ply, and Ingrain" along with satchels and trunks in the household department. The brothers sold "superior quality Kirk's soap," and in their grocery department White Rose Floor, granulated sugar, and "the best flavored and creamy cheese." The store also sold one-pound packages of a specially blended dark coffee bearing the Jaffa Brothers' label and boxes of imported Cuban blended cigars with the Jaffa Brothers' band.

Henry Jaffa became one of the political leaders in the newly emerging Peoples Party and in the summer of 1885 was elected the city's first mayor under the American system. During his mayoral tenure, Jaffa dealt with a number of issues marking the transition of Albuquerque from a frontier town to a modern city. He oversaw the creation of professional uniformed police and fire departments and a much needed water distribution and sewerage system, and started a road improvement program. He also sought to close the opium dens and dance halls. Following his term as mayor in April 1886, Henry and his family traveled in Europe for three years before returning to the West. Henry again settled in Trinidad and oversaw the brothers' corporate offices, but in 1890, he and his wife returned to Albuquerque, where he established the city's first large-scale grocery store, located on Central between First and Second streets. At this time, the Henry Jaffa family moved into a new house at 718 West Copper. This was the neighborhood where Albuquerque's first synagogue would also be constructed.

The Jaffa family was devoted to their Jewish heritage. Henry Jaffa led the effort to build Temple Albert, the first synagogue in Albuquerque, and became the first president of that newly organized reform congregation. His wife led the Ladies Benevolent Society. Jaffa was also a leader in B'nai B'rith (Children of the Covenant), the Jewish fraternal, social, and aid society formed in 1883, and helped to organize the Jewish cemetery in the Duke City. The Jaffa family donated the funds for a stained-glass window and purchased the Eternal Light that adorned Temple Albert. The light and the window are still in use in the prayer chapel of the current reform synagogue constructed in Albuquerque's northeast heights in 1950. Albuquerque is also home to an Orthodox and a Messianic synagogue, and a large active Jewish family center.

Henry Jaffa had two sisters who married and lived in Prussia and one sister who settled in New York City. In 1877, Henry married Pennsylvania-born Bessie Oppenheimer and together they had four sons; Benjamin O. (1879–1945), Walter M. (1880–1965), Aron, called Ronie (1884–1919), who became a Chicago-based artist and died in the national flu epidemic following the First World War, and Edger O. (1892–1900), who died young. Only Benjamin, a banker, raised a son to adulthood. Bessie Jaffa survived her husband by forty-two years and later moved to California to be near her sons and their families. She died in March 1943.

William S. Prager arrived in the Duke City, according to the April 24, 1880, *Albuquerque Advance*, "to open a store for the Jaffa Bros. and opens out [*sic*] with an immense stock of goods" in a temporary location on the Westside of the Old Town Plaza. The newspaper mentioned Prager again in its May 1 issue as being "a very popular clerk" and "well known to all Vegasites." During the time of the Earp posse's visit in New Albuquerque, Willie Prager's residence was in the Old Town area.

The Jaffa brothers completed the purchase of land in the New Town development for their new Duke City enterprise on June 28, 1880. According to old Bernalillo County land records, the brothers paid "$233 and 33⅓ 100 dollars" to the New Mexico Town Company for the property. It would be interesting to know how the businessmen brothers provided the land salesman with the "third of a cent." In the spring of 1880, the *Albuquerque Advance* had told its readers, "The Jaffa Bros. are well known to everybody on the line of road (the Santa Fe Railroad) by reason of having large dry goods stores at Las Vegas and Trinidad." In May 1882 the Jaffa brothers were considered among "a few of the rich men in this city (Las Vegas)," according to the city tax rolls published in the *Las Vegas Daily Optic*: "Jaffa Bros., $10,000."

Thirty years after New Mexico became a United States possession Las Vegas and Santa Fe were the two largest communities, with New Albuquerque engaging the two older cities in a political and social power struggle to be the economic center of the territory. In volume two of his autobiography, Miguel Otero noted the rapid growth of the Duke City: "[New] Albuquerque had grown from an odd collection of a few stores and shanties grouped around Railroad Avenue and First Street to a city of large buildings, gas works, street cars, and a population of over two thousand." The federal census for 1880 lists 35 Jewish-owned mercantile firms and specialty emporiums, like the Jaffa Brothers' company, in the tri-city trade area of Las Vegas, Santa Fe and New Albuquerque; that was one fifth of the total general merchandise establishments operating within the whole of the New Mexico Territory.

On Saturday, April 8, 1882, the *Albuquerque Morning Journal* noted that Willie Prager left Friday for a ten-day visit to Trinidad. The newspaper did not cover Prager's return to the Duke City, so it is possible that he returned to Albuquerque just ahead of the Earp posse's arrival on Monday morning, April 17. It is unclear if Prager's trip was for business or pleasure.

The Jaffa brothers refocused the business nature of their New Albuquerque store in November 1882. The grocery division closed and the business sold only dry goods, clothing and household furnishings. Henry Jaffa later established a separate grocery store along with a bakery and delicatessen in the 1890s. The new operation offered "hot rolls around the clock" for patrons, plus a specialty blend of Jaffa Brothers Coffee.

Since they had sold their camp gear in Silver City, Wyatt Earp's posse could no longer camp out along the trail or seek shelter at a friendly ranch house where they could post a sentry to keep watch for intruders. The posse was now in unfamiliar country, in a strange new city, and among few friends. These conditions changed the dynamics and it was no longer necessary to remain together for defense against an ambush from the Cow-boys. The men still needed a safe and secure place to sleep, but where? A boardinghouse could cost up to a dollar a day, including bed, breakfast and supper. A first-class hotel was $2.50 per day for sleeping quarters.

It is believed that Wyatt Earp paid his federal posse the standard high rate of five dollars per day for their service with no per diem. It seems, however, from reviewing the support payments that Wyatt Earp received and the posse's known actions, that the deputy U.S. marshal seems to have also unofficially covered the cost of food and shelter for his men and their horses.

Don Miguel Antonio Otero knew Henry Jaffa from business dealings and social events in Las Vegas and Trinidad. Otero also knew about Jaffa's business expansion into Old and New Town Albuquerque. Henry N. Jaffa held a reputation as a shrewd business manager. Don Miguel also held confidence in his son Gillie, his "man Friday," whom he sent to Albuquerque to restart arrangements for the arrival of special guests. Young Mr. Otero arrived in the Duke City on Monday, April 3, 1882, and quickly completed his mission. Within a few days a revised New Mexico sanctuary plan had been developed and set into motion.

It is unclear why or how Gillie Otero would later recall that Wyatt Earp was quartered in Jaffa's home, because there is some evidence to suggest that Jaffa did not move his family to the Duke City's new town section until late in 1883 or early 1884. Land records show that in early November 1883, Henry Jaffa purchased three town lots on Copper Avenue from his business associate W.S. Prager. Jaffa's residence on the deed record is "Trinidad, County of Las Animas and State of Colorado." On February 6, 1883, the *Las Vegas Morning Gazette* noted the Jaffa family had been in Albuquerque and spent the next two weeks in Las Vegas at the St Nicholas Hotel before "leaving for their home in Trinidad." The *Morning*

Gazette of February 3, 1881, noted that Henry Jaffa had sold a residential lot in New Town (East) Las Vegas for $475. This housing data does not mean, however, that Henry Jaffa did not have a rented house or apartment in Albuquerque prior to this residential land purchase yet maintained his primary residence and family in Trinidad.

It is possible that after almost sixty years and a lack of contemporary notes to help him recall the events of yesteryear, Gillie Otero's memory was limited. He could have also confused these 1882 events with other, later, activities between Wyatt Earp and Henry Jaffa. These 1884 and 1885 events are recounted in our companion book *Wyatt Earp and Doc Holliday: Their New Mexico Adventures.*

> **Author's Perspective:** Contrary to the Otero Letter's statement, logic suggests to me that Wyatt Earp would have felt more comfortable and secure sleeping near an old friend like Frank McLean or his brother Warren than in the strange environment of a man little known to him. According to the 1882 *Albuquerque Directory*, Frank McLean had a room at the Armijo Hotel; Charlie Ronan also lived at the Armijo. It is, however, possible that Jaffa and Earp had met in New Las Vegas in 1879, since they did have mutual friends. Logic does not preclude Henry Jaffa, or one of his employees, from having in fact made the advance arrangements for secure housing for Marshal Earp and his posse. It is possible that Wyatt did stay at some place associated with Jaffa's operation in Albuquerque without the man himself being present. We may never know the answer to this housing question.

"I remember that Blonger and Armijo kept watch over the boys. I was able later, when governor, to reward Armijo for that favor to my father."

Old Albuquerque was the county seat of Bernalillo County in 1882, so the county sheriff and his deputies had an office in the courthouse and maintained the nearby county jail. The county also had four constables, one for each justice court precinct. Old Town and New Town each had a town marshal and deputies to police their communities and it is very likely that the Santa Fe Railroad had a few special officers patrolling its extensive property in the area. Excluding a territorial ranger—the birth of the New Mexico Mounted Police was a quarter-of-a-century in the future—or the occasional visit of a federal officer to the area when federal court was in session, this would mean that the greater Albuquerque community was home to at least a dozen or more peace officers. Surely one of these men learned about the presence in the jurisdiction of Wyatt Earp and his posse.

Wyatt Earp carried an active commission as a deputy United States marshal in Arizona Territory. He was employed to rid the territory of outlaws who broke federal law or threatened the peace and safety of commerce along the international border with the Mexican Republic and he worked with Commandante Felipe Neri of the Mexican Rurales to accomplish that mission. Deputy marshal Earp commanded the full law enforcement authority of the federal government and while traveling in New Mexico Territory was shown due respect but not as recognition that he held any actual law enforcement authority within that territory.

The United States Marshal's Office in New Mexico Territory did not interact with the fugitive federal posse from Arizona. John E. Sherman, Jr., the chief federal marshal since 1876, had been forced to resign his post on March 2, 1882, because he was a heavy drinker and could not handle the enforcement duties of his office. Marshal Sherman was connected with the Santa Fe Ring. He was the nephew of Senator John Sherman of Ohio and commanding general of the army William T. Sherman and a brother-in-law of Senator Simon Cameron of Pennsylvania and General Nelson Miles. Before he came to New Mexico Territory, John Sherman had been a banking partner of Fredrick Grant, son of the former president.

New Mexico's new federal marshal, Alexander L. Morrison, Sr., appointed by President Chester Arthur, was still trying to organize his operation and had appointed only one deputy, his son, by the time the Earp posse arrived in his jurisdiction. During his years as chief federal lawman, Morrison and his deputies became a strong hammer against the New Mexico–Arizona border bandits. The Irishman was a second-tier member of the Santa Fe Ring and good friends with James A. Garfield, Chester A. Arthur and William McKinley. After leaving the marshal's office, he served as the joint United States Internal Revenue collector for Arizona and New Mexico territories. He died in Arizona in 1917.[2]

New Albuquerque served as the regional headquarters for David J. Cook's highly respected Denver-centered Rocky Mountain Detective Association. Tony Neis, a former deputy U.S. marshal under Marshal John Sherman, was the superintendent for New Mexico Territory and his brother Albert acted as his assistant. Two years earlier, in 1880, Tony Neis had killed three robbery suspects in a shootout near Ancho in Lincoln County while assisting postal inspectors with their investigation of the men as mail thieves. Sam Blonger worked with Cook's detective agency for a short time after he was replaced as marshal of New Albuquerque.

Cook's detective agency possessed a solid reputation as finders of missing persons and fugitives and other cases involving the right sum of money. Hundreds of dollars in reward money were allegedly offered for the arrest and return of Wyatt Earp and his posse to Arizona, yet none of Cook's detectives attempted to collect the reward. Maybe these men's reluctance was because the agency's founder—a retired major general of the Colorado National Guard, former tough Denver city marshal and Arapahoe County sheriff—had expressed his support for the deadly actions of the federal posse from southeastern Arizona. Cook's advice to fellow officers, published in his autobiography, *Hands Up! Or Twenty Years of Detective Work in the Mountains and on the Plains*, was simple: "To hell with crooks. Keep after them. Knock them around until they yell for mercy. That's the only treatment they understand." Wyatt Earp had done just that in his ride against the Cow-boys.

The officers of the Albuquerque Board of Trade, through their offices in the Central Bank Building, functioned as the quasi-government of New Town and paid the salary of the town marshal and his deputies. Since New Town was unincorporated, it had no town ordinances, so under territorial law the sheriff of Bernalillo County appointed the town's marshal and give him his law enforcement authority. The New Town Marshal, as well as his deputies through him, was accountable to the Board of Trade for his law enforcement actions. Because of this structure some misguided historians have called these officers Merchant Police, implying they were not real lawmen.

In the spring of 1882, a man named Colonel Molyneaux Bell led the Albuquerque Board of Trade. It is possible that Henry Jaffa had not yet joined this businessman's organization, because his name does not appear among the membership roll published in a local newspaper at that time. Jaffa would later become leader of the merchant group.

In his letter, Miguel Otero made the startling statement quoted above concerning law enforcement in Bernalillo County and Albuquerque. These comments could be taken to mean powerful influence was applied to the top law enforcement officials of the county and the twin cities in order to safeguard the personage of Wyatt Earp and in turn his posse.

Anti-Earp historians have claimed that local lawmen kept the seven-man federal posse under surveillance in order to make sure that they committed no crimes while staying in the area. They support their argument with a story published in the Democratic Party's newspaper the *Albuquerque Evening Review* on May 13, 1882, which said the Earp posse's "appearance in the city speedly [*sic*] became known among the rounders and [was] talked about." The term "rounders" was used in the 1880s to describe crooked gamblers, con men, and drifters. It is unclear why these writers have jumped to the conclusion the statement was negatively directed toward Wyatt Earp or his guards. The Duke City "rounders" may just as rightly have been concerned that Wyatt Earp and his men were not in town to join them but to deal with them as they had done with the less-than-honest gamblers in Tombstone's "Gambler's War." It is easy to forget that during this frontier era Wyatt Earp held a solid reputation as a top-tier professional gambler in the Rocky Mountain West.

Ed Bartholomew claimed in *Wyatt Earp II: The Man and the Myth* that the "Earp gang" ran to Albuquerque "hoping to bask under the protection of City Marshal Sam Blonger." When I first addressed Bartholomew's claim I used the official Albuquerque Police Department records to prove that Sam H. Blonger became New Town's marshal on August 5, 1881, and that the board of trade had the sheriff fire him on February 2, 1882. Archie Hilton replaced Blonger that same day and served as New Albuquerque's marshal until October 30, 1882. I used this information to show that Blonger was not town marshal in April 1882 at the time the Earp posse stayed in New Albuquerque.

Later, I conducted my own in-depth search of contemporary city records and determined that the Albuquerque Police Department's in-house history is incorrect as to Sam Blonger's tenure with the department. The territory's newspapers that covered Albuquerque's civic affairs contain numerous accounts of New Town police officers in action. According to these accounts, Sam Blonger did serve as the marshal of New Town Albuquerque, but for a much shorter and different period then claimed by official APD information. Blonger headed the small New Albuquerque police force from Wednesday, February 1, 1882, until discharged from duty on Sunday, July 9, 1882. During this research I also learned that the name Blonger is pronounced as if it rhymes with conjure.

Old Town's Marshal Archie Hilton replaced Sam Blonger as New Town's marshal on Monday, July 10, as Blonger was leaving Albuquerque for a business trip to Kansas City. Hilton was a 41-year-old Canadian laborer living with a 22-year-old female boarder in the 1880 census. No one seemed to question the morality of the town marshal living with a woman he had not married. (Marshal Hilton's father was a physician who had been born 69 years earlier and immigrated to New Mexico Territory from Maine.)

Following a detailed reading of both the *Albuquerque Evening Review* and the *Albu-*

querque Morning Journal for the weeks prior to and following the Earp posse's stay in the city, it becomes evident that Sam Blonger was an active and respected peace officer. One newspaper called Blonger "one of the most efficient officers in the territory and certainly the best marshal New Albuquerque ever had." On his 43rd birthday (one newspaper story mistakenly said that it was his 35th celebration), March 15, 1882, his friends in the business community gave Sam an engraved gold shield that bore the words "Marshal—New Albuquerque." The local merchants pledged $100 per month to a fund large enough to provide Sam's salary along with up to three deputies, each earning $75 per month. The board of trade and the sheriff also allowed the officers to supplement their salary by earning a fifty-cent bonus for each stray dog they killed that was roaming free around town.

A contemporary description of Sam Blonger noted he was a powerful man of over 200 pounds, standing six-foot-three. As a Colorado officer he had lost an eye in a gunfight, a deformity he hid behind blue-tinted glasses. Sam's curse was a quick temper and a penchant for brutally beating men with little provocation. He was especially renowned for beating on women. Sam was married three times and lost his only son when the boy was age fifteen.

The five Blonger brothers were French Canadian by heritage but had been born in Swanton, Vermont. They grew up in the lead-mining community of Shullsburg, Wisconsin, where they were members of the Universalist church. None of the brothers had a son who reached adulthood. In their youth, three of the brothers ran away from home and journeyed south to the Kansas cowtowns in order to learn about life. Here the Blonger brothers learned quickly the ways of the sporting life. Lou Blonger, who was ten years younger than Sam, was short and heavy-set, with big eyes. He was a fast talker and seemed to be the smarter brother and with a propensity toward patience and cunning.

Wyatt Earp knew both Sam and Lou as members of the "Knights of the Green Cloth" in Dodge City. The Blongers continued to pursue this style of living in the Colorado and Utah mining camps before settling in New Albuquerque just after the railroad reached the Rio Grande. Brother Joe was a miner at Cerrillos, south of Santa Fe, before coming to work for Sam.

Marshal Sam Blonger had ample reason to have affinity for the Earp posse. Days before the Arizona officers arrived in Albuquerque a man named Jones tried to assassinate Marshal Blonger, but Jones' shotgun blast missed its target. Officers captured the would-be killer. A month earlier, two men had shot at the marshal from ambush, but they also missed. The marshal and his would-be assassins exchanged eighteen shots before the men made their escape, only to be captured the next day. In the week before the Earp posse arrived in New Albuquerque, Marshal Blonger "sent five suspicious characters out of town" and "gave warning to seven more" to seek a new home. A few days later, he arrested one of "the notorious women of the town" who "under took to advertise herself ... in too bold a style" along a public street not in the red light district. Blonger was also dealing with an outbreak of smallpox in the Albuquerque jail. A Negro waiter, a prostitute, and a trainman died from the disease, while 14 other citizens lay deathly ill in the hospital.

Don Miguel A. Otero, Sr., and some associates organized the Duke City's first telephone company, with an original fifty-member subscription list. The Board of Trade of New Albuquerque provided the city marshal's office, in room 3 above the Star Clothing Store, with one of these new telephones in February 1882. Sam Blonger's office connected to the other telephones in the town and the railroad depot so that the police could respond quickly to requests for help. Blonger could also access the rest of the territory and the "outside" world via the new long distance line to Denver. This quick form of communication between business areas and the police was a distinct advantage for law enforcement in the early 1880s.

On the Saturday after the Earp posse arrived in New Albuquerque, Marshal Sam Blonger left the city to go to Denver. In the Mile High City, the marshal displayed ore samples and a location map to potential investors in the Star Mine. The mine was located in Hell Canyon on the west side of the Manzano (Apple) Mountains east of Isleta (Little Island) Pueblo in Bernalillo County. This mining district had great potential and most prospectors believed it could become a high-level strike. Sam Blonger was able to negotiate a sales contract for his claim in the sum of $120,000. He returned to New Albuquerque on Thursday, April 27, a very happy man. The marshal's estranged wife lived in Denver, but it is unknown if he visited her on this trip.

In the Otero Letter it says that "Blonger and Armijo kept watch," but the sentence does not identify the Blonger brother to whom it is referring. I assume that the writer meant the town marshal. However, it is also possible that the reference meant the deputies within the marshal's office and the sheriff's office.

During the few days that Sam Blonger was in Denver, deputy sheriff and deputy town marshal Lou Blonger was the acting police chief in New Town. On April 19, the *Albuquerque Evening Review* said that Lou Blonger "holds the peace and quiet of the town in the hollow of his hand." Lou Blonger was a close friend of Carlotta and Frank Thurmond, as was Wyatt and Doc, and when the couple moved from Silver City to Deming Lou left the Albuquerque area to help his friends establish their new ranch. There is no hard evidence to suggest that Lou Blonger and Wyatt had any intercourse during Earp's stay in the Duke City, but the odds seem against such a notion.

It is possible that Otero did not know that Earp or Holliday knew Lou and Sam Blonger. Young Gillie may not have personally known the acting marshal. It is also of note that Otero did not mention Old Town marshal Archie Hilton as one of the lawdog watch force, considering that Earp visited the Old Town Plaza on at least one occasion. Hilton, like the Blonger brothers, was one of Armijo's deputies and as such took orders from the Bernalillo County sheriff.

A sidebar note to Hilton's life took place on May 14, 1908. Hilton was working as a Wells Fargo express agent guarding a $35,500 mine payroll being shipped from Albuquerque to Dawson, in Colfax County, for the workers in the town's coal mining and coking business. Three men robbed the mining company payroll shipment at the depot of the railroad junction farming community of French. Hilton's friend Fred Fornoff, a former marshal of Albuquerque, was then captain of the New Mexico Territorial Mounted Police and served as the chief investigator of the robbery. At the time, officers suspected the hold-up was an inside job. The money was never recovered and no one was ever convicted of the crime.

Not long after the Earp contingent left Albuquerque, the Blonger brothers also left town. Sam attempted to open a hotel in booming Prescott, Arizona, but found the venture a weak prospect, so he continued with his gambling and horseracing. One can only speculate as to whether Wyatt and Sam ever took the time to discuss their love of the ponies. Sam was back in Albuquerque in time for the November elections, so Republican Party bosses drafted him as the candidate for constable of the Albuquerque precinct. He received only 130 votes in a three-way run with the Independent candidate Tony Neis (320 votes) and Democrat Con Caddigan. Deputy sheriff Caddigan won the election with 990 votes and used the office to conceal his "gold brick" swindles until the newly formed Citizen's Safety Committee ran him out of town in early 1883.

Sam and Lou Blonger finally settled in Colorado, operated a mine at Cripple Creek and opened a second-rate dance hall and saloon, with a side hall for gambling, in downtown Denver. They both became part of the Mile High City's gambling fraternity. Ed Bartholomew wrote that Lou became "the Mr. Big of vice in Denver" in the 1890s, and by added innuendo implied that Wyatt Earp also had questionable integrity because he had once associated with the brothers. Bartholomew meant for his innuendo to add a layer of black smut on Wyatt Earp's integrity.

Sam Blonger died at seventy-six years of age from "hardening of the spine" at his Denver home in February 1914. A Colorado jury convicted Lou Blonger of criminal activity and give him a 7- to 10-year sentence. He died in the state's Canyon City Prison in 1923 when he was seventy-four years old.

There is much yet to be uncovered about the Blonger clan of lawmen, gamblers and con men. Current-generation Blonger descendants Scott and Craig Johnson have embarked upon this yeoman task and may help bring these brothers to the forefront of important secondary western personalities.

"I was able later, when governor, to reward Armijo for that favor to my father."

Francisco Perfecto de Jesus Armijo was the sheriff of Bernalillo County in the spring of 1882. He was born on February 10, 1845, into a prominent Valencia County family of blue-blood Castilian descent. His father, Ambrosio Armijo, Sr., was a freighter along the Santa Fe Trail. The gray-eyed, sandy-haired Perfecto studied at St. Louis University, like the Otero brothers, and after the War Between the States he and his brother Jesus established a freighting business centered in Las Cruces. Perfecto Armijo fought against Kiowa and Comanche Indians on the Kansas plains and the Mescalero Apaches in southern New Mexico. The *Santa Fe Weekly New Mexican* of May 25, 1869, told how, during a running fight with some Apache raiders in the Organ Mountains, young Perfecto Armijo received a dangerous wound and almost lost his life. Wishing to be nearer to the family homestead, Armijo moved north in the late 1870s and established a mercantile company near Albuquerque's Old Town Plaza.

The 1880 federal census listed Armijo as a sheep raiser with a Mexican-born wife and three daughters, but it did not say he was also the Bernalillo County sheriff and a territorial militia commander. He was first elected sheriff in 1878 and served in that office until 1884. Sheriff Armijo proved to many a misbehaving Anglo miner and range hand that not all Mexican lawmen were cowardly when faced by rowdy *Americanos*. During his six years as sheriff, Armijo single-handedly held off two lynch mobs, bucked a rowdy group of cowhands on the main street of New Town Albuquerque and led the effort to capture the murderers of Col. Charles Potter in 1881. Potter was on a mission for the U.S. Geological Society gathering data concerning the profitability of the territory's mining industry. On a return trip across the Sandia Mountains to Albuquerque, Mexican bandits killed him for his few personal possessions. The bandits all died violent deaths.

Sheriff Perfecto Armijo had few reasons to shoot a man, but there are numerous old timers' stories of his lightning fists. Armijo legally hanged one of the prisoners he had saved from a lynching after a jury found the man guilty of murder and sentenced him to death.

Contemporary newspaper accounts called Armijo "absolutely without fear" and record that he once arrested "the Kid" without trouble; however, the young man quickly escaped from the adobe county jail near the Old Town Plaza. In his last months in office, the sheriff feuded with the county commissioners concerning $14,000 in tax collections. After leaving public office, Armijo and his brother became successful real estate developers in the Old Town area.

On Saturday, February 25, 1882, Don Manuel Otero died at his home in Valencia County. He was just short of his sixty-seventh birthday when a bout with typhoid pneumonia killed him. Former Governor Miguel Otero wrote about his uncle's death years later: "My father [Don Miguel] was almost heartbroken over the death of his only brother and never fully recovered from the shock." Just over a month later, on Easter Sunday, April 9, 1882, young Miguel lost another uncle. The sixty-five-year-old Don Ambrosio Armijo left a wife and five children. Maria Candelaria Otero-Armijo was Don Miguel A. Otero's youngest sister. Perfecto Armijo, businessman and long-term sheriff of Bernalillo County, was one of her children.

When the present-day reader understands the depth of sorrow felt within the Otero and Armijo families at this time their ability to deal with the political storm of the Earp sojourn is little short of amazing. This feat of coping must have made a lasting impression upon young Miguel, so much so that he hinted at it nearly six decades later in a letter to a friend.

In 1905, Governor Miguel A. Otero kept a personal promise to his cousin Perfecto and appointed him to fill a vacancy in the office of Bernalillo County sheriff. It had been 21 years since he had first held the sheriff's post. Armijo won the next general election and continued to serve as sheriff until 1909. In 1890, voters had selected Armijo as one of the first aldermen after Albuquerque incorporated as a city. Perfecto Armijo died peacefully in his sleep in 1913 at age sixty-eight and is buried in Albuquerque's Mt. Calvary Catholic Cemetery.

Some historian-researchers have questioned the authenticity of the Otero Letter because Miguel Otero referred to his cousin Perfecto Armijo by his family name and not by his first name. This practice is hard to appreciate until the modern reader understands the Victorian formality of Governor Miguel Antonio Otero. This proper society gentleman even addressed his two wives by their formal "Mrs. Otero" title and his son as "young Master Miguel."

Wyatt Earp most certainly had business contact with a few other men during his stay in New Albuquerque. W.C. Nixon was the Santa Fe station agent in town and D.W. Cobb was the Wells Fargo Express Company agent in New Albuquerque; each man had a long distance telephone line to his home office. F.O. Hurst managed the Western Union Telegraph Company office and Harry Burris operated the New Mexico News Company's newsstand in the post office building on Railroad Avenue. The postmaster was a former New Mexico legislator and friend of Don Miguel Otero named John A. Hill. E.W. Bowen operated a fresh fruit and newsstand on the corner of First and Railroad avenues.

"Jaffa gave Earp an overcoat from his store, Earp's had been ruined in a fight with the Cow-boys. I remember that cold wind even today."

Young Miguel Otero most likely never saw Wyatt Earp's shot-up topcoat during his visit to New Albuquerque in 1882, but he most certainly later heard about it. The bottom half of Wyatt Earp's riding coat was shredded and the coat's sleeves contained holes made by bullets and buckshot intended to kill the man who wore the overcoat. His shotgun duel at Iron Springs is a keystone of Wyatt Earp's gunfighter legend.

Contention City saloon helper George Hand mentioned the Cow-boys in his diary for March 24, 1882: "The cow boys, twenty or more, have been prowling around all the morning. They are well mounted, well armed and seem intent on biz. They are searching for the Earp party who took breakfast 2 miles above here this morning." Hand also took note of the area's weather conditions: "We had a light shower of rain and a wind storm this afternoon."

The windy afternoon ride had been long, dusty and monotonous for Wyatt Earp and his posse as they moved through the foothills of the Whetstone Mountains where the Mustang Mountains joined to form a swale about 35 miles northwest across the San Pedro Valley from Tombstone. During the ride, Wyatt had loosened his two heavy cartridge belts around his waist to relieve some of the strain. When the posse reached a fork in the trail, they stopped a few minutes so Wyatt could give his brother Warren some last-minute instructions before riding on up the narrow rocky pathway to the mountain spring. Wyatt left Warren at the trail divide to await a messenger from the Tombstone Citizen's Safety Committee with the latest news and some much needed cash for supplies. The main trail split here and Wyatt did not want the courier to miss the rendezvous.

Unknown to Wyatt Earp, Sheriff Behan had learned that the Citizen's Safety Committee was sending a messenger to them so he arrested the courier before he could leave Tombstone. It is likely that the sheriff had a confederate among the committee that kept him informed of their activities. It is also likely that Behan knew that he could not reach Iron Springs in time to corner the Earp posse, so he sent some lackeys to ambush the federal officers. I admit this idea is pure conjecture on my part, but I have based it upon sound reasoning considering the facts. George Hand noted in his diary, "3 P.M.—they [the men hunting the Earp posse] again came from the direction of Tombstone, watered their horses here and started again at the double quick for Kinnear's ranch [at Ash Spring at the base of the Whetstone Mountains]."

Deputy marshal Wyatt Earp and his strike force were making a systematic search of the water holes in Cochise County hunting for the Cow-boys. The team was about five miles from a spring they intended to search, but they had seen no fresh signs all afternoon. A relaxed mood had settled over the federal officers as they anticipated setting up their camp at the mountain spring and cooking a hot meal for supper. In the Arizona foothills, these March afternoons could still become cool as the sun moved west.

Now it was Friday, March 24, 1882. Wyatt Earp was in the lead as his men rounded a rocky shoulder and cut across a sandy slope leading down to the dry arroyo and a mountain spring. I am cognizant of historical researchers' debate surrounding the proper name (Burleigh Springs, Cottonwood Springs, Mescal Springs or Iron Springs) and location (I have been to two possible locations) for this spring. I have chosen to use the name Iron Springs in this narrative because Wyatt Earp used that name to describe the location of the firefight.

It had been a long dry ride from the San Pedro River bottom and it was now about mid-afternoon. Wyatt dismounted yards from the eroded bank that hid the natural water supply from his view and unbuttoned his overcoat as he slowly walked his horse forward. The rest of the posse followed him, still mounted and strung out for yards along the trail, winding their way up the arroyo. The wind was blowing lightly. Suddenly the sounds of nature became still as death.

A decade after he looked into the face of the Death Angel, Wyatt spoke to a *Denver Republican* reporter about the fight at Iron Springs. Readers in the Rocky Mountain West were able to read the interview on Sunday, May 14, 1893. The reporter told readers that during their discussion Wyatt Earp wore a gray tailor-made suit, starched white shirt, fashionable neckwear, tan Russet shoes, and a derby hat: "His hair, which was once as yellow as gold, is beginning to be stranded with white." In 1893, Wyatt S. Earp was 45 years old.

Deputy marshal Wyatt Earp spotted the Cow-boy's camp, white sleeping tents near an old wooden structure and a small cook fire, situated on the edge of a cottonwood-covered sandy slope. Just as he saw the campsite, the rustlers spotted him. One estimate suggested as many as two dozen Cow-boys were at Iron Springs that afternoon. Wyatt said he saw nine men in the camp. Curly Bill was cooking a stew in a big pot, while Johnny Barnes, "Rattlesnake Bill" Johnson, Charles "Pony Diehl" Ray, Ed and Johnny Lyle, Milt and Bill Hicks, and "Babacomari Frank" Patterson were loafing around the camp.

Almost as if a movie director had given his actors the command, "Action!" Sherman McMaster cried out, "Curly Bill!" and the Cow-boy killer bees went for their guns. The posse, except for Wyatt Earp, quickly turned their horses and raced back along the road from the spring. They were seeking cover from the expected barrage from Cow-boy guns.

Over 40 years after the events at Iron Springs, Wyatt gave a physical description of Curly Bill Brocius to his friend John Flood. Following Wyatt's cryptic speaking style Flood's notes say, "Curly Bill, about 5'11½" straight, looked like a Cherokee Indian, heavy build, 180 lb., was solid." (A few years later, Tombstone diarest George Parsons described to Stuart Lake the relationship of the two men during the months prior to their last meeting: "The best of feeling did not exist between Wyatt Earp and Curly Bill and their recognition of each other was very hasty and at some distance.")

Curly Bill and Wyatt reached for their shotguns at the same moment. The roar must have been almost deafening as both men fired double loads of buckshot at each other. "I reckoned that my time had come," remembered Wyatt. "But if I was to die, I proposed that Curly Bill at least should die with me." Wyatt was a split second quicker: "His chest was torn open by the big charge of buckshot. He yelled like a demon as he went down." The blast knocked Curly Bill against the opposite bank of the arroyo as it nearly cut him in half. Curly Bill's shots had torn through Earp's overcoat: "I found that the skirts of my coat, which had been held out at my sides by my leather holsters, had been riddled into shreds." Following the roar of shotguns, the following seconds of silence was almost as stark.

Wyatt Earp stood his ground and faced the combined outlaw fire as the Cow-boys regained their composure following the shotgun duel. Earp quickly exchanged his empty shotgun for his long-barreled Colt and returned the Cow-boy's fire as he tried to remount his terrified horse. "My horse reared and tugged at the bridle in such wild fashion that I could not regain the saddle." The fact that he had loosened his cartridge belts and one had slipped below his waist and kept him from raising his leg high enough to reach the saddle stirrup may have exacerbated the situation. The *Santa Fe Daily New Mexican* described what happened next: "Earp returned fire, then charged upon the Cow-boys who ran, leaving 'Curly Bill' dead upon the field."

Wyatt Earp later said he saw one of his bullets hit Milt Hicks and another hit Johnny Barnes. Fred Dodge wrote Stuart Lake on September 30, 1929, that Barnes told him that he had been the would-be killer that shot Virgil Earp during the December 1881 ambush in Tombstone. The wound Barnes received at Iron Springs never healed properly and he finally died from the lingering effects of Wyatt Earp's bullet. Hicks survived his wound. Frank Patterson survived the Iron Springs fight only to have Apache raiders kill him as he carried the mail in July 1885.

A Cow-boy bullet hit Earp's boot heel and he lost his footing and almost fell, making the Cow-boys believe they had hit him. Seconds later, Wyatt was again trying to mount his horse as another bullet tore the leather from his saddle horn. Finally, Earp gave up attempting to mount and slowly backed his horse down the trail and away from the gunfire. It was then that Wyatt noted Texas Jack's dead horse a few yards away and saw that Vermillion was trying to free his rifle from the saddle for action. Wyatt Earp was the only member of the federal strike force to have fired a shot at the Cow-boys during the firefight at Iron Springs.

Doc and the others stood frozen in time as they watched Wyatt's duel with Curly Bill. He then stood and fought the rest of the outlaws until he had no more loads in his weapon. They had seen Curly Bill's blast hit Wyatt's overcoat; they had seen other bullets tear through his hat and clothes and believed that Wyatt was a walking dead man. Wyatt, Texas Jack and the rest of the posse now retreated from the depression that housed the muddy little spring and regrouped beyond the dunes at an outcropping out of sight and range of the of the Cow-boys' guns. The firefight was over and the bloody gun smoke-covered battleground was left to the Cow-boys.

The "Lion of Tombstone" checked himself for wounds, reloaded his weapons, pulled his ragged trail coat around himself, and backtracked the path he had so recently covered. The strike force's team cohesion would never be the same as before Iron Springs and they all knew it. I believe Warren regretted for the rest of his life that he had not been at Iron Springs beside his brother.

Stuart N. Lake wrote to a friend concerning the deadly firefight: "It was at his [George Robertson's] ranch that Wyatt got a horse for Texas Jack after the Iron Springs fight." The rancher was a member of the Tombstone Safety Committee.

Later, Wyatt took a few moments to write Virgil about the events at Iron Springs. He reassured his brother that, contrary to some current newspaper accounts, both he and Warren had been uninjured during the short ferocious gunfight. In a second interview with a reporter for *the San Francisco Examiner*, this time for the May 28, 1882, issue, Virgil said he had recently received a letter from Wyatt in which Wyatt said, "I killed Curly Bill, without a doubt." Today, this Wyatt to Virgil letter, if it could be located, would be a priceless frontier outlaw-lawman document.

Wyatt Earp should have died in his standup firefight with the Cow-boys at their Iron Springs camp, but the only "wound" he received was a numb leg from having his boot heel shot off. His guardian angel had worked overtime just as it had done during the Tombstone streetfight when he emerged uninjured. The day before the October streetfight in Tombstone Wyatt had picked up his special-order, dark blue, heavy greatcoat—with a special leather-lined pocket holster for his 10-inch-barreled Colt .45—from P.W. Smith's Store on the southwest corner of 4th and Allen streets between the Cochise County Bank and Doling's Saloon. Smith was a Republican, an Earp supporter, and a partner in the *Tombstone Epitaph* business. Wyatt's new greatcoat had suffered a hole from a bullet fired point-blank by the dying Frank McLaury as he closed the streetfight. Now the overcoat contained more lead-induced holes from Cow-boy bullets and shredded coattails from Curly Bill's shotgun blast.

"That was the closest call I ever had," said Wyatt a decade later when recalling the gunfight at Iron Springs. "How I came out alive is more than I can ever guess." At a different time, Wyatt said that he had heard a "voice"—he believed it might have been Morgan's spirit—warning him of impending danger as it had at the Tucson railroad yard a few days earlier. Weeks after the gunfight at the spring, the *Denver Republican* of May 22, 1882, quoted Doc Holliday as saying, "Our escape was miraculous. I think we would have been all killed if God Almighty wasn't on our side." Bat Masterson wrote about Wyatt Earp for the February 1907 issue of *Human Life* magazine and said, "No other man I know could do the things he did day after day and live. He seems to lead a charmed life."

When Wyatt's posse had regained their nerve and wished to finish the fight with the Cow-boys they wanted Wyatt to lead the charge back to the Cow-boy encampment. Wyatt told them, "If you fellows are hungry for a fight you can go on and get your fill." He had made his stand, served a death warrant on Curly Bill, a delayed sentence upon Johnny Barnes, and wounded others. The fight at Iron Springs made one fact very clear to troublemakers in Cochise County: Wyatt Earp would kill on sight. The tale of Wyatt's bloody stand, in a hail of outlaw bullets, put the fear of retribution into the Cow-boy ranks and all those who supported them. Researcher Tim Fattag discovered a letter dated shortly after the Iron Springs fight in which the writer reports having overhead Sheriff Johnny Behan, while he was at Contention City, imply that more Cow-boys had been wounded during the fight than the two publicly acknowledged and Curly Bill had not been the only outlaw killed at that desert water hole. At the time, Behan also believed that Wyatt had been badly wounded or maybe was dead because the Cow-boys' reported seeing him stumble during the exchange of fire. Even if one disregards this information as hearsay, one fact is very clear. Following the fight at Iron Springs, Sheriff Behan went out of his way to avoid an open clash with Wyatt Earp and his federal posse.

George Hand was a pioneer settler in southern Arizona. The native New Yorker had come west seeking gold during the California rush of 1849 and had been one of the volunteers who fought for the Union cause during the War Between the States. In 1867, he settled in Tucson and with his friend George Foster operated a butcher shop for two years before giving up that venture and establishing a saloon. In the spring of 1882, Hand was in the mill town of Contention City tending bar for a friend. The settlement served as the junction railroad station for Tombstone, located about eight miles southeast of the mill site.

The fifty-two-year-old bachelor lived with his dog Rip and kept a diary of his three months in Contention City. Hand recorded two items of interest to this narrative. In his diary, George noted the daily weather and wind conditions and made frequent remarks about the number of corpses that had suddenly started to populate the rural countryside. He also made reference to the bravado of Behan's Cow-boy posse "prowling around the town" searching for the Earp posse, while the federal marshals were visibly camped just a couple of miles outside of Contention City. On March 19, 1882, George Parsons noted in his diary, "Mileage still counting up for our rascally sheriff. He organizes posses, goes to within a mile of his prey and then returns. He's a good one."

During the twenty-three days Earp's posse rode across southern Arizona, George Hand recorded the weather as cold and windy for 18 of those days. On two of these 23 days, the sky dumped hard rain and hail on the Tombstone area. Earp's federal posse suffered over a fortnight of weather unfavorable for mountain horseback riding. The cold winds from the south or southeast made a cold-weather resistant topcoat a must to protect a rider from the elements.

The Otero Letter is unclear as to when Jaffa provided Wyatt Earp the new coat or what style of coat it was. Wyatt's customized long coat worn at Iron Springs was only about five months old, having been bought just before the streetfight in October 1881. Doc had also bought a new jacket just before that incident. Holliday purchased a grey wool overcoat on sale for eight dollars at a Tombstone store.

It is not surprising that Miguel Otero would remember that fall's weather after so many decades; even the *Las Vegas Daily Optic* had commented upon the Duke City's weather during the spring of 1882. In its Thursday, April 20, 1882, issue, the newspaper commented, "Heavy winds at Albuquerque." Earlier the *Albuquerque Evening Review* had reported that a "blizzard visited us last night," and, if that was not enough, high winds fanned a devilish fire in the downtown business distinct. The *Daily Optic* of April 14, 1882, mentioned that another snowstorm hit the city, at the Glorieta Pass area, and then had swiftly moved west and slammed into the Sandia and Manzano mountains east of Albuquerque.

In the late 1970s, Kenneth Belcomb, a retired employee of the Soil Conservation Service, fondly recalled his youthful years in early New Town Albuquerque before large gatherings of the Albuquerque Historical Society. Once, he discussed the Duke City's wind problem, saying, "The effects of wind are no longer as distasteful as when the village had relatively few structures, facing dirty streets, and nestled in a valley surrounded by vast stretches of unprotected sandy soil. When the wind comes, blowing sand begets blowing sand. Each particle, as it dislodged, serves to scour and dislodge other particles, until the air is full of wind-blown sand that tears at structures, penetrates cracks, windows, and doorways, and lodges in one's ears and eyes." Belcomb also explained "the wind does blow in Albuquerque, especially during March, April and May—to the point of distraction for the sick and elderly."

One must ask how this wind-blown sand affected the health of Doc Holliday's consumptive lungs. The wind may have been an additional reason for Holliday's leaving Albuquerque ahead of Wyatt and the rest of the posse. In July 1880, Clara Brown described Tombstone's weather as being much the same as that at Albuquerque: "The soil is loose upon the surface, and is whirled into the air everyday by a wind which almost amounts to a gale; it makes the eyes smart like cinders from an engine, it penetrates into houses, and covers everything with dust." This could help explain why Doc Holliday spent relatively little time in Tombstone in the spring or summer months.

Among the wild tales circulated by Cow-boy supporters, including former Cochise County deputy sheriff Billy Breakenridge, in the aftermath of the fight at Iron Springs was that Wyatt Earp had worn a steel bullet-proof vest during the fight. When Wyatt read this fable in *Helldorado* he laughed: "Can you imagine [me] riding around the Arizona desert in one of those [heavy confining steel vests] on one of those nice spring days at about 90 degrees?" Vest or no vest, records seem to indicate Cochise County had, in fact, few warm days in April 1882.

The *Tombstone Daily Nugget* reported that the Stockraisers' Protective Association paid the Earp posse the $1,000 bounty offered for Curly Bill Brocius. The reward was supposedly paid "in horses and money" by the groups' president, Henry C. Hooker, but Wyatt always claimed he never received any such reward.

That same issue of the *Daily Nugget* contained a differing account of the fight at the Cow-boy camp: "Wily William is beyond question of doubt alive in New Mexico." The *Daily Epitaph* posted a substantial prize payable to Curly Bill if he would just show up in person to collect it. He never again appeared in Tombstone after the water hole fight.

One item of interest concerning the fight at Iron Springs appeared four years before Wyatt Earp became the hero in the popular ABC-TV series about his "life and legend." The *Tombstone Epitaph* of Thursday, March 8, 1951, carried an article entitled "Photo of Curly Bill in Possession of Lillian Troy Solves His Death." This article claimed that the outlaw's corpse was photographed before burial "because the men who killed Curly Bill wanted proof of his death." To my knowledge, historians have not followed up on this lead and the present location of the alleged Curly Bill death photograph is unknown and unpublished. In addition, no one has named the photographer or explained who took him to Iron Springs or to the Patterson Ranch so the photograph could be made. Who was Lillian Troy and how did she come by the alleged Curly Bill photo?

> **Author's Perspective:** Did Wyatt Earp kill Curly Bill at Iron Springs in March 1882? The question has become almost a modern day shibboleth for law and order enthusiasts and students of the Tombstone era. Yes, I believe that Wyatt Earp killed Curly Bill Brocius.
>
> There is one historical document often overlooked during a review of the incidents at Iron Springs. In September 1978, Dr. Robert J. Chandler, Wells Fargo Company historian, located a line item notation in Wells Fargo Express Company's General Cashbook for April 1882 of a $150 payment made to Wyatt Earp for killing "Curly Bill," by Chief Special Agent John N. Thacker. The express company founded in 1844 by Henry Wells and William Fargo was not in the habit of paying rewards or expense money not earned. On September 16, 1926, John Flood, Jr., asked his friend Wyatt Earp what he would say to someone who questioned his claim to have killed Curly Bill. Wyatt replied, "Well, Flood, he never knocked on my door."

"I do not remember that the boys had much money."

Even as a young man, Miguel A. Otero, Jr., had a strong appreciation for a dollar and throughout his life was a respecter of the finer things in life. He quickly developed a lifestyle to match his quest for fame and fortune. Over a half century after the events of 1882, Otero recalled that Earp's posse did not have an excess of money for a high-level lifestyle.

During the winter of 1881–82, the Cochise County Cow-boy supporters had kept Wyatt Earp tied up in court hearings defending himself and paying his own legal fees while taxpayers paid for the prosecution's case on behalf of the Cow-boy element. Taxpayers paid the public bill for the three courtroom attempts made to convict Earp and Holliday of murder for their part in the streetfight. Wyatt spent days hunting down and arresting Virgil's would-be killers and bringing them before a judge, only to see the suspects released because of perjured alibis. Wyatt Earp was drifting toward financial ruin.

To truly understand Wyatt's frustration with the legal system one should also consider how Earp funded his Cow-boy campaign. Wyatt held a federal deputyship from Arizona's U.S. marshal Crawley P. Dake, not the federal or territorial government. He was not a federal employee but worked for Marshal Dake, who expected his deputies to give him a 25 percent kickback of all court fees they collected and to also give him all bounty or reward money they received. Wyatt Earp had to pay his possemen's expenses from his own resources, unless Marshal Dake chose to reimburse him, or received private support for his posse. There was one more concern; Arizona Territory had no shield laws protecting peace officers from personal lawsuits for their actions while performing their duty.

Virgil and Morgan Earp had mounting medical bills resulting from the wounds received doing their duty as Tombstone police officers because the city did not cover the cost of their medical care. James and Warren were the only Earp brothers earning any regular income in early 1882. Wyatt Earp gave an interview to a reporter for the

Gunnison Daily-Democrat in June 1882. He told the Colorado newspaper, "I sold out my place, but we have some mining property back there yet." Earp had not sold his Tombstone home but in fact had only mortgaged the property to James Howard for $365, at 2 percent interest per month, on February 13, 1882. Spending most of November 1881 in court hearings and lodged in jail had provided Wyatt with precious little time to earn money. In February 1882, he was again jailed and forced to defend himself for the Tombstone streetfight in the justice court in Contention. Ike Clanton even attempted to have the case reheard in Tombstone before probate judge J.H. Lucas. All three attempts proved an exercise in futility. With his savings gone and business dealings on hold, Wyatt Earp needed the loan to pay the family's mounting legal and medical fees.

Two years after the mortgage was executed, Wyatt had not repaid his house loan, so James Howard sued Wyatt and Mattie in the district court of Arizona's Second Judicial District for forfeiture of the property and was awarded the house and town lot in Cause 8911 on March 10, 1884. It is very likely that Wyatt Earp, now living in Idaho Territory, knew nothing about the legal action and had he known might have considered the loan on the house a fair return on his investment and accepted the "loan" as payment for his house and moved on with his life. As if enduring contracted preliminary hearings on possible murder charges were not enough, Wyatt Earp had become ill while incarcerated in the makeshift Cochise County Jail on Toughnut Street near Third, for a few weeks in November 1882. The drafty jail, located on the southern edge of the 4,539-foot plateau the town sat upon, was not a warm place to spend cold winter nights. The location did provide a splendid view of the Dragoon Mountains when the wind was not blowing dust around.

"Some days later, Earp and Holliday had a falling out at Fat Charlie's one night. They were eating when Holliday said something about Earp being a Jew boy. Something like Wyatt are you becoming a damn Jew boy? Earp became angry and left. Charlie said that Holliday knew he had said it wrong, he never saw them together again."

Before the Otero Letter discovered me, I had written an article for the summer 1999 issue of *Old West* magazine wherein I postulated that the "Albuquerque disagreement" and the "Trinidad break up" may have been part of a master public relations plan to confuse Wyatt Earp's political enemies and maybe even to help stimulate a pro–Earp public opinion campaign. I reasoned that Wyatt would need this positive law enforcement image in case he faced a jury in a future murder trial. Doc Holliday had been painted by Cow-boy supporters with a "badman" image and Earp still sought to cultivate a law and order persona so he could return to Tombstone and run for sheriff of Cochise County in the fall election. I also expressed the concept that the newspaper reports describing the deaths of McMaster, Tipton and Wyatt during their retreat out of Arizona Territory could have originated with the Earp posse or its supporters. At the time, I felt the breakup idea had all the elements of a simple, "good guy–bad guy" public relations spin. Even with the knowledge contained in the "Otero Letter," the idea is still worth further review.

In the early 1880s, Old and New Albuquerque held a reputation as a center for fine dining establishments. In the December 22, 1876, issue of the *Santa Fe Daily New Mexican*, William D. Dawson, one of the editorial staff, wrote about his visit to Ed Branford's orchard near Old Town. Dawson said Branford made "a vegetable sauce which in the estimation of connoisseurs is fully as good if not superior to the famous Worcestershire, and can be bought at least one half cheaper. I found the sauce on the hotel table at Albuquerque, as well as his 'chow-chow,' a pickle relish of exceedingly fine flavor." (I myself enjoyed Branford's Territorial House salsa up until the late 1990s when the family sold their recipe to a major soup company conglomerate that buried this tasty salsa in preference to their own in-house product.)

On May 13, 1882, the *Albuquerque Evening Review* reported on the Earp posse's visit in the Duke City, proudly reporting, "The party, while in Albuquerque, deported themselves very sensibly, performing no acts of rowdyism, and this way gained not a few friends for their side of the fight." The Republican Party–supporting *Albuquerque Evening Review* also reported that Doc Holliday "became intoxicated and indiscreet in his remarks, which offended Wyatt and caused the party to break up. Holliday going with Tipton [northward to Trinidad]."

In reply to a reporter's question two days after the *Evening Review* story was published, Doc Holliday told the *Pueblo (CO) Chieftain*, "We [he and Wyatt] had a little misunderstanding, but it didn't amount to much." If the disagreement was so minor, why would a newspaper reporter located hundreds of miles from the scene of the row find it newsworthy? Following the Earp–Holliday misunderstanding, Wyatt ordered Dan Tipton to escort Holliday to Trinidad so Bat Masterson, the city marshal, could keep Doc out of trouble until the rest of the posse joined them or all the extradition and pardon questions were settled.

Doc Holliday's supposed "Jew boy" comment brings to mind an earlier incident, contained in the apocryphal information about a youthful Wyatt in Illinois during the spring of 1869. Young Earp had an altercation with a man named Tom Piner at a hotel in Bardstown. The man had called him a "California boy," a frontier euphemism for coward, as in he ran to the West Coast to avoid serving in the army during the War Between the States. It should be recalled that Wyatt was in his early teen years during the war and had in fact run away from home to enlist alongside his older brothers but was stopped by his father. When Wyatt Earp was 15 years old he joined his family for the westward trek to the West Coast. The Illinois tale also claims that Wyatt Earp shot the man after the bully had attempted to shoot him. If the Illinois incident is true it provides a framework for Wyatt Earp's not appreciating a derogatory remark concerning his character, especially from a person he considered a close friend.

Upon first read, I was not sure if the term "Fat Charlie" referred to a real person or a business establishment, but more research has provided some clues. Some "place" possibilities present themselves in contemporary newspaper advertisements. One such ad was for "Charlie's Sideboard" operated by a B.W. Clair: "The cleanest and neatest resort for gentlemen in the city. All drinks mixed in plain sight. Finest liquors and cigars. South side Railroad Avenue, between First and Second Streets."

Charlie's Sideboard does not seem to have been a standard restaurant, but it was customary for high-class saloons in the 1880s to furnish a food buffet during certain hours of the day. This "resort for gentlemen" was the type of place that a young man like Gillie Otero might have visited while in New Albuquerque. "Any one who was ever in Las Vegas knows Gillie, and when once acquainted friendship springs up," commented a reporter for the *Lincoln Golden Era* in the summer of 1885. Thus, Gillie may have visited Charlie's Sideboard on a business or social level enough to hear about the Earp–Holliday "misadventure" firsthand. Gillie Otero was a social animal. In 1884, he was one of the organizers of the Montezuma Club, a private membership establishment in New Town Las Vegas. The club had a dance floor with a grand piano, a library sitting room, and billiard and pool tables. The young Otero had his own two-room apartment attached to the club area.

Another possible location for "Fat Charlie" was the White House Billiard Parlor on Railroad Avenue near Third Street hosted by Charley Montaldo. An early Albuquerque newspaper advertisement suggests another possibility. The notice says that "Fat Charlie" managed the Retreat Restaurant, "the best place to get a square meal," but contemporary newspaper advertisements imply the place was a pool hall with the "only fifteen ball pool table in the city." The Retreat was located on the south side of the Old Town Plaza and served "free lunch every morning and night" with "beer on draught." The proprietor of the White House Billiard Parlor was Jessie James' friend W.S. Munroe. I find it hard to believe that Wyatt Earp would have hung around a pool hall so soon after Morgan's murder in such a place. It is possible that Wyatt never entered another pool hall the rest of his life.

One more idea requires a closer review. Miguel Otero's older brother Page was a championship pool player and lived in Albuquerque during the early spring of 1882 before he moved to the Magdalena Mountains to go prospecting. In late March and early April, the *Albuquerque Evening Review* promoted an effort among the Duke City sporting community to stage a formal billiard tournament between Page Otero and Albuquerque's champion, Charlie Ronan. In 1879, Charlie Ronan had been one of the New Town Las Vegas gamblers collectively called the Dodge City Gang because they had all come south from that cowtown. In July 1877, Charlie Ronan had been arrested in Dodge City by city marshal Larry Deger as part of his crack-down on the "sporting element" supported by his political rivals Mayor James "Dog" Kelley and the city council. Dodge City may be where the youthful Otero brothers and Ronan first became acquainted. Charlie Ronan was also friends with Miguel Otero's Las Vegas friends Scott Munroe and Doc Holliday. Bat Masterson biographer Robert K. DeArment claims that Ronan, like Holliday, was consumptive.

In April 1881, Ronan and James Masterson took Bat Masterson's side in the famous Dodge City Plaza shootout with Al Updegraff and A.J. Peacock. On December 12, 1881, Ronan killed a man in a shooting affair at the Albuquerque train depot. He was cleared of murder in court the next morning on a self-defense plea. The somewhat physically rotund Charlie Ronan used Old Town Albuquerque's Retreat Restaurant as his headquarters. Was the "Fat Charlie" of the Otero Letter the pool-player, gambler, bartender, and gunman Charlie Ronan?

Finally, if "Fat Charlie" was a real person and not a place then the best choice is

Charles Exley. A story published in the *Albuquerque Evening Review*, on November 14, 1882, said that "Fat Charlie" was Exley's nickname. Exley was the host and chief at the Holladay House a hotel and restaurant located in Bernalillo, 17 miles northeast of Albuquerque on the east bank of the Rio Grande. Doc Holliday and Will Sanguinette owned the establishment. This partnership is discussed in the author's book on Wyatt and Doc's New Mexico adventures.

> **Author's Perspective:** If the "Fat Charlie" of the Otero Letter was meant to be Charles Exley, then maybe Doc Holliday's "Jew boy" remark took place in Doc Holliday's own establishment. Before a definitive pronouncement concerning who "Fat Charlie" really was or wasn't, I feel researchers need to investigate the subject more extensively.
>
> The "Jew boy" comment attributed to Doc Holliday provokes the question of whether Doc was an anti–Semite. The question has no simple answer. Bat Masterson said that Holliday, when provoked, could "cuss like a sailor," as could most other western hard-cases on the frontier. Masterson, who was also a great disseminator of colorful language, said that Doc also used racial slurs especially addressed towards blacks and Mexicans. These indictments may seem harsh in light of the present climate of social correctness, but during the frontier era these racial epitaphs were an accepted convention of common conversation.

When Holliday was a dentist and fledgling gambler in Dallas, Texas, he had a dispute with a professional gambler named Henry Kahn in nearby Breckinridge. Kahn came from a pioneer Jewish merchant family in Dallas County. The Kahn family had a store on the same block as the office that Holliday shared with his dental partner. In early July 1877, the *Dallas Weekly Herald* reported Holliday and Kahn had a disagreement over a poker game and that Doc attacked Kahn with his cane. Officers arrested both men and a judge fined them. Later the two met again and the argument resumed but quickly ended when Kahn seriously wounded Holliday. George Henry Holliday came from Atlanta to help his cousin with his convalescence at Fort Worth's upscale Trans-Continental Hotel. When George Holliday returned to Georgia a much improved John Holliday left Fort Worth and traveled southwest to Fort Griffin and a fortuitous first meeting with Wyatt Earp.

Henry Kahn escaped arrest for shooting Doc Holliday and went into hiding from a forgery indictment in nearby Shackelford County. The Texas Rangers listed Kahn on page 168 of their *List of Fugitives from Justice, 1878*: "Kahn is a Jew, 5 feet, 8 inches high, slim build, no whiskers, light complexion, dark eyes; last heard of in Fort Worth; has relatives living in Dallas, (Kahn Bros.) doing business there." Most likely, the two men never saw each other again. Did John Holliday harbor anti–Jewish sentiments because of this incident? The reader should also remember that Doc, for most of his adult life, had a Jewish banker friend, but this is not to say that a person cannot be friendly with an individual and still generally dislike their race or religious creed. A point in case is Gillie Otero. He was condescending to African Americans, calling them "coons" and believing their only worth was as servants. He also displayed open contempt for Native Americans and expressed the need for the genocide of their race.

> **Author's Perspective:** I met Jeanne Cason Laing—daughter of one of the two sisters who ghost-wrote Josie Earp's memoirs—while we were both attending an Old West outlaw-lawman history conference in Sacramento in July 2002. She was a very gracious

elderly lady and joyfully discussed Josie as she recalled her from when Josie lived with the Cason family in the late 1930s. Ms. Laing told me that Josie loved to attend romance movies and song and dance productions with her and her teenage girl-friends. Josie owned a small nightstand radio and listened to it in the evenings. Her favorite radio show was the frontier adventures of *The Lone Ranger* and Tonto, while the misadventures of *Amos 'n' Andy* was a close second. Ms. Laing was uncertain what happened to the radio when Josie died.

During a discussion about the Otero Letter Ms. Laing recalled that Josie Earp "was not very sorry to see the rift develop between Wyatt and Doc, but claimed she was not nearly as upset over it as Wyatt. Josie and Doc did not have the warm relation-ship the two men had." Ms. Laing speculated that Doc's supposed "Jew boy" com-ment contained in the letter "may have been the last straw between the two men" as part of a possible long-smoldering disagreement of some nature.

In Albuquerque, Wyatt Earp made his first attempt at a preemptive public relations effort to combat his recent negative press. He visited a New Albuquerque newspaper office and offered to give an unrestricted interview on one condition: no publication until after he and his men had left the city. Wyatt did not wish to alert his enemies of his location and risk a party of Cow-boy supporters descending upon the Duke City in an attempt to kill or capture him.

It is a remarkable fact that none of Albuquerque's four major newspapers carried a story about Wyatt Earp and his posse being in the Duke City during their ten-day sojourn. What makes that media silence nothing short of remarkable is all the national and regional press coverage concerning the bloody Cow-boy Campaign and the spec-ulation concerning the current location of deputy U.S. marshal Wyatt Earp. Where would he strike next?

On April 2, 1882, the publisher-editor of the *Albuquerque Evening Review*, the city's Republican partisan newspaper, which claimed to have the "largest circulation of any paper in New Mexico," printed an editorial critical of the territorial government at Prescott and the lack of support for law and order. W.E. Bailhache wrote, "If the people and gov-ernment of Arizona cannot, through the laws of the United States and of the territory, trample upon ruffianism, the territory is not worth the money asked for by the governor to assist in putting down the almost anarchy with which it is now afflicted. If Tombstone is controlled by desperados, the county and the town have only themselves to blame."

Wyatt Earp's presence in town a couple of weeks later was common knowledge on the streets of New Albuquerque, yet nothing appeared in the local newspapers, espe-cially the *Evening Review*. A simple explanation is that Henry Jaffa might have accom-panied Wyatt Earp to the newspaper office for an off-the-record background interview. The astute publisher of a newspaper whose motto was "No News Escapes Us" would quickly perceive the financial implications attached to Jaffa's presence and wisely chose to cooperate with Marshal Earp's request.

The *Evening Review* published its story only after Arizona newspapers had erro-neously reported Wyatt Earp's death. The *Review* told its readers that Earp and his posse had recently been in their city but did not quote Earp in the story. Thus, future historians missed an opportunity to hear directly from Wyatt Earp his impressions of the moment. Maybe, unknowingly, the *Evening Review* recorded the real reason they had not printed a comment from Wyatt Earp; "Your true fighting man talks very little of his exploits." Deputy United States marshal Wyatt Earp was a true fighting man.

The *Evening Review* reporter told readers, "Removed from the scene of their conflicts with [Arizona] enemies, they [the Earp brothers] became no more rioters than the frontiersman in general, and from their deportment those unacquainted with them would have taken them quicker for hard-working miners than for the men the results of whose work called out a proclamation from the president." A few months later, the *Evening Review* again commented on Wyatt Earp and said he was "withal a much more peaceable man than people would imagine one of his name to be," since Wyatt Earp's bloody reputation was still being discussed in barrooms across the Southwest.

Author's Perspective: The *Albuquerque Evening Review* reported that deputy United States marshal Wyatt Earp had also given an interview to the city's morning daily newspaper, and some recent writers have made this same claim. A press conference often has reporters from numerous news media in attendance. However, I have not been able to locate any firsthand Wyatt Earp interview published by the Democratic Party–leaning *Albuquerque Morning Journal*, *Albuquerque Daily Democrat*, or the Spanish language *La Revista* during the spring of 1882. In fact, a few days after the *Evening Review*'s Earp story was published the *Albuquerque Morning Journal* indignantly stated on May 18, "At no time in their lives, did the Earp desperadoes call at the *Journal* office. They seem to have consorted with the sandy sorehead on the sundown sheet while they remained in hiding in this city." This statement does not mean that Earp did not speak to a *Journal* reporter or editor W.S. Burke at some other location. It just shows that the town's evening newspaper had already covered the event.

The *Evening Review* and the *Morning Journal*, New Albuquerque's two largest newspapers in circulation, were engaged in partisan political, editorial, and economic warfare for control of the newly developing community's advertising revenue and nothing was fair about their reporting. The "Albuquerque Newspaper War" roared on for months after Wyatt Earp and his posse left the area. Ironically, the two newspapers shared the same pressroom.

"One afternoon I drove Earp and Jaffa to the river to see them building the new bridge. Earp remarked how it reminded him of the big bridge at Wichita."

It is unclear why Otero included the above sentences in his letter since it is almost certain that the event did not happen in April 1882. A question has been raised concerning young Gillie Otero's ability to have personally escorted Wyatt Earp and Henry Jaffa to view the Rio Grande bridge project. Scott Johnson has suggested that this incident is most likely recorded incorrectly, since strong evidence contained in public records, newspapers and Colorado court documents suggest that Otero was physically in Denver during most the Earp posse's 10-day Albuquerque stay. It is possible that Gillie Otero's 1940 comment is a telescoped recollection of events from Wyatt Earp's 10-day 1882 sojourn and Wyatt and Josie Earp's 1884 visit to Henry Jaffa's New Albuquerque home to celebrate a Jewish holy festival. This later event is discussed in our book on Wyatt Earp and Doc Holliday's New Mexico adventures.

Miguel Otero held a long-term fascination with water and big building projects. During his tenure as governor, he watched the construction of a new territorial capitol building modeled after the national capitol complex. After his tenure as governor of New Mexico, Otero spent a number of years as United States marshal for the Panama Canal Zone and afterwards considered that period a highlight of his life. The advent of the Second World War and his failing health prevented him from writing volume four of his autobiography containing his Central American adventures.

The Douglas Avenue toll bridge over the Arkansas River at Wichita, Kansas, was a controversial project when Wilhelm "Dutch Bill" Griffenstein, a founder of the town, undertook the project. The building site for the bridge spanned the area used by the annual cattle drives to cross the river. The $29,000 expanse, constructed in 1872, was a 1,000-foot-long, ten-span bridge built with iron piles on stone piers, providing a 16-foot-wide roadway with a tollhouse at each end. It would be interesting to know what it was about that bridge that caused Wyatt Earp to remember it almost a decade later. Surely it was not its size, because Wyatt had seen a larger and longer bridge span under construction crossing the Mississippi River at St. Louis when he worked as a bouncer on a riverboat bordello near Peoria, Illinois, in 1871. The steel arch Mississippi River bridge begin service in July 1874 following seven years of construction.

Maybe Wyatt Earp had recalled when he, backed by ten riflemen, had halted a massive cowboy raid on Wichita. Earp, a policeman under Mike Meagher at the time of this incident, had faced the raiders as they were seeking to leave the bridge and enter the city. Wyatt's determined action ended the confrontation peacefully. Contrary to later-day Earp debunkers, Jim Cairns, a deputy marshal who served with Wyatt Earp, remembered that event in a newspaper interview shortly after Earp's death in 1929. Jim Cairns married Bat Masterson's sister Nellie.

On June 8, 1880, E.W. Deer, the editor of New Albuquerque's *Daily Golden Gate* evening newspaper, told readers, "Bernalillo is advertising for proposals for a new bridge, how would it pay to build a toll bridge over the Rio Grande here?" Bernalillo is a community dating from the 1600s located 17 miles north of Albuquerque on the east bank of the Rio Grande. In 1880 it, like other river towns, was also a new station on the advancing Santa Fe Railroad. Today, there is a massive Rio Grande bridge that connects the small community of Bernalillo with the sprawling new west bank city of Rio Rancho. One of New Mexico's fastest growing upscale cities sprang from the old Alameda Land Grant in the 1960s.

It is hard to determine the exact nature of Otero's bridge comment. It is impossible to determine exactly which of the area's four spans the former governor was referring to in his 1940 statement. Two Rio Grande bridges already served the Old and New Albuquerque business area when a new bridge company undertook its construction project in the early 1880s.

In 1882, Barelas was an old Spanish settlement located west of the railroad shops in New Albuquerque and the two towns were connected by a small horse-drawn rail coach. Stover and Hazeldine streets connected the settlement to the Santa Fe Railroad shop area. The federal census of 1880 had listed about 350 residents for Barelas. The little trading center, today a part of Greater Albuquerque's extended South Valley area, had a river bridge and many people used this structure to walk or drive small carts across the wide, shallow, swift-flowing waters. Today, the street that still crosses the river is called Bridge Boulevard.

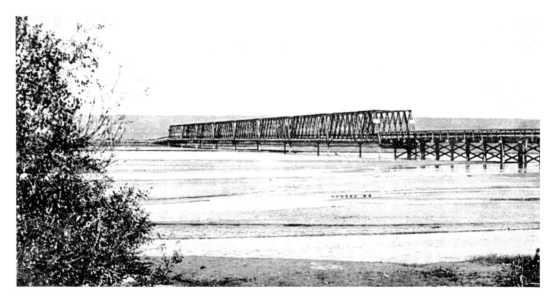

Wagon bridge across the Rio Grande at Old Town Albuquerque (author's collection).

The second bridge, a smaller footbridge for horse and human traffic, connected the east-west banks of the river just west of the Old Town Plaza, but the seasonal floods would often disable this wooden span built a few feet above the river's normal height. The Albuquerque Bridge Company had designed their new structure to accommodate the growing wagon traffic seeking to cross the river safely. The new structure design was stable enough to withstand the occasional high water of fall and spring mountain runoffs.

A third bridge was located a couple of miles north of the Old Town Albuquerque Plaza located between the Spanish-Mexican farming settlements of Los Ranchos de Albuquerque and Alameda, founded in the early 1600s. Early information about this structure is sparse.

Another crossing about 18 miles downriver from the Albuquerque area was the Atlantic and Pacific Railroad bridge across the Rio Grande near the Isleta Indian Pueblo. People and animals could cross when no trains were due, but a wagon had difficulty crossing the rough railroad ties that held the steel rails in place. The bridge was little help in expanding the area's trade westward.

The Bernalillo County River Commission, established by an act of the 1876 territorial assembly, controlled commerce and trade along the Rio Grande near Albuquerque. The commission levied a tax on riverfront property owners to fund maintenance of the riverbanks, irrigation locks and commercial bridges. Four prominent men, Jose Montano Candelaria, Jose Armijo y Ortiz, Santiago L. Hubbell and Thomas F. Phelan, composed the commission in 1882 and they approved all the bridge-building projects. In the spring of 1880, the *Albuquerque Advance* had bragged, "When the big bridge is finished Albuquerque will be the only town on the river [for north-south and east-west trade routes]."

The Rio Grande bridge project was a private business venture of the Albuquerque Bridge Company, with Henry Jaffa's friend J. Franz Huning, a Jewish beef contractor and flour mill owner, as the major investor and company president, as well as partners Judge William E. Hazeldine as secretary and W.K.P. Wilson, a banker, as the company treasurer. Huning was a German immigrant forced to stop in Albuquerque during the winter of 1854. There he forgot about California and decided to plant roots in the old plaza business community. His brothers Louis and Henry soon joined the new resident in the mercantile business and land development. (Huning descendants Erna and Harvey Fergusson became respected regional authors.)Huning and Hazeldine were also partners in the Albuquerque Publishing Company, the parent company of the *Morning Journal* newspaper. The newspaper's editor was W.S. Burke, a Civil War veteran and a devoted Republican who worked on papers in Iowa and Kansas before coming to New Mexico in 1881. Burke would one day become the first superintendent of public instruction in Bernalillo County. Burke hired Edmund G. Ross, a former U.S. senator from Kansas, to do the editorial work on the *Morning Journal*. Ross, whose vote saved President Andrew Johnson from being removed from office during his 1868 Senate impeachment trial, was now a Democrat and would become governor of New Mexico Territory in May 1885.Hazeldine served in the Territorial Council of the 25th Legislative Assembly that met in January 1882 at Santa Fe. He served as chair of the council's powerful Railroad Committee and chair of the Privileges and Election Committee. He was also vice-chair of the Judiciary Committee and the Agriculture and Manufactures Committee. These important leadership positions gave Hazeldine an influential voice in legislative matters. As chair of the upper chamber's Railroad Committee, Hazeldine enjoyed a friendship with many of the nation's foremost capitalists and leaders of the nation's political structure. The judge founded and operated the Street Railway Company, which ran a route connecting Old Town and New Town Albuquerque and these two towns to Barelas. He was also a founder of the First National Bank of Albuquerque, with his friend former congressional delegate Mariano Sabino Otero, nephew of Don Miguel and cousin of Gillie Otero, as president. His friends Elias S. Stover and three of the Armijo brothers were directors. Judge Hazeldine and Will Wilson served with Huning as members of the board of trustees for the Albuquerque Academy, which was an adobe building owned by Huning that served as the schoolhouse, located on the east side of the plaza. They served on the territorial fair committee as well and were also the founders and officers of the Albuquerque Gas Company in addition to the bridge company. Hazeldine married a teacher from the Albuquerque Academy staff. Later, the couple moved to Prescott, where the former judge became the cashier at the Bank of Arizona. In 1885, Leigh Chambers interviewed the banker, who along with many other businessmen swore to affidavits demonstrating how Arizona's former United States marshal Crawley P. Dake misused government funds, not Wyatt Earp. It is possible that Hazeldine met Wyatt in Albuquerque. This is another one of the chain of relations and business dealings that build alliances.

Henry Jaffa was a friend of Huning and Hazeldine. He also knew their business partner Elias Sleeper Stover, an ex–lieutenant governor of Kansas, owner of a large wholesale grocery concern in New Albuquerque and a member of the Bernalillo County Commissioner's Court. Huning, Hazeldine and Stover owned all of the land between the road connecting Barelas to the Albuquerque Plaza and the new railroad tracks, New Albuquerque's town site. Stover was also one of the founders of the First National Bank of Albuquerque. Stover had left Kansas before Wyatt Earp made his Dodge City reputation, but he most likely knew of the former lawman. In later years, Stover became the first president of the Uni-

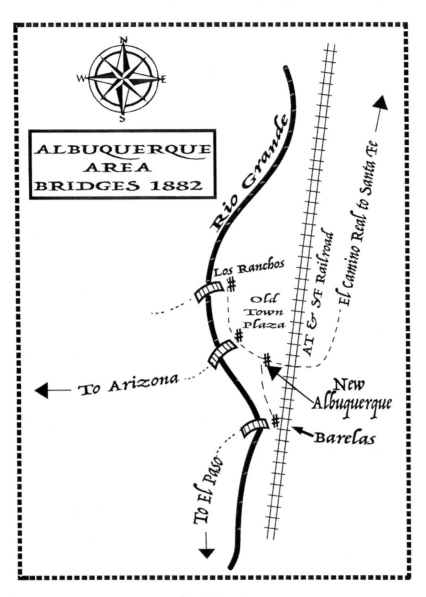

Map by Ashley Gray.

versity of New Mexico, located at Albuquerque. Today, Henry Jaffa, Franz Huning, William Hazeldine, and Elias Stover have Albuquerque streets named in their honor.

Elias Stover was an original founder of the city's Board of Trade, which supported the bridge project as a means to expand commerce westward. The board even had its own Bridge Committee, chaired by R.C. Vose. (Mrs. Vose was a music teacher at the Albuquerque Academy.) The new bridge had a 500-foot approach span that rose across the marshy bottomlands before connecting with the 600-foot span that provided travelers a dry river crossing. There was a tollhouse located about halfway across the bridge so a toll collector could assess a five-cent one-way crossing fee. The Huning Bridge had a ribbon cutting on Tuesday, December 12, 1882.

15

Destination: Colorado

An officer doing his duty must rely almost entirely upon his own conscience for encouragement. The sympathy of the respectable portion
of the community may be with him but it is not openly expressed.—
Virgil Earp, *San Francisco Examiner*, 27 May 1882

One of the most misunderstood events in the saga of Wyatt Earp and Doc Holliday
is the dentist's arrest in Denver during May 1882 and the botched attempt to extradite
him back to Arizona Territory for the murder of Frank Stilwell. This adventure is a tale
of political horse trading at its best.

"Wells Fargo arranged safety in Colorado and the road [the Santa Fe Railway] gave them passage to Trinidad."

Charley Bartholomew, a Wells Fargo express messenger who worked with Wyatt
Earp, enthralled a reporter about his Tombstone days, reported as "Battling Road
Agents," in an 1888 interview published in the August 3 issue of the *Phillipsburg (KS)
Herald*: "I never saw a braver nor a more efficient man than Wyatt Earp. He was gen-
tlemanly and kind in his conduct toward his men and rendered me very valuable service."
The old guard added, "Wyatt Earp is a man who believes in right and justice, and he
was always ready at anytime to render his assistance in warfare upon thieves and holdups."

Following a fortnight of tension seeking a safe sanctuary, Wyatt Earp's fugitive federal posse left New Mexico Territory when the special 16-wheeled mountain engine of
the Atchison, Topeka & Santa Fe Railway pulled its passenger coaches through the
7,650-foot-high mountain tunnel atop Raton Pass. The Raton Pass railroad tunnel was
2,011 feet long, 14.5 feet wide and 19 feet tall. Wyatt and his companions entered the
state of Colorado and shelter from the political storm raging in Arizona Territory when
the train headed down the northern slope of Raton Mountain toward Trinidad.

Colorado governor Fredrick W. Pitkin and Don Miguel A. Otero were two of the
original incorporators of the Atchison, Topeka and Santa Fe Railway. They also were

very good friends. In the end, it was mutual business interests and close personal friendships that sealed the deal for deputy marshal Wyatt Earp, and by extension his federal posse, to be granted a safe harbor in Colorado. Pitkin also implied that if he conducted an extradition hearing he would view these proceedings in light of the best interests of the state of Colorado, which is to say Pitkin's best interests. A month after Don Miguel and the governor held their last meeting, Pitkin led the Colorado delegation to Otero's graveside service in Denver's Riverside Cemetery. The highly respected Don Miguel Antonio Otero, Sr., had only been fifty-two years old.

Don Miguel Otero had gone to Denver in April on business. During this visit to the Mile High City, the senior Otero attended a social function and "was swindled" out of $2,550 by Doc Baggs, a "lottery man." A couple of days later, Gillie Otero was in Denver and recovered part of his ailing father's financial loss. Upon his return to New Mexico, young Otero was ready to celebrate and spent the first weekend in May at the festive Knights of Pythias convention at Santa Fe. Gillie Otero omits mention of this "bunko incident" in any of his autobiographies.

Meanwhile, Don Miguel Otero returned to Las Vegas from a few days at the Jemez Hot Springs, north of Santa Fe, and was planning a return trip to Denver. Fate stepped in and he developed pneumonia and died on Tuesday, May 30, 1882. Wyatt Earp may never have known the depth of Don Miguel Otero's involvement in his life during the spring of 1882.

The early morning northbound Santa Fe engine pulled out of the station at New

Raton City, New Mexico Territory, "The Gate City," 1882 (Fred Lambert collection).

Town Albuquerque headed up the Rio Grande for Bernalillo, east across the hills to Cerrillos and on to Galisteo Junction, the backdoor to Santa Fe now called Lamy. The train continued on east up over the 6,478-foot Glorieta Pass and along the Pecos River Valley to New Town Las Vegas. Wyatt and Doc and their female companions, along with James Earp and his family, had made this same trip in a covered wagon in the fall of 1879.

At about 2:00 p.m. the northbound train spent a 20-minute meal stop at New Las Vegas. It is fun to speculate whether Wyatt and Doc looked around the expanding New Town business section and ate a late lunch at the new Harvey House dining room or stayed on the train, keeping out of sight. Holliday's former saloon was located a block west of the railroad station. Next on the northward route were railroad stations at Wagon Mound, Springer, and, finally, Raton City. "Raton in 1880 had been a border town, existing only on the most detailed scale maps," wrote former territorial governor Miguel A. Otero in 1935. "In a year's time, it became a flourishing city, as a result of its centralized position in the heart of the northern coal region."

Across the nation, the economic outlook for 1882 was not overly optimistic, because 1881 had been a year of poor crop harvest resulting in food price increases. The year had also witnessed the beginning of numerous labor and mining strikes for higher wages and better working conditions. The *Raton Guard*, in early March 1882, published some humor about the town's future: "We learn from t'other sheet [*New Mexico News and Press*] that there are lewd women in Raton. The local [editor] on that sheet keeps himself well posted on such matters, and we take his word, for once." The opening of a bordello in a frontier community was a sign of economic growth because

COPR. FRED HARVEY

H-1561   RATON TUNNEL, THE HIGHEST POINT ON THE SANTA FE BETWEEN TRINIDAD, COLO., AND RATON, N. M.

Raton Mountain railroad tunnel on the Colorado–New Mexico border (author's collection).

it took a large pool of men with disposable income to sustain a house of sexual entertainment.

Telling its national readership about Raton's growth, the *Saturday Review*'s western correspondent wrote, "The substantials of life, beef, flour and potatoes are cheap, clothing ditto, coal $3.25 per ton, labor is demanded at high prices. Money lenders get eighteen percent without a murmur and borrowers say they make more profit than the lender."

Fifteen years after he left his farm in the Commonwealth of Kentucky, my great-great-great-Uncle Augustin Hornung wrote his brother back home about his arrival in newly established Raton City, commenting, "The community's name is Spanish for rat, and we have a few living here." Uncle Gus managed the Raton office of a major business in the community. The *New Mexico News and Press*, published in Raton on May 6, 1882, reported on the success of Uncle Gus's management: "The shipments of the Raton Coal and Coking Company for the month of April were 8,432 tons." Raton Coal was sold in faraway Tombstone in the same building that housed the Safford, Hudson & Company bank operated by M.B. Clapp as cashier.

Following Confederate service during the War Between the States, Uncle Gus settled a small ranch in west Texas and fought raiding Comanche and Kiowa as a ranger on the frontier. In the late 1870s, he sought new opportunities and acquired a new ranch in New Mexico Territory. Two years after settling in Colfax County, the new *Raton Guard*, in early March 1882, published a lengthy story featuring Gus Hornung: "A meeting for the purpose of creating a building and loan association here was held at the Moulton House last night [March 9th]. Mr. Horning [*sic*], of the Coal and Coking Co., together with many other such men, are agitating and working the matter up." The lengthy newspaper article described the savings and loan concept and ended with an endorsement of the effort: "The laborers and others of Raton, whose means are limited, and who pay exorbitant rents and receive but little satisfaction there from, will do well to consider the many comforts they could receive by entering into such an arrangement which otherwise they are deprived of."

Raton City's first depositor-owned savings and loan company operated much like a modern credit union. The new investor company was looking to finance low-cost house building in Raton City like the Raton Coal and Coking Company, which had already built a low-cost housing complex in the nearby mining camp of Blossburg. Over a century after its birth, the financial institution Uncle Gus helped to start was still operating, but, sadly, the business has not survived into this century.

My great-great-great-uncle's letters home contained numerous personal references, such as, "Tell Mom that I get Buckwheat flour here [at Pace's Grocery Store] and try to make 'um like her." The Widow Hornung lived with her oldest son's family on farmlands along the banks of Bear Grass Creek. Family preferences must run deep, because I also enjoy buckwheat waffles with red raspberry jam. In one of the letters Uncle Gus sent to his brother back in the Commonwealth of Kentucky, he described the saloons in Raton City in 1882: "The saloon owners lock the front door on Sunday, but leave the back or side door open for their best customers. You use the honor system and mark your drinks on your ledger sheet and settle up on the next trip. The best Bourbon is had at the [Little] Brindle [Saloon] down from the office. I have one after supper before going to my room. Please tell Mother that I never use on the Sabbath and I go to the Methodist Mission often. I could use another can of your tobac [tobacco] for Christmas." Uncle Gus was a true Kentuckian. He appreciated quality Kentucky bourbon and the commonwealth's strong tobacco. After Tombstone, Wyatt Earp added bourbon to his like list along with a cigar. Uncle Gus once wrote, "Earp is a first class gentleman, he likes Bourbon. He is aces high."

Gus Hornung first met Wyatt Earp in Texas when Wyatt was on the gambling circuit working undercover for the Wells Fargo Express Company. In its March 30, 1882, issue, the *Raton Guard* published an account of the fight at Iron Springs, Arizona, where Earp killed the Cow-boy leader Curly Bill Brocius in a shotgun duel. On Wednesday afternoon, April 26, 1882, a railroad messenger delivered a heavily wrapped package and a note from Santa Fe Railroad headquarters to Uncle Gus. The memo provided him with instructions for what to do with the package. Later on that cool crisp Wednesday evening, Gus Hornung walked across Railroad Avenue from his office to meet the northbound Santa Fe train as it puffed up to the new Raton depot. He was looking for Wyatt Earp.

At Raton City's newly constructed railroad depot, many travelers disembarked for a 40-minute rest stop and a quick meal at the year-old Fred Harvey's restaurant. Meanwhile, the railroad crew made an engine change. The trip from Raton City, located at about 6,700 feet above sea level over the 7,622-foot Raton Pass required a sixty-five-ton, sixteen-wheel engine to replace the standard workhorse locomotive. The average grade on the Colorado side was about 121 feet to the mile, while the steepest grade was 185 feet to the mile. Near the summit, the train traveled through a half-mile tunnel blasted through Raton Mountain. Raton City was located about ten miles south of the New Mexico territorial and Colorado state border.

About 8:30 p.m. Uncle Gus and Wyatt left his posse at the Harvey House and walked over to J.B. Neely's Ten-Cent Lunch Counter for a private conversation and some food. "J.B. Neely has added, in connection with his Denver beer saloon, a handsome lunch counter, well supplied with ham sandwiches, cold meats, and coffee, so if you are hungry, go to Neely's ten cent lunch counter and be refreshed," advised the *Raton Guard*. "His lunch counter is in a separate room from the bar, where you can eat in peace and quiet."

Neely's was Gus's favorite "fast food" place and was an ideal locale for him to talk to Wyatt and eat cold meat sandwiches and drink hot coffee, a favorite of both men. Wyatt Earp was showing signs that he was ill with a spring cold or mountain hay fever. The *amigos*, who had not seen each other in years, visited for about half an hour until the train whistle announced departure time. A few minutes later the train moved north again.

A couple of times during his Cow-boy Campaign Wyatt Earp received cash to maintain his posse in the field. During their supper, Uncle Gus delivered the Santa Fe Railroad package and message to his friend. The package contained $1,000 worth of "Double Eagle" $20 gold coins. The fifty coins were appropriate because in many parts of the West paper banknotes were unpopular as they could so easily be counterfeited; thus gold coins were often preferable. These Double Eagles were the strike force's final payment, courtesy of the cabal that supported their mission against the Cow-boys.

Uncle Gus knew that his friend enjoyed the writings of Mark Twain and he figured Wyatt might appreciate the opportunity to enjoy some humor in addition to the newspaper accounts he had been reading.[1] Gus gave Wyatt his copy of *The Adventures of Tom Sawyer* he had purchased at the Raton book and newsstand operated by W.B. Asher in Raton. A few days after Earp left Raton, the *Las Vegas Daily Gazette* of May 3, 1882, editorialized about Mr. Asher, calling him a "level headed young man," and welcomed his recent move to join the business fraternity of the twin cities.

The fugitive federal officers boarded their coach and began the final leg to Trinidad, Colorado. A couple of weeks after the Earp posse passed through Raton City, Uncle Gus wrote to his Kentucky relatives: "Tuesday was the dullest day that I have ever seen. We need more rain and someone to clean the streets as the high winds blow the garbage about." Wyatt Earp and Uncle Gus would meet again in December 1884 and this incident is recounted in our book on Wyatt Earp and Doc Holliday's New Mexico adventures.

Trinidad, Colorado, is located on a 4,700-foot-high plain some 651 miles west of Kansas City and 266 rail miles from Albuquerque. In the summer of 1882, Trinidad was a city the size of Tombstone, with about 6,500 residents.

When John Conkie, a Republican, took office as mayor in April 1882, he appointed Bat Masterson as the new police chief, at $75 per month salary plus the extra fees earned by making arrests and serving process papers. Bat donned a silver badge engraved "City Marshal" and the city council allowed him three deputies to help with his duties. Bat's younger brother Jim had served under Bat's predecessor, but he was not reappointed as a policeman under his brother. Jim did, however, serve as a constable by appointment from the county commissioners in October 1882. A year later, a new Trinidad mayor and council did not extend Bat's tenure as city marshal and returned his predecessor to the post.

On Sunday, April 16, 1883, the popular Lou Kreegler, a mean-tempered carpenter, again became Trinidad police chief. Kreegler would remain in Colorado law enforcement for another three decades. Jim Masterson returned as one of Trinidad's city police officers. Bat Masterson was not in the city for the transition of authority, as he had left Trinidad for Denver on Wednesday, April 11, 1883.

It is unknown if Wyatt saw Jim Masterson upon reaching Colorado, but Bat was on hand to meet Wyatt and his posse at the El Moro train station near Trinidad. The fugitive federal officers had spent ten hours riding the train up from New Town Albuquerque. The Trinidad marshal helped his friends locate suitable accommodations in his town. Doc Holliday and Dan Tipton had been enjoying Marshal Masterson's tutelage while awaiting the arrival of Wyatt and the rest of his federal posse.

Wyatt and Bat's friend George C. "Shotgun" Collins, an undercover operative for Wells Fargo, was also in Trinidad. He had worked with Dan Tipton to make arrangements for Wyatt's stay in Gunnison. Tipton had worked in the mining camp in 1879 before Lou Rickabaugh, Earp's Tombstone gambling partner, sent for him to come to Tombstone and help Wyatt deal with the Cow-boy menace. Collins, who had also been in Arizona, would join Wyatt and Bat in Kansas in June 1883 as part of the famous Dodge City Peace Commission. Collins killed a man in 1885 and was sent to prison at Cañon City, Colorado, where he stayed until he was pardoned by the governor in 1891 via a petition from Wyatt Earp, Bat Masterson and others.

Once again, Wyatt's close connections with the Neff family were to prove helpful. In a previous chapter we discussed D.P. Neff, who managed the branch operation in Silver City that served New Mexico's Southwest mining camps for the mother company based in Trinidad. M.W. Neff, the senior partner of the mercantile operation, was a Mason and a leader in the Trinidad business community. As a coal merchant, Neff sold this product to the Santa Fe Railway at Pueblo and to the Denver Gas Company monopoly in the capital city. Households and blacksmith shops in southeastern Colorado were also his steady customers. M.W. Neff enjoyed access to the right political circles in the state capital. There is no clear-cut answer to how big a part Neff played in the aftermath of the Cow-boy Campaign. However, I believe that he at least assisted Holliday and Tipton until Wyatt Earp arrived and may have spoken to key state officials on Doc's behalf during his extradition fight.

Within days of Wyatt Earp's entering Colorado, he had a conference with his friend Edward Colborn. The lawyer had been the city attorney at Dodge City when Wyatt was part of the police force. The men reviewed Wyatt's legal situation and that of his posse under the laws of Colorado. Colborn may have advised Earp that it was too dangerous for the men to stay together any longer, so shortly after he received his last payment as a federal posseman Holliday boarded a train headed north to South Pueblo. Colborn would later serve as a judge at Salt Lake City in Utah Territory.

At first glance, South Pueblo would seem like an odd locale to choose due to Doc's delicate health; North Pueblo was the center for a smallpox outbreak in early May 1882. But upon deeper inspection, we discover that Bat Masterson's friend Henry Jameson was the city marshal at South Pueblo; since protection was a larger concern than possible health issues the choice seems sensible. Also, Doc's Royal Gorge War friend Pat Desmond, a former South Pueblo police chief, was now the local constable and the two men spent a considerable amount of time together after Holliday arrived in the community.

On the first Saturday of May 1882, the *Trinidad Daily News* reported that Wyatt and Warren Earp were still in town but that the other Earp men had "gone south Wednesday morning [May 3]." Sherm McMaster and "Turkey Creek" Jack Johnson had completed their mission of escorting Wyatt safely to Colorado; they now got on with their own lives, returning to New Mexico Territory to renew old friendships with the gamblers in New Town Las Vegas. The Trinidad paper concluded by noting, "Again the *News* takes pleasure in saying they [the Earps] are all 'way up' boys—gentlemen of the first water."

The political maneuvering began in earnest after Wyatt Earp arrived in Trinidad. Some historians believe that representatives of Wells Fargo's management now completed plans to circumvent Earp's extradition to Arizona Territory on any charges resulting from his Cow-boy roundup. On that subject, the *Albuquerque Evening Review* had an editorial comment: "The [*Tombstone*] *Epitaph* believes that the Earp boys are not half so much desperadoes as the present officers of Cochise county and it is probably right." A few months later the *Albuquerque Daily Democrat* reported, "Titles to town lots in Tombstone, Arizona, are recognized by a shotgun in the hands of a determined man." Where were the Earp brothers when you needed them?

While staying in Albuquerque, Wyatt Earp received a letter from a friend in Gunnison, most likely George "Shotgun" Collins, informing him about the mining camp as a place to rest and regain his fortunes. Early in the week following the disbanding of his posse, Wyatt was ready to visit the Gunnison region. He, Warren, and the faithful Texas Jack and Big Tip left Trinidad and settled into a two-tent campsite along the river outside of Gunnison.

The remote Colorado mountain community was still mourning the murder of Sheriff J.H. Bowman by cattle thieves when the fugitives arrived. The killing of the popular county officer by rustlers may have helped local citizens accept the Earps as "heroes," because they had fought the kind of men who had murdered their sheriff and friend. Wyatt spent a few days in bed, stuffed with medicine from Dr. C.F. Hart's Pharmacy, recovering from a cold—or possibly allergies from the cold winds and blowing dust—he had contracted in Albuquerque.

Wyatt Earp established and financed a faro bank in Charlie Biebel's saloon in Gunnison, employing Warren, Big Tip, and Texas Jack as dealers. Where did Wyatt get the money to equip and back his Colorado gambling operation and pay to equip and supply his living quarters at his river campsite if, as some latter-day writers have claimed, he was financially busted? Did Lou Rickabaugh, John Meagher or the "Easterners" gambling cartel the Earps and Holliday had supported during Tombstone's recent "Gamblers' War" (or perhaps all of them) finance Wyatt's new start or did the funds come from some other source?

A few weeks after their arrival, Wyatt and Warren gave an interview to the *Gunnison Daily News-Democrat* and Wyatt volunteered his services should town marshal Sid Byers need his assistance. The brothers presented themselves as well-dressed gentlemen and law-abiding businessmen. The Gunnison sojourn was a public relations coup. The Earps, Big Tip, and Texas Jack were hiding in plain sight in a remote Colorado mining town.

16

The Legal Fight to Save Doc Holliday

[John Henry Holliday was described as] a man of light weight, rather tall, smoothly shaven, and is always well dressed. Streaks of gray can be seen in his hair, which grows from a head a phrenologist would delight in examining. His eyes are blue, sharp and piercing.—*Pueblo (CO) Daily Chieftain*, 17 May 1882

The writer of the Otero Letter asserts that *"Wells Fargo arranged safety in Colorado and the road [AT&SF RR] gave passage to Trinidad"* for Wyatt Earp and his posse. When this security commitment was made to Wyatt no one could have foreseen the firestorm that lay just over the horizon. Many political favors were called due and ruffled feathers were tenderly smoothed in a number of arenas and jurisdictions.

The *Tombstone Daily Epitaph* of May 20, 1882, now under ownership favorable to the Cow-boy element, reported, "It is pretty well understood that a row has taken place in the Earp camp." By the time people in Cochise County read this sentence, the Earp posse had broken up and each man had gone his own way. First, Wyatt and Doc had their "Albuquerque disagreement" in April and now in May they had their "Trinidad split." (They would, a few weeks later, have a "reconciliation at Gunnison" and then four years later a final tearful "farewell at Denver.")

Since leaving Albuquerque, Doc Holliday and Dan Tipton had been in Trinidad a few days awaiting the arrival of the rest of the posse. Contemporary information seems to suggest that Wyatt might have viewed Doc as a volatile loose cannon—"seems to have at all times a nervous frightened manner"—so the two men agreed to put some distance between themselves. Were hurt feelings over the disagreement at Fat Charlie's place in Albuquerque still an issue between Wyatt and Doc? Had Wyatt assigned Dan Tipton as a nursemaid to keep a watch over the "prematurely gray" Doc Holliday? Or was Big Tip an advance man to locate safe harbor for Wyatt? The answer is very possibly yes to all the questions.

Holliday had been in Colorado about three weeks before most of the hullabaloo concerning the Arizona troubles faded from the media. With the decline in publicity, Doc felt adventuresome. In spite of the dire warning Wyatt had given his men about keeping a low profile, Holliday joined gambler friends Sam Osgood and "Texas George"

226

Robinson for a trip to Denver to visit the racetrack. En route, the trio met Bat Masterson, Trinidad's city marshal.

When he reached Denver, Holliday checked in with chief of police James Lomery to let him know that he was in the city, where he would be attending to some business and would remain unarmed. At the racetrack, Doc visited with David J. Cook, chief of the Rocky Mountain Detective Association. Neither peace officer attempted to arrest the gambler-dentist on any outstanding fugitive warrant from Arizona Territory.

Later, Doc Holliday had a business appointment with John N. Vimont, a mining engineer friend from Tombstone. On May 15, 1882, the *Denver Daily Tribune* reported that "J.N. Vimont, Leadville," was staying at the Windsor Hotel. John Vimont, superintendent of the Big Pittsburg Mine in Leadville, was a business associate of H.A.W. Tabor, Colorado's lieutenant governor.

Horace A.W. "Haw" Tabor was the lieutenant governor of Colorado in 1882. Tabor owned profitable mining interests at Leadville, Colorado, and in New Mexico Territory, including the Terence claim in Socorro County. The Terence mine earned about $35 per ton and production costs averaged about five dollars per ton. The 1881 profits, in current dollar value, were over half a million dollars. Tabor's brother Maxie had been with Doc Holliday during the Royal Gorge War in 1879. When officers arrested Holliday on a Denver street in May 1882, Doc was planning a business venture with Lt. Governor Tabor and investment capitalist John Vimont in Colorado's Wood River country.[1]

Tabor, his doctor, and his personal secretary arrived in New Town Las Vegas on Thursday, May 4, 1882. The mining tycoon and his little support group spent about a week at the hot springs as he enjoyed the spa and its relaxing treatments. It would seem that even while vacationing for his health Tabor kept tabs upon his friend Wyatt Earp and was able to respond when needed. Josie Earp recalled in her memoirs a half-century later that it was in the magnificent Tabor Hotel in Denver that she and Wyatt saw Doc Holliday for the last time.

Doc did not keep his appointment with Vimont because a self-appointed bounty hunter named Perry Mallon, assisted by Arapahoe County deputy sheriffs Charles T. Linton and Barney Cutler, arrested Doc Holliday on a street in the "Mile High City" on Monday, May 15, 1882. They escorted Doc to the county jail based upon the outstanding Pima County murder warrant charging him as a participant in the Tucson killing of Frank Stilwell. Mallon had presented himself to the Colorado officers as a deputy sheriff from Los Angeles who had been tracking Holliday for nine

Horace A.W. Tabor, lieutenant governor of Colorado, 1882 (author's collection).

years. He was in fact a minion working on behalf of Cochise County sheriff Johnny Behan. The *Pueblo Daily Chieftain* took up Holliday's defense publicly proclaiming, "The arrest is a plot of the Cow-boys against his life."

Why did Arizona authorities charge Holliday with Frank Stilwell's death and not Wyatt Earp? In his 11-page handwritten letter to Walter Noble Burns, dated March 15, 1927, Earp said, "Doc and I were the only ones in Tucson at the time Frank Stilwell was killed. Others remained in Benson." Wyatt never denied that he had shotgunned Stilwell in the Tucson railroad yard when Doc was not present. Earp was a deputy United States marshal and Holliday was his posseman. The answer to the above question is "simple politics." Doc was the weak link. He had a tarnished image as a person with a sour disposition and a troublemaker reputation whom few potential voters liked. The Cochise County Cow-boys' political strategy was to destroy Doc and hurt Wyatt by association, thus knocking Wyatt out of the upcoming sheriff's race.

Bat Masterson heard the news of Holliday's arrest and quickly hatched a plan to rescue him. Stuart Lake, who as a youthful press agent for President Theodore Roosevelt had known Bat, once wrote researcher Robert Mullin concerning Masterson: "There's a lot of stuff to be written about Bat, too much of it bad. Always he [Bat] was a fixer, a conniver, and for personal profit. He lacked Wyatt's integrity and the older he grew the more he connived."

Following his Denver arrest on murder charges from Arizona Territory, Doc Holliday granted an interview to a *Pueblo Daily Chieftain* reporter. On May 17, 1882, the newspaper reported, "When questioned as to his doings in Arizona, said he had nothing to fear from that quarter, as he had received full pardon from the governor [of Arizona] for his bloody work, in consideration of the effective service he had rendered the author-

F.W. Pitkin, governor of the State of Colorado, 1882 (Public Domain).

ities." Doc's big mouth almost ruined the gentlemen's agreement between Arizona's territorial governor Fredrick A. Tritle and Colorado's governor Fredrick W. Pitkin. The tongue slip caused a momentary panic among Earp supporters, leading to a flurry of activity to save Holliday's hide and also protect Wyatt Earp from arrest in Colorado.

On May 18, 1882, the *Las Vegas Daily Gazette* published a San Francisco exchange story from a Tombstone dispatch: "The sheriff of Arapahoe county, Col., has telegraphed here that Warren and Wyatt Earp and Doc Holliday have been arrested there (Denver). They will be brought back (to Arizona) for trial." This was a tall tale; only Holliday was under arrest. The Earp brothers were safely out of the jurisdiction of the authorities at Denver. The sheriff's telegram was testing the reward waters before he moved on his quarry. Even Colorado's new federal marshal, Walter A. Smith, journeyed to

Gunnison to check on the Arizona men, but he had no luck in catching sight of them and returned to Denver frustrated by the journey. Word finally reached both Sheriff Spangler and Marshal Smith to stop poking the Wyatt Earp hornet's nest.[2]

Ohio-born Michael Spangler was a friend of Don Miguel A. Otero. In 1882, Spangler was sheriff of Arapahoe County and had his office in the courthouse at Denver. He also oversaw the function of the county jail and it was in the lockup that Spangler had a disagreement with Masterson about the custody of Holliday and the status of the conflicting charges leveled against the gambler-dentist. Masterson lost this debate, but the sheriff's attitude seemed to change a few days later when he became supportive in his stance toward Doc Holliday's legal troubles.

Sheriff Spangler, a staunch Republican, found it inconvenient to be in Denver when Doc had his extradition hearing before Governor Pitkin. He was enjoying a few vacation days at the Montezuma Hot Springs and looking forward to a fishing trip arranged by his friend Don Miguel A. Otero. Otero had also invited another old friend on the same trip, J.M. Studebaker from South Bend, Indiana. The Studebaker Company manufactured quality work wagons and buggies; in the future, they would pioneer in the production of the automobile. The 34-year-old Spangler became vice president of the Union National Bank of Denver when his term as sheriff ended in 1883. He died in 1897 at age 48, leaving a widow and six children. His oldest son became a lawyer and later the judge advocate general of the Colorado National Guard.

Gillie Otero was the host for the Spangler–Studebaker trout fishing expedition. The trip ended abruptly so that young Otero could return to Las Vegas. He had experienced a premonition of something being wrong at home and when he reached the old Las Vegas Plaza, he found his beloved father gravely ill. Don Miguel Otero died a short time later. "I was scarcely twenty-three years old when my father died," Gillie Otero wrote decades later. "And at that tender age had to assume many responsibilities which were forced upon me, not at all to my liking or desire."

On Wednesday morning, May 17, 1882, South Pueblo city marshal Henry Jameson presented the Colorado governor with a habeas corpus warrant charging Doc Holliday with larceny. The Pueblo warrant charged that Doc had obtained money "under false pretenses" from a Pennsylvania traveler named Charles White in the sum of $115. District judge Victor A. Elliot scheduled a habeas corpus hearing for Tuesday, May 23. In the meantime, Pima County sheriff Bob Paul, of Tucson, arrived in Denver on Friday, May 19, complicating matters with his murder warrant for John H. Holliday.

At Doc's first habeas corpus hearing, the judge released him because evidence showed that Perry Mallon was not a bona fide California deputy sheriff and had no authority to make an arrest. Sheriff Paul presented the court with his new warrant and had Holliday again arrested for murder. A new habeas corpus hearing was set for Friday, May 26, but the judge rescheduled it for Monday, May 29. On Thursday, May 25, Sheriff Paul received an official Arizona requisition to escort Doc Holliday back to Arizona Territory to stand trial for the murder of Frank Stilwell. Pima County sheriff Bob Paul presented the Arizona extradition papers to Colorado's Governor Pitkin for his review and official action.

On Thursday evening word also reached Denver that a fire had destroyed a large section of Tombstone's business district, including the O.K. Corral stable complex.

George Parsons wrote in his diary that he suspected arson by the Cow-boy crowd in retaliation for Earp's murderous ride through the countryside.

Roy Young, an Oklahoma preacher, and California attorney John Bossenecker have done a creditable job of helping to rescue Bob Paul from the shadows of the Earp saga and to present him as the stalwart officer he had been. Robert "Bob" Havlin Paul had been born in Massachusetts in 1830 and before turning eighteen made three whaling voyages around Cape Horn into the Pacific Ocean. Bob became part of the California 49ers stampede, but he was not a successful gold seeker. He never gave up his dream of wealth and over the years invested in many mining ventures.

In 1854, Bob Paul began his law enforcement career by winning election as constable in a Sierra Nevada mining camp called Campo Seco. Next, he became a deputy sheriff and then won election as the sheriff of Calaveras County, California. In 1874, Bob started his long association with Wells Fargo Express Company as a shotgun messenger and later as a special agent working for chief of detectives James B. Hume. Wells Fargo's general superintendent John Valentine sent Paul to Arizona to protect the express company's interests in the territory's southwestern mining district. Paul once rode with the Earp brothers on a sixteen-day, 400-mile, manhunt over some of the most arid and rugged terrain in southern Arizona searching for the would-be robbers of the Benson–Tombstone stage.

Bob Paul's law enforcement career was not damaged by his failure to bring the Earps or Holliday back to Arizona for trial. He continued as Pima County sheriff until 1887, when he went to work for the Southern Pacific Railroad as a detective. He was appointed United States marshal for the Arizona Territory in 1890. Bob Paul ended his days as a lawman serving as the undersheriff of Pima County. He died of Bright's disease in March 1901 at his humble home in Tucson.

The deck was stacked against the justice process during Doc Holliday's extradition hearing on Monday, May 29, 1882. John H. Holliday and his attorney W.S. Deckard, a former federal judge and the honored dean of the Denver bar, met Governor Frederick Walker Pitkin in his capitol office. Attorney General David J. Cook, Lt. Governor Horace A. Tabor, and Bat Masterson spoke in Doc Holliday's defense. Two other men also weighed in on Doc's behalf. They were Denver banker and mining investor Lee Smith, a former Georgia liquor and tobacco wholesaler and Holliday family friend, and George W. Crummy, the governor's own business partner in the San Juan Mining District and a friend of deputy United States marshal Wyatt Earp. The Republican governor already understood the position of his good friend Don Miguel Antonio Otero, Sr. Each of these men held sway with the chief executive.

The Colorado governor was very cognizant of the powerful political and economic forces standing behind John Henry Holliday, DDS. E.D. Cowen of the influential *Denver Tribune* had publicly stated his support of Doc's effort to avoid returning to Arizona. The *Denver Republican* and *Pueblo Chieftain* also joined the effort. The *Rocky Mountain News*, however, did not get "the word" about Holliday and the Earps, so W.N. Byers, the editor, became the voice in support of returning the fugitive federal posse member to Arizona Territory.

Wells Fargo Express Company was still active behind the scenes. The *Las Vegas Daily Optic* reported that John J. Valentine made a visit to Denver during the week prior to Governor Pitkin's final decision in the Holliday extradition matter. Since appointment records no longer remain, it is unclear if Superintendent Valentine spoke with the Colorado governor.[3]

On Wednesday, May 31, 1882, Governor Pitkin denied the requisition request from Governor Tritle to have Sheriff Paul bring John Holliday back to Arizona, saying the document had not been properly prepared. This action caused Arapaho County authorities to discharge Holliday and witness the dentist's arrest on the larceny warrant issued at Pueblo. Later that day, Arapaho County deputy sheriff Charles T. Linton, Sheriff Bob Paul, and Bat Masterson escorted Doc Holliday to Pueblo. The next day, Justice McBride arraigned Holliday, who waived examination, on the charge of stealing over $100 in a confidence swindle. The justice allowed Holliday to post a $300 bail bond to appear for trial at the July term of court and he would be a free man if he stayed within the court's jurisdiction. Legally Doc Holliday could roam freely anywhere within the confines of the state of Colorado.

On Thursday, June 2, 1882, the *Las Vegas Daily Gazette* reported on Holliday's bail hearing held in Pueblo on Wednesday. In the same issue the newspaper noted in a June 1 dateline that there had been great excitement in Denver: "The remains of Don Miguel Otero arrived here this morning on a special train. The funeral will take place tomorrow (Thursday)." The man who had played such an important behind-the-scenes leadership role in the exile of the Earp posse from Arizona Territory had died before he saw the fruits of his labor. It is possible Gillie Otero, at some point, considered that the stress of arranging sequester of the federal marshals and the added personal disgrace of being robbed by a confidence man had broken his father's spirit.

Pima County sheriff Bob Paul had journeyed to Pueblo to witness Doc's hearing and to take him into custody if the Colorado court dismissed the larceny case. Paul returned to Tucson without Holliday. Upon his arrival back home, he made a public pronouncement against the two sham hearings he had attended and gave his unflattering opinion about Colorado justice for the local press. Years later, in 1898, when the political hostilities had cooled, Bob Paul wrote a letter to Tucson's *Arizona Citizen* defending the actions that Wyatt Earp had taken over fifteen years earlier. Earp and Paul had been friends from the time Wyatt had been a very active Pima County deputy sheriff and Bob a Wells Fargo Express Company shotgun messenger. Earp had helped Paul prove his challenge to election vote fraud during the Pima County sheriff's race in 1880.

In early June 1882, Doc Holliday traveled to Gunnison to spend a few days with Wyatt, Warren, Big Tip and Texas Jack. Wyatt and Doc may have finally discussed Wyatt's feelings about his posse's deserting him at Iron Springs and the "Jew boy" remark Holliday had made in Albuquerque. Certainly, they discussed Doc Holliday's legal troubles. In 1930, Judd Riley, a Gunnison police office during the months the Earp group was living in that community, said that Wyatt was always armed with "two guns high up under his arms, but he never used them here." He added that Earp "told us boys on the police force we could call on him if we needed help at any time." Riley noted that Doc Holliday was the only member of the Earp circle "that seemed to drink much, and the minute he got hilarious, the others promptly took him in charge and he just disappeared." It is possible that personal strain, political pressures, media attention, and Holliday's own unpredictable nature had become too much for Wyatt Earp, because Doc soon left

Gunnison and returned to Pueblo. Later that summer regional newspaper stories placed Holliday in the Colorado mining camps of Salida, Leadville, and Silverton.

Territory secretary H.M. Van Arman, acting governor of Arizona Territory during June and July 1882 in the absence of Governor Tritle, innocently sent Governor Pitkin a revised requisition for Doc Holiday dated June 9, 1882. The dentist was no longer in police custody and the same power base that had supported Doc Holliday in May was still active on his behalf in June, so the Colorado governor ignored this new document. Van Arman, an appointee of the new president, Chester A. Arthur, was a strong Republican partisan, so when he learned the "truth" of the Holliday situation he decided not to follow up on his "misguided" requisition request. Arizona territorial authorities made no further effort to extradite the gambler-dentist. After his term as Arizona governor, F.A. Tritle received a presidential appointment as the register of the United States Land Office at Prescott.

17

Wyatt Earp vs. Johnny Ringo

I promised my brother [Morgan] to get even and I have kept my word so far. When they shot him he said the only thing he regretted was that he wouldn't have a chance to get even. I told him I'd attend to it for him.—Wyatt Earp, *Gunnison (CO) Daily News-Democrat*, 4 June 1882

Many discussions concerning Deputy United States Marshal Wyatt Earp's campaign against the Cow-boys conclude when he and his federal posse ride out of Arizona Territory in April 1882. In fact, the campaign did not end until after a final, less publicly acknowledged second surgical strike mission was successfully carried out in July 1882.

The Otero Letter contains this sentence with no explanation as to its meaning: "*Earp had a long talk with the president of Wells Fargo, but I can not say about the direction of the talk.*" It is possible, in light of later events that involved Wyatt Earp and Miguel Otero in 1885 when 26-year-old Otero was the chief deputy United States marshal for New Mexico Territory, that Otero knew such a meeting held relevance but only later learned the nature of the agreement reached between Wyatt Earp and John J. Valentine that April day in 1882 and at that time found it too sensitive to divulge.

Author's Perspective: I believe the groundwork for a second phase of the Cow-boy Campaign was formulated at that morning conference in Superintendent Valentine's private railroad car. This chapter will examine the evidence for and against this belief.

Walter Noble Burns, a spinner of western folktales from Chicago, revived the Johnny Ringo mythology when Doubleday, Page and Company published his landmark history of the "Town to Tough to Die" in December 1927. Two years earlier, he had resurrected Billy the Kid from an early grave and made his name a household word. Burns hoped to do the same for another western bad boy when he wrote, "John Ringo stalks through the stories of old Tombstone days like a Hamlet among outlaws.... His somber eyes seemed brooding upon a fate that had changed a life of bright promise into a career of sinister futilities." A Cow-boy sympathizer wrote a letter to the editor of the *Tombstone Epitaph* in November 1929 and opined, "If anyone wants to know who the real lion of Tombstone was, tell them that it was John Ringo."[1]

Josie Earp cut through the mythmaking in old age when she wrote, "Ringo seemed reserved and gentlemanly to me. I doubt, on my own observation, that Ringo was as wantonly murderous as some have tried to portray him, through he was admittedly a killer." Josie knew Ringo from his business association with her onetime fiancé Sheriff Johnny Behan, who had once been Ringo's roommate. Josie and Ringo were friends enough that she called him Jack in her memoirs and the Cow-boy leader seems to have willingly given or loaned Josie Marcus some money during her stay in Tombstone after her breakup with Johnny Behan and prior to her association with Wyatt Earp. Strange as it may seem to present-day readers, Wyatt Earp and John Ringo were friends enough that Wyatt also called Ringo by his nickname.

Who was Johnny Ringo? He was born John Peters Ringo in Washington, Clay Township, Wayne County, Indiana, in May 1850. Green's Fork is the present-day name of Ringo's small-town birthplace. The future killer spent his youth in the James-Younger outlaw country around Liberty, Missouri, and later moved to California with his family. By the mid–1870s, he was "raising hell" in central Texas. Ringo was a key figure in the Hoodoo, or Mason County, War conflict over sectionalism and ethnic prejudice masquerading as a dispute over livestock ownership. During this blood feud, Ringo learned the fine art of back-shooting and murder. Released due to a lack of witnesses willing to testify against him, John Ringo escaped a murder charge, and the German farmers of Precinct 4 (Loyal Valley) in Mason County, Texas, elected him constable in November 1878. A few months later, the former Lone Star peace officer was causing trouble in the New Mexico Territory before heading on west to meet his destiny in Tombstone, Arizona Territory. In that wild region Ringo was crowned "King of the Cow-boys" in those pre–Roy Rogers years.

San Simon was one of many small trading centers established in Arizona during 1880; that same year John Ringo and Ike Clanton located a ranch in the San Simon Valley. Ringo also staked out some mining locations. The Cochise County Cow-boys were trying to organize control over the valley by electing Ike Clanton justice of the peace and Joe Hill/Olney as constable in November 1880. A territorial court, however, overturned the election due to voter fraud; there were more votes cast than residents living in the precinct. The three men formed a cattle operation partnership in the valley.

In discussing Johnny Ringo, biographer Steve Gatto has raised questions concerning Ringo's relationship with a couple of men named Price. The former range-war killer sold a mining claim to John E. Price of New Mexico, and on another property he gave his power of attorney to a James Price of Missouri. The Price and Ringo families had ties rooted in post–Civil War Missouri and Reconstruction politics. John Price was involved with building the railroad from New Mexico into Arizona. Gatto makes no claims about this relationship, but could there have been a "gentle-

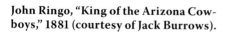

John Ringo, "King of the Arizona Cowboys," 1881 (courtesy of Jack Burrows).

man's agreement" to develop the San Simon Valley livestock and mining resources by constructing a rail line on Cow-boy lands? Had such a successful development venture taken place the Cow-boy–railroad cabal might have become wealthy. This idea is yet another Tombstone saga possibility that needs more research.

In the first decade of the twentieth century, writer Frederick Ritchie Bechdolt visited with Wyatt Earp and then composed an unflattering tale that appeared in the *Saturday Evening Post* and was reworked for inclusion in his 1922 book, *When the West Was Young.* He quotes Wyatt as admitting he killed Ringo. Bechdolt wrote his friend Billy Breakenridge on December 23, 1927, and recounted his visit with Earp: "He [Wyatt] speaks with considerable respect of John Ringo, and with much less of Curly Bill."

In 1920, in reply to Bechdoth's article, Wyatt Earp provided Mrs. Forrestine Cooper Hooker, the daughter-in-law of Arizona rancher and Earp supporter Henry C. Hooker (she was also an author of children's books), a first-person defense of his actions in Arizona. One of the incidents described is the killing of Johnny Ringo on Wyatt's way out of Arizona headed for New Mexico. This story was never published in Wyatt Earp's life time.[2]

Wyatt's latter-day confidante John Flood, in his 1926 biography manuscript, recounts the Ringo killing. He didn't supply a date for the killing but inserted the account in the chapter telling about the hunt for the outlaw in April 1882. This chapter leads into the narrative of the posse leaving Arizona. Josie Earp, in her 1930s collaborative autobiographies, tells how Wyatt returned to Arizona and killed Johnny Ringo. These three firsthand accounts contain many similarities about how Wyatt killed Ringo, yet they also contain major differences.

Arizona historian Dr. Frank Lockwood also visited Wyatt and Josie at their home and later published the claim that Wyatt told him how he had ended Ringo's life. As had Bechdolt before him, Lockwood believed that Wyatt Earp was a "cold and cruel killer." He had read Mrs. Hooker's account a few years before he visited with Wyatt.

"Jack Ringo's Death" is the title of Josie Earp's account of how her husband killed Ringo in one version of the Cason/Ackerman manuscripts. Interestingly, the chapter on Earp's killing of Ringo was omitted from Glenn G. Boyer's edited and novelized Cason/Ackerman manuscript, published in 1976 by the University of Arizona as *I Married Wyatt Earp.* Boyer claimed that the university's editors cut the chapter for length. This tale is difficult to accept because the details of how Wyatt killed Ringo, told by the wife of the man who pulled the trigger, is explosive drama. This revelation would have made Boyer's version of Josie's autobiography even more marketable and the movie adaptation more dramatically Hollywood.

Josie's Ringo death chapter, as edited by Glenn Boyer, first saw publication in 1974 in the local edition of the *Tombstone Epitaph.* This was two years before publication of Boyer's book *I Married Wyatt Earp*, and it was published again in 1975 in the National Edition of the *Tombstone Epitaph*. In February 1987, *Real West* magazine published Josie's Ringo killing story in an expanded version of the two *Epitaph* publications. In his 1993 "historical novel," *Wyatt Earp's Tombstone Vendetta*, Boyer once more used Josie's account of Ringo's death as the basis for a section in this work. In 1997, Boyer privately printed an editorialized version of Josie's Ringo death tale as a booklet titled *Who Killed John Ringo?* Josie Earp made no money on publication of her memoirs, but Glenn D. Boyer did.

Tucson's *Arizona Daily Star*, on Sunday, January 26, 1964, published an interview with Earp artifact collector John Gilchriese. During the conversation, Gilchriese explained how he felt Earp could have killed Ringo, based upon Wyatt's own description contained in chapter 45, "Where There's Smoke," from John Flood's manuscript. It is unclear if Gilchriese had seen the Hooker manuscript at this time, but it is likely, since John was researching his massive, as yet unpublished, Wyatt Earp biography at the time.

Robert L. Thomas, the reporter who interviewed Gilchriese for the Tucson newspaper, revived the Wild West collector's thesis for a new article published in the fall 1972 issue of *Old West* magazine. In "I Think Earp Took Johnny Ringo," Thomas quotes from John Flood's work and adds Gilchriese's thoughts that Wyatt had left Colorado on the Santa Fe Railroad and entered New Mexico via Raton Pass but had traveled only as far as East Las Vegas: "That would be a day and night by train. Then he could have ridden horseback from there to Roswell, skirting the Mescalero Apache country and the western fringes of the Staked Plains. From Roswell, another horseback ride would take him to Lordsburg and from there he would ride straight to the Chiricahua Mountains. That means about six days by horse and one by train. It could be done."

Following the publication of the Thomas article, Robert Mullin wrote to ask his friend John Gilchriese about some of the comments in the story. Strange as it might seem, Gilchriese claimed that he did not know Thomas had repackaged their earlier interview and that he had never meant to convey the idea he believed Earp really killed Ringo, only that he could have done the deed. John Gilchriese always wanted others to view him as the foremost authority on Wyatt Earp. He never achieved his desire because he was constantly shifting his storyline and historians lost confidence in his credibility. Gilchriese's death seems to have ended any attempt to publish his "definitive" work-in-progress manuscript, "The Man Called Wyatt Earp."

John Gilchriese used his friend John Floods' manuscript as the main source for speculation of a covert strike against Johnny Ringo. He got the central idea correct, but he woefully misunderstood the topography and travel logistics in Colorado and New Mexico during the summer of 1882. First, it would be hard to believe that anyone would have rented a horse to a stranger for a trip across two territories, an extended length of time, not to mention the renter's being able to identify Earp's use of the horse, thus placing Wyatt in New Mexico and Arizona. Did Wyatt buy a horse? It's doubtful, as quality horse purchase was not as easy as it is portrayed in the movies. This horseback ride idea presents a major flaw in Gilchriese's thesis. I suggest Wyatt Earp's return foray into Arizona after Johnny Ringo happened a different way.

Gilchriese has Earp doing too much horseback riding in the wrong direction. After leaving the train at East Las Vegas Wyatt heads toward Roswell, located in eastern New Mexico near the Texas line, for no purpose. It should be noted that Roswell was not platted as a village until 1885; before that time it was a simple adobe trading post on the Pecos River. On this route, Earp would have had to cross open plains, skirt the massive Apache Indian Reservation with few routes across the mountains, navigate the great lava flow fields in western Lincoln County, ford the Rio Grande, pass through the western mountains, and cross the desert before reaching Lordsburg for the jump into Arizona.

Author's Perspective: In the summer of 1882 the Chiricahua Apache renegade leader Nana brought his warriors out of Mexico to raid southern New Mexico. Gilchriese's suggested Earp trip totally disregards the danger of a white man traveling alone near the vast 460,000-acre Mescalero Apache Reservation due to the trouble with the Jicarilla, Mimbres and Mescalero Apache. In June 1882 it had taken four troops of cavalry from nearby Fort Stanton to contain a reservation uprising and the Apaches were still mourning their dead and wounded, so non–Indians did not travel the area and remained in a state of high alert into July.

The Apache Indian agent William Henry Llewellyn, future Rough Rider hero during the 1898 War with Spain, received two wounds during the June riot. The chief of the reservation's Indian police was James L. "Whispering" Smith,[3] famous in Nebraska and Wyoming as a railroad detective and ferocious foe of road agents, was trying to maintain the fragile truce. Wyatt would have understood the personal travel danger and kept wide of the Apache reservation.

One last point is that Wyatt Earp was a fine equestrian, but for long trips he preferred a buggy or a wagon. Earp was a pragmatic man who sought convenient ways to accomplish his ends. A good example is that, when he was Dodge City's assistant city marshal, he saved his shoe leather and fatigue by riding a mule while patrolling the length of the Front Street plaza in the Queen of the Cowtowns. It would be characteristic of Wyatt to have taken the easiest and fastest way to reach southwestern Arizona Territory on any covet mission launched from southern Colorado.

Mark Twain could have been discussing the death of Johnny Ringo when he wrote about a mystery murder in his second volume of *Early Tales and Sketches*. The renowned humorist wrote, "Nothing in the world affords a newspaper reporter so much satisfaction as gathering up the details of a bloody and mysterious murder, and writing them up with aggravating circumstantiality." After an extended review of 1880s Colorado and New Mexico stagecoach route maps and timetables, railroad route maps and timetables, along with Arizona and New Mexico topographic maps, I have pieced together a more realistic possibility of what could have happened in July 1882. My "aggravating circumstantiality" thesis of how Wyatt Earp killed John Ringo rests upon a set of facts and informed projections.

On Sunday, July 2, 1882, Wyatt Earp departed from his secluded Colorado campsite outside of Gunnison, leaving his brother Warren, Texas Jack and Dan Tipton to attend the July 4th celebration and to operate Wyatt's faro game at Biebel's Saloon. He boarded a Denver, South Park and Pacific Railroad (Denver and Rio Grande Railroad subsidiary) passenger or freight train, traveling 73 miles east over the continental divide via the 10,856-foot-high Marshall Pass headed for Salida (the narrow gage had reached Gunnison in August 1881).

At Salida, Wyatt boarded the Wells Fargo Express car on the Royal Gorge Canyon route of the Denver & Rio Grande Railroad, traveling east across Colorado's Sangre de Cristo Mountains 95 miles to Pueblo. The train traveled the 80-mile stretch across the high mesa country on the narrow gauge line headed toward Trinidad. At Trinidad, Wyatt Earp transferred from the D&RGRR to the Santa Fe Railroad system to enter New Mexico via the Raton Tunnel. Once in New Mexico the rail line was owned and maintained by the New Mexico and Southern Pacific Railroad Company, a subsidiary of the parent company, for the trip to New Las Vegas and on to New Town Albuquerque, continuing on south along the Rio Grande to San Marcial, where he connected with the Santa Fe's other division, the Rio Grande, Mexico and Pacific Railroad, to go west toward Deming. Following a two-hour cargo transfer there, Wyatt Earp boarded the westbound Southern Pacific headed to Arizona. Just as in his stopover in April, there is no record that he had any contact with deputy sheriff Dan Tucker.

Before we continue this scenario, the reader should understand the relationship of the Southern Pacific Railroad system with the Wells Fargo Express Company in 1882. The partnership began in 1869 when the Southern Pacific Railroad received a one-third interest in the Wells Fargo Express Company for the exclusive right to operate the express business along the Southern Pacific system. The two companies renewed this agreement in 1878, with an additional $1,250,000 in Wells Fargo Express Company stock being given to Southern Pacific. The railroad management had a vested interest in protecting the commercial success of their express company partner by eliminating the lawless element that might do financial harm to their investments in the express company's ability to provide quality customer service.

The Wells Fargo Express Company shipments carried on the narrow gage D&RG system would have been offloaded onto the wider wheel-based freight cars used on the standard gage rail systems of the Santa Fe and the Southern Pacific. This layover to unload and reload the cargo at Trinidad was the real danger point in the covert plan for Wyatt Earp to get out of Colorado, across New Mexico, and into Arizona. However, he and the mission were vulnerable at this juncture only if someone was seeking the deputy federal marshal.

The Twentieth New Mexico Territorial Legislative Assembly enacted a comprehensive railroad law in early February 1878. This legislation specified the travel order in which each style of car followed the passenger coaches: mail car, express car, baggage car, and then freight cars, ending with a caboose. This order for rolling stock travel would have helped insure some security from observation by general passengers. Wyatt Earp, acting as a special officer, would have attracted little or no attention had he traveled, eaten, and slept inside a Wells Fargo Express Company coach. On a coach carried over one of three interlocking railroad systems used during the mission, Wyatt Earp could have accomplished the whole trip from Gunnison, Colorado, to some point inside eastern Arizona Territory without incident.

The steam locomotives in the 1880s would have averaged about 22 miles per hour with selected passenger, freight, and water/coal stops; a locomotive could burn a cord of wood every 35 miles. The covert trip outlined above took three days, so on July 5 or 6 Wyatt Earp would have joined his awaiting posse.

Josie Earp claimed that the staging area for Wyatt's new strike force was on Col. Hooker's vast Sierra Bonita Ranch. Wyatt may have chosen to use one of the same camps he had utilized a few months before during the original mission—a secluded site away from possible outside observation. Josie Earp's idea puts the posse way north of Ringo's suspected location in the Chiricahua Mountains. A location in the remote Texas Canyon or along San Simon Creek is more logical and secure.

Since 1881, the Atlantic and Pacific Railroad had started its westward route from A & P Junction, near the Isleta Pueblo on the west side of the Rio Grande south of

Albuquerque, at a terminal with the Santa Fe Railway. From there it ran westward toward Arizona and on to present-day Flagstaff. In 1882, this route took 60 hours to complete and was 795 miles shorter than the route used by the Southern Pacific Railroad to reach the West Coast.

Josie Earp believed that Wyatt had used the A&PRR route to reach Arizona. However, I think her scenario is inaccurate because it places Wyatt in remote Indian country too many miles north of her supposed rendezvous site on Henry Hooker's Sierra Bonita Ranch. It is possible Josie Earp surmised this was the route used for "the return" because she had traveled this northern Arizona route on her 1937 trip to visit Fred Dodge at his Texas ranch.

Returning to the southern route theory for the way Wyatt returned to Arizona, one Earp biographer has stated that an unnamed Lordsburg blacksmith, an undercover Wells Fargo operative, aided Wyatt by providing him with horses to get him into Arizona undetected. This is a possibility for how Wyatt acquired his horse, but there is a second account with more possibility.

In 1984, I began working with Mrs. Cipriana Baca Randolph compiling information for my biography of her father, titled *Cipriano Baca: Frontier Lawman of New Mexico*. During this research stage Mrs. Randolph told this author her California-born father, before settling in New Mexico Territory, had worked on the Sanford farm/ranch north of Tombstone. It was at Sanford's that Baca saw Morgan Earp at a dance held on the homestead. Another time, while buying supplies in Tucson, Baca's boss pointed out Wyatt Earp as a prominent Tombstone businessman, gambler and sometime lawman. In Stuart N. Lake's research notes, there is a reference to Morgan Earp's having had

some disagreement with William "Curly Bill" Brocius and Charles "Pony Diehl" Ray while he was attending a social at Sanford's place. This incident is possible because Morgan operated a gambling concession in Tucson, enjoyed social functions, and was disliked by the Cow-boys.

In the early 1880s, a cattle growers' association recruited Baca as an undercover agent to assist association range riders in gathering evidence against suspected rustlers. Baca's cover job was as a meat contractor selling Arizona beef to Southern Pacific Railroad construction crews building across Arizona, racing eastward to connect with the Santa Fe Railway in New Mexico Territory.

One of Cipriano Baca's New Mexico friends was Charley Bigsby, a Silver City livery stable operator and undercover Wells Fargo operative. One day Bigsby asked Baca to do him a favor and deliver two horses to a campsite in the canyon on the Southern Pacific Railroad grade west of Strain's Pass near the Arizona–New Mexico line. The animals were for use by a deputy United States marshal:

Cipriano Baca, New Mexico's premier frontier Hispanic lawman (Chuck Hornung, New Mexico Mounted Police Collection).

Father spent two days camped out watching for the man. Then one day he saw a man step off the train up in the pass. That man was Wyatt Earp. Father gave him the horses and gear and Earp gave my father a twenty-dollar gold piece and Earp rode off for Arizona.

I remember that Earp story because I was visiting Father for Christmas about a year or so after he left the rangers [Captain Herb McGrath's New Mexico Mounted Police Company] after the Great War. I saw him in Albuquerque at the other place [Baca's rented house] and he showed me a copy of a *Saturday Evening Post* story he was reading about old Tombstone [Frederick Bechdolt, "Tombstone's Wild Oats," 13 December 1919]. Then he said he had helped the man in the story. I asked who and he said Wyatt Earp. I was a teenage girl and the name Wyatt Earp didn't mean anything to me, so I asked who he was.

Father seemed to think very highly of Earp. I thought it was funny when he said he would like to see a book or movie about Earp's life. Years later every time I saw that TV show [*The Life and Legend of Wyatt Earp*] I would think about that visit with my father and wish that I had asked him more about his life [in Arizona Territory].

Mrs. Randolph was unable to place a date to this Baca–Earp incident that would connect it directly with a possible Earp–Ringo killing scenario in July 1882. The Baca–Earp encounter could have taken place at some other time or not at all. However, the circumstance does fit with other possibilities and the Wells Fargo Express Company could easily have arranged to have Wyatt Earp's stabled horses transported from Silver City to Deming.

The reader might recall that Wyatt Earp left two horses at Silver City in April during the posse's journey to New Albuquerque. Although Cipriana Randolph did not mention a second man with Earp, that does not preclude the man's presence. The focus of her father's story was Earp and not the horse delivery incident. If Earp had a traveling companion that should not have caused Baca any concern. Many officers, including Baca during his own law enforcement career, traveled with a deputy or posseman and Baca did bring a second horse, so he may have anticipated a second rider.

Mrs. Randolph said her father told her "Earp was tall and blond and had a commanding manner." Wyatt Earp probably never knew that the young Hispanic who gave him the horses and gear that summer day in 1882 would become famous as an outlaw-hunting sheriff, deputy United States marshal, and, later, the lieutenant of the first company of New Mexico's Territorial Mounted Police, commonly called Fullerton's Rangers after their captain.[4]

Author's Perspective: What was Wyatt Earp's authority to lead a special strike force in search of Johnny Ringo? As we have discussed earlier, in early 1885 United States district attorney James A. Zabriskie finished his special field investigation into the operation and fiscal management of the United States Marshal's Office under the stewardship of Crawley P. Dake.Zabriskie mailed his five-page typed report to United States attorney general Benjamin Harris Brewster under the date of Sunday, January 22, 1885. The special investigator had interviewed Marshal Dake as part of his review, and in the last sentence on page two of his report Zabriskie noted that Dake claimed that Wyatt Earp "sent his resignation to Marshal Dake, by mail"; but he provides no date for Wyatt's self-termination as a deputy federal marshal for Arizona Territory.

Wyatt Earp's actions would seem to support the concept that he considered himself a federal deputy at the time he conducted part two of his Cow-boy Campaign. Dake was still the United States marshal for Arizona Territory and he had not revoked Wyatt Earp's deputy commission or accepted his February 1882 resignation offer. Many Colorado newspaper stories refer to both Wyatt and Doc as federal deputy marshals during the summer of 1882. Without the actual dated resignation, it is conceivable that Wyatt Earp did not relinquish his appointment until after he killed Johnny Ringo on July 13 and successfully returned to Colorado. This scenario works, since Marshal Dake left office on Tuesday, July 18, 1882, the same day that the *Tombstone Daily Epitaph* reported Ringo's death. Zan L. Tidball, of New York State, replaced Dake as the chief federal law enforcement officer in Arizona Territory.

On November 17, 1884, the *Albuquerque Evening Democrat* reported that Zabriskie was in the city "for a short visit and can be found at the Armijo [Hotel]." The newspaper called him "the talented federal attorney for Arizona" but did not state his purpose for being in the Duke City. Staying at the Armijo at this time was former deputy United States marshal Wyatt Earp and his wife Josie Marcus. Was this the time and the place where the two men met and discussed the Dake funding investigation?

Here are some additional facts to ponder. During the time that the Earp brothers were in Tombstone, James A. Zabriskie was a prominent Tucson attorney in partnership with Benjamin H. Hereford. In fact, Wyatt recommended Zabriskie as a defense lawyer to Curly Bill Brocius during his hearing on the charge of killing Tombstone city marshal Fred White in October 1880. Brocius told Earp that Zabriskie had prosecuted him for a crime while they lived in Texas. Hereford's son was a deputy sheriff under Johnny Behan. When men traveling on the road along Turkey Creek found Johnny Ringo's corpse sitting in the V-notch of a double oak tree along the stream, there was a letter from the Hereford & Zabriskie law firm in his pocket. The content of the lawyer's communication is unknown.

In spite of diligent searching the Earp posse could not locate Johnny Ringo in March–April 1882, so how did Earp expect to local him in July? Wells Fargo Express Company had many informants in Cochise County during the Cow-boy roundup. These spies, some of them turncoat Cow-boy supporters, had seen the new way the wind was blowing and wanted to be in the good graces of the law and order element; some simply wanted the bounty money offered.

According to Josie Earp there were three men especially seeking John Ringo in the summer of 1882. One spy was Tombstone saloonman and lady's man Nashville Franklin "Buckskin Frank" Leslie. This Texas native had been an army scout with Tom Horn and Al Sieber and an informant for Wells Fargo. Leslie served as a special policeman to legalize his employment as a bouncer in a Tombstone saloon and rode with the Earps on posses trailing suspected stagecoach robbers. He was a drinking buddy of Johnny Ringo and may have been among the last to see him alive before Ringo met his fate. (Some writers have claimed that Leslie confessed to killing Ringo. It is true that Leslie was a deadly man with a pistol. In later years, he served six years in Arizona's Yuma Territorial Prison for murdering his lover. Upon release, Buckskin Frank joined the long list of frontiersmen whose final days became a mystery of the Old West.)

The second lookout was Lou Cooley, an undercover operative for Wells Fargo whose public job was as a troubleshooter and range enforcer for Henry C. Hooker's ranching empire. He was an expert tracker and would join Wyatt Earp's posse on the final hunt for Johnny Ringo.

The third scout was Sheriff John Behan's civil process server–tax collector–jail janitor, William Milton "Uncle Billy" Breakenridge. This son of New York spent his youth in Wisconsin and was part of the rabble that perpetrated the Indian village slaughter at Sand Creek in Colorado Territory. Breakenridge worked as a storekeeper, a freighter, and a railroad construction worker. He held numerous public servant jobs before ending his career as a special officer for the Southern Pacific Railroad. Billy was honored as "Colonel Breakenridge, the Tombstone Deputy," during his final years. Fred Dodge wrote Stuart Lake about Breakenridge in 1929 saying, "He was a nice young lady then [in Tombstone] and I suspect is a nice old woman now." Buried in Tucson's Evergreen Cemetery, Breakenridge died in February 1931 at age 85.

Who was the man who earned the blood money for locating Johnny Ringo? Josie Earp says Breakenridge pinpointed Ringo's location. "Uncle Billy" claimed to be Johnny's friend in his self-serving 1928 autobiography, yet he was the person who set him up for a bullet and earned the Wells Fargo bounty money. Josie Earp had known Breakenridge in Tombstone, but she turned sour on Billy after he dumped on Wyatt in his autobiography after her husband had befriended Behan's deputy, down on his luck and needing money, and helped him gather information for his book. In her own autobiography Josie discussed the man she called "Billy Blab" saying, "I do not accuse William Breakenridge of evil intent. He was merely a weak, talkative man, of a sort, unendowed with great intelligence, untroubled by any scruple of conscience, and unchecked by any sense of loyalty to friend or enmity to foe, could, in life, present disarming appearance of friendliness to all. He made a good tool for the outlaws of Cochise County."

What was Johnny Ringo doing in the Chiricahua Mountains in July 1882? Researcher Lynn Bailey has suggested that he was trying to locate a new site for his cattle ranch operation. In the summer of 1882, Ringo had nothing to fear from local law enforcement officers and he believed that Wyatt Earp was long gone. He knew two men from Abilene were in the San Simon Cienega region buying up land claims and water rights for wealthy Texas cattle ranchers Claiborne Merchant and James Parramore so the men could expand their operation into Arizona. The Texans spent in the vicinity of $22,000 for their purchases. Ringo, in partnership with Joe Hill and Ike Clanton, owned a place at the lower end of the Cienega where the trio ran about 1,000 beef and dairy cattle as well as growing alfalfa and garden vegetables by use of an irrigation system. On the partners' property was a small trading post for area residents. If they sold their property, at a profit, the new owners would allow 18 months for their resettlement. This was a good reason for Ringo to come out of seclusion and search for new acreage.

Johnny Ringo had misjudged Wyatt Earp. The federal marshal was back on the manhunt and when he was provided an update on Ringo's location Wyatt is quoted as telling his posse, "Well, if Ringo is in this valley, he certainly is entitled to stay." The full implication of Wyatt Earp's comment, as recorded by John Flood on page 321 of Wyatt's 1926 autobiographical manuscript, was that Wyatt Earp felt his old friend Jack Ringo had earned the privilege to stay permanently in the Sulphur Springs Valley or any other place Wyatt's bullet discovered him.

Who were the men who rode with Wyatt Earp on this final hunt for Johnny Ringo? In her autobiography, Josie Earp says that Tombstone gambler and Wells Fargo informant Fred Dodge was one of the new strike force team. Dodge never publicly admitted involvement in Johnny Ringo's death, but he did make a halfhearted admission to certain knowledge when he wrote Stuart Lake in the late 1920s. The nominally talkative Dodge said simply, "I was riding in that part of the country quite a little bit right at that particular time."

Josie Earp identified other posse members as Wyatt's old Wichita friend, now a Tombstone Safety Committee member and Earp gambling partner, John Meagher of the Alhambra Saloon. The third man was the faithful O.C. "Hairlip Charlie" Smith. The fourth stealth rider was Lou Cooley. Johnny Green, the fifth member, was a good man with a card deck or a pistol. Green was nicknamed "Crooked-Mouth" because he once had a bullet pass through his cheek and the healed wound distorted the appearance of his mouth. Green had also earned the moniker of "Cathouse Johnny." When Wyatt was the Pima County deputy sheriff stationed at Tombstone in 1880 he had cause to arrest Green, but the men soon became friends and in later years they would be traveling companions on the gambling circuit. I believe that if Wyatt had a traveling partner when he left Colorado in July 1882, it was most likely Johnny Green and not Doc Holliday.

> **Author's Perspective:** The United States Marine Corps has a credo composed of ten character points. I believe that Wyatt Earp may have unknowingly used some or all of these measurements when selecting his new strike force-posse; dependability, courage, decisiveness, endurance, initiative, integrity, judgment, proficiency, selflessness, and loyalty. I also find it revealing that none of the possemen who had been at Iron Springs and left Wyatt Earp to face death alone rode with him on this deadly mission to kill Johnny Ringo.

> Why wasn't Doc Holliday part of this second strike force team? Josie Earp and others have claimed that Doc Holliday was a member of the "Return Posse." Mrs. Earp said in the late 1930s, in her ghost-written autobiography, that Wyatt and Doc left their Colorado retreats "sporting beards to disguise their well-known features, traveled west on the Atlantic and Pacific R.R., then made their way south through the mountains by horse." I have one problem with the disguise proposition. There is little doubt that by the summer of 1882 the public had heard of both "Wyatt Earp" and "Doc Holliday," but to think that the average traveler or peace officer was familiar with their "well-known features" stretches the imagination. Newspapers and magazines printed few pictures in the 1880s due to the limited availability of the illustrations and the cost of making wooden die cuts for the printing process. Due to these factors, the public did not become familiar with the standard headshot photographs of Wyatt and Doc popularized until after their widespread publication during the early twentieth century.

> During her declining years, Josie Earp wrote that Holliday and Doc's Texas friend, a man she called "Goober," was part of this new posse. Because both John Flood and Forrestine Hooker tell of Wyatt killing Ringo on his way to refuge in New Mexico and finally Colorado, some writers have assumed that Holliday was part of the Return Posse. "Goober" could have been a code name for Fred Dodge, who in the 1930s lived in Texas and had supplied Josie with a lot of background information concerning Tombstone and her husband's life in the community. Wyatt Earp's letter to Stuart N. Lake dated October 21, 1928, said, "Doc was not with me after we left Trinidad, Colo." I take Wyatt Earp at his word concerning Doc Holliday. Thus I have a problem accepting Doc's presence on this manhunt, but I have no problem with the presence of the mysterious "Goober" if he was in fact Fred Dodge.

Public records seem to support Wyatt Earp's claim that he and Doc did not ride together again after May 1882. Doc had spent most of June with Wyatt and Warren in Gunnison. However, during the first week of July 1882, according to the *Salida Mountain Mail*, Holliday was in that Colorado community. On Monday, July 10, Holliday appeared before a grand jury hearing in Pueblo. The next day the court issued a criminal indictment based upon the larceny complaint concocted by Bat Masterson. The district judge issued a corpus warrant for Holliday's arrest. The court docket listed the case as Cause #1851, *The People vs. J.H. Holliday.* Doc Holliday, "in his own proper person as well as his counsel, W.G. Hollings, Esq., also came" into the district court and entered a not guilty plea. Holliday's release was upon a $500 bond to appear at trial when summoned. Holliday was again a free man, subject only to the call of the Pueblo County District Court.

The *Pueblo Daily Chieftain* of July 19, 1882, reported that Doc Holliday "is now in Leadville and is being interviewed by the carbonate reporters." Doc had been planning a trip to Leadville in May when arrested in Denver on the warrant from Arizona. However, no Holliday interview appears in the *Leadville Daily Herald* during midsummer 1882. Was the Pueblo newspaper item one of misinformation to cover Holliday's true movements or did Doc just change his plans and not go up to Leadville? He may have gone to Leadville and attended to business and his visit was not newsworthy. Doc's legal troubles were hundreds of miles south in Tucson and Pueblo, not in Leadville.

Writers like Glenn G. Boyer, Ben T. Traywick and Karen Holliday Tanner tried to explain that the legal language of the Pueblo court records quoted above mean that Doc Holliday's attorney was present representing him in court at the July 10, 1882, court hearing. Furthermore, they claim the Pueblo newspaper story concerning the legal action was a planted notice by friends to provide Doc with an alibi, if he ever needed one. Other researchers like attorney-historian Steve Gatto and Holliday biographer Dr. Gary Roberts have disproved the "Holliday returned to help Wyatt Earp kill Ringo" contention based upon the actual language of the legal documents and contemporary newspaper accounts. They present a strong case that Doc Holliday did not make the cut for this covert mission and really was present in the Colorado courtroom at the appointed hour. I believe that Holliday's court appearance could have been part of a larger covert action plan, hatched during Holliday's June visit to Gunnison, as a subterfuge to draw attention to Doc's location and thus removing suspicion from Earp. Most people believed the myth that Wyatt and Doc were connected at the hip, musketeers together. The ruse seems to have worked—and is still working over a century and decades later.

There are three additional odd facts to consider when discussing the death of John Ringo. Among the numerous items in John Gilchriese's western history collection was a paper credited to Kate Holliday titled "Character Picture of the Late John Riggold [*sic*]." William B. Shillingberg, in his book about Tombstone, quoted from Kate's manuscript concerning the warm relationship between the Hollidays and Ringo. Kate wrote, "Every time I think of Ringgold, my eyes will fill with tears, he was a loyal friend to my husband, Doc Holliday, and to myself." This "loyal friend" comment disregards the near lethal Holliday–Ringo confrontation in January 1882, but Kate, who was not in Tombstone, might not have known of this encounter.

A small newspaper item publicized by Kate Holliday biographer Anne Collier adds another question to the "Did Doc return with Wyatt?" debate. Originally published in the June 3, 1882, issue of the *Tombstone Daily Epitaph* is a list of then-recent stagecoach passenger arrivals that contains Kate Holliday's name. In addition to her name appearing on this list, Kate told the *Daily Epitaph* reporter she was en route to her home in Deming, New Mexico, from a visit to California; yet the reporter did not ask why she had taken a detour to Tombstone when Deming was on the direct Southern Pacific Railroad route from the west. It may be just a coincidence that Kate claimed to be living in an area populated by Cow-boy supporters and in a community where Mr. and Mrs. Frank Thurmond planned to establish their new business enterprise.

One more fact to add to the mix is that Colton, the city where the senior Earp's California homestead was located, was the western slope terminus for the SPRR and Deming was the eastern point where the SPRR connected with the Santa Fe rail system. In time, more in-depth investigation may provide a better understanding concerning why Kate Holliday claimed she was living in New Mexico in the summer of 1882 and who she had been visiting in California. One source has suggested that Kate was in the Golden State visiting her friend Mattie Blaylock (who was still waiting for Wyatt to arrive in Colton) about joining her in a "ladies entertainment" business in Deming secretly backed by Frank Thurmond and operated by Lou Blonger. Deming was the junction point for three major railroads and was the trade center for area miners, stock growers, farmers, speculators, and transcontinental travelers. Easy money and single men.

Author's Perspective: I have a few observations concerning Mrs. Earp's version of Doc Holliday's supposed return to Arizona. It makes no sense to believe that Doc would jeopardize his freedom and his life by being seen—or worse, being captured— in Arizona during his legal battle to avoid extradition back to that territory. What is more important, Wyatt's supporters did not want any more of John H. Holliday because he had already caused too much unwanted publicity. Some would argue that Wyatt Earp also had outstanding murder warrants for his arrest in Arizona Territory, but in July of 1882 he was not under imminent threat of arrest. He had followed the sanctuary game plan and kept a low profile and maintained a peaceful image. But most important, Wyatt Earp had very powerful men backing his efforts.

How did Wyatt Earp kill John Peters Ringo? Near dusk on what had been a clear hot mid-summer day, Thursday, July 13, 1882, following a tiresome hunt along unbroken paths in the western foothills of the Chiricahua Mountains, the man hunters finally located John Ringo's trail. Forrestine Hooker recorded Wyatt's recollection of that day: "On the third day a faint grey thread of smoke rose against the sky, telling of a distant campfire. A deep wash cut by cloudbursts during the rainy season, twisted below the spot where the smoke crept upward."

The man hunters had spotted a small puff of smoke from Ringo's campfire located in the mesquite in a small canyon north of the present-day Sanders Ranch in Cochise County. The posse moved in on Ringo from both sides of the canyon walls and surprised him as he was making coffee. The strike force kept Johnny's attention while Wyatt slipped around behind him to block his exit from the canyon. The wanted man or his horse finally saw or heard Earp and Ringo made a break for freedom over a nearby ridge just as the last rays of light set over the canyon's west wall. Wyatt Earp had John Ringo in his rifle sights and dropped him with the first shot. A few feet more and Ringo would have escaped.

After drinking Ringo's coffee, the covert man hunters, now in closing darkness, packed the corpse down the canyon and posed it in the fork of two blackjack oaks growing together along the bank of West Turkey Creek. Wyatt Earp wanted the outlaw's body found and identified so that no one could claim Johnny Ringo still lived in Old Mexico or Montana, as had happened in the controversy surrounding his killing of Curly Bill Brocius. John Flood wrote that after Wyatt Earp's man hunters had arranged Ringo's body, the federal deputy marshal mounted his horse and said, "He won't kill any other man's brother." The manhunt was finished, so each man rode away to confront his individual destiny.

On the day a coroner's inquest was held and Johnny Ringo was buried, Tombstone citizens saw Fred Dodge, John Meagher, and "Hair-Lip Charlie" Smith on the streets of their fire-damaged city. When the three men slipped out of Tombstone in early July, the community was still reeling from the massive late June fire that destroyed six blocks of the eastern part of the city centered on Allen Street. A whiskey barrel had exploded and, aided by a hot, dry, windy afternoon, the fire left 800 people homeless and caused hundreds of thousands of dollars of property damage. Fortunately, no one was killed but the *Tombstone Daily Epitaph*'s new owner, Charles D. Reppy, was injured. The other posse members were also seen in public. Lou Cooley was hard at work on the Hooker Ranch when news of Ringo's death reached that place. Cooley sued Sheriff Behan and his bondsmen for false arrest for the incident at Benson in the spring and asked for $5,000 in damages. But, as always, Gentleman Johnny escaped justice.

Johnny Green had stayed in the mountains with Wyatt Earp until they were satisfied that the current mission was completed. Then they left the Sulphur Springs Valley and headed toward the Southern Pacific tracks extending across southern Arizona Territory. At a water stop or station along the route, Wyatt Earp boarded an eastbound Wells Fargo Express car and reversed his trip of two weeks earlier. He was soon back in Gunnison. Johnny Green disappeared for a while, but a few weeks later, minus two saddle horses and gear, he joined Wyatt and Warren at their Colorado political sanctuary.

Wyatt Earp got his vengeance, some retribution, and a Wells Fargo bounty, and continued his well-earned reputation as, to use a modern metaphor, a "go to" man when big-business interests needed some extralegal assistance. There are numerous tales about Wyatt and his partner for hire, former Los Angles policeman Arthur M. King, doing extralegal work, called "black ops" in today's special operations lingo, for the Southern Pacific Railroad, Wells Fargo Express Company, the Burns Detective Agency, and the sheriff's office and police departments in Los Angeles and San Diego counties well into the 1920s.[5]

Johnny Ringo's body was discovered by John Yoast's dog as the teamster was passing some oak trees on the road near the mouth of Morse's Canyon headed toward the sawmill in the Chiricahua Mountains. The Smith-Sanders Ranch headquarters is located a few hundred feet off the road at this spot and two women from the ranch headquarters had noticed the body earlier in the afternoon, but they had assumed the man was asleep sitting on a large rock and resting in the big tree's V-notch. For safety reasons they had not investigated.

A Cochise County coroner's jury was impaneled by Dr. H.M. Mathews and a verdict of death rendered. Dr. Mathews, in his official coroner's report, wrote, "Cause of death unknown, but supposed gun shot wounds." Johnny Ringo's blackening, bloated, and putrefying body was buried just before sundown at the spot where the body was found. Today, the creek side gravesite of Johnny Ringo is located on private property.[6]

"There was [sic] few men in Cochise county, or southeastern Arizona better known [than Ringo]," the new pro–Cow-boy owners of the *Tombstone Epitaph* editorialized. "Many people who where intimately acquainted with him in life have serious doubts that he took his own life, while equally large numbers say that he frequently threatened to commit suicide." A reporter for the same newspaper wrote that Ringo had told him a couple of weeks prior to his death that he felt he was a marked man. The newspaperman wrote about the Ringo conversation in his piece "Death of Jack Ringo," published on July 18, 1882: "He was certain of being killed as he was of being living then. He said he might run along for a couple of years more, and may not last two days."

Within weeks of Johnny Ringo's demise, Arizona territorial governor Frederick Tritle remarked that the Cow-boy difficulties had ended in Cochise County. He and other influential like-minded believers had provided the support and funding needed for the completion of Wyatt Earp's seek and destroy mission to restore law and order; a quiet and civil environment was good for the business development of Arizona Territory.

Researcher Bob Cash located an obscure recollection of Ringo's death published in the *San Francisco Daily Alta California* on June 12, 1886. The reporter had questioned an old Tombstone resident concerning Ringo's death: "The community [of Tombstone] was about equally divided in its opinion between suicide and murder, and the dead man's friends were probably nearer the truth when they vowed that Ringgold [sic] never took his own life."

"Whoever it was that killed him, and propped him up in the position in which he was found, left nothing behind by which he could be identified," said the *Tombstone Prospector* on March 14, 1890, eight years after the event. "There is more than one man living in Cochise county who knows who did it but with them the mystery is a secret." Cow-boy supporter John Plesent Gray wrote, in *When All Roads Led to Tombstone: A Memoir*, "It was never divulged who did this [killing] or caused it to be done but many of Ringo's friends felt they knew."

Over a century of debate has still not settled the cause of Johnny Ringo's death and other questions. Was the corpse wearing or not wearing a hat when discovered? What happened to Ringo's boots and why had he wrapped up his feet in his undershirt? Why had Ringo's horse run off? Why did it take days to locate the horse? What happened to Ringo's camp gear? Most of these questions are fun to debate but do not change the fact that Johnny Ringo's death helped to seal the fate of the Cochise County Cow-boys.

Author's Perspective: I believe Wyatt Earp killed Johnny Ringo and his motive seems simple to me. The Earp brothers must have felt that their universe was in shambles in the summer of 1882. Therefore, Wyatt Earp sought justice for the violence perpetrated against his brothers, the ruin of his own political career in Cochise County, and the destruction of the Earp family's financial base. It is easy for me to imagine Wyatt Earp justifying his posse's action as completing unfinished public business. Only in his twilight years did he express some concern that his hunting and killing Johnny Ringo might be viewed by some sensitive people as having been committed outside of the legal framework of a peace officer doing his official duty. That said, however, I do not believe that Earp lost much sleep regretting having pulled the trigger on Johnny Ringo, the "King of the Cow-boys."

I believe what Wyatt Earp wrote Stuart Lake: "For my handling of the situation at Tombstone, I have no regrets. Were it to be done over again, I would do exactly as I did at the time." Wyatt Earp had told a reporter for the *Gunnison Daily News-Democrat* the same thing 46 years earlier, in June 1882: "Everybody in Tombstone knows that we did nothing but our duty. Anyway, I'd do it over again under like circumstances...."

If Wyatt Earp killed Johnny Ringo, why didn't Stuart N. Lake tell the story in his Earp biography? Earp gave Stuart Lake a copy of Forrestine Hooker's biographical article containing an account of Wyatt's killing of Ringo. Lake also had a copy of the Flood manuscript Earp had given him to review. Lake later claimed Flood's manuscript contained nothing about a hunt to kill Ringo, yet I have in my collection a version of the Flood manuscript that does contain a detailed chapter of how Wyatt Earp killed Ringo. We may never know why Lake's copy of the Flood manuscript did not contain the Ringo killing chapter, if in fact it did not. In my copy, the chapter before the Ringo killing ends with a lead into the search and the chapter following begins with Ringo's death and Wyatt's leaving Arizona. Lake must have been mystified because he had read Walter Noble Burns' tales of Earp and Ringo in Cochise County and found no mention of Wyatt's being involved in the death of Ringo. Shortly before Wyatt's death, he evaded Lake's questions on the subject of Ringo's death. During his own extensive research, Lake had not located any contemporary records to suggest that there was truth to the "Earp killed Ringo tale."

Lake once presented Earp with a list of men the author believed Wyatt had killed or assisted in killing. He wrote asking Earp if the list was complete and if it was not who was missing. Ringo's name was not on Lake's list, nor was the Indian Territory fugitive killed by the federal marshal's posse that Earp accompanied nor the would-be stage robber who died while attempting to raid the Wells Fargo Express box Wyatt was guarding nor the man who attempted to steal an elderly Wyatt's horse while he was prospecting in the Mohave Desert. Wyatt, or most likely Josie, who acted as her husband's scribe during his last years, did not add any additional names to Lake's list. Josie did not want Wyatt's would-be biographer to portray her husband as a "gunfighter" with a killer reputation; she desired a "clean story" with few or no killings. Nine months after Wyatt's death, Lake was completing his research and writing. He needed a definitive answer to the question, "Did Wyatt kill John Ringo?" On September 5, 1929, Lake wrote to Forrestine Hooker at her home in Washington, D.C., and told her he had read her *An Arizona Vendetta* manuscript. He questioned her account of Wyatt killing Ringo: "In all his talks with me, and we went over and over the Arizona battles, he never mentioned that he had killed Ringo." Lake also admitted that he and Wyatt were seldom alone to talk frankly: "Left to himself, Wyatt Earp would 'have come clean' for me, I am well satisfied." Lake asked for her help to clarify the Ringo account: "I do hope that you will understand the spirit in which my inquires are made...." If he received a reply from Mrs. Hooker that latter is no longer in his research papers.

Lake knew that his biography subject's grieving widow would be no help in providing information on this possible murder for hire since she wished for a nice clean tale minus all the killings; so he turned to Fred Dodge a second time to inquire about the killing of Ringo. Dodge had been assisting Lake in locating documents and people who could help provide colorful background information concerning Wyatt's law enforcement career.

Dodge replied to Lake on September 30, 1929: "I did know H.C. Hooker, but do not know anything about his daughter in law [Forrestine], but I am willing to bet all cheap pools that she never got the Ringo end [killing story] from Wyatt." It is very likely that Dodge was unaware that Wyatt had previously discussed his killing Ringo with authors Frederick Bechdolt and Frank Lockwood, as well as John Flood, Mrs. Hooker, and Josie. In his September 15, 1929, letter to Lake concerning Ringo's death, Dodge probably believed he was helping the memory of his friend by continuing the myth that Earp was not involved in Ringo's death. He told Lake, "No, Wyatt did not kill John Ringo. You are right Wyatt had left Arizona some little time." Dodge neglected to mention that Wyatt Earp returned three months later and did what Hooker and Flood said he had done.

In the late 1920s, Walter Noble Burns wanted to write a biography of Wyatt, but Earp explained he was already working on such a project with John Flood. Burns then changed his request and asked for assistance with a biography of Doc Holliday. Wyatt gladly agreed to assist with that project. Since Wyatt believed that Burns was seeking information on Doc's life it is reasonable to assume that Wyatt would have felt no need to volunteer details about Ringo's death since Doc was not a participant in that incident. Burns used Earp's information as a cornerstone to construct his monumental tome, *Tombstone: An Iliad of the Southwest*, and made Wyatt Earp the legendary "Lion of Tombstone." Josie disliked the book's gunfighter tone and Wyatt felt Burns had betrayed his trust. In a letter to his cousin George Earp, February 13, 1928, Wyatt mentioned the Burns book: "[I'm] sorry to know that you read the book called Tombstone, so many things that are untrue ... and so many things that never happened. But I guess I will have to stand for it."[7]

Lake had located no contemporary documentation to support the Ringo killing tale as reported by Mrs. Hooker, Dr. Frank Lockwood, and Frederick Bechdolt. However, other books by Burns and Billy Breakenridge had not mentioned Wyatt as a possible killer of Ringo, so Lake used Dodge's statement as his excuse to exclude the inglorious Ringo homicide from his myth-building biography of Wyatt Earp as a frontier knight.

Some believe that Fred Dodge was covering up for his dead friend, his former employer and himself when he introduced a "red herring" into the mix by writing Stuart Lake on September 15, 1929, stating, "[Michael] 'Johnny-Behind-the-Deuce' [O'Rourke] murdered him [Ringo]." The Earp brothers had been part of the posse that had saved Mike O'Rourke from a Tombstone gathering that some historians believe wanted to lynch the gambler for the murder of Phillip Schneider, chief engineer of Charleston's Corbin Mine. Tombstone writers, both for and against the Earp brothers, have made this incident in front of Vogan's Bowling Alley and Saloon into one of the premier events of the Tombstone saga. Wyatt Earp, however, never considered the incident a big deal. In fact, he told Walter Noble Burns, "I faced five hundred of 'em [in a mob] and just didn't let them get him. That's all."

Pink Simms, a cousin of the man who killed Ben Thompson, wrote a letter to Jay J. Kalez concerning the death of O'Rourke on September 30, 1934. The letter was published in *Frontier Times* magazine in May 1968 and quoted Simms as saying, "Eleven years ago [1923] I sat at the bedside of Johnny-Behind-the-Deuce, while he was dying. I had known the old tinhorn for many years." If the details of the letter are true, it is possible that Dodge was also privy to the circumstance of O'Rourke's death and used the information six years later to protect the real killer of Ringo, his friend Wyatt Earp. By blaming a dead man for murder, Dodge was in no danger of the man's refuting the charge. Dodge might also have felt he needed to protect himself, because there is no time limit on a murder charge.

Tombstone historian Ben Traywick wrote in the *National Edition of the Tombstone Epitaph,* June 1987, that an aging Fred Dodge wanted to finally set the record straight concerning the Johnny Ringo killing. Dodge changed the story he told Stuart Lake by describing how Wyatt Earp planned on "offing" the target during the manhunt. According to Traywick, Dodge no longer feared prosecution. Fifteen years after the Tombstone troubles, Fred Dodge and Wyatt Earp had their last meeting, on February 15, 1897, in San Francisco.

Some historians have quoted Wyatt Earp's remarks from his 1893 *Denver Republican* interview to support their claim that Earp had nothing to do with Ringo's death: "I never succeeded in finding Ringo. He got out of the country and was killed by someone else." A careful reading of these two sentences provides the reader with an underlying message. Wyatt was truthful when he said that he did not find Ringo on his final search before he and his strike force left Arizona in April 1882. Earp also said Johnny was "killed by someone else," implying that Ringo had not committed suicide.

One final fact needs examination. Chapter 13 of Jose Earp's memoirs, titled "Wandering with Wyatt," contains a comment on her husband's brushes with death. "In all our years together Wyatt never once described a gun-battle to me." She then added, "He considered it a great misfortune that he had lived in such a time and under such circumstances that guns had figured at all in his career." In her memoirs, Josie Earp describes Wyatt's arrest of Ben Thompson in the plaza at Ellsworth, Kansas, the Tombstone streetfight and the Ringo killing based upon information she gathered from other people who had witnessed or taken part in the events.[8]

> **Author's Perspective:** True historians must ask a few questions concerning this covert action to hunt Johnny Ringo. Who paid for this extended manhunt? Who organized the posse membership? Who did the logistical planning needed to assemble and equip such a secret operation? Why did no one, except Wyatt Earp and Fred Dodge, provide firsthand accounts of this manhunt? Why is there no paper trail? The answer to these and many other questions surrounding the death of Johnny Ringo always seems to lead back to the Wells Fargo Express Company and the fact that there is no statute of limitations on first-degree murder.

18

Wyatt Earp and Josephine Marcus

A capable wife is the crown of her husband, but an incompetent one is like rot in his bones.—Proverbs 12:4, The Jewish Study Bible

Following Morgan's funeral, Virgil Earp went to the "City by the Bay" to seek medical treatment for the arm that had been severely wounded in the December 1881 ambush. Money was a pressing issue with Virgil and Allie as his medical bills continued to accumulate. Early in August 1882, the San Francisco police arrested former deputy federal marshal Virgil Earp for dealing an illegally conducted faro game in his hotel room.

In early October 1882, Wyatt Earp left Gunnison, Colorado headed to California. He had left his brother Warren and Dan Tipton to operate his gambling concession. Wyatt stopped a few days in Salt Lake City to visit with James and Bessie and catch up on family affairs that had occurred since Tombstone. On Sunday, October 15, 1882, a Salt Lake City newspaper published the name "W.B. Stapp" among the list of persons with telegrams being held for delivery at the telegraph office. This innocuous notice would have little meaning for most readers unless they knew that it was a code name used by Wells Fargo Express Company to contact Wyatt Earp.

When Wyatt learned that Mattie Blaylock had left Colton and returned to Arizona, he decided not to seek her out but to just let the relationship die. Nor was he ready to face his mother and father over the loss of Morgan. He went to San Francisco to confer with his contacts at the Wells Fargo Express Company's headquarters and make a final accounting of the Arizona troubles.

On October 20, 1882, the *Sacramento Daily Record-Union* noted, "Ex–United States Marshal Virgil Earp arrived in this city last evening from Tombstone, Arizona. He is here for the purpose of meeting his brother W.B. Earp, who will arrive from the east this morning." Virgil had come from Colton to update Warren, who had left Colorado's impending winter, about events at their parents' home. The brothers went on to check with medical specialists to reexamine Virgil's wounds. On November 1, 1882, the *Los Angeles Herald* reported that Wyatt and Virgil passed through Fresno on Halloween Day aboard the train headed "south or east." No destination was specified. Adelia

251

Edwards said in later years that Wyatt and Warren roomed for a short time with Virgil in an upstairs apartment on Pine Street in San Francisco, while Allie stayed at the Earp homestead in Colton.

"The latest news from the Quondam [former] Albuquerqueans, the Earp crowd, is that Wyatt, Warren and Virgil Earp are in San Francisco, engaged in dealing faro," reported the *Albuquerque Evening Review* in November 1882, noting the location of the rest of Wyatt's strike force: "Texas Jack is in Colorado, Doc Holliday in Leadville, McMasters [*sic*] and Johnson in Mexico, and Tipton in the Gunnison country."

On a rainy afternoon in late 1882, Wyatt Earp reconnected with a young woman he had met months before in Tombstone, Arizona Territory. He began intensely courting Josephine Sarah Marcus and her family.

The Otero Letter contains an explosive revelation, for 1940, concerning the ethnic heritage of Josie Marcus. Stuart N. Lake's landmark Wyatt Earp biography had been published only nine years earlier and it contained no reference to the Marcus family being Jewish. It would be almost two more decades before Josie's Jewish heritage became common knowledge, even among the legion of Wyatt Earp fans created by the popular 1950s-era television series. The detail came to light following the theft of the old lawman's tombstone from a Jewish cemetery in 1957.

"Jaffa told me later that Earp's woman was a Jewess."

A consummate politician of the Victorian Age like Miguel A. Otero, Jr., would normally err on the side of politeness and assume that a woman escorted about town by a man was either his wife, his "lady friend" or a relative. The words "woman" and "Jewess" used in his 1940 letter almost have a condescending tone in their usage. The sentence seems somewhat discourteous and insensitive to our modern era that's accustomed to hearing "girlfriend" or "BFF" used to acknowledge a man's special female companion. However, on the American frontier "his woman" was not a derogatory expression but an explanatory term.

In the 1880s, especially in the northeast part of the United States, the term "Jewess" was synonymous with prostitute, since many of the New York City brothels were operated by Jews who also controlled a major portion of the vast white slave trade in central Europe and supplied the New York City brothels with Jewish girls from Russia, Poland, and some German states. The speculation that Josie Marcus had been a teenage runaway turned prostitute in Prescott and had Johnny Behan as a client was not common historical discussion unto a half-century after the Otero Letter was written.

Does Miguel Otero's comment imply an unspoken dislike of Jewish women or of women as a gender or a disapproval of a "mixed relationship" between a Jew and a non–Jew? Otero was a practicing Roman Catholic communicant in an era of religious persecution of "Israelites" by his church, especially those "Christ killers" who crossed social or class lines. Josie Marcus had two strikes against her. We may never know the true meaning of Gillie Otero's choice of words, but the intent is worth examining in light of common usage in that era.

On May 22, 1882, the *Denver Republican* published a long interview with Doc Holliday, carried on page 5. In the article the former dentist discussed why Sheriff Johnny Behan did not like him and would pay to have him killed. Their mutual dislike started during a disagreement at a faro game. Doc says at one point, "In the quarrel I told him [Behan] in the presence of a crowd that he was gambling with money which I had given his woman." It would seem that Holliday's use of the phrase "his woman" was not an unusual or disrespectful reference at the time. The reason why Doc Holliday gave Johnny Behan's woman money is not clear. It could have been a loan or a payment for some service rendered.

Some historians have suggested that John H. Holliday's remark refers to Sadie Mansfield, the 15-year-old Prescott prostitute that 23-year-old Mrs. Victoria Zaff Behan named in her 1875 divorce action as her 34-year-old husband's paramour. Behan had served a term as sheriff of Yavapai County and representative for Prescott in the 1874 territorial legislature. The late Roger Jay took this information one more step and claimed his in-depth research proves that Sadie Mansfield was the "professional" name used by Josephine Sarah "Sadie" Marcus when she was a teenage runaway working as a prostitute in Prescott. An interesting fact related to this discussion is that all their married life Wyatt called his wife Sadie, but after his death she would never answer to that name. History is unclear as to when or how Doc Holliday and Miss Marcus first became acquainted. The research and debate on Marcus and Mansfield as the same person theory continues.

There are some undisputed facts about the Marcus–Behan relationship. In 1880, Marcus and Johnny Behan were living in Tip-Tops in southern Yavapai County and later she moved to Tombstone as his live-in-fiancée and nursemaid for the divorced sheriff's young son. Josie even paid for a house to be built for them, as friends warned her that Behan would never follow through with a marriage and would likely again consort with prostitutes. Behan did both and even had an affair with one of Josie's friends. He also contracted syphilis. Josie left the philandering sheriff but continued a close friendship with his son. Sometime in mid–1881, Josie Marcus was introduced to Wyatt Earp.

Author's Perspective: A major discussion among Earp researchers has centered on the fact that no one has as yet discovered an official government marriage record for Wyatt Earp and Josie Marcus. Some anti–Earp writers have even implied sinister reasons for this lack of legal documentation. The time-honored and historically legal practice of common law marriage on the American frontier has come under the stain of the tar pit and those who lived under this arrangement branded with a scarlet letter. A younger generation of Wild West historians have tried to place the actions of people settling the American frontier under our current code of law and social customs. This misdirected concept will never provide a clear picture of any era, because to truly understand the truth of historical events they must be viewed through the prism of standards that reflex that historic era.

To marry and rear a family is the first commandment addressed by God to his creation: mankind. In Rabbinic Judaism marriage is a sacred union blessed by God: "*Baruchatah, Adonai Eloheinu, Melech haOlam....* We praise You, Adonai our God, Ruler of the Universe, who has made us holy with commandments and commands us to marry and be holy together." The Marriage Service in the Jewish *Prayer Book* contains the phrase "Adonai [the Jewish name for the creator—God] hast instructed us concerning illicit marriage, and hast forbidden us to unite ourselves with our betrothed until they are wedded unto us under the *Chupah* by sacred rites of matrimony."[1]

Josie Marcus's older half-sister Rebecca married Aaron Wiener, an insurance salesman. The ceremony became a major family production. Father Marcus was dressed in long tails, a stovepipe hat and a formal white tie. The bride's mother wore a custom-made, wine-colored silk gown with tight bodice and long close-fitting sleeves. Rebecca was the center of attention in her pale lavender silk dress with velvet-trimmed basque. Josie recalled that she and her younger sister wore fashionable new high-button shoes.

The *Chupah*, or wedding canopy, is the central symbol of the Jewish wedding setting, representing the home the newlyweds will build. Rebecca's Chupah was purple and held by four of the groom's friends. Following the vocal exchange Wiener crushed a wine-glass with his foot, to recall the destruction of the Holy Temple in Jerusalem, and the crowd joined as one in shouting *mazal tov*, good fortune. In her memoirs Josie expressed two sentiments concerning Rebecca's wedding. Josie later recalled that she didn't understand many of the wedding traditions and could find no one who could give her "a satisfactory answer concerning the origin of some of the old rites." Josie found the festivities "thrilling" and "wondered how patient she could be while she waited for her own turn taking part in such a ceremony." Historians have asked for decades whether Josie had such a traditional Jewish ceremony, a civil ceremony or no formal ceremony at all.

"Osculation" is a first-class word to express the act of kissing. This act of affection has its roots resting in the creation of Adam and Eve, and in Jewish tradition a kiss is considered both a physical and spiritual union because a kiss is the sharing of the breath of life. It is unknown how Wyatt Earp and Josie Marcus viewed this act of human intimacy on religious grounds, but they most certainly engaged in the physical act. By the 1880s Judaism had developed many *minhags*, or social customs, binding upon believers. Many of these concerned the *mitzvoth* of marriage. Interfaith marriage, even today, is discouraged.

We may never know the depth of the concern felt by Josie's parents over her past affairs. Their headstrong daughter had run away to Prescott in Arizona Territory and may have worked as a teenage prostitute, returned home ill, recovered her health, and now a few years later planned to leave again. Josie had been courted by the dapper-dandy Johnny Behan, who was a divorcé, Roman Catholic, and livery stable operator. Now she went to Tombstone intending to wed Behan. She had sold her jewelry, purchased a house, and set up a residence for Johnny and his young son, Albert. But there never was a wedding, even though Josie signed letters home as Mrs. Behan. She split with Behan over his affair with a married woman, the wife of one of his business and political partners. Behan had shown the Marcus family his courtly side and impressed them with his charm only to betray their daughter's trust in him.

Josie left Tombstone and returned to San Francisco in the fall of 1882. The senior Marcuses lived with their daughter Rebecca Weiner and her husband, Aaron, at 720 McAllister Street. Within a short time the Marcuses' 22-year-old vagabond daughter was being courted by another gentile. Now Mr. and Mrs. Marcus had the notorious "blood-thirsty killer" Wyatt Earp at their doorstep.

Nekamah (revenge) and *shefikhat damim* (bloodshed) are key elements of belief in Judaism. The Torah, the first five books of the Jewish scriptures and the Christian Old Testament, prohibits both the act and the thought of vengeance, even though there is no specific penalty for such conduct. These scriptures recognize that the perpetrator of vengeance eventually becomes victim to his own feelings of indignation. The drive for vengeance can often lead to the shedding of human blood. The Decalogue, the Ten Commandments, forbids murder and this willful act of taking human life is regarded as the worst kind of criminal act against mankind and against God.

The twin shadows of *nekamah* and *shefikhat damim* followed Wyatt Earp to the Marcus house. No record survives to relate the inner feelings of Henry and Sophie Marcus toward this "Lion of Tombstone" and his violent ways. It is possible that Henry Marcus detected strength of character, a sense of honor, maturity, maybe even love for his daughter, in this new mild-mannered, "older-man" suitor. Earp held a national reputation for personal courage and fulfillment of duty. He was a man who projected an air of trust. In Hebrew he would be called *gibor hayil*, a man of valor.

It would be interesting to know if Henry Marcus saw a news item that appeared in many newspapers a couple of weeks before Christmas 1882. The article from the *Kansas City Journal* indicated that a Russian envoy was in the United States to hire a special team of bodyguards for the czar. He was looking for "nervy, quick, and active men" with "undaunted courage, quick and sure with the pistol and rifle who have had great experience in killing." The report said the Russian envoy was seeking guardsmen of the caliber of the Earp brothers. It is doubtful that the battle-tested brothers would have entertained the idea of moving to St. Petersburg, but the story does accentuate the reputation that was now attached to the surname Earp.

The most important question to ask about a marriage between Wyatt Earp and Josie Marcus is whether or not she wore a wedding band given to her by Wyatt Earp. The essential part of a Jewish wedding ceremony is the "the bride's purchase price," the groom's love, not his wealth or station in life. The bride's wedding ring, a simple band without jewels and little market value, is a symbol of the obligation the husband assumes in the union and the bride's acceptance of the ring signifies her acceptance of the groom's proposal of a life together. The union takes place when the groom places the ring on the bride's finger and recites the wedding pledge: "Behold, you are consecrated unto me with this ring."

In the private archive of the Arizona Historical Society is a collection of personal items that belonged to Wyatt and Josie Earp. Following Wyatt's death, Josie had given Artic explorer Lincoln Ellsworth, an admirer of her husband, some personal items. The Earp collection was presented to the historical society by Ellsworth's heirs following the explorer's death. One of these treasures of interest to this discussion is a small gold band identified as Josie's wedding ring. Wyatt is said to have worn a dark suit with a tan vest that Josie kept until her death. There are photographs of the jacket and vest, but their current location is unknown.

It may seem strange to non–Jewish people, but during Josie's lifetime a rabbi, someone knowledgeable in the Torah, was not required to perform a Jewish marriage. The only purpose a rabbi served was to act as a witness to the marriage covenant made between a man and a woman. The couple married each other by their action, thus any valid witness of age could serve as the wedding witness. In fact, a witness was not absolutely required.

Eventually federal and state tax laws required that a civil marriage license be issued and formally filed with the local government upon the solemnizing of the wedding ceremony by someone authorized by law to perform such ceremonies. In the Talmud commentary on the Jewish scriptures it is written, "The law of the land is the law." So in the early 1890s Judaic congregations began to select certain "qualified clergy [rabbis]" to conduct formal Jewish wedding ceremonies according to the new civil laws requiring such officials. The civil wedding license is a form of local tax and was instituted in the late 1880s to raise operating funds for local government.

In all the western states and territories the arrangement known as common law marriage, a man and woman living before humanity as a couple, was accepted as a legal agreement. During the height of the anti–Mormon fever of the 1870s and 1880s Congress passed, and President Arthur signed into law, the Edmunds Anti-Polygamy Act of 1882 that was specifically intended to punish followers of the Church of Jesus Christ of Latter Day Saints, headquartered in Utah Territory, who practiced polygamy. The new national law made polygamy a felony, but it also made both bigamy and "unlawful cohabitation" federal misdemeanors punishable by a minimal fine of $300, six months imprisonment or both.

In most states and territories in 1882, a civil marriage certificate was not required to live as husband and wife. In fact a religious ceremony was the most common form of marriage, and in many cases the only place that marriages, births and deaths were recorded was in the family Bible or a book of other scriptures or religious writings. A divorce differed somewhat since it often required a civil court or legislative action to dissolve a contractual obligation.

The Edmunds Act was never intended to alter the time-honored tradition of the marriage bond that had been established under English common law, which the United States inherited from Great Britain at the founding of the nation. Nor was the Edmunds Act meant to alter the treaty obligations protecting French law that governed the lands of the Louisiana Purchase prior to 1803 or Spanish law that had covered most of the Southwest territory prior to 1848, since neither French nor Spanish law required a civil notice of marriage, because it was a religious function under authority of the Roman Catholic Church's canon law or other religious bodies' marriage customs and traditions.

Wyatt and Josie's marriage should be examined in light of the marriage laws in force in 1882. California was a common law state until 1895. So if Wyatt and Josie wed prior to 1895 no civil record was required in the Golden State. However, Wyatt seems to have supplied a legal record of his marriage when he testified in a California civil court trial in December 1896 concerning a controversial prize fight he had refereed. Under cross-examination he was asked if he was a family man. Wyatt answered under oath, "I have a wife. She is Jewish." The trial record doesn't record a question concerning Josie's ethnic heritage, so it is unclear why Wyatt Earp felt the need to mention that fact. A psychologist or psychoanalyst could very likely make a case study of these remarks. But it is clear that Earp claimed he was lawfully married.

The Edmunds-Tucker Act of 1887 required all U.S. territories to issue civil marriage licenses and record the document after the ceremony was solemnized by the proper authority to conduct a wedding. This new federal law did not affect Wyatt and Josie, because California had become the 31st state on September 9, 1850. The state's Office of Vital Records was not established until 1905, and it began collecting marriage record information at that time.

If the couple wed in Colorado there never was a problem, because the Centennial State is one of eleven states that still recognize common law marriages contracted within that state as binding and legal if the couple (1) consent to the union, (2) represent themselves as being married, and (3) live in cohabitation, and (4) the community where they live believe them to be married. Even today all 50 states recognize a common law marriage as legal if it originated in one of the eleven states that still allow for this form of marriage arrangement.

Much hullabaloo has been made over the fact that no official wedding document has surfaced to confirm a Marcus–Earp union, but the reader must remember that what is legally mandated now and what was required to be married in 1882 are vastly different. Second, the Marcus and Earp families, the couple's friends, the general public, and, most important, Wyatt and Josie themselves considered that they were lawfully and honorably wed.

Mark Twain is often erroneously credited with saying that the "coldest winter I ever spent was a summer in San Francisco." In February 1928, Wyatt wrote his cousin George Earp that San Francisco was the city he liked "best of all," but he didn't specify why. A few years later, Josie wrote about the "City by the Bay" in her memoirs: "This was where we [she and Wyatt] married and our life began." Some historians and novelists have proposed various dates for this occasion ranging from 1882, 1888, 1896—and never. I disagree with never. One source has attempted to put a location to Wyatt and Josie's exchange of marriage vows. The claim made is that the deed was done before the captain of Luck Baldwin's yacht while the ship was at sea off the California coast. Pam Potter has dealt with this claim and proves it is false.

In Rabbinic or Orthodox Judaism the woman cannot initiate a divorce, but in the present era she must agree with her husband's action before he can proceed. In Josie's lifetime an Orthodox Jewish woman was *mesureve get* (shackled) in a relationship that only her husband could end by granting her a *sefer k'ritut* (scroll of cutting off) or a written divorce document called a *get*. Since an Orthodox Jewish woman can't initiate a divorce and in such circumstances where her husband cannot or will not grant the *get*, this poor woman is *agunah* (anchored) to a dead marriage. No rabbi would ever remarry her for fear of taking a chance of condoning an adulterous marriage. It is a terrible state of limbo for an Orthodox Jewish woman and her family.

Romance aside, Josie Marcus must have known about Mattie Blaylock. It is very possible that, at first, Josie may not have wanted to face the issue of marriage to Wyatt. Religion was not a problem for Josie Marcus because she was not an Orthodox Jewess. Her family came from the more liberal-minded reform sector of Judaic belief. To a free-spirited, self-liberated woman like Josie the real threat to her long-term well-being was desertion or abandonment. Wyatt was a living embodiment of her most dreaded fear and Josie didn't have a great track record of keeping her men faithful.

Custom over the centuries has dictated that the head of a Jewish household read a portion of the Book of Proverbs (31:10–31) to his wife during the family's Friday evening *Shabbat*, or biblical Sabbath, dinner service. These beautiful passages set the pattern for what constitutes an ideal wife, *eishet hayil*—a woman of valor—and how she should be a partner with her husband in their life together. Contrary to what many people might think, this ancient portrait of womanhood depicted an active helpmate, not a passive wall-flower woman who "knew her place" in society. These verses described a married woman's active involvement as a wife, as a lover, as a mother, as a homemaker, as a businesswoman, as a charity worker, and other positive virtues. It is doubtful that Wyatt ever performed the Shabbat remembrance service by candle lighting, a meal, and family blessings with Josie, but he may have read the Proverbs verses and recognized some of those traits in her. One can only wonder if Wyatt ever measured the Proverbs qualities of Josie against the character of the former women in his life: Urilla Sutherland, Sally Haspel, and Mattie Blaylock.

It is uncertain how well Josie knew Wyatt's parents, but she did refer to them as "Ma and Pa Earp" in her memoirs and noted that Wyatt cried upon learning of his mother's death. On the other side of the family tree "Mom and Dad Marcus" seem to have grown to have accepted Wyatt as a match for their daughter. Wyatt developed a "brother-sister" relationship with Josie's older sister Rebecca as well as one with Rebecca's husband. The old lawman especially enjoyed visits with Josie's younger sister Hattie, and her children exhibited a special fondness for their Uncle Wyatt, if not always for his wife.

Josie's older brother Nathan became like another brother to Wyatt. Maybe Nathan was able to fill the void left by Morgan's death. To him Wyatt was *"Zev Barak"* (Wolf Lightning), who defended his family with swift action and championed frontier justice. Nathan was with Wyatt and Josie during part of their turn-of-the-century Alaskan adventure and worked as a porter at Wyatt's Dexter Saloon in Nome. Wyatt and Nathan were arrested during an altercation at that saloon in September 1900. Nathan died six years later and today is buried in the Marcus family plot with his parents, near the joint grave of Wyatt and Josie, in the Hills of Eternity Memorial Park at Colma, California.

Years after Wyatt's death Josie wrote that Bat Masterson, "a handsome man with blue Irish eyes and long curling eyelashes," was the person who told her the most about "my husband's history as Wyatt would never talk of himself." Josie knew little about Urilla and her lost child, nothing about Sarah, and too much about Mattie. It is possible that Wyatt Earp's Victorian-era Methodist doctrinal upbringing was much like that of President Chester A. Arthur, who once told a reporter; "I may be President of the United States, but my private life is nobody's damn business."

In Jewish culture *Shalom Bayit*, or household peace, is a way of life and a young girl learns this principle from her mother. The husband and father was to be treated with dignity and respect by all the family. He was to be honored into old age. This is a tradition that Josie would have been taught and most likely practiced in her family. Despite this Jewish teaching and contrary to many fiction writers and movie scriptwriters, Wyatt did not live "happily ever after" with Josie Marcus. It was, at best, a tumultuous rollercoaster relationship.

In the later stages of their relationship Josie became the cause of Wyatt's obsession with a reclusive life on the high desert away from his former friends. Josie had so embarrassed him before his professional colleagues, shamelessly hocking her jewelry or conning money from them in his name only to lose it at gambling, that he preferred to hide. As he grew older, Wyatt would escape Josie by attending church, where he enjoyed listening to the sermons; taking long trolley car rides; and visiting Old West friends among the stuntmen extras hanging out at the western sets on the back lots of the movie studios. Wyatt would also have visited with his friends, western motion picture heroes, William S. Hart and Tom Mix.

One of William Hart's last films was a 70-minute bio-pic of Wild Bill Hickock that he produced, wrote the screen story for, and in which he was the lead. Paramount Pictures premiered it in New York on November 18, the week before Thanksgiving in 1923, to less than rave reviews. The public release was two weeks later. On January 15, 1924, Wyatt wrote Hart: "I hardly think I merit the little screen surprise, which made her [Josie] very happy, and I am sure makes me more conscious of your generous spirit." Bert Lindley made motion picture history as the first actor to play Wyatt Earp on the big screen; it was a bit part in a crowd sequence. No matter, Adelia Edwards recalled that the whole San Bernardino area Earp clan went to see the silent film and applauded the scene. A copy of the film is housed in the silent film collection of the Museum of Modern Art in New York City.

Over time there developed family rumors that Wyatt and Josie had "marital difficulties" and that they separated at different periods of their relationship because Wyatt was a "skirt-chaser." But Josie seemed to have a special hold on Wyatt, because he always returned to her. Maybe he was simply unwilling to deal with more than one woman at a time or maybe the Wyatt–Josie relationship was true love from Wyatt's point of view. An ancient Jewish rabbi named Saul (Paul to the Christian) caught this point when he wrote, "In this life we have three great lasting qualities—faith, hope and love. But the greatest of them is love."[2]

As Josie grew older, she seemed to always be in a state of disagreement or a prolonged stage of menopause. One of Wyatt's relatives once commented that no one could ever convince him that Wyatt Earp was a cold-blooded killer, because he put up with Josie for almost a half-century. Another relative felt that Wyatt stayed with her because she blackmailed him with something from his past, and although there is no real evidence of this, the idea makes a point.

The Hebrew word *balagan* can be translated as "foul-up," "fiasco" or "mess." The term could most certainly be applied to Josie's gambling addiction. This disease cost Josie and Wyatt the wealth she so deeply craved. In the early 1920s, during one of Wyatt's debilitating illnesses, he gave her the signed legal papers and the filing fees to record an oil lease claim on some Kern County, California, property. Josie lost the filing fee money gambling and then lied to Wyatt about what happened to his proposed lease on what became valuable oil production property.

Wyatt Earp had brokered a business relationship between Josie and her sister Henrietta Lehnardt that lasted until Hattie's death. The Lehnardt siblings did not like their Aunt Sadie and voided the verbal agreement between their mother and Wyatt for the care of his widow. Josie was muscled out of her rightful royalties from additional Kern County oil field claims that Wyatt had discovered. Wyatt had put the leases in Henrietta's name in trust for Josie because he didn't think Josie would be able to manage the investment after his passing. It would seem here that the Arab proverb was proven right: "Oil has always been thicker then blood."

Josie always blamed Wyatt for the near-poverty existence that they lived during his final years. In fact it was due to Josie, who had gambled away the money Wyatt had earned during the San Diego land speculation, the Alaska gold rush and the Nevada mining venture. "Josie was a very suspicious woman," recalled her great-niece Alice Greenberg. "She would never talk about the [Happy Days or the Colorado River Indian Reservation] mining claims and was suspicious of anyone's suggestion about getting Wyatt's story in print." She mistrusted Stuart N. Lake even after he and Wyatt had negotiated a rewarding publication agreement.

Sometimes the Earps were forced to stay with Josie's wealthy sister and her family. Other times they sojourned with other, more distant relatives. One of these second-degree relations remembered that Josie would often leave Wyatt sitting at the house without food to eat while she went off on one of her "social" junkets, gambling away what little they had to live on.

Robert Mullin wrote fellow researcher Carl Breihan, in July 1978, concerning his boyhood friend Bud Rutherford, a *Los Angeles Times* sports writer, and his frequent evenings visiting with Wyatt Earp: "Wyatt had long been a prize fight fan. The American Legion, which sponsored weekly Friday evening boxing matches, had favored Wyatt with a pass and a seat in the ringside press row. Bud, sitting beside Earp, and sometimes affording him a lift in his car to and from the stadium, said that the old gentleman was always courteous and friendly, but often seemed deeply depressed, living in obscurity after years in the limelight of popular acclaim."

> **Author's Perspective:** In summation, Josie wore a wedding band, thus meeting the major requirement for marriage under Jewish custom in 1882. Using deductive reasoning, I believe that Wyatt and Josie married each other before her family at her sister Rebecca's San Francisco home. Josie's mother and father lived in the Aaron Wiener household to share the living expenses. The likely time was December 1882. If Josie had a written record of the occasion it was most likely in the keepsake trunk, along with her family photo album and Wyatt's "fan club" letters, that the Earps lost during their many travels.

"Earp did [unclear word, but could be .mezuzah] when entering his house."

In his 1963 book, *Strength to Love*, civil rights leader Martin Luther King, Jr., wrote, "Nothing in the world is more dangerous than sincere ignorance and conscientious stupidity." For centuries, many faithful followers of the Christian and Muslim faiths have persecuted the Jewish people and their religious faith under a misguided belief that they were doing God's work. Hatred of Jews was very much alive and well in America during Josephine Sarah Marcus Earp's lifetime. It is a sad fact, but the hate lives still.

In Jewish rabbinical teachings, there is a belief that God made a "multiple-covenant" with humankind. God's first covenant was not with Abraham and the Jewish people but with Noah and his progeny—all of humanity—throughout the ages to follow. The

Noahic Covenant given after the Great Flood involves a universal mandate with seven precepts of human decency given to all humanity: (1) don't commit idolatry; (2) don't practice incest; (3) don't commit murder; (4) don't profane the name of God; (5) establish a system of justice; (6) don't steal; and (7) never tear off flesh or a limb from a living animal. A covenant made with God constitutes a covenant made with all of creation and the sign of this eternal Noahic Covenant is the rainbow in the heavens.

Later, God made a holy covenant, in addition to the Noahic Covenant, with Abraham, Sarah, and their progeny for a special relationship with their creator, and the Ten Commandments given to God's prophet Moses are implicitly a special pact for the Jewish people and the Holy Land throughout all the ages. Jews and non–Jews have their own covenant relationship with the Creator God and all believers will receive an eternal reward for their faithful righteousness within their own covenants.

As suggested in the Otero Letter, there is evidence that Wyatt Earp made an effort to understand Jewish culture and Jewish religious beliefs, but there is no evidence that he ever sought to convert to Judaism. In our book *Wyatt Earp and Doc Holliday: Their New Mexico Adventures*, we discuss Wyatt Earp's 1884 visit to Albuquerque when he was accompanied by Josie. On this occasion Henry Jaffa became acquainted with the pretty and charming Josephine Marcus and that would explain why he might recall her in later conversations with Gillie Otero. This visit could also explain how Henry Jaffa knew that "Earp's woman was a Jewess." Since it is believed that Wyatt and Josie visited the Jaffa home, the future mayor would have had firsthand knowledge that Earp tried to honor Jewish customs such as touching and then kissing the fingers that touched the mezuzah upon entering a Jewish home, especially on a high holy celebration like *Pesach* (Passover).

Wyatt Earp and his brother-in-law Bill Edwards held numerous political and philosophical discussions and often reviewed for each other the latest books they had read. Edwards once gave Wyatt a copy of Owen Wister's 1902 classic, *The Virginian: A Horseman of the Plains*. Earp also enjoyed reading the novels of Jack London and Rex Beach; he had known both men during his gold rush days in the District of Alaska.

Wyatt often quoted the one-liners of Samuel Langhorne Clemens, AKA Mark Twain. One of the many clips attributed to the renowned humorist was this one: "Outside of a dog, reading is a man's best friend, inside a dog it is too dark to read." Stuart Lake wrote, "Wyatt had an excellent [worldly] background, was much better educated and read more than most men of his time and place." A review of Wyatt Earp's correspondence supports Lake's contentions.

Adela Rogers St. John, an accomplished journalist, had known Wyatt and his friend cowboy movie star Tom Mix and in the May 22, 1960, issue of *American Weekly*, she wrote, "I knew Wyatt Earp, it dates me—but I'm glad I had the privilege." St. John also wrote that Earp and Mix would have lengthy and passionate discussions concerning the real meaning of William Shakespeare's plays and other works. Josie Earp supported St. John's observation when she wrote, "Wyatt was fond of the theater and was especially partial to Shakespearian [sic] plays." Biblical stories were another issue for serious debate and St. John said that Earp was a very effective lay evangelist and even witnessed to her. In his later years, Wyatt Earp became a student of the Bible and kept a copy of the scriptures on his bedside reading stand.

In 1831, the French statesman, historian and social philosopher Alexis de Toc-queville and a traveling companion toured the United States studying the American culture. Upon their return home DeTocqueville wrote a two-volume account of his observations entitled *Democracy in America*. The Frenchman had noted something unique about America: "The safeguard of morality is religion, and morality is the best security of law as well as the surest pledge of freedom." It is unclear if Wyatt Earp ever read the thoughts of DeTocqueville, but it is easy to see how he lived the ideals and val-ues the Frenchman had witnessed.

Wyatt Earp's ancestors had a long tradition of church attendance. The descendants and relatives of Walter Earp, Wyatt's grandfather, had a history of providing clergy for the Methodist-Episcopal Church and of naming their sons in honor of legendary pastors of that faith. The Earp siblings were taught the creed of Methodism's founder, John Wesley: "Do all the good you can. By all the means you can, in all the ways you can, in all the places you can, at all the times you can, to all the people you can, as long as ever you can." John Wesley's creed became part of the Earp Family creed.

Wyatt's mother first joined the Methodist-Episcopal Church in 1842 "and lived as an exemplary member" for decades. Wyatt and his siblings attended Sunday school and worship services of the Congregational Church while growing up in Iowa in the 1850s. Late in the 1860s, while living in Lamer, Missouri, Wyatt attended both the Southern Baptist Church and the Methodist-Episcopal Church–South. When he married Urilla Sutherland in January 1870 it was his justice of the peace father, not a clergyman, who officiated at the ceremony. We do not know the religious heritage of the Sutherland family.

Wyatt Earp became friends with the Rev. J.W. Stogdill, a Methodist-Episcopal Church pastor, while living in Wichita, Kansas, in the mid–1870s. According to articles in the *Wichita Eagle* and the *Wichita Beacon* during those years, the pastor taught that evil came upon mankind because they disregarded the spiritual truth of right and wrong. Stogdill believed that Wichita was a regional hub of intemperance, gambling, licen-tiousness and lawlessness. One of his sermons centered upon the 29th chapter of Jer-emiah. The Reverend Stogdill used verse seven as the point of his message: "Seek the welfare of the city ... [and] pray to God on its behalf; for your welfare is bound up in its welfare."

A few years later, in Dodge City, Wyatt became a deacon of the Union (Presbyter-ian) Church, where the Rev. O.W. Wright considered Earp "a high-minded, honorable citizen ... kind and courteous to all ... brave, unflinching, and on all occasions ... the right man in the right place." Novelist Frank Waters made the central theme of his *The Earp Brothers of Tombstone* the idea that Wyatt had been a church deacon while also being a "card-shark gambler." Waters considered this two-sided behavior as sanctimo-nious playacting. When Wyatt's estranged common law wife Mattie died in July 1888, his New Testament was discovered among her possessions. Today this little book, which had been presented to Earp by the Dodge City law firm of Sutton and Colborn, is housed in the Arizona Historical Society collection. The flyleaf gift inscription said the scrip-tures were "a slight recognition" of Wyatt's "many Christian virtues and steady following in the footsteps of the meek and lowly Jesus."[3]

Frank Waters rained condemnation upon Wyatt for having once possessed this treatise of the life and teachings of Jesus Christ and then deserting his wife to live a life of degradation. There are other facts to consider when discussing Wyatt Earp's faith and his actions. According to Allen Barra, Wyatt would say in his later years that his father taught his children to think for themselves and that the senior Earp held a simple philosophy; "Religion is a matter which every man must settle for himself." It would seem that Wyatt Earp spent much time sorting out his personal spiritual beliefs.

Some writers have suggested that the Sutton & Colborn inscription was meant as sarcasm because of Wyatt's less than saintly ways. Edward Colborn was Dodge City's town attorney and his partner Michael W. Sutton was the Ford County district attorney during Earp's police service in the community. Sutton was nicknamed "St. Michael of the Oily Tongue" because of his eloquent and forceful prosecuting abilities. He was a political force in the Kansas Republican Party and a voice of the state's temperance movement. He was also an attorney for the Santa Fe Railroad and had at first opposed Wyatt Earp's mission during the Dodge City Peace Commission incident in 1883.

Edward Colborn later became a justice of the peace at Trinidad, Colorado, and provided some legal assistance to Wyatt and Doc when they reached Trinidad in the aftermath of the Cow-boy Campaign. He ended his days as a church and political leader in Salt Lake City. I don't believe that Edward Colborn would have found anything satirical in giving a New Testament as a gift to a friend and fellow believer.

While in Tombstone, Wyatt Earp may have visited Endicott Peabody's Methodist-Episcopal services because many of Wyatt's strongest supporters were members of the new church. But it is doubtful that Earp and Peabody became the close friends some writers have asserted they were. The two men were acquaintances, but the opportunity for a deep friendship was limited because they had only a few months in early 1882 to get to know each other, since Marshal Earp spent much of this time dealing with legal issues and leading a federal posse chasing Cow-boys.

Peabody, however, wrote about the Earp brothers in 1925, six years before Lake's book and two years before Burns wrote *Tombstone*, saying, " The Earps, brothers who were guardians of the town, and, I may say, in my opinion were trustworthy officers." Peabody, who became the renowned founder of Groton School and pastor to President Franklin Roosevelt, returned to Tombstone in 1941 for a nostalgic visit. A newspaper reporter asked him if he had known the killer Wyatt Earp. He replied, "Young man, I don't think you realize the type of person we needed as law officers sixty years ago. The Earps were very good law officers." It has been said that a man's character is best judged by the character of the people who knew and admired him. Endicott Peabody knew and admired Wyatt Earp.

In 1955, Dan Thrapp discussed how Wyatt Earp "dropped away" from regular church attendance following his Cow-boy Campaign. Stuart Lake recalled it was not until Wyatt had settled in California during his "golden years" that he returned to attending the church of his youth. Sometime during the early 1920s, Wyatt Earp renewed his interest in studying the Bible and became a semi-regular attendee at the Congregational Church located at Wilshire and Plymouth boulevards near his Los Angeles home. Following Wyatt's funeral service at the Pierce Brothers' Funeral Chapel, Dr. Thomas Harper recalled Wyatt Earp as being so quiet and unassuming that most of the other people attending the service took him for a retired businessman. Harper also said he always knew when Wyatt had been at a service, because a $20 gold piece was found in the offering plate.[4]

In 1913, Harper and Brothers issued a "modern English" translation of the New Testament produced by Dr. James Moffatt, a British Biblical scholar, who would also publish an Old Testament translation in 1924 and both testaments together in 1926. The publisher presented Professor Moffatt's work in a parallel column edition with the popular King James version of 1611 and one review said, "They have given us old truths and a new beauty." This translation was very popular in the Congregational Church and it is very possible that Wyatt Earp spent the dollar asking price for the book and used it for his biblical study.[5] Wyatt Earp and western movie star Tom Mix often sat together and discussed the meaning of certain Bible stories. Researcher Roger Peterson fondly recalled that when he and Adela Rodgers St. Johns once discussed Wyatt Earp she told him, "I remember he was always reading the Bible."

The Earp mythology has embraced Josephine Sarah Marcus. The renowned award winning motion picture director John Ford is credited with a tale about Mrs. Earp's religious values. Ford directed the classic mythmaking *My Darling Clementine*, with two cinematic myths depicting Wyatt Earp tales. In one scene Wyatt is depicted dancing at a Tombstone church social and in the second creative scene a stagecoach is shown racing into town at dawn and creating a dust cloud right in the middle of the showdown at the OK Corral.

Ford explained that the actor Harry "Dobe" Carey, Jr., told him about the former frontier marshal and introduced the two men. John Ford recalled, "His wife [Josie] was a very devout religious woman and a couple of times a year she'd go to these religious conventions in Utah and eastern Arizona and Wyatt would get on a streetcar [from Los Angles to Hollywood] and come up to Universal Studios and join us." Ford also claimed that Earp told him about the stagecoach racing by during the streetfight and even drew him a layout sketch of the shooting. On another occasion Ford said that Earp would often get drunk with the studio stuntmen and wranglers. There are two glaring mistakes with these Ford tales; Josie Marcus was not overtly religious and Wyatt's family and his oldest friends agreed Wyatt was not a heavy drinker.[6]

The Marcus family's religious heritage was based upon a belief in the God of Abraham, Isaac and Israel. The *Tanach*, the Jewish scriptures, refers to the study of the Torah, the five books of Moses, and the Land of Israel as a *morasha* (heritage) that is a *yerusha* (inheritance) which has the directive to be handed down from generation to generation. The sage Rabbi Rashi interpreted this to mean both men and women have this *yerusha*. The *Sefer haHinukh*, Negative Commandment 152, confirms that a knowledgeable woman may render religious-legal decisions within her sphere of influence, but sadly it seems that Josie Marcus was not overt in living her Jewish heritage or faith. As an elderly woman, she recalled that her mother and father were not *haredim* (pious people) but that her mother did celebrate some religious customs and taught her daughters to love their family.

The Jewish heritage is passed between generations by the women of the faith. German Jewish immigrants helped to bring the new Jewish reformation movement to America. This new wave of religious change rejected the Mosaic rules of diet and purity in dress and asserted that Jews were no longer a special chosen nation but a religious community. Messianism was now interpreted as a personal struggle for truth, justice and righteousness that could flourish alongside other religions and people of good will.

In 1880, there were two hundred synagogues spread across the United States and reform congregations used 190 of these Jewish houses of worship. Even the small Jewish community in Tombstone came together for celebration of the festivals of God. Reform Rabbinic Judaism was the religious belief the Henry Marcus family seems to have accepted.

Josie's parents and her relatives were members of San Francisco's Sherith Israel Synagogue, populated by working-class Polish and German Jewish immigrants. As a girl, Josie had been a member of the synagogue and she married Wyatt Earp in a manner allowed by that body.

"I was not reared within the fold of any creed or church, though my Mother was, within her heart, a deeply religious woman. She observed some of the formal ceremonials of the faith of her childhood [Judaism] but few of them remained with me," wrote Josie Earp in old age. "Only the spirit that underlay these forms and that made such an inspiration of her life before her family, stayed with me and colored, to a greater or less extent, my own life." Josie did not take part in any of the activities or services of the Jewish community in Tombstone or with the "Frozen Chosen" in Nome, Alaska. It would seem that Josie did not attend synagogue services as a woman in San Francisco, Los Angeles or San Diego, but she did attend Jewish festival celebrations with family and friends.

Josie wrote that her mother had an unbounded faith in "a good and all-wise God" with "complete confidence in His power to guide and guard those she loved." Mrs. Marcus demonstrated this faith in a nightly prayer that she had said since her youth. Josie learned that prayer: "It is a brief plea to the *Lieber Gott* for protection and guidance and an expression of confidence that He would wake me to health on the morrow. This I have never failed to utter at night before I close my eyes nor append a special mention of each of those dear to me." In a sad close to her discussion on prayer Josie added, "But alas that list has diminished as the years have taken those ones from me until only the prayer remains now." Her father died in January 1895 and her mother in August 1912. Josie once described how the prayer she had learned as a child grew with her: "In earlier and more thoughtless years it was no doubt a formal gesture on my part, or in great stress, an instinctive clutching at some Power that I only hoped could hear and answer me." Josie seems to have believed that she reached an age of accountability for her actions. Today, American Jewish girls look forward to the day they celebrate their Bat Mitzvah with family and friends.

As Josie grew older her faith became more real and personal: "The experiences of life have disciplined and ripened me, it [the prayer she spoke nightly] has taken on a deeper and fuller meaning and has become at once the strength and the expression of my faith." Josie understood enough about Judaism to believe she had free will to champion her *yetzer ra* (evil inclination) or her *yetzer tov* (good inclination). She also knew about *teshuvah* (repentance for misdeeds) as outlined in Ezekiel 18:21–22. Her autobiography reveals her concern that her husband had exercised God's right (Deuteronomy 32:35) to *lex talionis*, the Latin term for the Law of Retaliation, when he sought the ancient "eye-for-an-eye" justice for his brother Morgan's murder and the crippling of his brother Virgil.

The Jewish festival of Shavuot is celebrated for two days. In Hebrew, these holy days are called *Hag haKatzir* and translate as the Festival of the Harvest in recognition of the gathering of the summer wheat. Another name for these days is *Yom haBikkurim* ,which means the Day of First Fruits. The main celebration concerns the remembrance of the time when the Israelites were gathered in the desert before *Har Sinai* (Mount Sinai) and God gave his people the oral and written Torah (scripture) and the 613 *mitzvoth*, divine negative and positive commandments, of the Jewish faith, including the *aseret had'varim*, the Ten Words or Statements of Conduct called the Ten Commandments by Christians.

Another injunction of the Torah is *Lashon haRah*, disparaging speech or gossiping about others. Josie did not observe *Lashon haRah*. In old age she was known to lie and gossip about her relatives and those she believed were "out to get her" or divulge her past. Some of Josie's Earp relatives recalled that she was cheerfully ignorant about the beliefs of Judaism. She would not indulge in conversations about Jewish food or tell Jewish jokes and would generally call Jews cheap low-class people, except for her two wealthy sisters. Her worst insult was to call a person a "kike."[7]

Shavuot is a special time of reflections but also a close family time that centers upon food. If Wyatt and Josie ever celebrated this festival it most likely did not contain any religious reference, but it is fun to speculate about them eating the dairy-based desserts they both enjoyed. The festival's two main dishes are cheesecake and blintzes, the latter a folded pancake filled with cheese and fruit preserves.

While they were touring the 1893 Columbian Exposition held at Chicago, it is very likely that Wyatt and Josie witnessed the storytelling show and cooking demonstration by Kentucky-born Nancy Green. The former slave was pioneering her role as "Aunt Jemima," the marketing spokesperson for the new ready-mixed, self-rising pancake mix. Josie fondly recalled that Wyatt loved flapjacks and all types of desserts, especially pie. In their golden years together on the high desert Wyatt cooked just to keep his "hand in at it." He would jokingly tell Josie, "Let me cook the hot cakes. You don't quite have the hang of it." It is unknown if Wyatt Earp ever used the Aunt Jemima pancake mix. Josie later claimed that Wyatt introduced her to Buffalo Bill Cody during their visit to this Chicago world's fair.

Like her biblical matriarchal ancestors, Josie often found spiritual comfort and peaceful serenity in the high desert country. "It still has that power for me," wrote Josie a few years before her death. "It is to the wilderness that I return when the pressure of life and its sorrows become too great for me. It had the same effect upon my husband and it would have been hard to find two people with less need for a nerve specialist [a psychiatrist] than we in those years."

Did Josie and the Marcus family speak Hebrew? "Definitely not" would be the right answer. During Josie's lifetime Hebrew was *loshen ha-kodesh*, the sacred language, and was rarely spoken other than during religious observances or by yeshiva, religious students studying the Torah and other sacred Jewish writings. The drive to resurrect the Hebrew language to popular usage gained strength with the rise of the Zionist movement in the late 1880s and 1890s. Eliezer ben Yehudah spearheaded the revival by infusing the ancient vocabulary with updated terminology and thus rescued Hebrew to become the official language of the State of Israel.

It is possible that the Hyman Henry Marcus family spoke Yiddish at home. Yiddish was *mame loshen* (mother's language), the social-street means of conversation in Askenazic Jewish enclaves of immigrants from eastern and northern Europe. In a draft of her memoirs, Josie Earp wrote that her mother always met her when she returned from school and her dance or music lessons with a hug and the warm greeting, "Come in, *liebchen*." Data from the 1920 census indicates that Josie's parents were both born in Hamburg, Germany, and immigrated to America. Yiddish is composed of Middle-High German, Old French, Old Italian, Russian, Polish and touches of Slavic. Yiddish is a social language adaptable to the locale of the speaker. It is replete with terms of endearment, like *liebchen*, nicknames, and expletives. The language has a collection of proverbs, curses, and idioms. Yiddish reached its zenith in the late nineteenth century and started to decline in popularity following the *Shoah,* the Holocaust of the late 1930s and early 1940s, when most of its native speakers became victims of Nazi Germany's Jewish genocide.

Josie attended the wedding of her younger sister Henrietta, called Hattie in the family, to a candy manufacturer named Emil Lenhardt. It is also possible that Aunt Josie and Uncle Wyatt were invited to the Bar Mitzvah of Hattie's son. This religious and social occasion marks the "coming of age or age of accountability" for a young man of Jewish faith. The current Bat Mitzvah celebration for girls did not gain popularity as a Jewish custom until the mid–1920s, so it is doubtful that Josie and Wyatt would have been invited to see her nieces "coming of age" in their faith. In 1900, Alice "Peggy" Cohn (Greenberg), from an observant Jewish family, lived in Nome, Alaska, with her Aunt Josie and Uncle Wyatt as her guardians. Later, Wyatt and Josie would attend Passover celebrations with other Marcus family members.

Emil Lenhardt committed suicide on January 26, 1912, the eve of the Holy Sabbath, in the basement of his Oakland candy company. He had been suffering from a mental disorder and his son-in-law had taken over much of the company management. In a move opposed by Jewish religious custom, Emil's body was cremated by his wife. Lenhardt was not a practicing Jew but was a leader in the Unitarian Church in San Francisco.

Josie's family was part of San Francisco's lower middle class working community that lived on the flatlands in an area nicknamed the "Slot" in the city's Forth Ward. It is unclear if the extended Marcus family ever suffered any mistreatment due to their ethnic heritage, but in that era Jews were often discriminated against socially and economically. The concept of egalitarianism was just a dream. It is doubtful that Josie Marcus gave much thought to a Jewish homeland or the growing Zionist movement of the early 1900s, but she did contribute to the Jewish Fund. She did charity work in Nome, Alaska, and later in Tonopah, Nevada. (A year before his assassination Martin Luther King, Jr., caught the true meaning of the American Jew's plight in an open letter published in the *Saturday Review*. In his "Letter to an Anti-Zionist Friend" Dr. King said, "You declare, my friends, that you do not hate the Jews, you are merely anti–Zionist. And I say, let the truth ring forth from the highest mountaintops. Let it echo through the valleys of God's green earth. When people criticize Zionism, they mean Jews. Zionism is nothing less than the dream and ideal of the Jewish people returning to live in their own land.") It is doubtful that much anti–Jewish prejudice was expressed or displayed openly within Wyatt Earp's presence, but during their life together Wyatt and Josie would have experienced some social prejudice, if only subtly expressed. Anti-Semitism was boldly asserted by national leaders like Supreme Court justice William Strong. In a speech given in 1870, the justice proclaimed that Judaism as practiced in the United States was "a cult only weakly tolerated within this mighty Christian nation."

Charlie Welsh was Wyatt Earp's good friend from Dodge City days and later his prospecting days in Alaska and California. Welsh eventually build a house in Needles, California, and later in Los Angeles. He and his wife Elena had eight sons and three daughters. Two of the girls, Grace and Alma, were very attached to Wyatt. In fact, Grace lived with the Earps during one of their summer stays in Colorado and later in San Diego. She was a teenager and the childless Wyatt was a surrogate father. Grace Welsh Spolodori said in a 1996 interview that Wyatt and Josie would often spend Thanksgiving and Christmas with her family and that Josie was "very Jewish." It is evident that Josie Earp understood some Christian doctrine. In her memoirs she used an analogy from that faith, saying, "Like certain travelers two thousand years ago we found no room in the inn."

It would seem that Wyatt and Josie Earp took some notice of the social activities of the Christmas season. They spent the 1885 Christmas holiday season with Henry and Mary Lambert in Cimarron, New Mexico. When Wyatt wrote to his actor friend William S. Hart, in January 1929, about the loss of Wyatt's brother Newton he mentioned that he had received the news "mingled with the Holiday cheer" of Christmas and the New Year celebration. At the end of his letter Wyatt wrote, "Mrs. Earp wishes to thank your sister for the nice card at Christmas." Five years earlier, in January 1924, Wyatt had been at his California desert mine site near Vidal when Josie joined him. Wyatt wrote, "Mrs. Earp brought your Christmas telegram out on the desert for me to read. Yours is a kindly thought and I thank you for it and with all the appreciation of a good friend."

> **Author's Perspective:** The nature, personage and the timing of the earthly arrival of *HaMashiach*, the Anointed One of Adonai, is the central difference between the two great monotheistic beliefs of Judaism and Christianity. A secondary gap between the two faiths is the Christians' missionary zeal to convert the Jew from his special covenant with God. Jews do not proselytize. One can only conjecture whether Wyatt and Josie ever discussed the physical and spiritual nature of *Y'shua ben Josef, HaMashiach*—Jesus, the Christ of the Christian faith.
>
> It is fairly clear from the historic record that Wyatt Earp accepted and intermittently practiced the Christian doctrine. It is equally clear that his wife Josephine honored, even if she did not always practice them, the ancient rituals and festivals of the Jewish faith. In First Samuel 16:7 of the Jewish scriptures we find these words: "For not as man sees [does the Lord see]; man sees only what is visible, but the Lord sees into the heart." Wyatt and Josie's individual beliefs concerning the Creator of the Universe or the nature of *Y'shua* are no longer of concern, because their individual deaths settled that issue for each of them.

19

Final Observations

"Whenever you're certain that you're dealing with downright vicious-ness, the complete disregard for human rights and decency, remember that such lawlessness is the greatest enemy of mankind. Any man who is honestly combating such lawlessness is justified in going to any lengths to which lawlessness forces the fight. When you know you have a fight with viciousness on your hands, hit first, if you can, and when you do hit, hit to kill."—Nicholas Earp's admonition to his sons

Five years after the Earp era in Tombstone ended, a Scottish doctor gave the world its first Sherlock Holmes adventure. In this 1887 novel called *A Study in Scarlet*, the budding consulting detective made this profound observation: "What you do in this world is a matter of no consequence. The question is, what can you make people believe that you have done?" The question asked by Sherlock Holmes is applicable to the con-frontation between Wyatt Earp and the members of the Cow-boy confederation.

In May 1882, the semi-invalid Virgil Earp was in San Francisco seeking extended medical care for his wounded arm. An enterprising newspaper reporter for the *Examiner* located him there on May 26 and asked for some comments about the Cochise County troubles. The next morning the newspaper quoted Virgil: "Concerning the fights between the Cow-boys and myself and [my] brothers, it has been stated over and over again that there was an old feud between us and some of our enemies and that we were fighting only to revenge personal wrongs and [to] gratify personal hatred. All such state-ments are false." "We went to Tombstone to do our duty as officers," Virgil Earp proudly told a California reporter about the brothers' actions in Tombstone in a story reprinted in Tucson's *Arizona Daily Star* on May 30, 1882. This is a thought-provoking statement in light of the fact that Sheriff John Behan would later tell special federal investigator Leigh Chambers, during the agent's review of Crawley Dake's operation of the U.S. mar-shal's office in Arizona Territory, that he believed Wyatt Earp had been "sent to Arizona to get the 'Curly Bill' gang" and that he accomplished his mission. Behan did not specify what authority he believed had "sent" Wyatt to Tombstone. The Department of Justice via the U.S. marshals? Wells Fargo?

Virgil continued his comments: "To do that [their duty as peace officers] we were put in conflict with a band of desperados, and it resolved itself into a question of which side could first drive the other out of the country, or kill them in it. Today my brother Morg is dead and I am a cripple for life. My other brothers [Wyatt and Warren] are fugitives." Virgil also commented about the odds the brothers faced: "The Cow-boys numbered at one time nearly 200 but during the last two years about fifty of them have been killed." There was no mention of how these half a hundred "saddlers," or range riders, had met their fates.

Former Cochise County sheriff John Behan's private praiseworthy comments about Wyatt Earp's war against the Cow-boys mentioned above were made prior to the hubristic sheriff's later public efforts to discredit the deputy federal marshal's accomplishments in corralling his "honest rancher" friends.

The Cow-boy sympathizers had begun their relentless excoriation campaign against Wyatt Earp during the justice court hearing concerning the Tombstone streetfight in November 1881 and the anti–Earp crowd did not end their violent denunciation once Wyatt left Arizona in April 1882. The rewriting of Cochise County history and the rehabilitation of John H. Behan began anew shortly after the sheriff lost his own party's primary nomination for sheriff in the 1882 election. The vanquished had begun to rewrite Arizona history.

In March 1885, the *Southwestern Stockman* of Wilcox published an editorial proposing that President Grover Cleveland appoint fellow Democrat Johnny Behan as the United States marshal for Arizona Territory. The newspaper said, "He drove the cow thieves, murderers, stage robbers and the lawless element generally from the county, and to him more than any man in Arizona is it due to-day that the stockman may enjoy their ranges and possessions in peace." The former sheriff added to the historical rewrite effort in 1897 when he told a *Washington Post* reporter "warrants were issued for their [the Earp posse] arrest, and summoning a posse, I went out to bring the Earps in. They were chased entirely out of the country and Tombstone knew them no more."

In the spring of 1888 the *National Police Gazette* contained a story about Wyatt Earp. On March 7, 1888, the *Hartford (KY) Herald* reprinted the story while reminding readers that Nicholas Earp, Wyatt's father, had been born in the county and married his second wife in the community and noted that her relatives still lived in Ohio County. This is the article's description of a 40-year-old Wyatt: "He is a quiet, unassuming gentleman, about six feet in height, broad shoulders, and wears a large blonde moustache. He is dignified, self-contained, game and fearless, and no man commands greater respect where he is known than Wyatt S. Earp. If he has been a man-killer and avenger, he has been so in the cause of justice and in a conflict with the most dangerous and treacherous elements of life in wild communities of the frontier."

In the early 1900s, a new breed of writer discovered the two-decades-old Cow-boy accusations about the Earp brothers and began to question their "heroic actions" in Tombstone. The new avenue of sensational exposure centered on the old Cow-boy smear campaign that the Earp brothers had been thugs and killers with badges, that the brothers were just another "gang" of shifty operators who had a good press agent. On September 9, 1903, the *Los Angeles Herald* published a letter to the editor from George Parsons. The former Tombstone miner, member of the Council of 10 for Tombstone's Committee of Vigilance, and community booster wrote to rebut the misinformation recently published in the newspaper concerning the Earp brothers' actions in Tombstone two decades earlier.

In his letter, Parsons claimed that Wyatt Earp and his brothers had always supported the effort to uphold law and order, except for one action: "When their brother Morgan was assassinated, Virgil Earp shot and Wyatt's life attempted, then they took the law into their own hands and did what most anyone would have done under the peculiar circumstances existing at the time, and what anyone reading *The Virginian* [a very popular western novel by Owen Wister first published in 1902] would consider their right to do." Parsons ended his comments by saying, "Wyatt Earp, who is older now but none the less gritty, I believe, I state this in justice to a much maligned man who, as a public character, was a benefit and protection to the community he once lived in."

On August 9, 1911, the *Searchlight* published in the small community of Cushing in Oklahoma Territory carried an exchange story about Wyatt Earp. The last paragraph summed up the revisionist version of the old gunman tale: "Earp fulfilled to the letter Mark Twains' description of the typical and western bad man and 'guntoter.' He was mild, quiet, soft spoken and inoffensive. All he asked was to be [left] alone, but he knew of only one way to resent [sic] an injury, and that was to shoot the aggressor. A casual glance would convey any impression except that he was a desperate character. But he was quick on the trigger, brave according to his lights, and without a scruple concerning the sacredness of human life."

The *Tombstone Epitaph* editorialized, on September 5, 1915, about a gathering of old-timers in town who were recalling the "Homeric days of empire founding." In yet another historical rewrite the editor categorized the 1881 streetfight as "the savage gun fight between the Earp gang and the Clanton and Lowrys [sic], a battle which might more properly be called an assassination."

Behan's civil process server was William M. "Billy Blab" Breakenridge. As an old man in 1928, Breakenridge wrote a self-serving autobiography called *Helldorado* that championed his former boss's job performance. "Tombstone's Deputy" wrote that Johnny Behan "was a brave and fearless officer, who could see some good in even the worst of men. He did not persecute any one, but would try to serve any warrant that was given him." Wyatt, unlike Behan and others in Tombstone, had treated Breakenridge with respect and even helped him find work when they were old men. However, for reasons known only to Breakenridge, he cast Wyatt as a villain in this heroic tale of "bringing the law to the mesquite."

Col. John S. Mosby, leader of a famous unit of Confederate cavalry in the War Between the States, in a June 11, 1902, letter to a man named Reuben Page, addressed man's need to justify his past actions. The old warrior postulated, "Men fight from sentiment. After the fight is over they invent some fanciful theory on which they imagine that they fought."[1]

In the 1990s, when Wyatt Earp regained a certain new credibility among the general public, Patrick Ford, son of John Ford, the renowned motion picture film director, claimed his father had known Earp in the early 1920s. He quoted Wyatt as once telling his father, "The only way to be a successful marshal in those days was to carry a double-barrel 12-gauge and don't shoot until you know you can't miss." I doubt Earp uttered these words, but, fact or fiction, Frank Stilwell and Curly Bill would not argue with the success of the statement's philosophy.

The rewrite of history continues. In 1989, Dr. Frederick S. Calhoun, the first official historian of the U.S. Marshals Service, using John D. Gilchriese as his consultant on the Earp brothers section of his book, wrote a denigrating account of the Earps' conduct in persecution of the rambunctious Cow-boys, which was published by the Smithsonian Institution Press. Two examples of the many distorted statements used by Calhoun include perpetuating the myth that Wyatt Earp used Gilchriese's fake Smith and Wesson .44 pistol to murder Frank McLaury in the Tombstone streetfight and that Wyatt refused to provide Marshal Dake with any accounting for the "thousands" of dollars he had provided to fund the Cow-boy Campaign.

In his taxpayer-supported agency history Dr. Calhoun wrote, "The Earps had no real evidence of any complicity by either the Clantons or the McLaurys in Mexican cattle rustling or stagecoach holdups." He continued, "Although Wyatt never found the riches he so desperately sought, he stumbled into American myth and legend. The bullet he fired into Frank McLaury carried him into the romantic, unreal realm of frontier hero. The remembrance was as underserved as it was enduring." The misguided efforts of rewriting the history of the Cow-boy troubles continues.

Author's Perspective: Once a western author has formulated an opinion concerning Wyatt Earp, there is a tendency to protect that belief, as if the universe revolves around that interpretation. Few are willing to step back and reassess their line in the sand. I was once part of this group and that is why it took over a decade to complete this investigation. New discoveries, like the Otero Letter, refocused my thinking and caused a reexamination of old information.

In the Hooker (1920) and Flood (1926) accounts, as well as later retellings, the

Ringo killing is the final action of the Earp posse before they rode for New Mexico Territory; it is reported as a legitimate killing by federal lawmen doing their duty. The truth behind the Cow-boy Campaign and Wyatt Earp's covert return and planned murder of Ringo was overlooked, because in American folklore a champion of justice cannot meticulously plan to hunt and kill a villain, no matter how vile, and still be a folk hero. This ethical problem may be why Stuart Lake chose to reject inclusion of the bloody showdown with Ringo in his mystic hero-building 1931 Wyatt Earp biography. Although today it is commonplace to have fictional superheroes with a dark side to their persona, in the early 1930s the reading public was not ready for such a "good guy–bad guy" hero. It was still a couple of years in the future when the planned ambush of the killer-bandits Bonnie and Clyde by former Texas Ranger captain Frank Hamer and his posse of hard-core lawmen made national headlines and the FBI ambush killings of John Dillinger, Charles "Pretty Boy" Floyd, and Lester "Baby Face Nelson" Gillis made J. Edgar Hoover's "G-Men" national heroes.

Wyatt Earp in old age (courtesy Robert G. McCubbin Collection).

John Charles Frémont officially served as Arizona's territorial governor from 1878 until the spring of 1882. Since he was out of the territory for many months at a time the territorial secretary, John J. Gosper, served as the acting governor during the height of the Earp brothers' war against the Cow-boys. The acting governor generally supported the brothers' efforts to maintain law and order. After President Chester A. Arthur forced Frémont to resign he appointed Frederick A. Tritle, an Arizona lawyer and mining investor, as the sixth territorial governor. Tritle quickly joined the fight against the Cow-boy elements. Following deputy United States marshal Wyatt Earp's Cow-boy Campaign and the killing of John Ringo, the governor remarked, "The Cow-boy difficulties are all ended." John Gosper and Fred Tritle, and their well-placed supporters, had seen to that.

I believe the Otero Letter has provided the tools to perceive the master design behind Wyatt Earp's Cow-boy Campaign, often misnamed as Wyatt Earp's Vendetta Ride, across southeastern Arizona Territory in the spring of 1882. The puzzle is almost complete. I know that a few pieces are still missing or fuzzy, but the major scope of the picture is clear enough. Deputy United States marshal Wyatt Earp and his federal strike force enjoyed massive and powerful backing to seek out and destroy the Cow-boy menace that caused mayhem along the United States–Mexico border in the late 1870s and early 1880s.

Others finished the seek and destroy mission launched in the spring of 1882 as they dug the grave for the outlaw-snake that Wyatt Earp's two strike force teams beheaded. Today however, like the mythical Hydra, the outlaw-snake has risen stronger in its evil intent and again threatens the border country of the Southwest. Where is Wyatt Earp today? More important, where is the national courage, the collective will, and financial means to wage this new deadly campaign against evil? The eighteenth century Irish statesman Edmund Burke said, "The only thing necessary for the triumph of evil is for good men to do nothing." Where is Wyatt Earp today?

Epilogue by Jeffrey Wheat

"Where is Wyatt Earp today?" The question implies that the nations of the world could use a man like him to lead a new assault upon the evils of the modern world. It is amazing to think that one man could make such a lasting impression on the world at large. For nearly a century and a half, Wyatt Earp has been the subject of newspapers articles, books, magazines, comic books, TV shows and movies. In his honor, statues have been erected, and streets, elementary schools, and two oceangoing vessels have been named after him. Not a day goes by that there isn't someone either researching him, writing about him, or referencing his name. He has become the universal symbol for courage and justice.

In real life, the legendary Wyatt Earp was a quiet, unassuming, simple man. According to reliable sources around the time of his Tombstone years, he was physically fit, straight as an arrow, 165 pounds, had wavy blonde hair and a bushy blonde handlebar moustache; he was a handsome man. Wyatt was a Republican and a Protestant by faith. He was soft-spoken, slow and deliberate, with a deep voice, much deeper than most men of his era. Wyatt Earp possessed what many people would refer to as a poker face, with bright blue eyes that at times became steely and piercing—the demeanor of a no-nonsense kind of man. It was the kind of look that a professional gambler or a lawman needed to survive on the Western frontier.

Wyatt and Josie Earp were practical people, not very materialistic, never concerned with accumulating possessions. Throughout their lives they were very nomadic, constantly on the move, always searching for an economic enhancement scheme or a means of striking it rich in mining or oil. Wyatt was ambitious, hardworking, entrepreneurial, and had grandiose dreams of being accepted as an equal by America's developing capitalist society.

Wyatt Earp was a fairly rational individual, not a quick-tempered thug. Perhaps he was cut from the same cloth as Davy Crockett, whose personal motto was, "Be always sure you're right—then go ahead." Wyatt was a decisive decision maker and when pushed too far, he responded sometimes violently, purposefully, unwaveringly. Family honor always came first for him and following the assassination of his younger brother Morgan and the ambush attacks made on his and Virgil's lives he snapped. He had had enough. For Wyatt, retribution was the only answer and nothing was going to stop him.

The fallout from the arrest attempt gone deadly during the Fremont Street encounter, the verdict of the Spicer Hearing, the Cow-boy retaliations, and Wyatt's mission to terminate his foe changed his life forever. These events stained his reputation as a lawman, cost him his hard-earned investment fortune, and dissolved his troubled domestic relationship, while the freedom to live his life as a "normal person" slowly drained away. Wyatt Earp paid a heavy price for his honor.

The legendary UCLA basketball coach John Wooden is credited with saying, "Your reputation is who people think you are ... [and] your character is who you really are." Wyatt Earp never wanted the celebrity status or man-killer reputation that was thrust upon him after his Tombstone adventures. It was an uncomfortable fit that he reluctantly grew to live with, if not enjoy. The lurid "blood and thunder" tales spun by overzealous writers never made life easy for Wyatt. He was so troubled with the inaccuracy of the wild stories that in a few instances he even tried to correct them. Finally, after years of aggravation, Wyatt decided to find someone to write his version of Tombstone. It too was filled with errors and fueled controversy. Historians today still struggle with this conundrum because of the discovery of new information like the Otero Letter or long-forgotten contemporary newspaper accounts, tax records, legal and business documents, diaries, and journals. The voyage of discovery continues.

Wyatt and Josie Earp shared 46 years together after the Tombstone saga was in their rearview mirror. They lived during the infancy of electricity, motion pictures, automobiles, telephones, radios, airplane transportation, and America's empire building. The couple were alive during the Great War, saw the beginning of America's experiment with the prohibition of alcohol and gambling, the rise of anti–Semitism in America and Europe, and the unbridled race toward a worldwide financial meltdown in 1929. After Tombstone, they traveled widely, racing their thoroughbred horses, and lived in mining camps in Colorado, Idaho, Alaska, Arizona, Nevada, and California. Wyatt often served as a peace officer in areas where he lived.

The discovery of the Otero Letter is just another step in the grassroots pursuit to locate more information about the Tombstone saga and the man whose legend has become larger than life. There is still more to be discovered and the letter should serve to encourage others to be persistent in their search for historical truth.

Good guy? Bad guy? No matter how you look at him, Wyatt Earp has become an important figure in the historic fabric of this country. There will always be more interesting things to discover about this man who is at the center of a chapter in American history that will never be closed. Keep searching.

Jeffrey Wheat is an Emmy Award–winning cameraman and director in Los Angeles. He serves on the board of directors at the William S. Hart Museum and is an avid Earpiana researcher. He is working on a book about the death of Morgan Earp and a documentary involving some living friends of the Earps.

Chapter Notes

Chapter 1

1. To better understand the massive Tombstone puzzle, here is a small piece to help form the bigger picture. Wyatt Earp was traveling across north central Texas in the late 1870s looking over rangeland to purchase as a small cattle operation in partnership with his brother James. William Rowland McLaury, an older brother of two Cow-boys the Earp brothers would kill in Tombstone, was a Fort Worth attorney doing legal work on regional land transactions. What kind of a relationship might have developed if Wyatt and Will McLaury had discussed land options over whiskey and a game of cards?

Our friend Paul L. Johnson, a New York descendent of the McLaury clan, has done a creditable job of bring the brothers Tom and Frank to life in *The McLaurys in Tombstone, Arizona: An O.K. Corral Obituary.* Paul uses McLaury family archives to paint a broader, more colorful, and personal family centered tale then the standard bad guy image of the past.

2. The first non-regional information published about "Wyatt Erpe" appeared on page 13 of the August 10, 1878 issue of the *National Police Gazette* in an article titled "Lively Scene at a Variety Performance." A "Special Correspondent" to the magazine reported the July 25 shooting raid on Dodge City's Brown and Springer Theater by a group of Texas "cow-boys." The city police shot George Hoyt, who later died of the wound, during an exchange of lead. Many historians credit Wyatt Earp with the fatal shot. Jeff Morey provided me with a copy of this article and while I was editor of the Western Outlaw-Lawman History Association *Journal*, I used the *National Police Gazette* article to illustrate a point concerning Wyatt's status as a legend in his own lifetime. Hoyt was the son of former Texas Ranger James Kindred Hoy and a descendant of a founder, along with Daniel Boone, of Boonesborough and Hoy's Station in Kentucky.

3. In her old age, Mrs. Katharine Haroney-Cummings sought revenge for "Wyatt's comments" recently published in Stuart Lake's Wyatt Earp biography. She believed that Wyatt had made all the statements attributed to him in the book (unknown at the time many Earp comments had been fabricated by the author), so she dictated inaccurate and anti–Wyatt Earp laced autobiographies to Anton Mazzanovich in 1931–32, Joe Chisholm in 1934–35 and Dr. A. W. Bork in

1936. She also wrote a biographical letter to her niece Lillian Raffert on March 18, 1940. A hand written copy of the Anton Mazzanovich manuscript is in the J. Evetts Haley History Center in Midland, TX, while the other original documents are in the collections of Kevin and Bev Mulkins, Graig Fouts, and the Lowndes County Historical Society, Valdosta, Ga. Copies of the three works are in the author's collection.

4. Over the course of this work, I will utilize the recollections of many who knew Wyatt Earp and recorded his thoughts and actions. *A Wild West Remembrance of Wyatt Earp's Sister Adelia Earp Edwards*, as recorded by Dave Cruickshanks, is in the Earp Family Collection in the Colton (CA) Public Library and the original manuscript of "Aunt Allie's" (Mrs. Virgil Earp) story, *Tombstone Travesty*, is in the Frank Waters Papers at the Center for Southwest Research, University of New Mexico, discovered by Cindy Reidhead and Jeff Wheat. Forrestine Hooker's manuscript *An Arizona Vendetta: The Truth About Wyatt Earp and Some Other Facts Stated to Writer by Wyatt S. Earp*, located by Jeff Morey, is housed in the Sharlot Hall Museum and Archives, Phoenix.

5. Arizona historian John D. Gilchriese often bemoaned that Stuart Lake's book was full of fiction concerning Wyatt Earp's life, but he knew the real story and would someday reveal the facts. Interestingly, during the final sixth season of the Earp television series, when Lake was no longer a paid consultant for the production company and in fact was suing the company for not paying him for his services rendered during the filming of the fifth season, John Gilchriese provided chief screenwriter Fredrick Hazlitt Brennon with the story idea for that season's episode 16, "Terror in the Desert." In this drama Wyatt Earp meets a woman who claims that Sheriff John Behan has framed her husband and helped to send him to the territorial prison at Yuma. In this fairy tale, Earp saves the innocent man and exposes Behan's misdeed, but he receives no punishment for his misdeed and the innocent man and his wife must leave Arizona.

In truth, some prisoners never made it to the desert lockup because they "escaped" during transport only to be tracked by Indian bounty hunters and killed for reward money. Wyatt Earp did spend time prospecting in the desert around Tombstone and many years after he left Tombstone he did some prospecting along the Colorado River around Yuma. Johnny Behan did have political connections at the Yuma prison and would one day serve as superintendent there. However, Gilchriese's adventure yarn, combining all of these minimal facts, is pure fiction.

Chapter 2

1. Bat Masterson wrote his short biographic sketch of Doc Holliday's life for the May 1907 issue of Alfred Henry Lewis' *Human Life* magazine. In 1959, Ed Bartholomew used his Frontier Book Company printing press to reprint a limited edition of select Masterson magazine tales. The Holliday story became more available to the public twenty-three years later when Jack DeMattos published his 75th anniversary annotated edition of the complete Masterson series.

2. Contrary to Bat Masterson's often stated dislike of Doc Holliday, Kate Holliday, in old age, wrote, "Doc and Bat Masterson became good friends. And when we left Dodge, Bat Masterson presented Doc with a pearl handled .45 Colt." This 31 page handwritten letter is in the Haley Memorial Library and History Center in Midland, TX.

John Clum expressed his dislike for Doc Holliday and Wyatt's friendship with the gambler in a letter to a friend on 23 August 1929. "I think Wyatt hurt himself" with his public support for the gambler said Clum and continued "I will not appear as a supporter of Holliday." The Clum letter is in Ben Traywick's Tombstone history collection.

3. Doc Holliday makes his first appearance in the *Life and legend of Wyatt Earp* TV series in episode # 66 on April 23, 1957 near the end of season two in the story titled "Wyatt Earp meets Doc Holliday." The story and teleplay were written by the series' head writer Fredrick Hazlitt Brennan with Earp biographer Stuart Lake serving as historical consultant. At one point, Doc is discussing his college education and says that he earned a " doctorate of dental science from Johns Hopkins." In his 1931 *Frontier Marshal*, Lake has Earp recall that Doc studied dentistry in Baltimore. The private Maryland university was not founded until January 1876. John Holliday graduated from the Pennsylvania College of Dental Surgery in Philadelphia on March 1, 1872.

4. Mary Katharine Haroney Cummings aka Kate Fisher, Kate Elder, "Big Nosed Kate", and Mrs. Holliday was born on November 7, 1850 in Hungary and died at the Arizona Pioneers' Home on November 2, 1940. She disliked the way Stuart Lake's Wyatt Earp biography portrayed her. She believed Lake's claim that Wyatt had said all the comments attributed to him about her; "a dancehall girl better known as 'Big-Nosed Kate'" and "she'd get drunk as well as furious and make Doc more trouble than any shooting-scrape" and finally "that fool woman." Lake's book also omitted the fact that Kate traveled with the Earps to Arizona from New Mexico. This journey is covered in our book, *Wyatt Earp and Doc Holliday: Their New Mexico Adventures.*

5. In the spring of 1974, I was privileged to accompanied Father Stanley (Louis Stanley Francis Crocchiola), a chronicler of New Mexico and Texas settlement histories, on a research trip to the Panhandle-Plains Historical Museum on the campus of West Texas State University (now West Texas A & M University) at Canyon. He was working on his book *Rail-*

roads of the Texas Panhandle and I was searching for anything dealing with outlaws and lawmen. The archivist suggested I might like to review the newly accessible material in the H. C. "Hank" Smith Collection and here I found the *Day Ledger for Conrad & Rath, Fort Griffin, Texas.* I discovered the post trader's journal had a page containing Doc Holliday's bar room charge account for September 14 to September 21, 1877. Holliday's $22 charge account was paid in full; 44 drinks at 50 cents per drink. I gave this information to Karen Holliday Tanner for use in her 1998 family centered biography of Holliday. Sadly, since our discovery a vandal has stolen the journal page.

Chapter 4

1. General George Washington wrote this advice to his nephew Bushrod Washington in 1783. When the federal government under the current constitution was established young Washington was appointed an associate justice of the United States Supreme Court by the new nation's second president, John Adams, in 1798. Justice Washington served faithfully for the next 30 years. He and his wife are buried on his uncle's Mount Vernon estate in Virginia.

Chapter 6

1. On Saturday, September 8, 1900, Wyatt Earp's old friend and Tombstone ally George Parsons wrote in his daily journal that he and fellow Tombstone alumni John Clum had signed affidavits that Earp's recently written "account of his adventures" was a true depictions of the events. Assuming this account is a different project from Earp's 1896 *San Francisco Sunday Examiner's* three-part ghost-written newspaper autobiographical series, this 1900 revelation is exciting because it suggest that fours years after the newspaper stories Wyatt had made a serious attempt to record his memoirs. This account was two decades before Forrestine Hooker or John Flood had attempted to put Wyatt's recollections on paper. Unfortunately, for history this 1900 memoir seems to have been lost. What could we have learned if we were able to read the stories that a 52-year-old Wyatt Earp had wished others to remember about his life. Maybe some day someone will discover a trunk containing this 1900 manuscript, Wyatt and Josie's family picture albums, or Wyatt Earp's collection of "fan letters" that Josie said were in luggage the couple lost during one of their cross country trips.

2. From the day, I first read Frank Waters book *The Earp Brothers of Tombstone: The Story of Mrs. Virgil Earp* in 1960 I had a feeling of disgust. The writing was so anti–Earp in tone that it overflowed with a personal hate for the American Myth, Wyatt Earp. The book claimed to be the recollections of Alvira Packingham Sullivan, Virgil Earp's beloved Allie. Even an amateur historian knew that she was the fun-loving Irish wife of the equally fun-loving marshal of Tombstone. Yet, Waters presented a woman who described her husband's family as conmen, corrupt lawmen and stage robbers. They were the bad guys led by the evil Wyatt. My second point of contention was the author's deliberate misstatement of well-known facts to support his blatant plan to destroy the hero-image of

Wyatt Earp. Virgil and Allie Earp were relegated to background characters in her own biography.

During the years that I served as editor of the quarterly *Journal of the Western Outlaw-Lawmen History Association* (WOLA) we gave voice to a new wave of discussion in the ongoing search for the facts surrounding Wyatt Earp's life and times. Following the discovery, nearly four decades after it was written, of Frank Waters' original 1935 manuscript *Tombstone Travesty* containing the actual statements made by "Aunt Allie," by S. J. "Cindy" Reidhead and Jeff Wheat, I agreed to publish a comprehensive examination of the manuscript and the published version. I wrote the introduction and supervised publication of the 1999 series of articles by Jeff Wheat, Gary Roberts, Casey Tefertiller, and Cindy Reidhead that exposed the many falsehoods and pure fiction Waters used to distorted Mrs. Allie Earp's true comments into his anti–Wyatt Earp work of fiction. The *Tombstone Travesty* manuscript is now part of the Frank Waters Papers in the Center for Southwest Research at the University of New Mexico in Albuquerque. WOLA *Journal's* successor, the *Journal of the Wild West History Association*, continues to provide a non-partisan scholarly publication forum for new discoveries in the field of Wild West history.

3. Andy Neff managed the California Fruit and Produce Store or popularly called the California Fruit Depot for the J. C. Eastman Company of Los Angeles. An ad in the Tombstone *Daily Nugget*, November 12, 1880, proclaimed, "All fruit for this house is picked fresh from the vines and trees and packed by members of the firm in Los Angeles. [Andy] Neff always at home in the store and glad to see his friends."

4. On March 6, 1905, Wyatt and Jose Earp filed their first mining claim in the high desert country of southern California. They filed the last claim 17-years later on March 13, 1922. Between the two they filed claims on almost 90 pieces of mining property, not counting some clams they discovered on Indian lands and could not file on. They sold or traded at least six ore mining claims to friends or relatives. In January 1909, Josie Earp registered 15-claims in her name. The couple's first mining claims, the "Happy Day" and "Luck Day," were their favorite camp and work site; it was also the most productive. Wyatt and brother James built Josie a tree house at the "Happy Day" site so she could sleep away from possible rattlesnakes in her tent. This is also the site where James spent the night trapped in a tree sitting out a flash flood as Wyatt, sitting on the opposite bank, stayed up all night in the rain talking to James to keep him awake so he would not fall out of the tree. Death had already claimed Morgan and Virgil, so his widowed brother James was very important to Wyatt. Wyatt had named one of his claims "Virgil W." and intended that Allie would profit from it, but it proved to be an unproductive mine.

5. Tombstone's 1880s Chinese enclave, nicknamed Hoptown because of the opium dens in the community, consisted of a two block area between Second and Third Streets bordered on the north by Fremont Street and Toughnut Street on the south. Nothing remains of the community today. Sam Sing's Chinese Restaurant on Fourth Street was a popular eating and rooming establishment with miners. The business enterprises of Hoptown were "ruled" the China Mary.

Chapter 8

1. Atmospheric data was extracted from *George O. Hand's Contention City Diary, 1882, George W. Parsons' Private Journal* kept at Tombstone in 1879–1882, and *Endicott Peabody's Tombstone Diary 1882* and weather reports carried in the Tombstone *Daily Epitaph*. Publication information is contained in the bibliography.

2. In her autobiography manuscript, *She Married Wyatt Earp*, Josie Marcus Earp recalled Wyatt's love of horses. "Throughout his life wherever one found Wyatt Earp, there he also found a horse if it were at all possible for him to keep one. He bought only one car in his life, and although it was of an expensive make and though he learned to drive it in an indifferent manner, he took little pleasure in it. Horses were the love of his life."

3. William Dennison, Jr., was born and died in Ohio. During his 66 years he married into a wealthy family, fathered seven children, worked as a lawyer and railroad builder, served as the 24th governor of Ohio, served as the 21st postmaster general serving under President Lincoln and Andrew Johnson, before President U. S. Grant made him the first president of the new board of commissioners for the District of Columbia. He was a founder of the Ohio Republican Party.

4. The failed attempt to rob the stage at Drew's Station on March 15, 1881, caused a nine-man posse to seek the would-be hold-up artists and murderers. When the chase was over the three Earp brothers and Bat Masterson presented Sheriff Behan with a bill for their services. The sheriff claimed he had not deputized them, so he owned then nothing. This incident caused an even bigger trust riff between the Earps and Behan. Finally, Wells Fargo Express Company covered the Earp posse's expenses. The company's payment records indicate Wyatt and Morgan earned $72 each, Virgil and Bat each received $32.

5. In his very popular 1872 book *Roughing It*, Samuel Langhorn Clemens aka Mark Twain included a short story he called "Buck Fanshaw's Funeral." This tale concerned how the friends of a Virginia City, Nevada saloonkeeper gave a massive celebration that honored the man in a manner not reflective of his real status in the community. The Clanton–McLaury funeral parade is a good example of this public relations model.

6. I used *A Compilation of the Messages and Papers of the Presidents, 1789–1897*, Vol. 8, Chester A. Arthur to Grover Cleveland (Washington, D.C.: Government Printing Office, 1898) edited by James D. Richardson for President Arthur's December 6, 1881, message to Congress.

7. Thomas Gardiner, a founder of the Los Angles *Times*, was on the eastbound train that John Clum boarded at Benson. He sent a letter to his paper, published on December 30, 1881, describing Clum's actions as the train stopped at the new railroad depot in the Cow-boy friendly town of Deming, New Mexico Territory. Gardiner said Clum looked "paler than ever before." The newspaperman continued, "He had been shot at the night previous and was the worst scared man I have ever seen for some time." Gardiner said that while stopped in Deming, Clum "crawled under a seat, tramp fashion, to keep the cowboys from raising his hair in case they happened to pass through the cars."

National newspapers carried stories of the stage attack for weeks after the event and then the drama just disappeared for the larger tale of the attacks upon the

Earp brother and Wyatt's ride for justice. Even Billy Breakenridge and Walter Noble Burns overlooked the attack in the books about early Tombstone. Wyatt had even forgot to tell Stuart Lake about the attempt on Clum's life. In Stuart Lake's papers is a letter dated January 24, 1929 from John Clum saying Jose Earp had asked him to see if he was interested in a "thrilling story" of the affair at Malcolm's Station. "It is so old it will be new—even to the old—times." Lake said yes and a happy John Clum sent the author old newspaper clippings and his own recollections in a letter and packet dated January 30, 1929.

8. During November 1881, the *Tombstone Daily Epitaph* and the *Tombstone Daily Nugget* newspapers each took notice of the attempts by Sheriff Behan to serve jury summons to prospective grand jury members. A close reading of the accounts suggest that the sheriff or his process servers attempted to select the persons to compose the panel. The newspapers reported the missed opportunities to serve pro–Earp backers and the extra effort expended to hunt down suspected Cow-boy backers. Judge Stilwell reprimanded the sheriff, in an open court session, on this apparent attempt to "pack" the jury and ordered him to serve all the summons or be held in contempt of court. The Cochise County Grand Jury, randomly selected by lot from the prospect list, was empanelled on Tuesday, November 22, 1881.

Over the years, Cow-boy supporters have claimed the Grand Jury was composed of a majority of pro–Earp supporters. Carl Chafin is given due credit for the research done on the membership of the Grand Jury panel. The seven names listed in this paragraph with an * behind their name are known to have been in Tombstone's pro–Earp business faction. These seventeen Grand Jury members were, (1) Lewis W. Blinn, lumber dealer*; (2) Charles W. Harwood, tinsmith; (3) Edmond A. Harley, bookkeeper; (4) D. R. M. Thompson, harness maker; (5) Max Marks, clerk; (6) Taliaferro F. Hudson, pharmacist; (7) Abraham A. Barnett, merchant; (8) William A. Harwood, lumber dealer*; (9) David Calisher, merchant; (10) John D. Kinnear, farmer and former stage line operator*; (11) Rudolph A Cohen, merchant; (12) Oscar F. Thornton, newspaperman*; (13) Sylvester B. Comstock, co-owner of Grand Hotel (former chairman of county Democrat Party)*; (14) Thomas R. Sorin, mining speculator*; (15) Marshall Williams, Wells Fargo agent*; (16) Frederick Restig, miner, and (17) George W. Buford, trader.

A side note to the men named above, David Calisher was suspected of arson at his Allen Street store on 03 March 1882. The fire was a great treat to the Tombstone business district, but quick action by volunteer firefighters saved the town.

9. When Wyatt Earp began his Cow-boy campaign, Will McLaury may have had cause to rethink paying for any more attempts upon the lives of the Earp brothers. McLaury wrote his father about the Tombstone tragedy saying, "My experience out there has been very unfortunate as to my health and badly injured me as to money matters—and none of the results have been satisfactory." He also wrote the Tombstone troubles were "...a matter we ought to think about as little as possible."

The premature death of his wife and the killing of his two younger brothers a few months later had left W. R. McLaury a bitter man. One must wonder did

he ever stop thinking about the Tombstone events. Did Will McLaury really relegate those bloody months to history and move on with his own life?

10. In 1929, Stuart N. Lake located the long forgotten handwritten court reporter's record of the Spicer Hearing of the Tombstone streetfight in the fall of 1881. In the 1930s, Howell Pat Hayhurst produced a typescript of court reporter Fred W. Craig's handwritten Streetfight Inquest and Spicer Hearing documents as part of a Federal Works Progress Administration preservation project. In June 1951, Stuart N. Lake give this document to the Tombstone *Epitaph* for safekeeping. In February 1975, Tombstone historian Al Turner acquired this 60-page document when the newspaper ceased publication. Over forty years ago, I bought a copy of the document owned by Lake-*Epitaph*-Turner. Over the years the typescript had acquired margin notes written by Hayhurst, Turner, and Glenn Boyer; after I bought the document I added my own notes. Someone pasted clippings from the *Epitaph*'s courtroom testimony to the back of the typescript page containing that person's testimony.

In March 1966, a letter from Robert Mullin was published in *Frontier Times* claiming he owned a copy the Hayhurst Typescript he had typed from the original owned by Stuart Lake. I searched for that document for years and finally located it in Texas. In September 2001, I traded the Haley Library and History Center a copy of my Hayhurst Typescript for a copy of their variant Hayhurst Typescript once owned by Robert Mullin and now contained in his papers housed in the special collections at the Haley. The two versions of the document contain differences in verbal use and style.

11. In February 1937, Josie Earp, along with Vinolia Ackerman and her husband, made an nostalgic return to Tombstone. Her youthful recollections are discussed in her autobiography and one remark is of special interest. Looking down Fifth Street from Allen Street, Josie wrote she could sees the "crumbling adobe building in which Mrs. Young had her hotel—where I had met Mr. and Mrs. Tom Fitch—and had nursed Senator Hearst." It is unclear what kind of nursing Hearst may have required that Miss Marcus was trained to handle. Was she ill during his Tombstone trip?

In 1881–1882, Lucy Young operated the Palace Lodging House on the site Josie described. The building escaped distraction during the big fire in June 1882. only to fall into disrepair. Was this lodging place Josie Marcus' residence after she moved out of the house she had shared with Johnny Behan and his young son?

12. John Boessenecker, a California attorney, has done extensive research on Jonathan N. Thacker. This former Nevada sheriff turned express company detective who ended his illustrious career as Wells Fargo's chief special agent, is a person who has yet to receive full recognition for his skills. Thacker's most famous cases were the arrest of the stage robber Black Bart in California and the 1899 shootout at Turkey Creek Canyon near Cimarron, New Mexico against the Tom "Black Jack" Ketchum Gang.

13. Col. William Herring lost his son and law partner, Howard, to a tragic death on October 31, 1891. The 27-year-old attorney died from complications of a cocaine dose used to numb the young man so he could have some teeth extracted. The father never got over the lose of his son who was a rising star in the Cochise County Bar Association and leader in St. Paul's

Episcopal Church. Young Herring was buried in the new Tombstone City Cemetery. His sister marked the grave site in 1922. Col. Herrington would become the Chancellor of the University of Arizona.

Chapter 9

1. The Tucson depot and the railroad yard where Sheriff Behan's deputy was dispatched have been restored as a regional tourist attraction and is now the location of the Southern Arizona Transportation Museum. On March 20, 2005, the museum unveiled a set of life-size statues depicting Wyatt and Doc, each carrying a shotgun, marking the Frank Stillwell killing.

2. Sheriff Behan's January–April 1882 financial records are in File 83, Box 08 of the Cochise County Records (MS 180) at the Arizona Historical Society Library, Tucson.

3. During his youthful years on the Kansas plains, in the cowtowns, on the gambling circuit, and in Tombstone, Wyatt Earp was known as a teetotaler. He did not drank hard liquor, but he did drink cider and beer. He was also remembered for his proper use of language and lack of swearing. Wyatt was known to enjoy a fine cigar and was constantly reading something. He often attended church services or camp meetings as well as vaudeville stage shows and theater presentations; especially comedy or Shakespeare. He was a gentleman who respected females, but he also accepted brothels and saloons as a necessary service, and a profitable business, in frontier country sparely populated with women.

Wyatt changed after the spring 1882 Cow-boy Campaign or Vendetta Ride and as he got older, and less wealthy, took to drinking hard liquor, swearing, and fell away from regular church attendance. However, during his later years in the 1920s he reverted to the Wyatt of his youth. Josie Earp wrote on page 102 of her memoir manuscript that Wyatt "drank very little at any time in his life" and "never cared for liquor so he had always left it alone, which may account in part for the fact that his nerves were always steady and his health sound."

Chapter 10

1. In the original version of Frank Waters' 1960 *Earp Brothers of Tombstone* written in 1936 and titled *Tombstone Travesty* contains a paragraph in Chapter 7 of Part Five, not used in the 1960 published book, because it contradicts Waters' belief that Wyatt Earp deserted Mattie Blaylock for Josie Marcus. In fact, in the original narrative Allie Earp explains that Mattie Blaylock had a quarrel with Wyatt after Morgan Earp's death and left him. Mattie never reconciled with Wyatt, and when it was safe she left the Earp family homestead in California, and returned to Arizona in the fall of 1882. She reconnected with Doc Holliday's friend Kate Elder at Globe and started a new adventure. Wyatt Earp sent Mattie money to help her get started in her new life and she continued to use the Earp name, but they never met again after Tombstone. The inquest report concerning Mattie's death provides the source for the claim that Wyatt had deserted her. Earp researcher Mrs. William Irvine located this report in 1958.

In *Earp Brothers*, Frank Waters has Allie Earp describe how Wyatt and Josie Marcus conducted an open love affair in Tombstone to the humiliation of Mattie Blaylock. This fictional narrative has discolored the Earp legend since 1960 when, in fact, Allie Earp never mentions knowing anything about an affair between Wyatt and Josie in Tombstone in the original draft of her story. She also knew nothing about Josie's relationship with Johnny Behan and makes very plain her displeasure with present day (late 1930s) Tombstone residents who believed that Josie Marcus had lived in Tombstone during the early 1880s.

In fact, the Earp sister-in-laws, Allie and Josie, were friendly during their husband's lifetime, even going on prospecting trips together along the Colorado River in the early 1900s and living in Goldfield, Nevada were the brothers were once again lawmen.

2. The meteorological records taken at Fort Bayard, 10-mile east of Silver City, New Mexico, for 1882 were published in the *Silver City Enterprise* on August 15, 1884. These records indicate that the region received 7.10 inches of rain from late July to mid–September 1882 and this has remained a long standing record for the region.

3. The *Tombstone Daily Epitaph*, March 7, 1882, reported this news from New Mexico, "We hear that a steam road wagon is to be put on between Silver City and Deming." It is unknown if this new vehicle was in service yet. If so, maybe the Earp posse had fun riding in this "modern" conveyance over the sandy landscape to Deming.

4. On 22 August 1882, *The Argus*, published in Melbourne, Australia, contained the third part of a lengthy account recounting the recent adventures of Archibald Forbes, a world traveler. In this installment the writer describes his visit to Deming and the wait for change of luggage and express between the Southern Pacific and Santa Fe. He also mentioned the shotgun carrying killer sheriff who patrolled the depot area.

5. The Santa Fe Railroad maintained its own dedicated telegraph line along side its tracks to communicated from station to station quickly. In late 2005, a briefly worded Western Union Telegraph Company press release went nearly unnoticed. It simply read: "Effective January 27, 2006, Western Union will discontinue all Telegram and Commercial Messaging Services. We regret any inconvenience this may cause you, and we thank you for your loyal patronage." After 155 years, and millions of telegrams and Telex messages, a major part of American history quietly slipped into obscurity. Cell phone text messaging and emails had come of age.

Chapter 12

1. The first public discussion concerning the "Otero Letter" took place on *B.J.'s Tombstone History Discussion Forum* (http://disc.server.com/discussion.cgi?disc=39627) between 2001–2005. This site draws a wide spectrum of readers and participants, both amateurs and seasoned researchers, historians, and writers. Most of the time the discussions are insightful and informative since radicals and inciters are not welcome on this board.

Chapter 14

1. Before his untimely death, our friend and fellow researcher Mark Dworkin took an interest in this

book project and located present day Henry Jaffa descendents, four great-great-grandchildren. They told him that within their branch of the family there is no collective memory of Wyatt Earp being a friend of their ancestor. Mark was quick to recognize this lack of family recollection could simply mean that the one child of Henry Jaffa who has present day descendents found no special childhood significance to an Earp connection to his family, and thus the memory of an Earp–Jaffa friendship was lost in the Jaffa family history.

This phenomenon, while surprising to present day readers given Wyatt Earp's modern stature, is more common then one would think. I was home for a college holiday when I accidentally learned that my father's seldom talked about Great-Uncle Gus had known Wyatt Earp. The men first met in Texas when Gus was serving as a ranger, later renewed their friendship in New Mexico Territory and in turn of the twentieth century Nevada. Together, as a family, we had watched the 1950s Wyatt Earp television show and both Mom and Dad had encouraged my interest in Earp and the frontier west, but never mentioned Uncle Gus in discussion of these interests. Now, a decade later, the conversation hit the subject of old family letters written by Uncle Gus discussing Wyatt Earp. My parents had not made the connection between the TV hero Wyatt Earp and Uncle Gus' letters from "out West" mentioning a man named Wyatt Earp.

My father, a modest man, had accompanied General John J. "Black Jack" Pershing chasing Poncho Villa around Mexico in 1916 and fighting Germans in France in 1917–1918, protected the Philippines in the early 1920s during the sugar cane rebellion, and later served as a federal officer chasing "prohibition badmen" in the Depression Era. Dad had made history as a decorated hero and in his sunset years he had little interest in famous relatives or of past family relationships with famous people. The knowledge of an Earp–Hornung "Old West frontier days" connection would have been lost to our family's heritage except for a fortuitous afternoon conversation. Dad also never discussed Michael Joseph (Joe) Hornung, an early professional baseball player. I have always been a major league baseball fan. Go Angels!

I later discovered another Earp–Hornung connection. Carl D. "Dick" Sutherland, Wyatt's nephew by marriage to his first wife, teamed up with Frederick "Fred" Horning (Hornung) and committed a series of robberies and murders reaching from Missouri to California, in the 1890s through the early teens of the 1900s.

2. Alexander L. Morrison, Sr., had been born in Ireland in 1832 and immigrated to the United States in time to see action in the war with Mexico. He fell in love with New Mexico the first time he saw the land. However before he settled in the land of enchantment he first settled in Chicago and served in the Illinois legislature. He became friends with powerful Republicans in congress and championed the cause of Hispanics. Morrison was a strong adherent of Catholicism. He made his namesake son his chief deputy and established his headquarters in Albuquerque.

NBC-TV broadcast a different style western as part of their 1959–60 Thursday night lineup. The hero was a Harvard educated Apache named Buck Heart who Americanized his name to Sam Buckhart (Michael Ansara) and became a deputy United States marshal working for Andy Morrison (Dayton Lummis) head-

quartered on the plaza at Santa Fe. Buckhart was the guardian of a young Anglo girl and his landlady acted as a sort of governess. The *Law of the Plainsmen* series was a spin off from two episodes of the ABC-TV series *The Rifleman* concerning a single father raising a young son on a ranch near North Fork, NM. The *Plainsman* series was built upon a foundation of truth as New Mexico's U.S. Marshal Morrison did have great affinity for Hispanics, Indians, and justice. The two shows ended each week with the hero explaining a life lesson to their youthful charge.

Chapter 15

1. Wyatt Earp was a voracious reader and it is very possible that he owned some of the popular history books written by Hubert Howe Bancroft. G. W. Caldwell, one of Bancroft's research assistants, interviewed Wyatt in San Diego in 1888. The Bancroft team also interviewed Virgil Earp at his Colton home that same year. In his notes on Wyatt, Caldwell wrote, "To him more than any other man is due the credit for driving out the banditti of that territory (Arizona)." He added, "Socially he could be taken for a Minister. He has a heart as big as an ox and feelings as tender as a child." In describing his physical characteristics Caldwell observed that Wyatt was as "quick as a cat." These Earp interview notes are housed in the research files of the Bancroft Library on the campus of the University of California at Berkeley.

Chapter 16

1. Colorado's Lt. Governor Horace A. Tabor owned a railroad line in the state. This railway was the central figure in a Lone Ranger radio adventure ("H.A.W. Tabor" #1781) broadcast on 19 June 1944 over the NBC Blue Network. The Masked Man and Tabor ride the rails and fight outlaws to deliver a gold shipment to the Denver mint. The script was written by Bob Green.

2. Walter A. Smith, a Republican, was confirmed by the United States Senate as chief federal marshal for the District of Colorado on 13 March 1882.

3. The official papers from the administration of Governor Frederick W. Pitkin (61–399) are housed in the Colorado State Archives at Denver. There are no records concerning Arizona Territory's extradition request or the governor's hearing concerning the case of John H. Holliday, DDS listed in the detailed Public Records Register for the governor's papers.

Chapter 17

1. Johnny Ringo would have loved that one day he would rate three major biographers and a handful of Western novels and untold articles, fact and fiction, to chronicle his restless life. Nevertheless, John would have really laughed about becoming an Old West motion picture and television folk hero.

On Thursday, October 1, 1959, Johnny Ringo made his greatest leap toward lasting fame as the sheriff at Velardi, Arizona, when his fictional adventures appeared as a 38-episode CBS-TV series with his name as the title. This was the first television series produced by the now legendary producer Aaron Spelling. The handsome songwriter-singer Don Durant, who died at age 72 in 2005, played Ringo during the series' one season run. In the show, he called his horse Bingo. Durant is seen on screen occasionally picking out tunes on a guitar and in the series' 12th episode, "Kid with a Gun," broadcast on Christmas Eve 1959, Ringo sings his original "Child's Prayer" to a young girl orphan he is assisting to locate her father's killer.

As was the convention in that era of TV westerns, Durant composed the words and merchandise tie-ins were numerous, among which was a half dozen toy pistol sets, a Transogram Company board game, a coloring book, a paint-by-number kit, a toy town playset and a special issue Dell comic.

The show's gimmick was that Ringo, an ex-gunfighter turned sheriff, carried a Civil War era LeMat handgun. The pistol was equipped with a single .410 shotgun barrel mounted under the regular barrel of his six-shot .45-caliber revolver. This "seven-shooter" assisted Ringo each week in taming Velardi, Arizona Territory. The real LeMat was a British made cap and ball pistol equipped with a nine-shot .36-caliber cylinder and front-load shotgun tub; TV westerns never let facts get in the way of a good story. The famous Confederate cavalry commander General J.E.B. Stuart carried one of 200 LaMat pistols used by the southern army.

The Ringo TV series writers gave a nod to the Earp brothers as Johnny examines a copy of a nickel western magazine called *Bad Men of the Plains* during Episode 25, "The Gunslinger," where Ringo recalls his early days as a fast draw killer. ABC-TV's Wyatt Earp had moved to Arizona Territory at the end of the 1958–1959 season and Johnny Ringo (Britt Lomond) showed up in Tombstone during the fall of 1960 after CBS-TV cancelled Durant's Ringo series.

In Durant's TV show, Sheriff Ringo was a highly cultured individual. In back-to-back episodes, the new sheriff quotes from the works of the 17th Century British philosopher Sir Francis Bacon and 14th Century Sir Geoffrey Chaucer's "The Canterbury Tales" of prose and verse. It is doubtful that real Ringo possessed little more than a basic rural backcountry education. The highly educated Johnny Ringo is the product of fiction writers' fertile imaginations.

2. Forrestine Cooper married Henry Hooker's son and they had a daughter they named Forrestine. The Hooker's divorced and the elder Forrestine left the ranch and remarried. The daughter Forrestine married a man named Tom Froelich who she later divorced in 1933 before leaving Los Angeles and returning to the Sierra Bonita Ranch. She became enamored with ranch foreman Jess Gatlin and married him in August 1934. The new husband killed his bride at Ajo, Arizona, on February 24, 1935, and then took his own life.

3. Most people in the twentieth century assumed that "Whispering Smith" was a fictional creation after reading Frank Hamilton Spearman's 1906 novel and seeing the silent era movie adventures based upon the book, most notably H.B. Warner's Smith portrayal in 1926. Alan Ladd brought the soft-spoken "Luke" Smith, railroad detective, to life in a 1948 Paramount Pictures color classic. A number of movies have featured a character like Smith.

In 1959, a production company filmed 26 episodes of a TV series called *Whispering Smith* based upon the adventures of Denver police detective "Tom" Smith starring real life World War II hero Audie Murphy, but due to production problems the show did not reach viewers for two years. NBC-TV did not broadcast the show's last six stories due to complaints concerning the series' violent content made before a Congressional hearing on crime and violence.

It has taken decades to separate fact from fiction, but recent discoveries have added more information to the public knowledge of the real frontier life of James L. "Whispering" Smith. Thanks to Allen P. Briston's 2007 book we now know Smith was a peace officer in Wyoming, Nebraska and Colorado before spending a short time in New Mexico Territory.

4. The 25-year-old Cipriano Baca married Mary Linda Keefe, often called Marie, the 19-year-old daughter of Dr. Thomas and Kate Keefe, in Deming on Saturday, March 19, 1887. Keefe was Irish born and educated, while his wife was a native of New York State. The couple had migrated to California in the late 1860s and lived in the San Francisco Bay area where Keefe worked attending the troops stationed at the Presidio. In the 1870s, Keefe moved his family to Winters in Yolo County, about 15 miles north of Vacaville, where he operated as a druggist. It is here that Baca and his future wife first encountered each other. Keefe traveled the northwest and Trains-Sierra country seeking new business fields, including the infamous mining town of Bodie. Keefe served a few days in the Bodie jail because of a domestic dispute and soon left the Trains-Sierra Country in search of new adventure fallowing the Southern Pacific Railroad construction crews working eastward from California across Nevada to Arizona. This type of transient practice could be adventurous, but not always lucrative, so these "doctors" often had a second profession.

In the spring of 1882, Thomas Keefe opened an office on Pine Street in the new frontier settlement of Deming, New Mexico. He advertised a business card that said he was a "Physician and Surgeon" and that his office had "A supply of drugs and chemicals on hand." Keefe shared his office space with P. J. McGrath, a building constructor. McGrath's son Herbert would become a highly effective sheriff of Grant County and a captain of the New Mexico Mounted Police.

After the 1883 fire that destroyed his office, Doctor Keefe established his new facility on Gold Avenue next to the William Drug Store. The Keefe family was prominent in Deming society by late 1884. However, it would seem that Baca's father-in-law never lost his wanderlust. From time to time, he would seek business deals and employment that offered a high rate of return for his efforts. A short time after Marie's wedding; the Keefe family left Deming for the west coast.

It is worth noting that on October 26, 1881, a man using the name Thomas Keefe had been a witness to key events surrounding the deadly fight on Fremont Street near the back entrance to the O.K. Corral in Tombstone, Arizona. The Earp brothers—Chief of Police Virgil and his deputy brothers Wyatt and Morgan—assisted by special policeman Dr. John H. Holliday had attempted to arrest members of the Cow-boy gang. The encounter ended in the death of three of the suspected troublemakers, Tom and Frank McLaury and Billy Clanton, and the wounding of all the peace officers except Wyatt. This deadly, failed-arrest attempt spawned a series of killings that still cause heated debate among historians and Wild West enthusiast studying southeastern Arizona's rustler troubles and border depredations during the early 1880s.

Tombstone's Thomas Keefe was summoned, on Thursday, November 10th to testify at the preliminary hearing to determine if the city lawmen should be held for trial on a murder charge resulting from the exchange of bullets. In the aftermath of Tombstone's Fremont Street fiasco, Thomas Keefe assisted Dr. Nelson S. Gilberson with his initial examination of Billy Clanton and then later gave a detailed description of the Cow-boy's wounds at the Justice of the Peace hearing. He next helped Dr. William Miller as he injected Clanton with two shots of morphine to ease the dying man's pain. Keefe later seconded the county coroner, Dr. Henry Matthews, with his attempt to make the fatally wounded Tom McLaury comfortable during his final moments. The Tombstone "carpenter" had, in some manner, assisted all three doctors who attended to the Cow-boy wounded on that bloody Wednesday afternoon in late October 1881.

The Tombstone business directories of 1881 and 1882 list a "Keefe & Co, liquor saloon, 412 Allen," while an 1883 directory does not list the Keefe saloon, but has Keefe as a carpenter. He was a witness to Mrs. Mary Woodman shooting William Kinsman, an Englishman, in front of the Oriental Saloon and testified at he Coroner's Inquest held in February 1883.

Was the early 1880s Tombstone saloonkeeper and/or carpenter the same man who was a respected physician in early Deming? Did this man then become Baca's father-in-law? The known facts provide a tight timeline into which the actions of the Tombstone Keefe and the Deming Keefe could be judged as being the same individual. The jury of historical fact is still considering these questions. I discuss this issue in more depth in my 2013 biography of Cipriano Baca.

5. In her memoirs Jose Earp recalled, on page 170 of the manuscript, that her husband had a forgiving nature, "Wyatt was a nature that harbored no ill feeling toward anyone, even those who had done him real injury." However, Earp's employer Wells Fargo was a determined foe. The *Silver City* (NM) *Enterprise*, on March 6, 1885, published a story about the express company's determination to eradicate road agents and highwaymen operating in their business area. The account said that Wells Fargo & Company had suffered $415,312.55 in shipment losses in 378 stages and trains robbers during its 14 years in business and had spent $512,414.00 in reward money and posse expenses during the same period. The express company's efforts to assist law enforcement resulted in 240 court convictions or a three-fifths offender captured or killed ratio. It is not difficult to believe that if Wells Fargo wanted John Ringo out of business, he would be put out of business.

6. Corner's jury member Robert M. Bollier had witnessed Wyatt Earp's actions defending accused murderer Johnny-Behind-the-Deuce from a rumpus "band of concerned individuals" in Tombstone in January 1881.

7. When I was in my late 20s, I was able to purchase a first edition of Walter Noble Burn's *Tombstone*. The book came with a letter written in February 1928 by Wyatt Earp to his Missouri cousin George Washington Earp, who sometimes claimed that his middle name was Wyatt, discussing the Burn book and containing the often-quoted comment that

Wyatt's favorite city was San Francisco. In his imaginative 1976 book about the life of Josie Marcus, Glenn Boyer implies in a footnote that my Earp to Earp letter is in his collection. I had given him a copy. In August 1972, John Gilchriese tried to buy the letter. I still have the book and the letter.

George Earp lived an interesting life. He was a founder of Ulysses, Kansas where he served as mayor and constable. He was involved in the countyseat "war" to make Ulysses host to the new county government and later served as county clerk. In 1893, Earp moved his wife and three young children to Wichita where is served as deputy US marshal and as an agent of the US Revenue Service. In the early 1930s, George Earp served two years in the Kansas State Penitentiary for a "Crime against Nature (sodomy)" with several under legal age girls. He spent his last years living in Joplin, Missouri where he spent over two decades as a tax consultant. George fell under the spell of the late 1950s Wyatt Earp craze and provided *Reader's Digest* with a fantasy account of his working with Wyatt in Dodge City when he was a boy. He died just before Christmas in 1960 at age 96. George and Anna Earp are buried in Wichita's Maple Grove Cemetery.

8. The only time that Josie witnessed Wyatt use his pistol with lethal results, other then killing rattlesnakes at their desert mining camps, was in 1917 when he shot a very large bull that was charging their new automobile. Wyatt and Josie where driving up the road to John Clum's 20-acre date farm at Indio, California when they encountered the animal. The bull had already smashed the car's radiator in his first attack and was now set to do battle with the door on Josie's side of the vehicle. Wyatt dropped the bovine with one shot and Josie fainted in the front seat. When Clum heard the story from his foreman, he just roared with laughter. Did the one time Tombstone mayor hold a barbeque in the bull's honor?

It is hard for some present-day western romantics to picture the "Lion of Tombstone" driving an automobile or dueling with a bull like a matador. In her memoirs, Josie wrote about her husband's automobile. "He bought only one car in his life, and although it was an expensive make and though he learned to drive it in an indifferent manner, he took little pleasure in it."

Chapter 18

1. I depended upon *The Language of Judaism* by Rabbi Simon Galustrom, *Judaism* edited by Arthur Hertzberg, and the National Jewish Center of Learning and Leaderships (CLAL)'s *The Book of Jewish Sacred Practices* for a basic understanding of the Jewish faith and its customs and traditions. CLAL represents all denominations of Judaism and has the mission to help keep the Jewish faith relevant in the twenty-first century. Our friend the late Mark Dworkin was very helpful explaining contemporary practices of non–Israeli Jewish believers to me.

The Jewish Study Bible (1999 edition) was consulted for understanding the Hebrew scriptures used in this work. The Jewish Publication Society, utilizing the society's *Tanakh* translation of 1985, was published by Oxford University Press in 2004 as a commentary and verse by verse study guide for the Hebrew scriptures.

2. "Wyatt admired good-looking women, enjoyed the company of intelligent women," recalled Josie Earp on page 169 for her memoirs manuscript. "While I was proud when women noticed my husband and wanted him to meet sincere admiration with the proper courtesy, I realized that he was human and that not all of the attention with which they showered him were sprung from unmixed motives. I was fearful at times that some of the cleverly masked little feminine campaigns which I, being a woman, was quick to discern, might not meet with defeat." She added, "I was very young." Maybe she was recalling how she had once described Wyatt, "Added to the glamour of his background, he was in no way unattractive. Tall, and with a trim, erect figure, he always dressed neatly though inconspicuously." He was also prosperous and carried a mantle of fame about himself.

On the next page of her memoirs Josie wrote, "Jealousy and suspicion can create havoc in the human heart, indeed, in the whole body and they can ruin the loveliest disposition. Like any evil emotion they harm most the one who harbors them. I was some time in learning this, but the knowledge saved me such pain as well as to establish a wonderful bond between my husband and myself." Wyatt and Josie endured two separations during their long relationship due to the things she expressed, cloaked in proper Victorian language, in her remembrances.

3. In his book on the Earp brothers Frank Waters uses Wyatt Earp's New Testament as a means of attacking him as a hypocrite and the men who gave the testament to him as pranksters. Neil Carmony's *NOLA Journal* article on the subject continues in that dark vain. However, an in-depth examination of the men who presented Wyatt with the testament provides a more accrete assessment of the gift and the religious nature of the men who gave the book. Mattie Blaylock must have understood the sentiment Wyatt attached to the gift because she kept the testament during her darkest hours of drugged depression.

4. Dan L. Thrapp discussed Wyatt's return to church life as a senior citizen in his article titled "Religious Life of Wyatt Earp Told" published in the *Los Angeles Times* of 24 July 1955

5. I admit that it is speculative day dreaming on my part, but a few verses in the eleventh chapter of the second epistle the missionary Paul wrote Christian believers in Corinth addresses Wyatt Earp's Cow-boy roundup. One can envision Wyatt setting on his front porch, a cat resting in his lap, reading his parallel renderings of his new "modern language" translation of scriptures and reflecting on his Cow-boy Campaign. Dr. Moffatt translated the Greek text thus, "I have been in danger from rivers and robbers, in danger from Jews and Gentiles, through dangers of town and of desert, through dangers on the sea, through dangers among false brothers—through labour and hardship, through many a sleepless night, through hunger and thirst, starving many a time, cold and ill-clad, and all the rest. And then there is the passing business of each day."

6. John Ford often told his version of knowing Wyatt Earp and how the old marshal gave him the information about the stagecoach racing by during the OK Corral fight. Ford told the story to Henry Fond, co-host with John Wayne and James Stewart of a television special on the famous motion picture director's career, on film. The documentary, "The American West of John Ford," was broadcast on CBS-TV on December 5, 1971. Today, even amateur historians know that Ford's stories concerning Wyatt Earp are fables or at best very, very tall tales. The show is available on DVD or free viewing on the YouTube website.

7. The booklet *Lashon Hara: The Evil Tongue* by Dean and Susan Wheelock is the source for understanding this Jewish principle that any spoken or written word, or expression of the body, that causes another person to be hurt in any way is wrong. A friend of mine once classified the Book of Proverbs as Jewish bumper stickers. Proverbs 18:21 says, "Death and life are in the power of the tongue, and those who love it will eat its fruit."

Chapter 19

1. The comments of John S. Mosby, the Gray Ghost, are taken from the Comments of John S. Mosby, the Gray Ghost, are taken from *The Letters of John S. Mosby*, edited by Adele H. Mitchell for the Stuart-Mosby Historical Society in 1986.

Bibliography

Primary Books: New Mexico

Bartlett, Edward L. (Attorney General). *Compiled Laws of New Mexico 1884*. Santa Fe: New Mexican, 1885.

Catron, T.B., and W.T. Thornton, comp. *Railroad Laws of New Mexico*. Santa Fe: New Mexican Job Printing, 1881.

Chase, C.M. *The Editor's Run: New Mexico and Colorado in 1881*. Montpelier, VT: Argus and Patriot Steam Book and Job Printing House, 1882.

Dawson, William D. *New Mexico in 1876–1877: A Newspaperman's View*. Compiled and edited by Robert J. Torrez. Los Ranchos, NM: Rio Grande, 2007.

Kingsbury, John M. *Trading in Santa Fe: John M. Kingsbury's Correspondence with James Josiah Webb, 1853–1861*. Edited by Jane Lenz Elder and David J. Weber. Dallas: Southern Methodist University Press, 1996.

Otero, Miguel Antonio. *My Life on the Frontier, 1864–1882: Incidents and Characters of the Period When Kansas, Colorado, and New Mexico Were Passing Through the Last of Their Wild and Romantic Years*. New York: Press of the Pioneers, 1935.

_____. *My Life on the Frontier, 1882–1897: Death Knell of a Territory and Birth of a State*. Albuquerque: University of New Mexico Press, 1939.

_____. *My Nine Years as Governor of the Territory of New Mexico, 1897–1906*. Albuquerque: University of New Mexico Press, 1940.

Porter, Henry M. *Penciling of an Early Western Pioneer*. Denver: World, 1929.

Ritch, W.G. *The Legislative Blue Book of the Territory of New Mexico, 1882*. Facsimile. Albuquerque: University of New Mexico Press, 1968.

Robertson, Nancy, ed. *Colfax County Roots: Cemetery and Probate Records*. Raton, NM: Friends of Raton Anthropology, 1980.

_____. *Index [to] Marriage Records, Colfax County, NM, 1869–1905*. Raton, NM: Arthur Johnson Memorial Library, 1980.

Tice, Henry Allen. *Early Railroad Days in New Mexico, 1880*. Santa Fe: Stagecoach, 1965.

Ward, Margaret. *Cimarron Saga*. Private printing: c 1965.

_____. *Cousins by the Dozens*. Private printing: c 1966.

Primary Books: Arizona and Other Areas

Bell, Susan Groag, and Karen M. Offen. *Women, the Family, and Freedom: The Debate in Documents*. Vol. 1, 1750–1880. Stanford, CA: Stanford University Press, 1983.

Berlin, Adele, and Marc Zvi Brettler, ed. *The Jewish Study Bible*. Oxford, NY: Oxford University Press, 2004.

Boessenecker, John. *When Law Was in the Holster: The Frontier Life of Bob Paul*. Norman: University of Oklahoma Press, 2012.

Breakenridge, William M. *Helldorado: Bring the Law to the Mesquite*. Ghostwritten by William MacLeod Raine. Boston: Houghton Mifflin, 1928.

Brown, Clara Spalding. *Tombstone from a Woman's Point of View: The Correspondence of Clara Spalding Brown, July 7, 1880 to November 14, 1882*. Edited by Lynn R. Bailey. Tucson: Westernlore, 1998.

Cook (General), David J. *Hands Up!; or, Twenty Years of Detective Work in the Mountains and on the Plains*. Denver: W.F. Robinson, 1897.

Dodge, Fred. *Undercover for Wells Fargo: The Unvarnished Recollections of Fred Dodge*. Edited by Carolyn Lake. Boston: Houghton Mifflin, 1969.

Dun, R.G. *The Mercantile Agency Reference Book; Containing Ratings of the Merchants, Manufactures, and Traders Generally Through the United States and Canada*. Vol. 85. New York: R.G. Dun, July 1889.

Earp, Josephine. *She Married Wyatt Earp*. Edited by Karl Chafin. Riverside, CA: Earl Chafin, 1998.

_____. *She Married Wyatt Earp*. As told to Mable Earp Cason and Vinolia Earp Ackerman. Compiled by Glenn Boyer. Rodeo, NM: Historical Research Associates, 1999.

Earp, Wyatt S. *Wyatt Earp*. Recorded by John Henry Flood, Jr., 1926. Edited by Glenn G. Boyer. Sierra Vista, AZ: Yoma V. Bissette, 1981.

_____. *Wyatt Earp's Personal Diagrams of Prominent Historical Events*. Compiled by John D. Gilchriese. McLean, VA: United States Marshals Foundation, 1989.

Gray, John Plesent. *When All Roads Led to Tombstone: A Memoir*. Edited and annotated by W. Lane Rogers. Boise, ID: Tamarack, 1998.

Hand, George O. *Next Stop, Tombstone: George Hand's*

Contention City Diary, 1882. Edited by Neil B. Carmony. Tucson: Trail to Yesterday, 1995.

_____. *Whiskey, Six-guns and Red-light Ladies: George Hand's Saloon Diary, Tucson, 1875–1878.* Edited by Neil B. Carmony. Silver City, NM: High-Lonesome, 1994.

History of King Solomon [F & A Masonic] Lodge #5, Tombstone, Arizona. Np, 2003.

King, Martin Luther, Jr. *Strength to Love.* New York: Harper & Row, 1963.

Kula (Rabbi), Irwin, and Vanessa L. Ochs, ed. *The Book of Jewish Sacred Practices: CLAL'S [National Jewish Center for Learning and Leadership] Guide to Everyday and Holiday Rituals and Blessings.* Woodstock, VT: Jewish Light, 2001.

Martin, Douglas D., ed. *The Earps of Tombstone.* Tombstone: Tombstone Epitaph, 1959.

_____. *Tombstone's Epitaph: The Truth About "The Town Too Tough To Die."* Albuquerque: University of New Mexico Press, 1951.

Masterson, W.B. "Bat." *Frontier Gunfighters of the Western Frontier.* Annotated by Jack DeMattos. Monroe, WA: Weatherford, 1982.

Mosby, John S. *The Letters of John S. Mosby.* Edited by Adele H. Mitchell. Warrenton, VA: Stuart-Mosby Historical Society, 1986.

Parsons, George W. *The Devil Has Foreclosed: The Private Journal of George Whitwell Parsons; The Concluding Arizona Years, 1882–1887.* Edited by Lynn R. Bailey. Tucson: Westernlore, 1967.

_____. *The Private Journal of George W. Parsons.* Tombstone, AZ: Tombstone Epitaph, 1972. Reprint of a mimeographed book by Arizona WPA Project, 1939.

_____. *A Tenderfoot in Tombstone: The Private Journal of George Whitwell Parsons; The Turbulent Years, 1880–1882.* Edited by Lynn R. Bailey. Tucson: Westernlore, 1966.

Peabody, Endicott. *A Church for Helldorado: The 1882 Tombstone Diary of Endicott Peabody.* Edited by S.J. Reidhead. Roswell, NM: Roswell, 2006.

The Prayer Book: Weekday, Sabbath and Festival. Translated and edited by Rabbi Ben Zion Bokser. Springfield, NJ: Behrman House, 1983.

Richardson, James D., ed. *A Compilation of the Messages and Papers of the Presidents, 1789–1897.* Vol. 8, *Chester A. Arthur and Grover Cleveland.* Washington, D.C.: Government Printing Office, 1898.

Stephen, W. *Report for Congress: Federal Holidays, Evolution and Application, February 8, 1999* (98–301). Washington: Congressional Research Service, Library of Congress, 1999.

Stephens, John Richard, ed. *Wyatt Earp Speaks!* Cambria Pines by the Sea, CA: Fren Canyon, 1998.

Turner, Alford, ed. *The Earps Talk.* College Station, TX: Creative, 1982.

Walling, Emma, ed. *John "Doc" Holliday: Colorado Trails and Triumphs.* Told from old Colorado newspapers. Snowmass, CO: Private Printing, 1994.

Secondary Books: New Mexico

Alexander, Bob. *Dangerous Dan Tucker: New Mexico's Deadly Lawman.* Silver City, NM: High-Lonesome, 2001.

_____. *Sheriff Harvey Whitehill: Silver City Stalwart.* Silver City, NM: High-Lonesome, 2005.

Atheaon, Robert. *Rebel of the Rockies: A History of the Denver and Rio Grande Railroad.* New Haven: Yale University Press, 1962.

Ball, Larry D. *Desert Lawmen: The High Sheriffs of New Mexico and Arizona, 1846–1912.* Albuquerque: University of New Mexico, 1992.

_____. *The United States Marshals of New Mexico and Arizona Territories, 1846–1912.* Albuquerque: University of New Mexico Press, 1978.

Bancroft, Hubert Howe. *Bancroft's Works.* Vol 17, *Arizona and New Mexico, 1530–1888.* San Francisco: History, 1889.

Beck, Warren A., and Ynez D. Haase. *Historical Atlas of New Mexico.* Norman: University of Oklahoma Press, 1969.

Bryan, Howard. *Albuquerque Remembered.* Albuquerque: University of New Mexico Press, 2006.

Caffey, David. *Chasing the Santa Fe Ring: Power and Privilege in Territorial New Mexico.* Albuquerque: University of New Mexico Press, 2014.

Chappell, Gordon. *To Santa Fe by Narrow Gauge: The D and RG's "Chili Line."* Denver: Colorado Rail Annual, 1969.

Christiansen, Paige W. *The Story of Mining in New Mexico.* Socorro: New Mexico Bureau of Mines and Mineral Resources, 1974.

Cleveland, Norman. *A Synopsis of the Great New Mexico Cover-Up.* Private, 1989.

Deutsch, Sarah. *No Separate Refuge: Culture, Class, and Gender on an Anglo-Hispanic Frontier in the American Southwest, 1880–1940.* New York: Oxford University Press, 1987.

Fergusson, Erna. *Erna Fergusson's Albuquerque.* Albuquerque: Merle Armitage, 1947.

Fleming, Elvis E., and Ernestine Chesser Williams. *Treasures of History III: Southeastern New Mexico People, Places, and Events.* Roswell: Historical Society for Southeast New Mexico, 1995.

Gjevre, John A. *Chili Line: The Narrow Rail Trail to Santa Fe.* Espanola, NM: Las Trampas, 1884.

Grove, Pearce S., Becky J. Barnett, and Sandra J. Hansen, ed. *New Mexico Newspapers: A Comprehensive Guide to Bibliographical Entries and Locations.* Albuquerque: University of New Mexico Press, 1975.

Hatley, Allen. *Open Pit Porphyry Copper Mines and Other Grant County (NM) Treasures.* Private, 2009.

Hertzoz, Peter. *La Fonda: The Inn of Santa Fe.* Portales, NM: Bishop, 1962.

Horn, Calvin. *New Mexico's Troubled Years: The Story of the Early Territorial Governors.* Albuquerque: Horn & Wallace, 1963.

Inman, Henry. *The Old Santa Fe Trail: The Story of a Great Highway.* Topeka: Crane, 1916.

Janin, Hunt, and Ursula Carlson. *Trails of Historic New Mexico: Routes Used by Indians, Spanish and American Travelers Through 1886.* Jefferson, NC: McFarland, 2010.

Julyan, Robert. *The Place Names of New Mexico.* Albuquerque: University of New Mexico, 1996.

Langston, LaMoine. *A History of Masonry in New Mexico, 1877–1977.* Roswell: Hall-Poorbaugh, 1977.

Lehmann, Terry Jon. *Santa Fe and Albuquerque, 1870–1900: Contrast and Conflict in the Development of Two Southwest Towns.* Ann Arbor: University of Michigan Press, 1974.

Melendez, A. Gabriel. *Spanish-Language Newspapers in New Mexico, 1834–1958.* Tucson: University of Arizona Press, 2005.

Myrick, David F. *New Mexico Railroads: A Historical Survey.* Golden: Colorado Railroad Museum, 1970.

Poldervaart, Arie W. *Black-Robed Justice.* Santa Fe: Historical Society of New Mexico, 1948.

Riskin, Marci L. *The Train Stops Here: New Mexico's Railway Legacy.* Albuquerque: University of New Mexico Press, 2005.

Sherman, James E., and Barbara H. Sherman. *Ghost Towns and Mining Camps of New Mexico.* Norman: University of Oklahoma Press, 1975.

_____. *Ghost Towns of Arizona.* Norman: University of Oklahoma Press, 1969.

Stanley, F. [Stanley Francis Louis Crocchiola]. *The Duke City: The Story of Albuquerque, New Mexico, 1706–1956.* Pampa, TX: Pampa Print Shop, 1963.

_____. *The Grant That Maxwell Bought.* Denver: World, 1952.

_____. *"Raton Chronicle."* Denver: World, 1948.

_____. *Socorro: The Oasis.* Denver: World, 1950.

Stratton, Porter A. *Territorial Press of New Mexico, 1834–1912.* Albuquerque: University of New Mexico Press, 1969.

Tanner, Karen Holliday, and John D. Tanner, Jr. *Directory of Inmates, New Mexico Territorial Penitentiary, 1884–1912.* Fallbrook, CA: Runnin' Iron, 2006.

Tobias, Dr. Henry J. *A History of the Jews in New Mexico.* Albuquerque: University of New Mexico Press, 1990.

Tobias (Dr.), Henry J., and Sarah R. Payne. *Jewish Pioneers of New Mexico: The Ilfeld and Nordhaus Families.* Albuquerque: New Mexico Jewish Historical Society, 2005.

Tobias (Dr.), Henry J., and Tomas Jaehn. *Jewish Pioneers of New Mexico.* Santa Fe: Museum of New Mexico Press, 2003.

Twitchell, Ralph Emerson. *The Leading Facts of New Mexican History.* Vol. 2. Cedar Rapids, IA: Torch, 1912.

Unger, Patti, comp. and ed. *True Tales.* Vol. 1, 1882–1883. Articles from the "Silver City Enterprise." Silver City: NM: SunDog, 1991.

Walker, Mike. *Railroad Atlas of North America: Arizona and New Mexico.* Faversham, Kent, England: Steam Powered, 1995.

Westphall, Victor. *Thomas Benton Catron and His Era.* Tucson, University of Arizona Press, 1973.

Secondary Books: Arizona and Other Areas

Ackerman, Rita K. *O.K. Corral Postscript: The Death of Ike Clanton.* Honolulu: Talei, 2007.

Alexander, Bob. *John H. Behan: Sacrificed Sheriff.* Silver City, NM: High-Lonesome, 2002.

Aros, Joyce. *In Defense of the Outlaws.* Tombstone, AZ: Goose Flats Graphics, 2008.

Ashdown, Paul, and Edward Caudill. *Mosby Myth: A Confederate Hero in Life and Legend.* Wilmington, DE: Scholarly Resources, 2002.

Bailey, Lynn R. *Henry Clay Hooker and the Sierra Bonita.* Tucson: Westernlore, 1998.

_____. *A Tale of the "Unkilled": The Life, Times, and Writings of Wells W. Spicer.* Tucson: Westernlore, 1999.

_____. *The Valiants: The Tombstone Rangers and Apache War Frivolities.* Tucson: Westernlore, 1999.

Bailey, Lynn R., and Don Chaput. *Cochise County Stalwarts: A Who's Who of the Territorial Years.* 2 vols. Tucson: Westernlore, 2000.

Barra, Allen. *Inventing Wyatt Earp: His Life and Many Legends.* New York: Carroll & Graf, 1998.

Bartholomew, Ed. *Wyatt Earp, 1848–1880: The Untold Story.* Toyahvale, TX: Frontier Book, 1963.

_____. *Wyatt Earp, 1879–1882: The Man and the Myth.* Toyahvale, TX: Frontier, 1964.

Bederman, Gail. *Manliness and Civilization: A Cultural History of Gender and Race in the United States, 1880–1917.* Chicago: University of Chicago Press, 1995.

Bell, Bob Boze. *The Illustrated Life and Times of Doc Holliday.* Phoenix: Tri-Star Boze, 1994.

Borneman, Walter R. *Marshall Pass: Denver and Rio Grande Gateway to the Gunnison Country.* Colorado Springs: Century One, 1980.

_____. *Rival Rails: The Race to Build America's Greatest Transcontinental Railroad.* New York: Random House, 2010.

Boyer, Glenn G. *Suppressed Murder of Wyatt Earp.* San Antonio, TX: Naylor, 1967.

Boyer, Glenn G., ed. *Wyatt Earp: Family, Friends and Foes.* Vol.5, "Who Killed John Ringo," by Josephine Earp. Rodeo, NM: Historical Research Associates, 1997.

Brand, Peter. *The Life and Crimes of Perry Mallon.* Meadowbank, Australia: Np., 2006.

Brooks, Tim, and Earle March. *The Complete Directory to Prime Time Network and Cable TV Shows, 1946–Present.* 6th edition. New York: Ballantine, 1995.

Burns, Walter Noble. *Tombstone: An Iliad of the Southwest.* New York: Doubleday, 1927.

Burrows, Jack. *Johnny Ringo: The Gunfighter Who Never Was.* Tucson, University of Arizona Press, 1987.

Cahn, Yehuda. *Like a Reed: The Message of the Mezuza.* Baltimore: Private, 1994.

Calhoun, Frederick S. *The Lawmen: United States Marshals and Their Deputies, 1789–1989.* Washington, D.C.: Smithsonian Institution Press, 1989.

Cox, William R. *Luke Short and His Era: A Biography of One of the West's Most Famous Gamblers.* Garden City, NY: Doubleday, 1961.

DeArment, Robert K. *Bat Masterson: The Man and the Legend.* Norman: University of Oklahoma Press, 1979.

_____. *Broadway Bat: Gunfighter in Gotham; The New York City Years of Bat Masterson.* Honolulu, Talei, 2005.

_____. *Knights of the Green Cloth: The Saga of the Frontier Gamblers.* Norman: University of Oklahoma Press, 1982.

Degregorio, William A. *The Complete Book of U.S. Presidents, from George Washington to George W. Bush.* Revised and up-dated. New York: Barnes & Noble, 2004.

Dobson, John M. *Politics in the Gilded Age.* New York: Praeger, 1972.

Ellickson, Robert C. *Order Without Law: How Neighbors Settled Disputes.* Cambridge: Harvard University Press, 1991.

Fattig, Timothy W. *Wyatt Earp: The Biography*. Honolulu, Talei, 2003.

Fierman, Floyd S. *Guts and Ruts: The Jewish Pioneer on the Trail in the American Southwest*. New York: Ktav, 1985.

Fisher, Ron W. *The Jewish Pioneers of Tombstone and Arizona Territory*. Tombstone: Ron W. Fisher, 2002.

Fisher, Ron W., ed. *The Tombstone Business Directory, 1880–1884*. Ron W. Fisher, 2002.

Galustrom, Simon. *The Language of Judaism*. New York: Jonathan David, 1966.

Gatto, Steve. *Alias Curly Bill: The Life and Times of William Brocius*. Lansing, MN: Private, 2000.

_____. *Curly Bill: Tombstone's Most Famous Outlaw*. Lansing, MN: Protar House, 2003.

_____. *John Ringo: The Reputation of a Deadly Gunman*. Tucson: San Simon, 1995.

_____. *Johnny Ringo*. Lansing, MN: Protar House, 2002.

_____. *The Real Wyatt Earp: A Documentary Biography*. Edited by Neil B. Carmony. Silver City, NM: High-Lonesome, 2000.

_____. *Wyatt Earp: A Biography of a Western Lawman*. Tucson: San Simon, 1997.

Halaas, David Fridtjof. *Boom Town Newspapers: Journalism on the Rocky Mountain Mining Frontier, 1859–1881*. Albuquerque: University of New Mexico Press, 1981.

Hertzberg, Arthur, ed. *Judaism*. New York: George Broziller, 1962.

Hickey, Michael M. *The Death of Warren Baxter Earp: A Closer Look*. With political overview by Richard Lapidus. Honolulu: Talei, 2000.

_____. *John Ringo: The Final Hours: A Tale of the Old West*. With analysis and commentary by Ben T. Traywick. Honolulu: Talei, 1995.

Jahns, Pat. *The Frontier World of Doc Holliday, Faro Dealer, from Dallas to Deadwood*. New York: Hastings House, 1957.

John's Western Gallery Auction. *Wyatt Earp, Tombstone and the West*. Parts I, II, and III. *The John D. Gilchriese Collection*. Auction catalogue and narrative series, 2004–2005.

Johnson, David. *John Ringo*. Stillwater, OK: Barbed Wire, 1997.

_____. *John Ringo: King of the Cowboys*. Denton: University of North Texas Press, 2008.

Johnson, Paul L. *The McLaurys in Tombstone: An O.K. Corral Obituary*. Denton: University of North Texas Press, 2012.

Kirschner, Ann. *Lady at the O.K. Corral: The True Story of Josephine Marcus Earp*. New York: HarperCollins, 2013.

Lake, Carolyn. *Undercover for Wells Fargo: The Unvarnished Recollections of Fred Dodge*. Boston: Houghton Mifflin, 1969.

Lake, Stuart N. *Wyatt Earp: Frontier Marshal*. New York: Houghton Mifflin, 1931.

Lamar, Howard Roberts. *The Far Southwest, 1846–1912: A Territorial History*. New York: W.W. Norton, 1970.

Lewis, Alfred Henry. *The Sunset Trail*. New York: A.L. Burt, 1905.

Lynch, Sylvia D. *Aristocracy's Outlaw: The Doc Holliday Story*. New Tazewell, TN: Iris, 1994.

Martin, Douglas D. *The Earps of Tombstone*. Tombstone: Tombstone Epitaph, 1959.

_____. *Tombstone Epitaph: The Truth About "The Town Too Tough To Die."* Albuquerque: University of New Mexico Press, 1951.

Moody, Valerie. *The Feasts of Adonai: Why Christians Should Look at the Biblical Feasts*. Lubbock, TX: Gibbora, 2002.

Myers, John Myers. *Doc Holliday: The Life of the Famous Desperado of the Old West*. New York: Little, Brown, 1955.

Newlin, Deborah Lamont. *The Tonkawa People: A Tribal History from Earliest Times to 1893*. Lubbock: West Texas Museum Association, 1982.

Ormes, Robert N. *Railroads and the Rockies: A Record of the Lines in and Near Colorado*. Denver: Sage, 1963.

Osterwald, Doris B. *Cinders and Smoke: A Mile by Mile Guide for the Durango to Silverton Narrow Gauge Trip*. Denver: Golden Bell, 1989.

Pendleton, Albert S., Jr., and Susan McKey Thomas. *In Search of the Hollidays: The Story of Doc Holliday and His Holliday and McKey Families*. Valdosta, GA: Little River, 1973.

Poling-Kempes, Lesley. *The Harvey Girls: Women Who Opened the West*. New York: Paragon House 1989. Reprint, New York: Marlowe, 1991.

Posner, Richard A., and Katharine B. Silbaugh. *A Guide to America's Sex Laws*. Chicago: University of Chicago Press, 1996.

Reidhead, S.J. *A Church for Helldorado: The 1882 Tombstone Diary of Endicott Peabody*. Roswell, NM: Wyatt Earp, 2006.

Roberts, Gary L. *Doc Holliday: The Life and Legend*. Hoboken, NJ: John Wiley & Sons, 2006.

Ross, John F. *War on the Run: The Epic Story of Robert Rogers and the Conquest of America's First Frontier*. New York: Bantam, Random House, 2009.

Sarna, Jonathan D. *When General Grant Expelled the Jews*. New York: Schocken, 2012.

Shillingberg, William B. *Tombstone, A.T.: A History of Early Mining, Milling, and Mayhem*. Spokane, WA: Arthur H. Clark, 1999.

Tanner, Karen Holliday. *Doc Holliday: A Family Portrait*. Norman: University of Oklahoma Press, 1998.

Tefertiller, Casey. *Wyatt Earp: The Life Behind the Legend*. New York: John Wiley & Sons, 1997.

Theobald, John, and Lillian Theobald. *Wells Fargo in Arizona Territory*. Tucson: Arizona Historical Foundation, 1978.

Traywick, Ben T. *The Clantons of Tombstone*. Tombstone, AZ: Red Marie's, 1996.

_____. *John Henry: The Doc Holliday Story*. Tombstone, AZ: Red Marie's, 1996.

_____. *John Peters Ringo: Mythical Gunfighter*. Tombstone, AZ: Red Marie's, 1987.

_____. *Wyatt Earp: Angel of Death*. Honolulu: Talei, 2007.

_____. *Wyatt Earp's Thirteen Dead Men*. Tombstone, AZ: Red Marie's, 1998.

Van Cise, Phillip S. *Fighting the Underworld*. Cambridge: Riverside, 1936.

Wagoner, Jay J. *Arizona Territory, 1863–1912: A Political History*. Tucson, University of Arizona Press, 1970.

Walker, Henry P., and Don Bufkin. *Historical Atlas of Arizona*. Norman: University of Oklahoma Press, 1979.

Waters, Frank. *The Earp Brothers of Tombstone: The*

Story of Mrs. Virgil Earp. New York: Clarkson N. Potter, 1960.

Wheelock, Dean, and SusanWheelock. *Lashon Hara: The Evil Tongue.* Lakewood, WI: Hebrew Roots, nd.

White, Brooks. *Galeyville, Arizona Territory 1880: Its History and Historic Archaeology.* Raleigh, NC: Pentland, 2000.

Young, Roy B. *Cochise County Cowboy War: A Cast of Characters.* Apache, OK: Young & Sons, 1999.

_____. *James Cooksey Earp: Out of the Shadows.* Apache, OK: Young & Sons, 2006.

_____. *"Johnny-Behind-the-Deuce": Guilty Until Proven Innocent; The True Story of Mike O'Rourke and the Shooting of Philip Schneider.* Apache, OK: Young & Sons, 2007.

_____. *Pete Spence: "Audacious Artist in Crime."* Apache, OK: Young & Sons, 2000.

_____. *Robert Havlin Paul: Frontier Lawman; The Arizona Years.* Apache, OK: Young & Sons, 2009.

Articles

Anderson, Mike. "Posses and Politics in Pima County: The Administration of Sheriff Charlie Shibell." *Journal of Arizona History*, Autumn 1986.

Associated Press. "Western Union Ends Telegrams—STOP." February 1, 2006.

Ball, Larry D. "Pioneer Lawman: Crawley P. Dake and Law Enforcement on the Southwestern Frontier." *Journal of Arizona History*, Autumn 1973.

Banks, Leo W. "Wyatt Earp: Fearless Lawman, Loyal Friend, Deadly Enemy, Gambler, Boxer, Con Man, Lawbreaker, Womanizer." *Arizona Highways*, July 1994.

_____. "Wyatt Earp's Handwriting Tells All." *Arizona History*, November 1997.

Barra, Allen. "Who Was Wyatt Earp? From Law Officer to Murderer to Hollywood Consultant; The Strange Career of a Man Who Became Myth." *American Heritage*, December 1998.

Bartholomew, Ed. "Western Gunfighters Unmasked." *Westerner*, October 1962.

Belden, L. Burr. Neil Carmony, ed. "Close Friend of Wyatt Earp Tells of Latter's Life." *Quarterly of the National Association for Outlaw and Lawman History*, January-March 2004.

Beller, J. "Sanders of Turkey Creek." *Old West*, Fall 1972.

Bork, A.W., and Glenn G. Boyer, ed. "The O.K. Corral Fight at Tombstone: A Footnote by Kate Elder." *Arizona and the West*, Spring 1977.

Bossenecker, John. "John Thacker: Train Robber's Nemesis." *Real West*, September 1976.

Boyer, Glenn G. "Curly Bill Has Been Killed at Last." *Real West*, June 1989.

_____. "The Earps in Mohave County [CA]." *Arizona Highways*, March 1989.

Boyer, Glenn G. "Johnny Behan, Assistant Folk Hero." *Real West*, April-June 1981.

_____. "Johnny Behan of Tombstone." *Frontier Times*, July 1976.

_____. "Morgan Earp, Brother in the Shadow." *Old West*, Winter 1983.

_____. "Murder at Millville: A Century-Old Arizona Mystery Resolved." *Real West*, April 1983.

_____. "On the Trail of Big Nosed Kate." *Real West*, March 1981.

_____. "Postscript to Historical Fiction About Wyatt Earp in Tombstone." *Arizona and the West*, Autumn 1976.

_____. "The Secret Wife of Wyatt Earp." *True West*, June 1983.

_____. "Those Marryin' Earp Men." *True West*, April 1976.

_____. "Welcome to Wyatt Earp Country." *Arizona Highways*, November 1982.

Brand, Peter. "Dan Tipton and the Earp Vendetta Posse." *True West*, December 2001.

_____. "Daniel G. Tipton and the Earp Vendetta Posse." *Quarterly of the National Association for Outlaw and Lawman History*, October-December 2000.

_____. "Duty Bound: The Story of John Wilson Vermillion and the Myth of Tombstone's 'Texas Jack.'" *Wild West History Association Journal*, August 2010.

_____. "The Escape of 'Curly Bill' Brocius." *Western-Outlaw Lawman History Association Journal*, Summer 2000.

_____. "The Man Who Arrested Doc Holliday." *Wild West*, June 2009.

_____. "Sherman W. McMaster(s): The El Paso Salt War, Texas Rangers and Tombstone." *Western-Outlaw Lawman History Association Journal*, Winter 1999.

_____. "Wyatt Earp, Jack Johnson and the Notorious Blount Brothers." *Quarterly of the National Association for Outlaw and Lawman History*, October-December 2003.

_____. "Wyatt Earp's Vendetta Posse." *Wild West*, April 2007.

Burrows, Jack. "Ringomania: The Perpetuation of a Western Myth." *Western-Outlaw Lawman History Association Journal*, Spring 2000.

Carmony, Neil B. "Wyatt Earp's New Testament." *Quarterly of the National Association for Outlaw and Lawman History*, July-September 2001.

Cataldo, Nicholas R. "Nicholas P. Earp: Tough Frontiersman." *National Edition Tombstone Epitaph*, March 2005.

Chandler (Dr.), Robert J. "A Smoking Gun?: Did Wells Fargo Pay Wyatt Earp to Kill Curly Bill and Frank Stilwell?; New Evidence Seems to Indicate Yes." As reported by Mare Rosenbaum. *True West*, July 2001.

_____. "Under Cover for Wells Fargo: A Review Essay." *Journal of Arizona History*, Spring 2000.

_____. "Wells Fargo and the Earp Brothers: Cash Books Talk." *California Historical Quarterly*, Summer 2009 [also *Wild West History Association Journal*, April 2010].

Chaput, Don. "Fred Dodge: Undercover Agent or Con Man?" *Quarterly of the National Association for Outlaw and Lawman History*, January-March 2000.

Clanton, Terry "Ike," and Wyatt Earp. "Big Brother at the O.K. Corral: A Frontier of Gun Control and Federal Justice." *Harper's*, September 2002.

Clum, John P. "It All Happened in Tombstone." *Arizona Historical Review*, April 1929.

Coleman, Jane Candia. "Wyatt Earp Country." *Louis L'Amour Western*, July 1994.

Collier, Anne E. "Big Nose Kate and Mary Katherine Cummings: Same Person Different Lives." *Wild West History Association Journal*, October 2012.

_____. "Harriett 'Hattie' Catchim: A Controversial Earp Family Member." *Western-Outlaw Lawman History Association Journal*, Summer 2007.

Collins, Jan Macknell. "The Wife of Wyatt Earp's Sworn Enemy." *True West*, February 2015.

Cool, Paul. "The Capture of New Mexico's Rustler King." *Wild West*, April 2014.

_____. "Escape of a Highwayman: The Riddle of Sherman McMaster." *Western-Outlaw Lawman History Association Journal*, Summer 2000.

_____. "'With Murder Rates Higher Than Modern New York or Los Angeles': Homicide Rates Involving the Arizona Cow-Boys, 1880–1882." *Wild West History Association Journal*, August 2014.

_____. "The World of Sherman McMaster(s)." *Western-Outlaw Lawman History Association Journal*, Autumn 1998.

Crawford, Sybil F. "Morgan Earp's Louisa: Another Myth Exploded?" *Western-Outlaw Lawman History Association Journal*, Summer 2001.

Cubbison, Douglas R. "Newton Earp: The Forgotten Fighting Earp Brother." *Western-Outlaw Lawman History Association Journal*, Fall 2000.

_____. "The Service of James and Virgil Earp in the American Civil War." *Western-Outlaw Lawman History Association Journal*, Spring 1996.

Davis, Lance E. "The Investment Market, 1870–1914: The Evolution of a National Market." *Journal of Economic History*, September 1965.

De La Garza, Phyllis. "Texan Johnny Boyett Was the Man Who Gunned Down Warren Earp." *Wild West*, February 2014.

DeArment, Robert K. "Wyatt Whoppers." Newspaper Articles, 1897–1905. *Wild West History Association Journal*, October 2009.

DeMattos, Jack. "The Dodge City Police Commission Revealed." *Wild West History Association Journal*, April 2013.

_____. "Whatever Became of the Dodge City Peace Commission?" *Real West*, January 1977.

Diaz-Gonzalez, Darlinda. "Billy Claiborne, Arizona's Billy the Kid." *Quarterly of the National Association for Outlaw and Lawman History*, July-September 2005.

Dullenty, Jim. "Ike Clanton, Billy Byers and the Massacre." *Western-Outlaw Lawman History Association Journal*, Spring 1998.

Dworkin, Mark. "Henry Jaffa and Wyatt Earp." *Western-Outlaw Lawman History Association Journal*, Fall 2004.

_____. "Henry Jaffa and Wyatt Earp: Wyatt Earp's Jewish Connection; A Portrait of Henry Jaffa, Albuquerque's First Mayor." *Western-Outlaw Lawman History Association Journal*, Fall 2004.

_____. *New Mexico Jewish Historical Society Newsletter*, December 2005, March 2006, June 2006, and September 2006.

Dyke, Scott. "Clantons Had Reputations for Rustling and Running." *Wild West*, October 2013.

Earp, George W., and Frank Bruce. "I Rode with Wyatt Earp." *Reader's Digest*, December 1958.

Earp, Josephine. "Sinister Shadow from the Past." Edited by Glenn G. Boyer. *True West*, September 1975.

Eckhart, C.F. "The Sam Bass Connection in New Mexico." *National Edition Tombstone Epitaph*, May 2002.

Edwards, Harold L. "The Man Who Killed Ike Clanton." *True West*, October 1991.

Ernst, Robert. "Terminology Used to Refer to a Member of a Marshal's Posse." *Wild West History Association Journal*, August 2010.

Espinosa, J. Manuel, ed. "Memoir of a Kentuckian in New Mexico." *New Mexico Historical Review*, October 1933.

Evans, Bill. "Gunfight in the Whetstone Mountains." *Wild West History Association Journal*, December 2008.

Fattig, Timothy. "James Flynn: Tombstone's Two-and-a-Half Month Marshal." *Western-Outlaw Lawman History Association Journal*, Spring 2002.

Fisher, Truman Rex. "The Great Wyatt Earp Oil Rip-off." *Western-Outlaw Lawman History Association Journal*, Summer 1995.

_____. "Wyatt Earp's Multitudinous Tombstones." *True West*, April 1997.

Galbraith, Den. "The Lost Ledge of Governor Otero." *True West*, March 1964.

Gatto, Steve. "Johnny Ringo, Land and Cattle Speculator." *Quarterly of the National Association for Outlaw and Lawman History*, October-December 1994.

_____. "Justice Wells Spicer's Decision in the Preliminary Hearing About the Gunfight at the O.K. Corral." *Tombstone Times*, October 2006.

Gilchriese, John D. "Gunfight at the O.K. Corral." Franklin Mint Booklet, 1982.

_____. "The Odyssey of Virgil Earp." *English Westerner's Tally Sheet*, January-February and March-April 1973. Updated from *Tombstone Epitaph*, Fall 1968.

Harden, Paul. "Western Union and the Railroad Telegraphers." *Socorro (NM) El Defensor Chieftain*, 4 March 2006.

Hill, Gertrude. "Henry Clay Hooker: King of the Sierra Bonita." *Arizoniana*, Winter 1961.

Hitt, Jack, comp. and ed. "Big Brother at the O.K. Corral: A Frontier Fable of Gun Control and Federal Justice." *Harper's*, September 2002.

Hornung, Chuck. "A Confederate State of Kentucky?" *The Valley Viking*, Spring 1961.

_____. "Fact vs. Fiction: The Luther King Escape." *Western Outlaw-Lawman History Association Journal*, Winter 2000.

_____. "The Lynching of Gus Mentzer at Raton, New Mexico Territory." *Real West*, April 1985.

_____. "New Evidence for the 'Buntline Special' Found?" *Western Outlaw-Lawman History Association Journal*, Spring 2006.

_____. "Tombstone Travesty vs. Earp Brothers of Tombstone." Editor's introduction to the exposé of Frank Waters. *Western Outlaw-Lawman History Association Journal*, Fall 1999.

_____. "Wyatt Earp and Doc Holliday in Las Vegas, New Mexico." *True West*, May 1999.

_____. "Wyatt Earp's Birthplace." *Western Outlaw-Lawmen History Association Journal*, Spring 2000.

_____. "Wyatt Earp's New Mexico Adventures." *Old West*, Summer 1999.

Hornung, Chuck. With Dr. Gary Roberts. "The Split: Did Doc and Wyatt Split Because of a Racial Slur?" *True West*, December 2001.

House, R.C. "Wyatt Earp and the Civil War: He Answered the Call of Distant Drums." *True West*, October 1983.

Jay, Roger. "Another Earp Arrest?" *Quarterly of the National Association for Outlaw and Lawman History,* October-December 2004.

_____. "The Dodge City Underworld." *Quarterly of the National Association for Outlaw and Lawman History,* July-December 2007.

_____. "Face To Face: Sadie Mansfield/Josephine Sarah Marcus." *Wild West History Association Journal,* February 2013.

_____. "'The Peoria Bummer': Wyatt Earp's Lost Year." *Wild West,* August 2003.

_____. "A Tale of Two Sadies." Wild West, October 2014.

_____. "Wyatt Earp, Wichita Police." *Western-Outlaw Lawman History Association Journal.* Part 1, Fall 2006. Part 2, Winter 2006.

Johnson, Paul Lee. "Were the McLaurys Leaving Tombstone?" *Western-Outlaw Lawman History Association Journal,* Autumn 1998.

_____. "The Will of McLaury." *Wild West,* October 2013.

Kelley, Troy. "Tombstone's Unknown Marshal: Ben Soppy." *Western-Outlaw Lawman History Association Journal,* Winter 2003.

_____. "The Will of McLaury." *Wild West,* October 2013

King A.M. "The Last Man." *True West,* May-June 1959.

_____. "Wyatt Earp's 'Million Dollar' Shotgun Ride." As told to Lea McCarthy. *True West.* July-August 1958.

Lapidus, Richard. "The Youngest Earp: Strange Events Surrounding the Death of Warren Earp." *Western-Outlaw Lawman History Association Journal,* Fall 1995.

_____. "The Youngest Earp: The Troubled Life and Times of Warren Earp." *Western-Outlaw Lawman History Association Journal,* Summer 1995.

Lewis, Nancy Owen. "High and Dry in New Mexico: Tuberculosis and the Politics of Health." *New Mexico Historical Review,* Spring 2012.

Lockwood, Frank C. "They Lived in Tombstone! I Knew Them #4: Wyatt Earp." *Tombstone Epitaph,* March 8, 1945.

Lubert, Steve. "Should Wyatt Earp Have Been Hanged?" *True West,* February-March 2001.

McKinnan, Bess. "The Toll Road Over Raton Pass." *New Mexico Historical Review,* January 1927.

Mitchell, Carol. "Mrs. Josephine Earp: Lady Sadie, the Other Woman in Wyatt's Life" *True West,* February–March 2001.

Monahan, Sherry. "The Women of Tombstone." *Western-Outlaw Lawman History Association Journal,* Winter 1998.

Montoya, Maria E. "The Dual World of Governor Miguel A. Otero: Myth and Reality in Turn of the Century New Mexico." *New Mexico Historical Review,* January 1992.

Morey, Jeff. "Wyatt Earp's Buntline Special: The Real Story." *Guns and Ammo,* December 1997.

Mullin, Robert N. "Here Lies John Kinney." *Journal of Arizona History,* Autumn 1973.

Nash, Gerald D. "New Mexico in the [Miguel A.] Otero Era: Some Historical Perspectives." *New Mexico Historical Review,* January 1992.

Nelson, Scott. "Charleston, Arizona Territory: The Two-Gun Town of Red Dog." *Western-Outlaw Lawman History Association Journal,* Winter 2000.

_____. "Trailing John 'Jim' S. Sharp: Badman of Cochise County." *Western-Outlaw Lawman History Association Journal,* Winter 2000.

Nolan, Frederick. "Boss Rustler: The Life and Crimes of John Kinney." *True West.* Part 1, September 1996. Part 2, October 1996.

Otero, Miguel A. "Old Times." *Raton (NM) Morning Reporter,* unknown date in 1930s.

Palmquist, Robert F. "'Arizona Affairs': An Interview with Virgil W. Earp." *Real West,* January 1982.

_____. "'Good-Bye, Old Friend': The Last Meeting of Wyatt and Doc." *Real West,* May 1979.

_____. "Mining, Keno, and the Law: The Tombstone Career of Bob Winders, Charley Smith, and Fred Dodge, 1879–1888." *Journal of Arizona History,* Summer 1997.

_____. "Virgil Earp in Prescott, 1877." *Real West,* December 1980.

Parish, William J. "The German Jew and the Commercial Revolution in Territorial New Mexico, 1850–1900." *New Mexico Quarterly,* Autumn 1959.

Pendleton, Albert S., Jr., and Susan McKey Thomas. "Doc Holliday's Georgia Background." *Journal of Arizona History,* Autumn 1973.

Peterson, Roger S. "Wyatt Earp: His San Francisco Days Were Adventures, Too." *San Francisco Sunday Examiner and Chronicle,* 17 January 1982.

_____. "Wyatt Earp, Man Versus Myth." *American History,* August 1994.

Potter, Pam. "Murdered on the Streets of Tombstone." *Quarterly of the National Association for Outlaw and Lawman History,* October–December 1979.

_____. "Remembering the McLaurys," *Quarterly of the National Association for Outlaw and Lawman History,* October–December 2006.

_____. "Sadie's Fairy Tale Wedding." *Wild West History Association Journal,* October 2012.

_____. "Wyatt Earp: Aged, Potent Lion of Tombstone." *Quarterly of the National Association for Outlaw and Lawman History,* January–March 2006.

Rasch, Phillip J. "Exit Axtell, Enter Wallace." *New Mexico Historical Review,* July 1975.

_____. "The Resurrection of Pony Diehl." *Los Angles Westerners Branding Iron,* December 1957.

_____. "They Tried to Hold Up the Tombstone Stage." *Real West,* October 1984.

Reidhead, S.J. "A Close-up View of Wyatt Earp's Last Days." *Western-Outlaw Lawman History Association Journal,* Fall-Winter 1997.

Roberts, Gary L. "Brothers of the Gun: Wyatt and Doc." *Wild West,* December 2012.

_____. "The Clay Allison Vs. Dodge City Legend." *New York Westerners Newsletter #2,* 1961.

_____. "Doc Holliday: The Earps' Strangest Ally." *Wild West,* October 2006.

_____. "The Fight That Never Dies." *Frontier Times,* October-November 1965.

_____. "The Fremont Street Fiasco; or, How to Start a Legend Without Really Trying." *True West,* July 1988.

_____. "Mrs. John Holliday? Mary Katherine Haroney Fisher Elder Cummings." *True West,* December 2001.

_____. With Chuck Hornung. "The Split: Did Doc and Wyatt Split Because of a Racial Slur?" *True West,* December 2001.

_____. "The Wells Spicer Decision, 1881." *Montana,* January 1970.

Rose, John. "Twenty-Four Hours with Ike Clanton." *Wild West,* October 2006.

St. Johns, Adela Rodgers. "I Knew Wyatt Earp." *Arizona Weekly*, May 22, 1960.

Schoemehl, Frederick. "Cracking the Case of the Missing Earp Grave." *National Edition Tombstone Epitaph*, March 2014.

Seligman, G.R., Jr. "Crawley P. Dake." *Arizoniana*, Spring 1961.

Smith, Chuck. "One for Morg!" *Quarterly of the National Association for Outlaw and Lawman History*, October-December 2005.

Silva, Lee A. "Did Tom McLaury Have a Gun?" *Wild West*, October 2006.

_____. "In a Brother's Shadow [Virgil Earp]." *Wild West*, December 2009.

_____. "The Mysterious Morgan Earp." *Wild West*, October 2010.

_____. "They Were a Couple for Nearly 50 Years, but Were They Ever Legally Married?" *Wild West*, October 2013.

_____. "The Wyatt Earp/ Buntline Special Controversy." With supplementary research by Jeff Morey. *Quarterly of the National Association for Outlaw and Lawman History*, April-June 1993 and 1994, July-September 1993 and 1994, October-December 1993 and 1994, January-March 1994 and 1995.

Stevens, Peter F. "Wyatt Earp's Word Is Good with Me!" *American West*, February 1988.

Tefertiller, Casey, and Jeff Morey. "O.K. Corral: A Gunfight Shrouded in Mystery." *Wild West*, October 2001.

Thomas, Robert L. "I Think Earp Took Johnny Ringo." *Old West*, Fall 1972.

Thrapp, Dan L. "Religious Life of Wyatt Earp." *Los Angeles Times*, 24 July 1955.

Tobias, Henry J., and Charles E. Woodhouse. "New York Investment Bankers and New Mexico Merchants: Group Formation and Elite Status Among German Jewish Businessmen." *New Mexico Historical Review*, January 1990.

Traywick Ben T. "The Murder of Warren Baxter Earp. *Old West*, Winter 1990.

_____. "The Search for Florentino Cruz." *Western-Outlaw Lawman History Association Journal*, Winter-Spring 1995.

_____. "Showdown: Wyatt Earp vs. Curly Bill." *Western-Outlaw Lawman History Association Journal*, Summer 1995.

_____. "The Tombstone's Dragon Lady." *True West*, May 1999.

Troy, Lillian M.S. "Photo of Curley Bill in Possession of Lillian Troy Solves His Death." *Tombstone Epitaph*, March 8, 1951.

Turner, Alford E. "The Clantons of Apache County." *Real West*, March 1979.

_____. "The Florentino-Earp Affair." *Real West*, January 1979.

_____. "Guns of the O.K. Corral." *Real West*, January 1981.

Urban, William. "Wyatt Earp's Father." *True West*, May 1989.

Walker, Henry P. "Arizona Land Fraud Model 1880: The Tombstone Townsite Company." *Arizona and the West*, Spring 1979.

Weider, Eric, and John Rose. "The Making of Wyatt Earp's Legend." *Wild West*, April 2008.

West, Elliott. "The Saloon in Territorial Arizona." *Journal of the West*, Fall 1974.

Wittels (Dr.), Sylvia. "Doc's Disease." *True West*, April 1997.

Wright, Erik. "Looking for Doc in Dallas." *True West*, December 2001.

Young, Roy B. "The Assassination of Frank Stilwell." *Wild West History Association Journal*, August 2008.

_____. "Wyatt Earp, Outlaw of the Cherokee Nation." *Wild West History Association Journal*, June 2010.

_____. "Wyatt Earp Talks 'Pretty': A Look at Wyatt Earp's Interaction with Interviewers, Writers, and Historians." *Wild West History Association Journal*, December 2011.

Research Facilities

ALBUQUERQUE SPECIAL COLLECTIONS LIBRARY

Albuquerque Business Directory for 1882
Albuquerque and Las Vegas Business Directory for 1883
New Mexico newspaper collection (microfilm)

ARIZONA HISTORICAL SOCIETY LIBRARY, TUCSON

Arizona Historical Newspaper Collection
Cochise County Records (MS 180)
Earp Family Papers
George Parsons Papers and Diaries (MS 645)
Governor Fredrick Tritle Scrapbooks
John Pleasant Gray, "When All Roads Led to Tombstone" typescript
Mabel Earp Cason Papers
Nora Neff Hixenbaugh File
Pima County Records
Record of Commitments for the County Jail
Sheriff John Behan Financial Records, Jan-April 1882, File 83, Box 08
Walter Nobel Burns Collection
Wyatt Earp to Walter N. Burns, 08 November 1926

CENTER FOR SOUTHWEST RESEARCH, UNIVERSITY OF NEW MEXICO, ALBUQUERQUE

Frank Waters Papers and Collection: *Tombstone Travesty* manuscript and letter files
Maxwell Land Grant and Railroad Company Records
Otero-Stinson Collection and Papers (506)
Miguel A. Otero Personal Notebooks, 1882–1906
Miguel A. Otero Letters Received/Letters Sent Files, 1934–1944
Miguel A. Otero book manuscript drafts
Santa Fe Railway Company Collection
United States Marshal Records, Territory of New Mexico
William A. Kelleher Collection: New Mexico Territorial Newspapers (bound)

COLORADO STATE ARCHIVES, DENVER

Governor Frederick W. Pitkin Papers

COLTON PUBLIC LIBRARY, COLTON, CA

Earp Family Collection
Edwards, Adelia Earp, "Wild Western Remembrances by Wyatt Earp's Sister." MS, 1932.

HALEY MEMORIAL LIBRARY AND HISTORY CENTER, MIDLAND, TX

Hayhurst Typescript of Document 45: Coroner's Inquest, October 1881 and Document 94: Justice of the Peace Examination of Territory of Arizona vs. Morgan Earp, et al., November 1881, Tombstone, Cochise County.
J. Evetts Haley Collection:
Memoir, Mary Katherine Haroney (Mrs. John Holliday), 1932–1935,
Robert N. Mullin Collection:
Correspondence:
John Ringo to (Sheriff) Charles Shibell, 03 March 1880
Stuart N. Lake to Robert N. Mullin, 17 August 1953
Waldo E. Koop to Robert N. Mullin, 31 July 1964
Tombstone Evening Gossip, 29 March 1881 (only known copy of this newspaper).

HUNTINGTON LIBRARY, SAN MARINO, CALIFORNIA

Stuart N. Lake Research Papers

KANSAS STATE HISTORICAL SOCIETY, TOPEKA

E.P. Lamborn Papers, Special Collections

NATIONAL ARCHIVES, WASHINGTON, D.C.

U.S. Department of the Interior Records (Record Group 48):
John Gosper to James A. Garfield, 17 March 1881, President James A. Garfield Appointment Papers.
Report of the Governor of New Mexico Territory, 1879–1885,
"In the Matter of the Investigation of Charges Against S.B. Axtell, Governor of New Mexico, 1875–1882."
U.S. Department of Justice (Record Group 60):
Acting Governor John Gosper to Secretary of State James G. Blaine, 30 September 1881.
Acting Governor John Gosper to U.S. Marshal Dake, 28 November 1881.
Governor John C. Frémont to Secretary Carl Schurz, January 6 and January 26, 1879.
Joseph Bowyer to Acting Governor John Gosper, 17 September 1881.
Report from Leigh Chalmers, Special Examiner, 13 August 1885.
Report of Special Agent S. R. Martin, 19 April 1882.
Report of U.S. District Attorney James A. Zabriskie, 22 January 1885 (File 2725-1885).
Secretary of State Blaine to Acting Governor John Gosper, 15 November 1881.
Supplementary Report from Leigh Chalmers, Special Examiner, 3 September 1885.
U.S. Attorney E.B. Pomroy to Attorney General Wayne MacVeagh, June 23, 1881.
U.S. Marshal C.P. Dake to S.F. Phillips, Acting Attorney General, 3 December 1881.

NEW MEXICO STATE RECORD CENTER AND ARCHIVES, SANTA FE

Colfax County Records (1973–025): Sheriff's Journal 1869–1884 (C-6)
San Miguel County District Court Records, 1878–1881.

Special New Mexico Territorial Census 1885, Bernalillo County

NEW YORK HISTORICAL SOCIETY, NEW YORK CITY

Will McLaury Letter Collection

RIO GRANDE HISTORICAL COLLECTION, NEW MEXICO STATE UNIVERSITY, LAS CRUCES

Arizona and New Mexico newspaper collections (microfilm)
Stock Growers' Association of New Mexico Membership Book, 1884
Stock Growers' Association of New Mexico Records (MS 178)

SEVER CENTER FOR WESTERN HISTORY RESEARCH, NATURAL HISTORY MUSEUM, LOS ANGLES

Correspondence: William S. Hart to and from Wyatt Earp and Josephine Earp

SHARLOT HALL MUSEUM AND ARCHIVES, PHOENIX

Governor John J. Gosper Papers

SOUTHWEST MUSEUM, BRAUN RESEARCH LIBRARY, LOS ANGELES

Forrestine C. Hooker. "An Arizona Vendetta: The Truth About Wyatt Earp and Some Others; Facts Stated to Writer by Wyatt S. Earp." Manuscript. c. 1920

STEPHEN H. HART LIBRARY, COLORADO HISTORICAL SOCIETY, DENVER

Atchison, Topeka and Santa Fe Railroad/Railway Collection
William Jackson Palmer Collection

UNIVERSITY OF ARIZONA LIBRARY, SPECIAL COLLECTIONS, TUCSON

Cow-boy Depredations File
George O. Hand's Contention City Diary
Hildreth Halliwell (grandniece of Allie Earp) recorded interview, September 21, 1971
John Phillip Clum Collection, Marjorie Clum Parker manuscript
Johnny Behan Family Papers
Minutes of the Tombstone Common Council, 1880–1882
Walter Noble Burns Papers

WELLS FARGO AND COMPANY CORPORATE ARCHIVES, WELLS FARGO BANK, SAN FRANCISCO

General Cashbook
Loss and Damage Ledger

WILLIAM S. HART HOME, LOS ANGELES COUNTY PARKS DEPARTMENT, NEWHALL, CALIFORNIA

Correspondence: William S. Hart to and from Wyatt Earp and Josephine Earp

Private Collections

BOYER, GLENN G., COLLECTION (AS OF JULY 1995 AT HIS ARIZONA RANCH)

John Flood, Jr. Manuscript (Wyatt Earp autobiography), 1925.

Louisa Ann Houston (Mrs. Morgan Earp) Letters, 1880–1882.

Mabel Earp Cason-Vinnolia Earp Ackerman Manuscript (*She Married Wyatt Earp by Josephine Earp*) and research documents and letters.

Mary Katherine Haroney (Mrs. John H. Holliday) Research File.

Mrs. Charles A. Colyn (Ester Lillian Hulppieu Irvine) Research/Genealogical Collection.

HORNUNG, CHUCK, AND V.J. HORNUNG, WESTERN HISTORY COLLECTION

Dan Gordon, *Wyatt Earp* motion picture screenplay, revised 24 May 1993, unpublished copy.

Ed Bartholomew Collection, select research material on Tombstone.

Ester Lillian Irvine, "Data On The Earp Family" genealogical newsletter collection, 1958.

Gus Hornung Papers and Archives.

Hayhurst Typescript of Document 45: Coroner's Inquest, October 1881 and Document 94: Justice of the Peace Examination of *Territory of Arizona vs. Morgan Earp, et al.*, November 1881, Tombstone, Cochise County. Copy contains *Tombstone Epitaph* testimony clippings pasted on the back of the typescript page. Owned by Stuart N. Lake, *Tombstone Epitaph* office, Al Turner, and Glenn G. Boyer. Bought in 1977.

Henry Lambert and St. James Hotel Papers and Cimarron Photograph Archives.

Jeff Morey Study Papers:

"Blaze Away!: Doc Holliday's Role in the West's Most Famous Gunfight" (copy).

"The Streetfight: What We Know and Why We Know It" (copy).

Kevin Jarre, *Tombstone* motion picture screenplay, drafts 1–5, unpublished copies.

Miguel A. Otero to "Dear Friend" ("The Otero Letter"), 1940.

Version of Hayhurst Typescript owned by Robert N. Mullin via Stuart N. Lake (copy).

Wyatt Earp to "Friend Colburn," 19 April 1886.

Wyatt Earp to George Earp ("I like San Francisco best" letter), 13 February 1928.

SIMMONS, C. LEE, COLLECTION (AS OF JULY 1995 AT HIS SONOITA, ARIZONA, HOME)

Al Turner Research Collection.

Mabel Earp Cason-Vinnolia Earp Ackerman Manuscript (*She Married Wyatt Earp by Josephine Earp*) and research documents and letters (copy in the author's collection).

INTERVIEWS AND PRESENTATIONS (AUDIO/VIDEO)

Interview: Grace Walsh Spolorori by S.J. Reidhead, San Bernardino, California, 23 May 1996, copy.

Interview: Mary Lail by Chuck Hornung, Cimarron, New Mexico, 22 June 1967, notes.

Panel: "The Earp Controversies: The Range of Opinions." Roger S. Paterson, moderator, with Jeff Morey, Lee Silva, Michael M. Hickey, Ben T. Traywick, Gail K. Allan, and Glenn G. Boyer at WOLA Convention, Tucson, Arizona, 22 July 1995.

Panel: "O.K. Corral Gunfight Symposium [audio]." Terry "Ike" Clanton, moderator, with Ben T. Traywick, Sue Van Slyke, Wallace Clayton, Dana Skull, and Steve Gatto, at Clanton Gang Reunion, Tombstone, Arizona, 18 November 1995.

Presentation and Exhibits: "Trial of the Shootout at the O.K. Corral." At State Bar of Arizona, 14 July 2000.

Presentation: "The Earp Curse." Glenn G. Boyer, at WOLA Convention, Deadwood, South Dakota, 21 July 1994.

Presentation: "The Earp Debate." Jeff Wheat, moderator, with Casey Tefertiller and Jeff Morey, at WOLA Special Event, Phoenix, Arizona, 3 January 1998.

Newspapers

ARIZONA TERRITORY

Phoenix Herald
Prescott Arizona Miner
Tombstone Daily/Weekly Epitaph
Tombstone Gossip
Tombstone Daily/Weekly Nugget
Tombstone Prospector
Tucson Daily/Weekly Citizen
Tucson Daily/Weekly Star
Wilcox Southwestern Stockman
Yuma Times

CALIFORNIA

Los Angeles Herald
Los Angeles Times
Sacramento Daily Record Union
San Diego Daily Union
San Francisco Call
San Francisco Chronicle
San Francisco Examiner

COLORADO

Denver Republican
Denver Rocky Mountain News
Denver Tribune
Gunnison News-Democrat
Pueblo Daily Chieftain
Trinidad Daily News

KANSAS

(Dodge City) Ford County Globe
Dodge City Times
Phillipsburg Harold
Wichita Beacon
Wichita Eagle

KENTUCKY

Hartford Herald

NEW MEXICO TERRITORY

Albuquerque Advance La Revista de Albuquerque (Old Town Albuquerque)

Albuquerque Evening Review
Albuquerque Morning Journal
Cimarron News and Press
Deming Graphic
Deming Headlight
Las Vegas Daily/Weekly Gazette
Las Vegas Daily/Weekly Optic
(Lordsburg) Western Liberal
Otero Optic
Raton Guard
(Raton) New Mexico News and Press
Santa Fe Daily/Weekly New Mexican
Silver City Eagle
Silver City Independent
(Silver City) New Southwest and Grant County Herald
Silver City Southwest Sentinel

Socorro Chieftain
Socorro Industrial Advertiser

TEXAS

Dallas Weekly News
Fort Worth Daily Democrat
Jacksboro Frontier Echo

OTHERS

Cushing (OK) Searchlight
National Police Gazette
Salt Lake City Tribune
Saturday Evening Post
Washington Post

Index